PENGUIN BOOKS

KITH

'*Kith* could have been written by no one but Jay Griffiths. It is ablaze with her love of the physical world and her passionate moral sense that goodness and a true relation with nature are intimately connected. She has the same visionary understanding of childhood that we find in Blake and Wordsworth, and John Clare would have read her with delight. Her work isn't just good – it's necessary' Philip Pullman

'An impassioned, visionary plea to restore to our children the spirit of adventure, freedom and closeness to nature that is their birthright. We must hear it and act on it before it is too late' Iain McGilchrist

'An impassioned and well-researched plea for the spirit of adventure to be instilled in the young' *Sun-Herald* (Sydney)

'Jay Griffiths writes with such richness and mischief about the one thing that could truly save the world: its children' KT Tunstall

'A beautiful combination of expansive tenderness and fierce intolerance of pettiness. *Kith* is a call to live life intensely and authentically, vividly, and with grace, humour and passion. Griffiths has politicized awe and wonder and play' Niall Griffiths

'With a quotable quote on every page Griffiths invites the reader to tune into her wavelength and embark upon the high seas of the strong emotions associated with childhood memory. Her personal experience of indigenous cultures, and of the wilderness, is skilfully blended with her extensive reading across the spectrum of the humanities and the social sciences. Throughout the pages of this text, the need to re-connect with nature is presented with illuminating precision' *Social Artist*

'Packed with stories, histories, poetry and passion' *Big Issue*

'Jay Griffiths is one of our most poetic and passionate critics of the ways of civilization; provocative, illuminating and shamelessly romantic' Theodore Zeldin

ABOUT THE AUTHOR

Jay Griffiths is the author of *Pip Pip: A Sideways Look at Time*, *Wild: An Elemental Journey* and *A Love Letter from a Stray Moon*, a novella about the life of Frida Kahlo. She is the winner of the inaugural Orion Book Award and of the Barnes & Noble Discover Award for the best new non-fiction writer to be published in the USA. She has also been shortlisted for the Orwell Prize and a World Book Day Award. Jay Griffiths grew up in England and now lives in Wales.

KITH

The Riddle of the Childscape

Jay Griffiths

PENGUIN BOOKS

PENGUIN BOOKS

Published by the Penguin Group
Penguin Books Ltd, 80 Strand, London WC2R ORL, England
Penguin Group (USA) Inc., 375 Hudson Street, New York, New York 10014, USA
Penguin Group (Canada), 90 Eglinton Avenue East, Suite 700, Toronto, Ontario, Canada M4P 2Y3
(a division of Pearson Penguin Canada Inc.)
Penguin Ireland, 25 St Stephen's Green, Dublin 2, Ireland (a division of Penguin Books Ltd)
Penguin Group (Australia), 707 Collins Street, Melbourne, Victoria 3008, Australia
(a division of Pearson Australia Group Pty Ltd)
Penguin Books India Pvt Ltd, 11 Community Centre, Panchsheel Park, New Delhi – 110 017, India
Penguin Group (NZ), 67 Apollo Drive, Rosedale, Auckland 0632, New Zealand
(a division of Pearson New Zealand Ltd)
Penguin Books (South Africa) (Pty) Ltd, Block D, Rosebank Office Park,
181 Jan Smuts Avenue, Parktown North, Gauteng 2193, South Africa

Penguin Books Ltd, Registered Offices: 80 Strand, London WC2R ORL, England

www.penguin.com

First published by Hamish Hamilton 2013
Published in Penguin Books 2014

002

Copyright © Jay Griffiths, 2013
All rights reserved

The moral right of the author has been asserted

Typeset by Jouve (UK), Milton Keynes
Printed in Great Britain by Clays Ltd, St Ives plc

ISBN: 978-0-141-03945-9

www.greenpenguin.co.uk

CONTENTS

THE RIDDLE

While I was travelling for my last book, *Wild*, I encountered a deep riddle: a difficult riddle. It stuck in my teeth like a string of celery. I teased at it with my tongue and my fingertips played on it. Like all good riddles, it was tricky but glimpsable and, more than anything, it told me it was worth solving.

Why are so many children in Euro-American cultures unhappy? Why is it that children in many traditional cultures seem happier, fluent in their child-nature? Nature is at the core of the riddle: I began looking for the nature of childhood, whose quintessence is inextricable from nature itself. I was interested in how children belong, needing their kith, their local acre, as they need their kin. An entire history of childhood is in that one word 'kith', which is now used as if it means only extended family, whereas in the phrase 'kith and kin', 'kith' originally meant country, home, one's land. Childhood has not only lost its country but the word for it too: a country called childhood.

How has childhood become so unnatural? Why does the dominant culture treat young humans in ways which would be illegal if applied to young dogs? Born to burrow and nest in nature, children are now exiled from it. They are enclosed indoors, caged and shut out of the green and vivid world, in ways unthinkable a generation ago. Bit by bit, a pattern came clear – that children's lives have been subject to intolerable enclosure for the profit of others.

The riddle took me to that other natural world: human nature, a term so complex, so simple and so wise. Human nature in childhood asks for both freedom and closeness. A child's mind is constellated with animals as the night is with stars. Child-nature salutes the gods of play and pays homage to wild time. It needs autonomy and self-will. The riddle asked: who owns a child, anyway? Do children naturally create their own tribes? It is in the very nature of the child to want to learn, yet society has historically contrived a school system that is half factory, half prison, and too easily ignores the very education which children crave.

Then the riddle took me further in, to the spirit of childhood, its sense of quest; the importance of woodlands for the psyche; the faërie realm of metaphor; the secret world of a child's soul where the stories of childhood are whistled with the deft and fragile panache of poetry. Throughout, I had a hunch that Romanticism reflected the nature of childhood not as a period in cultural history but as a perennial truth, because children are themselves the first Romantics.

This book draws on my experience of children's lives among indigenous cultures in the Arctic, West Papua, Australia, North and South America and Northern Europe, and touches on the history of childhood in mainland Europe and Scandinavia, as well as the intriguing psychodrama of childhood played out when the Native American philosophy of childhood met Settler philosophy. Behind all of these, though, is the spirit of childhood itself, whose imagination knows no borders.

CHAPTER ONE

Kith

Stumbling on a bird's nest as a child, I was breathtaken. I gasped at the tenderness of it, the downy feathers, softer than my fingers, moss folded into grasses and twigs in rounds. My eyes circled and circled it, caught by the mesmerizing perfection of the nest. It was the shape of my dream, to be tucked inside a nest and to know it for home.

A nest is a circle of infinite intimacy, a field-hearth or hedge-hearth. Every nest whispers 'home', whether you speak English, Spanish, Wren or Robin. Part of a child's world-nesting need is answered seeing a rabbit warren, a badger sett or otter holt, as children's writers instinctively know, giving children a secret passage to dens, nests and burrows.

Through nests, a child's own hearthness is deepened and the child grows outwardly and inwardly into its world. Outwardly, children stare at a nest, fascinated. Inwardly, the nest reflects not just the body's home but the mind's. In the snug refuge of the nest, the psyche fills itself out from within, as round and endless as a nest, creating its infinite-thoughted worlds. Intertwined with the world of fur and feather is the world of metaphor where mind makes its nests. Metaphor weaves 'grass' and 'shelter' together. It ties 'twig' to 'refuge'. It knits 'moss' to 'home'.

Finding a nest is a homecoming for a child. In Greek, homecoming is *nostos*, the root of the word 'nostalgia' – an ache for home, a longing for belonging. Children, filthy little Romantics that they are, have an uncanny gift for nostalgia in nature; something inchoate, yes, but yearning, yearning for their deepest dwelling.

Every generation of children instinctively nests itself in nature, no matter how tiny a scrap of it they can grasp. In a tale of one city child, the poet Audre Lorde remembers picking tufts of grass which crept up through the cracks in paving stones in New York City and giving them as bouquets to her mother. It is a tale of two necessities. The grass must grow, no matter the concrete suppressing it. The child must find her way to the green, no matter the edifice which would crush it.

The Maori word for placenta is the same as the word for land, so at birth the placenta is buried, put back in the mothering earth. A Hindu baby may receive the sun-showing rite *surya-darsana* when, with conch-shells ringing to the skies, the child is introduced to the sun. A newborn child of the Tonga people 'meets' the moon, dipped in the ocean of Kosi Bay in KwaZulu-Natal. Among some of the tribes of India, the qualities of different aspects of nature are invoked to bless the child, so he or she may have the characteristics of earth, sky and wind, of birds and animals, right down to the earthworm. Nothing is unbelonging to the child.

'My oldest childhood memories have the flavour of the earth,' wrote Federico García Lorca. In the traditions of the Australian deserts, even from its time in the womb, the baby is catscradled in kinship with the world. Born into a sandy hollow, it is cleaned with sand and 'smoked' by fire, and everything – insects, birds, plants and animals – is named to the child, who is told not only what everything is called but also the relationship between the child and each creature. Story and song weave the child into the subtle world of the Dreaming, the nested knowledge of how the child belongs. The threads which tie a child to the land include its conception site and the significant places of the Dreaming inherited through its parents. Introduced to creatures and land-features as to relations, the child is folded into the land, wrapped into country, and the stories press on the child's mind like the making of felt – soft and often – storytelling until the feeling of the story of the country is impressed into the landscape of the child's mind.

That the juggernaut of ants belongs to a child, belligerently following its own trail. That the twitch of an animal's tail is part of a child's own tale or storyline, once and now again. That on the papery bark of a tree may be written the songline of a child's name. That the prickles of a thornbush may have dynamic relevance to conscience. That a damp hollow by a riverbank is not an occasional place to visit but a permanent part of who you are. This is the beginning of belonging, the beginning of love.

In the art and myth of Indigenous Australia, the Ancestors seeded the country with its children, so the shimmering, pouring, circling, wheeling, spinning land is lit up with them, cartwheeling into life. In bitter contrast to the iridescent lifefulness of this entrance to the world, during the years of the Stolen Generations, some Indigenous Australians were forced to give birth in morgues, surrounded by the dead, because the authorities did not consider them to be human.

The human heart's love for nature cannot ultimately be concreted over. Like Audre Lorde's tufts of grass, it will crack apart paving stones to grasp the sun. Children know they are made of the same stuff as the grass, as Walt Whitman describes nature creating the child who becomes what he sees:

There was a child went forth every day,
And the first object he look'd upon, that object he became . . .
The early lilacs became part of this child . . .
And the song of the phoebe-bird . . .

— 'There was a Child Went Forth'

In Australia, people may talk of a child's conception site as the origin of their selfhood and their picture of themselves. As Whitman wrote of the child becoming aspects of the land, so in Northern Queensland a Kunjen elder describes the conception site as 'the home place for your image'.

Land can make someone *who they are*, can create their psyche, giving them fragments of themselves. On losing this, Indigenous Tasmanian Errol West writes: 'There is no one to teach me the songs that bring the Moon bird, the fish or any other thing that makes me what I am.' Shatter the relation to land and you shatter personalities like a smashed wing-mirror kicked into the dust.

From song, from dream, from elements of earth and water, spirit-children are immanent in the land. They are left there by the Ancestors of the Dreaming, who sang their way across the land, leaving an imprint of music like an aural footstep. And sometimes a woman who has already physically conceived a child chances to step in that same footstep, and, if she does, part of the song and the spirit-child leap up into her so she feels a quickening, sharp as an intake of breath at a kick within, sweet as a night surprised by song. Sometimes it is the father who, seeing something unusual – a particularly large fish or an animal behaving strangely – may know it as an indication of a spirit-child. Or a man walking by a lake may find a spirit-child jumping into his mind, which he will send in a dream to his wife, inseminating the spirit-child within her. Then the Lawmen, the knowers of the songline which the father or mother was on, can tell which stanzas of the song belong to that child, its conception totem and, in that sinuous reflexivity of belonging, its quintessential home.

To be born is, in Latin, *nasci*, and the word is related to *natura*, so birth, nature, the laws of nature and the idea of an essence are related. It is as if language itself has embedded birth in the natural world. In the Amazon, people say childbirth should always take place in the forest-gardens so the condensed energy of the plants can nourish the child. In New Guinea, future generations are called 'our children who are still in the soil' and when I was in West Papua, the western half of the island, I was told that in the Dani language the expression for digging potatoes is the same as that for giving birth to a child. Women say they can sometimes hear the unearthed potatoes, which are always handled gently, calling out to them, the land singing things into being to be mothered into the world.

Legends of childhood across the world suggest whole landscapes lit with incipience. Everywhere is potential, beginningness. It may be the inheld energy of an acorn or the liquid and endless possibilities of water; it may be the fattening of a potato in the secret earth or the leaping of a salmon which is the child Taliesin – in whatever form it takes, the land itself is kindling children.

In Indigenous Australian culture, there is a common idea that the land is mentor, teacher and parent to a child. People talk of being 'grown up by' their land; their country as kin.

So do English-speakers – without quite realizing it. A child may be looked after by its 'kith and kin', we say, as if both terms meant family or relations. Not so. 'Kith' is from the Old English *cydd*, which can mean kinship but which in this phrase means native country – one's home outside the house – but no one I have yet met has known that meaning. This sense of belonging has nothing whatsoever to do

with a nation state or political homeland, but rather with one's immediate locale, one's square mile, the first landscape which we know as
children. W. H. Auden wrote of this as 'Amor Loci', the love of his
childhood landscape. Kith kindles the kinship which children so easily
feel for the natural world and without that kinship, nature also loses
out, bereft of the children who grow up to protect it.

Much of a baby's first knowledge is in the language of touch and
smell, the texture and feel of the materials which surround it. The
world to a baby appears like sight underwater, when it is hard to dis-
tinguish separate objects, when everything shimmers in varieties of
brightness, a vision of the Aurora Borealis in swathes of light and
curtains of colour. With this vision, a highland baby in West Papua
opens its eyes to a bagful of vegetables and the odd piglet, all of them
together in a string bag dangling down its mother's back, bouncing
as she walks or digs sweet potato or searches for frogs, or tucked into
a riverbank while she washes. Outside the mesh of the string bag, the
baby is enveloped in clouds. If it cries, its mother will swing the bag
round and feed the baby, maybe also feeding the piglet. The baby
hears its mother's feet on the ochre clay and the slippery gurgles of
ubiquitous mud. The mother wraps the child in a particular leaf,
known to be very cool in the strong sunlight, and may cover the baby
with an umbrella made of pandanus leaf to keep off both rain and sun.

Children are porous to nature, as Wordsworth describes: as a child,
a lake 'lay upon my mind' and the sky 'sank down/Into my heart'.
Created of lake and sky, he says, 'Thus were my sympathies enlarged.'
Before any sense of myself, before a mirror had meaning, before my
skin was a boundary, I remember nature as if it were inside me. Birds
sang and I heard it inside. It snowed: I snowed. It rained: I rained. As
if in some pre-verbal state, whatever 'it' was, I was too. I was warm
in May because the sun was: I couldn't tell the difference. I was all the

world and all the world was me, saturated with presence. Grass. Blue. Tree. Water. Wind.

It was a kinship so primary that the senses understood it long before the mind. Water was the touch of it; I could feel the sky and taste the dampness of leaves in the uninstructed mud the body knows. I had two older brothers, each of us a year apart, and our mother, a gardener, thought that children, like seeds, grew best unobserved in good black earth, so in daffodils we were crazy with yellow and by autumn we were brown and shiny as conkers, but all through the year we were frank and stout with dirt. Our mother dressed us in three little pairs of black tops and three little pairs of black trousers, so no one would ever complain about us being filthy for the very good reason that they would never see it. Every once in a while, six little bits of black clothing went in the laundry and three little bits of grubby childhood went in the bath.

~

The riddle of this book is that of a child's human nature, which includes a sense of quest, the need for identity and the demand to honour the ludic principle – the principle of play. It is about how that human nature is nested in nature which co-creates the child. That relationship is vital for the psyche, and shy, bullied, neglected or abused children, those without friends or those with difficult families, find that their sense of belonging in nature is itself a remedy. Nature near the home seems to be a significant factor in promoting the psychological well-being of children growing up in the countryside, but even in small ways access to nature positively influences children so, for example, playing on asphalt seems to generate more conflict among children while playing in greenery promotes more harmony.

Author Barry Lopez describes the lifelong consolation of nature first discovered in childhood: 'a long, fierce peace can derive from this knowledge.' In Flora Thompson's memoiresque *Lark Rise to Candleford*, the young Laura is trapped in a depression for months and it is nature which releases her in a long river-moment where the water itself seems to have a message for her. 'To what does the soul turn that has no therapists to visit? It takes its trouble to the trees, to the riverbank, to an animal companion,' wrote psychologist James Hillman.

Nature gives children a soul-acceptance smooth and valuable as silk. In nature, children learn they are watched over by something of stature and gravity, to which they can take their levity and mischief, something which will comprehend their sadnesses and stand witness to their secrets.

In West Papua, a mountain may be referred to as 'mother' to all the children who grow up in her foothills while the forests can be places of awe, as spirit beings are thought to guard certain trees. Sometimes, after a death, the body is laid out in the top of a tree, so local children hear the bass notes of their ancestor story in the air.

If it is therapist, friend, witness, mother and mystery, nature is also muse to children. Listening to stories, children conjure images of mountains or deserts, reaching into their minds for their kith, the country of their knowledge. Especially, says J. R. R. Tolkien, a child will make that picture 'out of The Hill, The River, The Valley which were for him the first embodiment of the word'.

Pablo Neruda recalls leaving Temuco, his childhood home, when he was exiled from Chile:

There was a creek far down the slope, and the sound of its waters came up to me. It was my childhood saying goodbye. I grew up in this town. My poetry was born between the hill and the river, it took its voice from the rain, and like the river, it steeped itself in the forests. And now, on the road to freedom, I was pausing for a moment near Temuco and could hear the voice of the water that had taught me to sing.

I met a forget-me-not on equal terms, as a child. We were introduced one afternoon in the garden. Its name was so understandable and so emotional, unlike its formal name, *myosotis*, and is so-named in many languages: *ne m'oubliez pas* in French, *Vergissmeinnicht* in German, *nontiscordardimé* in Italian, *nomeolvides* in Spanish, *vergeet mij nietje* in Dutch, *forglem meg ei* in Norwegian, *mi me lismonei* in Greek and *förgätmigej* in Swedish. I was delirious for hours, finding that such a little thing, a child's flower if ever there was one, had a voice, and a loud one – a voice which demanded never to be forgotten. And with that came the connotations of forgetting: to ignore, to pass by, to treat something as insignificant, to condemn, to refuse, to betray. From that afternoon on, the act of remembering has been bound for the rest of my life – faithfully – to this tiny, cherished flower. It was the ordinary and unforgotten symbol of the ordinary and unforgettable nature which surrounded me.

When I was in Australia, Indigenous Australians told me not only how children need land, but also how land needs children, to hear their voices and their laughter in order to know that it is not abandoned. In an eloquent report of the land's distress, anthropologist Veronica Strang is told how one lagoon, the Emu waterhole in the Cape York Peninsula, went dry with grief on the death of its owner. 'If the young people don't come back to this country, the country will feel that "Oh well, look like no one don't own me now," so this country will just sort of die away.'

'Forget-me-not,' the land says, in all the dialects of deserts or forests. Children don't forget that early promise and can be vociferous protectors of nature.

In 1964, Chairman Mao denounced gardens. Flowers were feudal. Children were ordered to get rid of grass – which was bourgeois – from school lawns. Mao ordered explicitly what modernity is now ordering implicitly: the removal of childhood from its home in nature. Consumer societies are stealing children away from their kith, their family of nature, in a stealthy alienation. This is not about some luxury, a hobby, a bit of playtime in the garden. This is about the longest, deepest necessity of the human spirit to know itself in nature, and about the homesickness which children feel, whose genesis is so obvious but so little examined. Writer on Native American spirituality Linda Hogan describes the term *susto* as a sickness of soul caused by disconnection from nature and cured by 'the great without'.

Children's first and greatest fear is abandonment. The effects of abandonment include low self-esteem, feelings of rejection, the suppression of emotion and possible suicidal feelings. The psyche-industries of the contemporary world construe this primarily as fear of maternal abandonment and understand separation anxiety in human–human terms. But if, as children themselves maintain and as listening adults confirm, nature is crucial in a child's sense of home, then the separation of children from nature in artificial societies must play an important part. Children, denied their home in nature, are denied the mothering of nature. They lose the original mother (*mater*) of matter; the nub of it all, the real, mind-mothering world. This is a primary abandonment which causes children so much unrecognized damage, for the spirit needs to feel rooted somewhere on earth, a need which has been denied in the West only very recently.

The Diagnostic and Statistical Manual, the bible of the American psychiatric profession, lists 'separation anxiety disorder' as 'excessive anxiety concerning separation from home and from those to whom the individual is attached'. But, says American commentator Theodore Roszak, 'no separation is more pervasive in this Age of Anxiety than our disconnection from the natural world.'

Between 1981 and 2011, over 625 Guaraní people in Brazil committed suicide: nineteen times higher than the national average. It is mainly children and adolescents who kill themselves, and the reason is land-loss. Evicted from their territory, as virtually all of their land has been stolen by farmers and cattle ranchers, Guaraní children suffer a land-orphaning. 'The Guaraní are committing suicide because we have no land . . . we are no longer free. Our young people look around them and think there is nothing left and wonder how they can live. They sit down and think, they forget, they lose themselves and then commit suicide,' says Rosalino Ortiz, a Guaraní woman. The youngest was Luciane Ortiz, aged nine.

Given indigenous cultures' attitudes to nature and given their experience of land-loss, it is perhaps no surprise that indigenous therapists have been first to examine this issue. In New Zealand, the Just Therapy team places nature and land at the heart of belonging. Attachment, the team insists, is not only the connection between the child and one or two individuals but also to the land. 'Whenever we Samoans speak,' says Kiwi Tamasese, a Samoan therapist, 'we are talking about the mountain, we are talking about the river, we are talking about the waters, so the primacy of attachment is to those things, to those markers, rather than to other human beings.' Therapy, then, might include the recovery of land for peoples and the restitution of nature to childhood so it can re-belong.

Both 'longing' and 'belonging' come from the Old English word *langian*. This sense of longing to belong, of yearning to be nested, this keening for nature, is audible in the accents of childhood. In his important work on what he calls Nature Deficit Disorder, Richard Louv spent years talking to nature-deprived children and wrote that they 'spoke of nature with a strange mixture of puzzlement, detachment, and yearning – and occasional defiance'.

I've seen this longing in children and how they are robbed of their belonging. They do not know how to describe what they miss because they have never had it, but their instinct knows. They know they have been cheated, terribly, and from the very start. They know the essential, vital world is just out of reach, though the need to grasp at it is still with them, leaving them snatching at substitutes, perpetually dissatisfied, without quite knowing why. I've seen the longing of the human soul for its home in nature, the homesickness of the psyche for its earth-hearth. I've seen a radiance of hope persist in children for many years, a hope that they will somehow approach that green song at the heart of things, and I've seen a dimness setting in, shadowing the radiance.

And when nature-deprived children grow up, they can demonstrate an anger which can turn against nature: furiously despising the very thing they first wanted, as anti-environmentalists do. The pattern is the same in a child who is temporarily abandoned by a parent, at first longing for them, then feeling cheated, searching for distraction. There is a persistence of hope and then sadness falls and, after the sadness, a fury, just as the parent, returning for the fond and filial welcome, finds their child hissing: 'I hate you.' When a society is inhospitable to nature, creatures lose their habitats, their dwellings – creatures *including children*. In this, modernity is dispossessing its own children. It makes the younger generation homeless, the adults making an undwelling for the children, unbequeathing them, unhousing, unsheltering, unnesting them. Childhood sent into exile.

CHAPTER TWO

The Patron Saint of Childhood

Reading the poetry of John Clare is like reading the autobiography of a robin. Perched on a spade, tucked into a hedgerow or gleaning seed-syllables in a field, England's 'peasant poet' sang the songlines of his native Northamptonshire.

Like a bird, he made nests for himself in particular trees including one called Lee Close Oak. When the robin sings 'A music that lives on and ever lives,' Clare could be writing of himself. The nightingale sang 'As though she lived on song' and in Clare's own life there were times when he lived on little more. Both boy and bird were 'Lost in a wilderness of listening leaves,' and his fledgling childhood was spent 'Roaming about on rapture's easy wing' in the circle of land around Helpston in the wheel of the year, as time turned in its agricultural cycles and reeled in its festivals.

It is hard today to imagine what children's lives were like before the Enclosures and it is impossible to overstate the terrible, lasting alteration which those Acts made to childhood in Britain. Although it is not, in the great scheme of things, so very long ago, we today are effectively fenced off from even its memory. My grandfather's grandfather would have known what it was like to make himself a nest on the commons of mud, moss, roots and grass but neither the experience nor a record of it is my inheritance and, for that, I hold a candle for John Clare, patron saint of childhood, through whose work we can see what childhood has lost: the enormity of the theft.

The commons was home for boy or bird but the Enclosures stole the nests of both, reaved children of the site of their childhood, robbed them of animal-tutors and river-mentors and stole their deep dream-shelters. The great outdoors was fenced off and marked 'TRESPASSERS WILL BE PROSECUTED.' Over the generations, as the outdoors shrank, the indoor world enlarged in importance.

PRIVATE: KEEP OUT

You see that sign in two places: on the bounds of the landowner's domain and on a child's bedroom door; and they are wholly related for, when children were banished from the commons, they lost their nests on the land. Over the years, as they came to be given their own bedrooms, a perfect and poignant mimicry evolved. Wanting some privacy but deprived of their myriad dens in the woods and on the commons, children have retaliated against the theft by sticking up signs on scraps of paper in wobbly writing: their last – unconscious – protest against the Enclosures which robbed them of all their secluded nests in the denning world, while giving them in return a prefab den, one small cage of a room. It was not, as children say, a good swap.

Born in 1793 to a sense of freedom as unenclosed as 'nature's wide and common sky', John Clare knew that the open air was his to breathe, the open water his to drink and the open land, as far as his knowledge of it extended, his to wander, and he began to write poetry of such lucid openness that it can best be described as light: his poems are translucent to nature, which shines through his work like May sunlight through beech leaves. Clare writes of the land as if he were a belonging of the land, as if it owned him, which is an idea one hears often in indigenous communities. His childhood belonged to that land and to its creatures; he knew them all and felt known in turn. One day, Clare writes, he wandered and rambled 'till I got out of my knowledge when the very wild flowers and birds seemed to forget me'.

And then, to his utter anguish, came the Enclosures, the acts of cruelty by which the common land was fenced off by the wealthy and privatized for the profit of the few. The Enclosures threw the peasantry into that acute poverty which would scar Clare's own life and mind so deeply. His griefstricken madness, alcoholism and exile as a result of this land-loss encapsulates in one indigenous life the experience of so many indigenous cultures.

In 1809, there was a parliamentary act to enclose his home territory, Helpston, and Clare saw the bitter effects at first hand as the Enclosers fenced off site after site of his memory. 'The axe of the spoiler and self interest' felled his beloved Lee Close Oak, and felled something inside himself. He lost one of his actual childhood nests but he also lost the metaphoric nest which is childhood itself where the young adult can, in a vulnerable moment, flit. Trying to console Clare for his loss, a local carpenter who had bought the timber gave Clare two rulers made from the tree. It is a poignant image for, despite the good intentions of the carpenter, the rulers represented the linear remodelling of Clare's world, wrenching the cyclical qualities of the commons (the rotation of crops and the slow cycles of time, the rounds of nests) into the strict fence-lines of Enclosure. 'Rulers' also suggests the ruling class of the Enclosers who invaded the land of the poor like an imperial army: Enclosure came 'like a Bonaparte,' wrote Clare.

One of the greatest poets of childhood, Clare is without rival as the poet of Enclosure in part because of his identification with his homeland. The Acts of Enclosure signified the enclosure and destruction of his spirit as well as his land. Winged for the simplest of raptures, he now limped at the fences erected by the 'little minds' of the wealthy. His own psyche had been as open as the footpaths of his childhood, paths which wend their way 'As sweet as morning leading night astray' but with sudden brutality 'These paths are stopt –' and

> *Each little tyrant with his little sign*
> *Shows, where man claims, earth glows no more divine.*

It is winter. It is always winter. In one of Clare's poems, the overarching metaphor is that the Enclosures have brought a bleak, cold, unseasonable season, 'strange and chill'. Partly, this was a direct description of the physical cold which children experienced when commoners lost their right to collect firewood for warmth; it was only because of common rights that people could 'maintain themselves and their Families in the Depth of Winter'. The Enclosures also brought a coldness of spirit, a winter of the heart. It was as if the wheel of the year had stopped turning, frozen at midwinter all year, and summer childhood would never roll round again.

Eastwell fountain never froze in winter and Clare describes how, every Whit Sunday from time immemorial, the young people of Helpston had gathered at that particular spring to drink sugar-water for good luck. He recalls tying branches together to make a swing and fishing with crooked pins, not catching anything. It's easy to picture the giggles, flirting and games. But after Enclosure, Eastwell fountain was made private property and the children were fenced out. Later, unchilded and unsung, the site had become 'nothing but a little naked spring', he writes, and it makes me wonder why he says 'naked'. I imagine that they literally clothed the spring with ribbons as children have so often garlanded wishing wells and lucky fountains, on the

Well-Dressing Days which used to be a part of a child's calendar but, further, I imagine that their custom clothed the spring with meaning and memory. Not only are the children bereaved but the land too, once possessed by children's voices, is now owned, as it were, by silence. Bereft of its children, the land is 'all alone'. The sense that a site may be lonely without its children recalls the beliefs of Indigenous Australians, the Emu waterhole grieving.

So the children of Helpston lost Eastwell fountain, site of their festival, and the festival itself died. This was one example of a widespread effect of the Enclosures, for carnivals typically had been held outdoors on the commons but when Enclosure stole those commons both the sites of carnival and the customs themselves disappeared. When the rights to the commons were abolished, the rites of the commons were lost: Enclosure made carnival homeless and it affected children badly because carnivals were once an enormous part of the glee of childhood. Today's few festivals are the shreds, the tattered remains, of the rites which once ribboned a child's year with dozens of carnival days and festooned it with Mischief Nights. There were Feasts of Fools, Apple-Tree Wassailings, Blessing-of-the-Mead Days, Hare-Pie-Scrambling Days, Hobby-Horse Days and Horn-Dance Days, the Well-Dressing Days which John Clare recalls, and Cock-Squoiling Days, Doling Days, Hallooing Largess led by the Lord of the Harvest, and all the variations of Hallowe'en (the Celtic festival of Samhain which archaeologists say has been celebrated for at least five thousand years), including Somerset's Punkie Night, when lanterns were made of mangel-wurzels. Mangel-wurzels. Give me mangel-wurzels, for the love of all that is good: mangel-wurzels.

It is not only a matter of the quantity of festivals but of their quality too. Carnival used to be a very public affair, sited outdoors with children playing a crucial role in this open, flamboyant theatre of exuberance. Carnival was public play but the Enclosures privatized it and over the years play moved indoors, so children today, enclosed in their bedrooms alone in an Xbox-fest with their PRIVATE: KEEP OUT signs on the door, cannot even know what used to lie on the other side of the fence, the public, excessive, inebriated, unbridled effervescence seizing a whole community.

When children were robbed of their carnivals, they lost a particular aspect of their relationship with nature, something at once intimate and political. For carnival renders political facts in personal ways, it plays its public roles in individual masks. Carnivals were part of children's political education in, for example, the joint-stock merry-makings which celebrated rights of grazing, gathering and gleaning on the commons, or in the 'beating of the bounds' by which a parish mapped its territories. In one case, at Scopwick in Lincolnshire, boys were made to stand on their heads in holes to make them remember the extent of their land.

Children lost the festivals, but they also lost something of the spirit of carnival, that ancient principle of reversal which subverts the *status quo*, which turns things upside down, as topsy-turvy as boys standing on their heads in holes. Carnival, rooted in the land, sends up its shoots of play, of rudeness and licentiousness, and sends up the authorities, too, with its days of misrule. But with the Enclosures, the authorities had a field day. Children suffered, not only from a loss of freedom and of carnival but because they were prosecuted under other laws passed to protect newly enclosed lands.

~

There was a small common near my childhood home, called Cow Common, one tiny patch which had escaped the historical Enclosures.

My first memories include the cow parsley there, which was taller than me, a parasol between me and the sun. In my memory, Cow Common was all commonness. It was the scruffy-normal from which all else diverged. It was what happened when things were left alone. It had no manners, no wealth, no restriction and no clocks. On the common, everything breathed easy and wild.

Particularly children. They are born commoners on the common ground of earth. Children, whatever their parents' class, are commoners; they come from beyond the ha-ha, beyond horticulture, decorum and dedicated grapefruit spoons. In landscape terms, they belong on the heath. They don't like the spirit of the Enclosures which mows its lawns and minds its manners, which strictly fences neatness in and untidiness out, and speaks of it all in clipped language. Nature under control. Paved patios. Miniature golf. Children prefer the spirit of the commons. Dirty. Open. The Unoccupied Territories.

And today? Does Cow Common still exist? I don't know. I don't want to go back. I don't want to see how, as an Internet search has just told me, 'most of Cow Common has gone.' I would feel robbed of a bit of my childhood if I met its absence. I would cry if I saw how the Cow Common of my very common childhood has been fenced off and privatized for the profit of the wealthy. The developers think it is valuable: we children knew it was priceless. Our wreck is long gone; developers nabbed it years ago. The Enclosures of the commons are still happening, from the profiteering bank which has seized the bank of the river in Jericho, Oxford, for luxury flats, to developers across America eyeing up worlds of childhood in disused plots of land.

The *Cow* Common of my childhood recalls the way that a peasant family could keep a cow (and perhaps geese) on the common, maybe tilling a little land. The commons had given people independence, but Enclosure threw the peasantry into pauperism. Prices rose. Wages fell. People starved. While the Enclosures drove people to starvation, they were forbidden from leaving their parish by the 'Settlement Acts', which from 1662 had prevented poor people's freedom of movement. Corralled within their parish, people turned to poaching and smuggling in huge numbers.

'All our family were smugglers,' one of my grandmothers once told me proudly, and they had to be to survive. Smugglers saw their work as legitimate trade and considered that the excise men were acting illegitimately in seizing profit from it. I have seen the man-traps used to catch smugglers in the town which my grandmother and all her ancestors were from, and a shiver runs through my genetic memory at the iron jaws, shattering bones and crippling someone for life. It could have been me.

By 1816, poachers, including children of nine or ten, were given punishments of imprisonment or transportation for offences against the Game Laws, enacted to protect the hunting rights of the wealthy. Transportation often meant a death sentence through abuse, cruelty and disease on the prison ships. Meanwhile, so widespread was the practice of poaching that, by 1830, one in three criminal convictions was for a crime against the Game Laws.

Pause a moment on this. In the 'Game' Laws, the clue is in the title. The games of the gentry – hunting for fun – were fiercely protected, while hunting for sheer starving necessity, engaged in by children and adults, was outlawed. The wealthy, engaged in sports and game shooting, were made wholly exempt from the Malicious Trespass Act of 1820, while a commoner's child, playing and breaking a branch, could be thrown in jail. Together, these acts amounted to a privatization of play. Common play – child's play – was privatized for profit.

Poaching, incidentally, something Wordsworth did as a child, has never died. Scottish artist Matthew Dalziel, from the age of seven in the 1970s, went out poaching with his dad and dog in rural Ayrshire. His mother did not always approve, tight-lipped as she cleaned the boy's clothes and berated her husband for stewing ram's horns in her jelly pan. As a boy it seemed 'a sort of human right to be able to take a fish from the river or a hare from the hill', says Dalziel. It was an adventure of the senses for a child. Chasing hares by moonlight, he recalls the rhythm of their paws 'quickening like a drumming across the earth's surface', with the grasses hissing as they ran. After the kill, the dog's heavy breath would be full of blood and sweat and would mingle with the oily woollen smell of his father's damp jumper, a madeleine of poaching.

Poachers are the hunters and the hunted. The boy feared the game-keepers who regarded them as trespassers. 'Like the animals you hunted, your senses would get highly tuned to seeing a shape behind a hedgerow that didn't quite look right, the sound of a gate squeaking, a steel wire fence lightly ringing, birds suddenly flying off, crows circling: all became voices saying someone was coming, something was not as it should be.' It was – and has always been – a nocturnal class war, where children could get a bit of their own back, their own commons, their own unenclosed freedom, trespassing a little against those who had so maliciously trespassed against them.

John Clare fears being told that his walking is 'trespass', saying that he 'dreaded walking where there was no path'. As a child, I shared that dread of the word 'trespass' and I still feel a fear which is wholly disproportionate to any punishment meted out today. Generations of children forced to recite the Lord's Prayer which uses the word 'tres-pass' instead of the Biblical 'sin' or 'debt' were further frightened off their own land. I learned my fear from my mother who learned it from hers: it would only need some six such transfers of fear, mother to child, to span the decades from the Malicious Trespass Act to my own wide-eyed fear at the fences. As a result of this act, children were sent to prison in large numbers. Mothers would have wanted to instil fear of trespass into their children as deeply as they would fear of poisonous snakes. As a girl, my mother misread the sign as 'TRESPASSERS WILL BE EXECUTED', and she was not alone. Another friend also mistook the word but not the threat, for, nailed next to the sign to frighten the children, a gamekeeper had hung a dead, executed, fox.

The figure of the Gamekeeper stalks children's fiction, acknowledging their persistent fear, so 'Giant Grum' in *The Little Grey Men* kills the animals in the woods; meanwhile TRESPASSERS WILL hangs over all the landscapes of childhood, from Winnie-the-Pooh to today's woodland privatizations, denying children their role as part of the wildlife.

The ideology of the Enclosures was driven by some of the less likeable attitudes of the Enlightenment: a loathing of wildness, a will to control nature, a love of hierarchies and subordination. Children suffered from these ideologies and childhood was to be enclosed as surely as land. This is not only a matter of shutting children off the land but also a matter of enclosing the playful spirit of childhood and prohibiting its carnival-heart and, further, subjecting it to domination, harsh discipline and punishment, as later chapters will demonstrate in more detail.

The experience of children was mirrored in the treatment of land. Although some early Enclosures had taken place in the thirteenth century, it was the fifteenth and sixteenth centuries that saw a wave of Enclosures, with an extreme peak in the eighteenth century, falling off by 1830. Map this with the history of childhood and something fascinating emerges: children were subjected to increasing discipline from the very end of the fourteenth century to the fifteenth and sixteenth centuries, reaching its height in the eighteenth century, until the tide began to turn by about, yes, 1830. The nature of the land and the nature of the child were both to be controlled, fenced in. Enclosure, both literal and metaphoric, was enacted against land and childhood.

~

Clare associated the commons with an everyday arcadia, so 'Nature's wild Eden' is found 'In common blades of grass'. Eden is here and how green is that valley, how evergreen, Eden, common as chaffinches, Eden-at-large, Eden-at-will, Eden belonging to everyone who will not wall others out. Clare welcomes everything; his Eden blesses thistles and embraces weeds, knowing that Eden is only truly Eden when the nettles are as welcome as the honeysuckle, when there is hard graft as well as moonlight, frozen well-water in winter as well as the zest of love in the zenith of summer.

His Eden is 'ruled' by nothing except 'Unbounded freedom' and, like all children given half a chance, Clare's sense of freedom included a quintessential freedom of time. He was a loafer, a dawdler, a *flâneur* of the fields, describing himself sauntering, roaming, lost in another time which existed before Enclosure:

Jumping time away
on old Crossberry Way.

Children today, peeping through the strict fences of their over-scheduled and clockworked lives, can only guess at his unenclosed sense of time. Steeped in, saturated with, drunk on the wine of time as if he had drunk it to the lees, the leavings, *laissez-boire*, the child Clare is rich on the leazings of life, the gleanings, the gatherings of memory, 'When I in pathless woods did idly roam.'

Ah, idleness, those long and lazy days when the clock is drowsy, the hours hazy and minutes erased, idleness is a friend to childhood and an enemy of the state. The 1794 Report on Enclosure in Shropshire states with nasty approval that a result of Enclosures would be that 'the labourers will work every day in the year, their children will be put out to labour early.' Children's hard labour would become necessary for survival, as families lost one right after another, including gleaners' rights to leaze after the harvest. 'Leazing' is a rich word which, like 'gleaning', means picking up what lies scattered after a harvest. Clare literally leazed in the fields but was also the poet-as-gleaner.

I found the poems in the fields
I only wrote them down.

He weaves together leaves and leazings, reading both language and nature; the birds and the words are interwoven as the yellowhammer weaves its nest of real sticks in the inspired air. 'And hang on little twigs and start again,' he writes, as if the infinite circle of a nest was a part-song sung by every bird.

Clare's was a nesting mind, delicate as tiny twigs, feathered with fellow-feeling and warm with tufts of grass tucked round the circle of his land in the cycle of the year. 'I've nestled down and watched her while she sang,' wrote Clare of the nightingale: the psyche which is well nested may sing the truest and when, as an adult, he writes about his childhood it is as if his childhood were a nest for his spirit. Nests within nests, his whole work is a nesting-place.

As a child, Clare nested in the lands which were his home and, charmed by nests, he wrote of the martin's nest, and a magpie's nest, the nests of linnet, blackbird, nightingale, pettichap or chiffchaff, skylark, landrail, yellowhammer, moorhen, thrush and robin. He includes the nests of hedgehogs and children's burrows, their little 'playhouse rings of sticks and stone'. His work seems to suggest that as a child he could feel safely nested only when the land around him was a safe nesting-place for every other kind of creature, knowing that the human mind can nest or make a home only when the ecology provides a home for all species. (The word 'ecology' comes from *oikos*, home.) Many children are disturbed by the idea that any animal, from a tiger to a snail, could lose its home, in a kind of instinctive ecological empathy.

It was the destruction of all the forms of home which unnested Clare's mind. He was evicted from his land by forces of undwelling and his madness and misery were written into his poems. I have been with Amazonian people when they have seen the searing brutality of their lands being ripped apart for gold in today's acts of corporate enclosure, and I have watched men weep while they say, aghast, 'We are the land,' a truth which John Clare would have effortlessly understood.

The Enclosures spiked the nest of Clare's psyche. Where moss and feathers had been, there was now a torque of barbed wire. When Clare writes of flowers or butterflies or birds being made homeless, he notes how they lose their depth of association so the landscape of the mind is pauperized by Enclosure.

> But, take these several beings from their homes,
> Each beauteous thing a withered thought becomes;
> Association fades and like a dream
> They are but shadows of the things they seem.
> Torn from their homes and happiness they stand
> The poor dull captives of a foreign land.

Language and meaning need to be nested in nature, and the immensity of the destruction Clare perceives is enormous. Enclosure, he tells us in various places, fenced off rapture and play, joy, customs, games, carnival and the past; it obliterated the glow of divinity, of generosity and kindness; it silenced songs and poetry; it prohibited lingering, lazing, roaming and straying; it closed the pathways; it brought the chill of winter into every season; it caged freedom, time and wildness; it ruined dwelling, refuge and shelter; it denied belonging and so stripped the psyche of every protection. It evicted childhood from its immemorial nest on the land and it exiled his adulthood from its nest of childhood memory.

Enclosure threatens the homes of all, whether a squirrel's dray, a mouse's nest or a badger's sett. Out on the heath, after Enclosure, the rabbits had nowhere to make a warren and were left to 'nibble on the road' while the moles became 'little homeless miners' and even the birds are ordered out of their homes in the woods by forbidding signs, so they must keep flying, from felled tree to felled tree, storm-driven and nestless.

Clare, in the sympathetic magic of poetry, gives a home to everything in the only commons he still had access to: the commons of imagination. If, as a result of Enclosures, creatures no longer had their nests on the common land, he would build nests for them in that other commons: language. One creature after another is given a home and shelter in Clare's writing and each of Clare's poems is a nest. The littlest twigs are caught, laid lightly, woven of thought and love; each gentle green adjective is like moss, each soft felt word a sheltering leaf, each verb a feather for a reverie of home. All poetry is dwelling, but Clare's are daydream dwellings for both creature and human, and when each nest-song is complete the bird of poetry alights there.

But in all these nested images – nests within nests – there is one more. John Clare, building his nests of land-poetry, has in fact made a nest for us all, a home and a flitting-place for every one of us to dwell in a while, in order to know what an unenclosed childhood was like and how the child's heart can find its nestness on the land.

CHAPTER THREE

Textures of Tenderness

There is a sensible way of treating children. Treat them as though they were young adults . . . Never hug and kiss them, never let them sit on your lap. If you must, kiss them once on the forehead when they say good night. Shake hands with them in the morning . . .

– American behaviourist John B. Watson, 1928

I felt as if I were an unwilling accomplice to torture. Echoes of the victim's screams rang sharply off the varnished walls. The door, tight shut though it was, could not block the cries of panic. At first the victim howled in raw terror, standing in her cage, shaking the bars in the fury of fear, her face mashed to purple with the force of her rage, while time itself seemed to stand still like an appalled witness till the roars which burned her throat gave way to the aghast grief of bereavement.

A baby, alone and imprisoned in a barred cot, shut into a room, alone, alone, alone. I felt sick and shocked by the cruelty of the situation. The baby's mother was visibly disturbed, pale and tearful. She was a good-hearted woman but a victim herself, preyed on by exponents of Ferberization, or Controlled Crying, that pitiless system, cruel to them both.

Controlled. Crying. The words speak of the odious aim: a bullying system controlling the feelings of a baby. The mother had been told the situation was the reverse, that the baby was trying to force her will on the mother, but all I could see was a one-year-old demented by abandonment. One American mother wrote poignantly on the Internet: 'Is Ferberization worth my heartache or am I truly torturing my child? It seems like cruel and unusual punishment.'

The idea is that babies can be 'taught' to stop crying by being left to cry alone. A parent will occasionally check on them, but will neither pick up nor stay with the infant. In time, the baby will learn that crying doesn't bring consolation and will cease the attempt. Parents are encouraged to schedule and limit the time they spend checking on the baby and may elect to use Graduated Scheduled Ignoring, whereby the more a child cries, the longer she or he must wait for a response. The Extinction method means letting a child cry indefinitely.

Does the system work? Of course it does. That is hardly the question. The real issue is why would such a thing be promoted? Why would it ever be accepted? What does it reveal about modernity's priorities? And how does it suggest answers to the riddle of unhappy children?

'They teach their children to cry!' was the appalled, disbelieving remark of a Lakota woman who, in the early 1930s, was confronted with the European belief that it was good for babies to be separated from their mothers in the government hospital and to cry until they were blue in the face.

Cuddled, snuggled and tended, most infants, throughout most of history, have known the world unlonely in that commons of tenderness unfenced from other human bodies. Among the Tojolobal-speaking Maya people of Chiapas in Mexico, children in the first two years of life are always close to their mothers, instantly appeased with toys or milk, to prevent them ever feeling unhappy. For infants under one year of age, among the Ache people, forest nomads in Paraguay, about ninety-three per cent of their daylight time is spent in tactile contact with their mother or father, and they are never set down on the ground or left alone for more than a few seconds. In India, and many parts of the world, children may share a bed with their mother until they are five; caressing, stroking and sensual pleasure is an important part of infancy among the Huaorani of Ecuador. In the infinite circle of arms, infants the world over have experienced that primary nest of human warmth.

For a typical European baby in the mid-seventies, the situation was, in a word, 'hell', says Jean Liedloff, psychotherapist and author of the influential book *The Continuum Concept*. 'He knows life to be unspeakably lonely, unresponsive to his signals and full of pain.' 'Deprived' is the term she uses – the infant given only intermittent physical closeness, as opposed to being constantly held in the arms of its mother or other adults. The terms 'lonely' and 'deprived' are telling: both hint at the dark side of individualism where privacy becomes emotional deprivation.

When Liedloff stayed with the Tauripan people in the Venezuelan forests, she was thunderstruck by happiness. 'They were the happiest people I had seen anywhere,' she writes, attributing this to people's childhood experience of being always held in arms. Ambushed by joy with the Yequana and Sanema peoples near the Brazilian border, she writes: 'much of the unreal quality of its people was accounted for by an absence of unhappiness, a large factor in every society familiar to me.' A huge number of anthropologists have similarly remarked on the happiness of children in traditional cultures. Likewise, whenever I have spent time in indigenous communities, I have never heard anything like the shrieks of fear and rage of the Controlled Crying child.

I have a memory of the cloudiest kind, an almost-lost feeling of sweetness experienced through a mist-covered haze, as if the earliest dawn of my life half lit something I can recall only with my sense of taste. So it is that I 'remember' the feeling of breastfeeding, drunk with milk, honey-suckled, all the round world mine and gentle, saturating me with love. This sense of immersion in the physical world – where 'mother' and 'world' are the same – is something which in-arms infants continue to experience: the rapt happiness nested in the lap of the world, wrapped in warm and living arms.

In a parka with a pouch and a large hood, a child – perhaps in a vest of velvet fawn skin – sits between the mother's naked body and the fur of her clothes. From here, the baby can see all the world and can drink all its sweetness on demand: so traditional Inuit infancy is recalled. Children of the !Kung people traditionally spent their first years in a sling, skin to skin with their mother, feeding on demand several times an hour, the relationship with both parents typically intimate and nurturant. !Kung people say that the closeness, the almost exclusive attention, unlimited love, food and comfort which each child receives in their first years provides strength and emotional security, the ability to handle the stress of the birth of a sibling.

If an infant is satiated with closeness, comments Liedloff, then as an older child he or she will need to return to that maternal contact only in emergencies. Such an infant will grow up to be more self-reliant, not because of the scarcity of early contact (as the Controlled Crying advocates argue) but precisely the opposite: from its abundance. By the age of about eight, the Ache children who as infants were never alone have learned how to negotiate the trails in the forests and can be fairly independent of their parents. In West Papua, I have seen how infants are deluged with closeness and grow into children who are fiercely, proudly independent.

Leaving a baby to cry will damage its confidence in its parents and in the world at large, making it more dependent rather than less, argues the psychotherapist Sue Gerhardt. Insistence on imposed sleep-times or feeding schedules is 'mental-illness-inducing', according to child psychologist Oliver James, and babies subject to this spend fifty per cent more time crying or fussing than babies given infant-centred care. He reports on an experiment in which some mothers, randomly selected, were asked to carry their baby regularly in a sling while another group were not. At the age of thirteen months, eighty per cent of the sling-carried babies were emotionally secure in their attachment to their mothers but only forty per cent of the others.

If, as an adult, one can feel the glimmers of varying radiances in the mind according to different touches – the harsh danger-light of being pushed aggressively or the glow when one is stroked by a lover – then how much more will touch matter to the mind of a baby for whom tactile knowledge is the first skill? Mind is kindled at the edge of the body, as are feelings.

High levels of maternal affection at the age of eight months are associated with significantly lower levels of distress, including anxiety and hostility, in adult offspring. On the other hand, if a baby is left to cry alone, high levels of stress hormones flood the infant, who is not developmentally equipped to deal with them. If there is no parent to de-stress the baby, she or he will end up becoming stressed at the least event and this stress is for ever: the baby's brain chemistry is changed for life. Human babies are born needing parents to protect them from stress, rather than force it on them, and if babies are consistently stressed through being ignored they will experience high levels of cortisol, which is hazardous to development, adversely affecting the immune system, memory and learning. There are strong links between high cortisol levels and depression, anxiety, suicidal tendencies, eating disorders, alcoholism and obesity. A baby's brain development is dependent on the baby being touched, on being held, on not being left to cry alone. The well-known studies of Romanian orphans show that those who were left untouched in their cots 'had a virtual black hole where their orbitofrontal cortex should be', writes Gerhardt.

There is a tradition of maternal separation among the aristocracy in Britain: Queen Victoria, buying three prams for her children from Hitchings Baby Stores of Ludgate Hill, popularized the bodily separation of the infant from the mother, and the wealthy have a history of abandoning even tiny children in boarding schools, with terrible emotional consequences. The social groups which impose separation on babies then often severely restrain older children, while (as the next chapter will discuss) children are happiest with first closeness and then freedom. Generations of Controlled Crying children (the idea began in the 1920s with New Zealand-born Truby King) have grown up with the precise opposite of what they need.

Many parents' reasons for using Controlled Crying can be summed up in one word: 'work'. Gina Ford, a famous British advocate of the system, stresses its importance for 'working mothers', and her consultancy service deals with 'women with high-powered jobs'. Parents who want 'routines' are keen on Controlled Crying, says Ford, and she comments that babies who have been forced into a routine will later adapt easily to a school routine and, one presumes, be more malleable to a workforce system.

While Gina Ford et al focus so heavily on the priority of work, tellingly, both Jean Liedloff, and Marjorie Shostak (working with !Kung people), draw the reader's attention to the connection between physical closeness in infancy and short working hours. !Kung women work perhaps two to four hours a day, spending the rest of their time making music, playing or telling stories. Short working hours, anthropologists say, is a feature of many indigenous societies. Liedloff, meanwhile, could discern no Yequana concept of work and became aware of an apparent absence of a word for 'work' in the Yequana vocabulary.

I've heard Controlled Crying advocates say a baby must learn to respect the parents' *boundaries*. Aside from the fact that a baby is about as well equipped to learn that lesson as it is to refute the theory of relativity, the very term 'boundary' is suggestive. The parents' psychological boundaries are illustrated in the 'limits' imposed on cuddling, the strict fencing off of time in routines and the emotional walls between parent and child – avoid even eye contact after 10 p.m., says Gina Ford. Mark the time, demarcate your territory, make the separation, erect the fence. And *No Trespassing* over the boundaries. A baby's open sense of time – the commons of its hours – is fenced by routines.

I can still see, in my mind's eye, the baby subjected to Controlled Crying, the hated bars of the cot like fence-posts, and the tiny hands gripping them as if this little Rebecca would overthrow the fact and the spirit of enclosure – hers and all children's. She was enclosed in a cot, enclosed in a room, fenced off from the tenderness she needed. In the historical Enclosures, the wealthy took what was common, erected fences around it and turned what had been public wealth into private wealth. So it is in these enclosures: limiting, fencing, restricting, marking boundaries, enclosing something common in order that private profits are made in those high-powered jobs, enclosing the commons of tenderness for the profit of wealthy corporations.

Closeness is food for a child's mind, feeding the spirit and leaving it satisfied, satiated with attention and tending. The world which that child perceives will be one of fullness and emotional abundance so the cup is brinkful to overflowing. But deprive a tiny child of that sense of abundance and you create an insatiable child – an emotionally needy, dissatisfied child who feels itself to be living in a world of depletion rather than abundance, learning that there is a scarcity of emotional resources. Such loss of essential well-being, writes Liedloff, 'leads to searches and substitutions for it', so 'happiness ceases to be a normal condition of being alive, and becomes a goal.' Deprived of the closeness of an infancy in-arms, 'One feels off-center, as though something were missing; there is a vague sense of loss, of wanting something one cannot define.' To Liedloff, the experience of constant closeness and the concomitant emotional warmth promotes a powerful feeling of one's lovableness. 'A person without this sense feels there is an empty space where he ought to be.'

This is a devastating psychological experience for an individual child who has suffered it. But I would argue that it has further political ramifications. Controlled Crying creates perfect conditions for consumerism. For if a consumer feels an unspecified but insatiable hunger, they will be manipulable by advertising. Marketing experts, we know, present objects as consolations for loneliness: products will comfort and befriend the consumer. Of course parents don't regularly set out to damage their children but, incrementally, society does so when it causes widespread emotional scarcity – an emptiness too deep and too early for words. So consumerist societies are formed, ever unsatisfied, greedy, needy and lonely, searching for substitutions.

The argument between Constant Closeness and Controlled Crying is profoundly linked to a centuries-old debate about human nature. Is the self a social being or an atomized individual? Advocates of Controlled Crying say it develops children's 'independent' sleep patterns and teaches children to 'self-soothe'. These responses are politically revealing, telling of a certain kind of individualism. Proponents argue for 'privacy' as if it were self-evidently good. For an older child, a sense of privacy in the intimate quiet of their own mind is ferociously important (and a later chapter will go into this), but an infant has no idea of, or need for, such privacy: rather, this system teaches it that it is ineluctably alone in the world – the hollow isolation of a baby alone in its bereft and inescapable canyon, hearing the echoes of no one except itself.

Controlled Crying advocates say it creates 'autonomy' within the child, but I would argue that it creates an anguished austerity, a bleak sense of deprivation – that word which is linked to the idea of a 'private' individual as one *deprived* of public life; here deprived of the public life of warm bodies and constant touch.

Advocates say it creates 'self-reliance': science tells us it creates a lifelong separation anxiety where the infant is taught that she is a lonely character in the theatre of abandonment which nightly re-stages her greatest fear. Controlled Crying advocates claim the system encourages independence and individualism. Me, I'm all for independence if that means true freedom. I'm all for individualism, where that means a genuine and wide diversity of character and the distinct voices of difference, but 'individualism' is one of the greatest lies of Western history. Ours is not a society that genuinely prizes individualism – note the dull conformity of politics, the dumb sameness of consumerism, the tabloid media's narrow focus on ubiquitous and identical drivel, society's intense hatred of the high notes of madness and the xenophobia against all kinds of border-crossers. This is not an individualistic society, rather it is a hyper-privatized one, removing the individual from the commons and privatizing communal life, privatizing the commons of tenderness and motherlove to create the hyper-privatized and innerly starved consumer.

When the private baby in her private room is screaming out her private hell, her first guess must be that her parents cannot hear, so she redoubles her cries, shaking the walls. After some time, her mother comes in, checks her and then leaves again. What will the child think? That her mother can hear but doesn't care. What does it mean for a child to learn that it is heard but intentionally ignored? I think it means teaching a child something of the annihilation of the self. In time, she may learn a subsequent lesson that she too should make herself deaf to the minds of others, repeating the legitimized cruelty.

In the States, developmental psychologist Dr James W. Prescott has studied the ill effects of sensory deprivation on infants, showing how a lack of closeness and bodily movement warps development, setting a child on a life path which may include depression, violence and suicide. The sheer unnaturalness of depriving infants of touch staggers Prescott, and he comments that, with the exception of Euro-American societies, 'there is no mammal that separates the newborn from its mother at birth or for any extended period after that. Yet we do that routinely.' In filmed experiments with baby monkeys, he shows how monkeys brought up touchfully will play, pet, hold and cling to each other, whereas touch-deprived monkeys refuse to play and avoid close contact, rocking endlessly in a form of self-soothing; growing older, they self-mutilate and exhibit signs of pathological violence. Prescott opens his observations out into the political sphere, commenting that children reared with 'affectional bonding' are likely to favour egalitarianism, while those reared with 'affectional deprivation' are likely to favour authoritarianism.

Infants perceive the warm and mysterious messages of the body, its pheromones and hormones, the baby's senses woven into the tapestry of other human beings, in cherished traceries of scent and excitement, feeling the textures of tenderness and the rhythms of love. This is the beginning of a politics far older – and kinder – than the selfish capitalism of today which would put the high-powered job before the anguish of a child; this is the politics of kindness, rooted from infancy in connectedness, in abundant empathy, the opposite of the deprived and hyper-privatized self.

The Controlled Crying baby is not only barred from the mother's closeness and her body, but from everything that is alive. The bodily senses, keen from birth to rub against the velvet skin of the living earth, are sealed in an artificial world with perhaps a piece of dead cloth for comfort and some plastic bars for companionship. An infant so treated has lost not only the world of its mother but the extended physicality of life, the motherworld.

Insecurely attached to its human parents, one can perhaps argue that such a child may also feel insecurely attached to the earth, to nature, and may respond by becoming un-empathic towards it and withdrawn from it. Is this also, in a complex underground process, one reason for modernity's terrible severance from, and lack of attachment to, the world of mothering nature? Wordsworth's intuition was that breastfeeding connects the baby to nature itself, and he writes of the unsundered relationship between infant and earth, describing a baby at the breast:

> *No outcast he, bewildered and depressed:*
> *Along his infant veins are interfused*
> *The gravitation and the filial bond*
> *Of nature that connect him with the world.*

It creates a form of empathy or pity 'cast from inward tenderness'.

Hannah Rachel Bell exquisitely describes the life of a newborn baby among the Ngarinyin people of Australia:

The child is suckled and continuously held by women until it can hold its head up on its own ... Touch, smell, the rhythm of the heartbeat, and breathing are considered 'food' as necessary for survival as mother's milk. Through these functions, the baby is attuned to its own humanity, and the rhythm or resonance of its group and culture. Alienation or separation from these rhythms of life are considered cruel, tantamount to deprivation and starvation of the child's developing spirit . . . If the child is going to grow to its potential, to be attuned to Earth, nature, the family, tribe, and Law, it must be nourished in this rhythmic life in infancy.

What better reasons could there ever be? To hold the earth close and be held by it, nested in the motherworld and intimate with the cosmos.

CHAPTER FOUR

By the Mark, Twain!

There is a direction beyond north, south, east and west: the mysterious fifth, the compass point for navigating one's daydreams, the star to steer them by. Speaking of her dream to circumnavigate the world, Laura Dekker repeatedly smiles as she turns her gaze to that point, up and to the side of her sights, to the lodestar of her freedom.

The child was born on a boat, as her parents were embarked on a seven-year voyage, and she lived at sea until she was four. When she was six, she had her own yacht and by ten she was solo-sailing. This was when she first set her heart on the far horizons, wanting to sail solo around the world, and by thirteen the Dutch girl was ready to attempt it.

But she found herself confronted by an implacable obstacle, worse than the Doldrums, worse than the Bermuda Triangle: she had the wind taken out of her sails by the forces of double dullness, the 'Office for Compulsory Schooling' which went to the law to prevent her. The court stepped in, making itself part-custodian of the child although her father, also her custodian, wanted her to be free to leave. In a series of rulings the court repeatedly prevented her from setting sail. (Laura did not turn up for one of the court sessions, as she had gone sailing instead.)

At one point, she sailed to England by herself but the British port authorities stopped her returning, insisting that her father must escort her home. Initially he refused, saying she was quite capable of sailing back alone. 'Capable' is the word. And resourceful, resilient and self-reliant.

At another point, she upped sticks and took herself to the Caribbean so she could start her round-the-world odyssey from there, but again the authorities prevented it, concerned with the risk of harm to the girl. If only the Dutch authorities, so apparently mindful of children's well-being, could consider the presumably trivial matter of the thousands of devastated childhoods in the former Dutch colony of West Papua, where Indonesia conducts a genocide against Papuans and where, I was told proudly, every child would be a freedom-fighter; and if only the courts could have left alone a child setting her sails for the freedom of the seven seas.

Tom Sawyer and Huckleberry Finn would have fought a duel over her on the spot, as they also are freedom-seekers, yearning for a freedom of time and of will, the freedom of the runaway slave and the freedom of the water. Mark Twain, as a young man, piloted steamboats on the Mississippi, that river which would become such a player – a character in its own right – in his most famous books. Born Samuel Clemens, Twain named himself after one of the river cries – 'By the mark, twain' – which the pilots would shout out when there were two fathoms of water below the boat, enough to steam away. It is, in other words, the call of the ship's own freedom.

Laura Dekker's ambition to be free, to run away to sea, newsworthy as it is today, is not such a remarkable desire. Aged fourteen and without his parents' knowledge, the future King Henry II hired a band of mercenaries, sailed to England and failed to take two minor castles. Ian Niall, in his 1967 autobiography, *A Galloway Childhood*, recalls:

'My mother's father was an adventuresome man. He had crossed the Atlantic as a boy, signing on as a member of the crew of a sailing-ship when he was no more than thirteen years of age. He sailed barefooted for he hadn't the money for seaboots.'

Paris, 1840. A thirteen-year-old boy called Béasse is having a run-in with the courts. Found without home or family, he is hauled before a judge and charged with vagabondage. Picture the cocky lad, his panache ringing out across the years, his elan running rings around the judge, turning on its head everything which Authority decrees.

JUDGE: One must sleep at home.

BÉASSE: Have I got a home?

JUDGE: You live in perpetual vagabondage.

BÉASSE: I work to earn my living.

JUDGE: What is your station in life?

BÉASSE: My station: to begin with, I'm thirty-six at least; I don't work for anybody. I've worked for myself for a long time now. I have my day station and my night station. In the day, for instance, I hand out leaflets free of charge to all the passers-by; I run after the stage-coaches when they arrive and carry luggage for the passengers; I turn cartwheels on the avenue de Neuilly; at night there are the shows; I open coach doors, I sell pass-out tickets; I've plenty to do.

JUDGE: It would be better for you to be put into a good house as an apprentice and learn a trade.

BÉASSE: Oh, a good house, an apprenticeship, it's too much trouble. And anyway the bourgeois . . . always grumbling, no freedom.

JUDGE: Does not your father wish to reclaim you?

BÉASSE: Haven't got no father.

JUDGE: And your mother?

BÉASSE: No mother neither, no parents, no friends, free and
independent.

Turning cartwheels on the avenue, he also turns cartwheels with the
judge's words, cock-a-hoop, cocking a snook as he challenges
the judge's assumption that he should have a home. A young expert
in the art of deliberate misunderstanding, he rephrases his lack of
parents as a positive – it makes him 'free and independent' – and in
this benign anarchy he is no one's slave and no one's master. Refuting
the judge's idea of law and order, he alludes to freedom as an inali-
enable right, part of the robust life force, and does so with the chutzpah
of a juvenile Dionysus. Against the stasis of establishment he opposes
the vehement nomadism of vagabonds with an effervescence both
cheeky and stubborn: he is an escapee from the dreary bourgeoisie
('always grumbling, no freedom') and refuses to be owned or controlled, domesticated or bored. Béasse stood (or cartwheeled) for
liberty. The judge imprisoned him in a reformatory for two years.

Vivacity glints in these runaways, from Tom and Huck to Laura
Dekker, the stray kings and footloose sailors, all those cut from that
patched and motley cloth, running colourful flags of freedom from the
masthead. It is as if all these children suggest the tenets of freedom as a
political right: freedom of thought, freedom of expression and freedom
of movement. 'Give me liberty or give me death!' are the exultant
words Tom Sawyer chooses for his school recital, supposedly from the
speech of Patrick Henry, a major figure in the American Revolution.

When the moon is a vagabond in the vagrant heavens, children
dream of escape. For some, it is the circumnavigation of the garden
at midnight, or leaving safe harbour and scudding over the bin bags,
heading for the out-of-bounds, seafaring across parks and neighbours'

gardens. 'The world's not such a bad place,' says Calvin, of *Calvin and Hobbes* fame, 'when you can get out in it.' A teenager told me recently (and with gusto) that the most 'real' thing he'd ever done was to shit in the woods under a full moon.

Climbing, running, sailing or sauntering with the swagger perfected by Richmal Crompton's 'Just William', children have seized freedom in any way they can, grinning with, green with liberty. What was common once can be common again, so children may know their own freedom, on the land and in the mind, turning starwise for liberty until horizons themselves somersault backwards off the map.

Playing 'games that the night demanded', writes Laurie Lee, was a priceless part of his childhood and he describes a game called Fox and Hounds, which began with two boys, on a five-minute head-start, loping away through farmyards, hills and woods.

> They had all night, and the whole of the moon, and five miles of country to hide in . . . we chased them through all the world, through jungles, swamps and tundra, across pampas plains and steppes of wheat and plateaux of shooting stars, while hares made love in the silver grasses, and the large hot moon climbed over us, raising tides in my head of night and summer that move there even yet.

Wordsworth in *The Prelude* describes nights of frost and wind on mountain slopes when ''twas my joy':

> *To range the open heights . . .*
> *. . . Through half the night . . .*
> *. . . I was alone . . .*

He was alone. He was nine. It was winter. It was normal.

Compare this with a big media story in England in October 2005, when an eight-year-old boy got lost in the woods and spent a night alone. His 'survival' was treated as a miracle and widely reported. Clearly, any unfamiliar situation may be frightening but, across the world, throughout history, eight-year-olds would be expected to be able to spend a night in the woods alone without anyone fussing.

Children's desire for freedom seems unquenchable. I recently gave a writing workshop in Kolkata for street children who had been temporarily corralled into a school where they were clearly well looked after and, in the main, happy, but they thirsted for the one thing which the school would not allow them: freedom. 'They want the freedom they knew on the streets,' said a teacher, 'to go anywhere, anytime.' In spite of the troubles on the street – poverty, abuse, hunger and violence – the children 'miss their freedom and keep running away'.

Once out of infancy, Native American children were traditionally free to wander wherever they wanted, through woods or water. Lakota children 'roamed far and wide over the countryside. They grew up without a sense of restriction and confinement. Their faculties became accustomed to space and distance, to skies clear or stormy, and to freedom in its full meaning,' writes Luther Standing Bear in *Land of the Spotted Eagle*; he recalls days – entire days – roaming the land. They would have appreciated D. H. Lawrence's rules on childcare: 'How to begin to educate a child. First rule, leave him alone. Second rule, leave him alone. Third rule, leave him alone. That is the whole beginning.'

'By the time he is five, he is grown up, beaming with health . . . delirious with liberty,' writes Roger P. Buliard in *Inuk*, describing an Inuit boyhood of 'freedom unlimited'. By about the age of seven, the boy handles knives and wants a rifle and a trap line, and from then on, 'travels with the men, as hardy a traveller as any of them.'

When I spent some days reindeer herding with Sámi people, I saw how the children were free not only out on the land, but indoors in the summer-huts. They rummaged around for food, finding a strip of cooked reindeer meat or a freshly caught fish or a tub of biscuits, feeding themselves as soon as they could and deciding what and when they would eat: a situation which averted that major source of family conflict – mealtimes.

Autonomy over food from a very young age seems a feature of childhood in many traditional societies. Young children in nineteenth-century Oxfordshire would catapult birds and go 'spadgering', casting a net over a whole hedge to catch sparrows. Alacaluf children of Patagonia fend for themselves early, using a shellfish spear and cooking their own food from the age of about four. Very young Inuit children may use a whip to hunt ptarmigans, with a flick of the wrist lopping off their heads. Ache children of Paraguay learn early how to collect fruit, and boys are given a bow and arrow when they are around two. By the time they are ten or twelve, they carry a bow all the time, learning to hunt, and by this age have become very independent of their parents. When Tom Sawyer runs away with Huck and Joe Harper, they take hooks and lines for fishing and they light a cooking fire: it seemed to them 'glorious' 'to be feasting in that wild free way'.

Travelling through the highlands of West Papua among the Yali people, I often saw village boys going off together, bristling with bows and arrows, to hunt birds, catch frogs and roast them in fires they would build themselves. From about five years old they would grow their own sweet potatoes, no longer asking their parents for food. At this point, they would leave their mother's house to live in the men's house: again, food is a marker of maturity.

Meanwhile, in England, an environmental play project called 'Wild About Play' asked children what they most wanted to do outdoors, and the answer was to collect and eat wild foods, to make fires and cook on them. This is exactly the sign of independence demonstrated by children everywhere, controlling their own food and their own bodies. I stress this because it seems that modern Euro-American children have two unusual food-related experiences: firstly, they *don't* have early autonomy with respect to food and, secondly, they *do* experience eating problems. While the desire to control one's own food seems a widely shared need among children, the issue of 'control' is one possible contributory factor to eating problems.

For years of evolutionary history, children have trapped, grown, found, hunted or fished for themselves and cooked on their own fires. The instinct to control one's own food and fire is blocked by the life-style of the dominant culture, which discourages children lighting fires or finding food outdoors, which categorizes food as something coming from shops rather than directly from the land, and which stipulates that food must be cooked, indoors, by an adult who often makes a child eat at their command. Is this part of the reason why some children, deprived of such an age-old freedom, are vulnerable to developing distorted relationships with food?

~

The sea. That was where I first learned the word 'horizon'. My brothers were pointing to something and I started looking for a boat. 'Not a boat,' they said, 'the *horizon*': it was as if I had never seen it before. That actual horizon would later extend into ideas of horizons: far horizons, horizons of time, past and future, horizons of hope and possibility. But it began there. My brothers and I spent weeks with our grandparents by the sea where we learned so much more than it may have seemed. Not because we saw an actual shipwreck but because we saw the potential for it. Not because we actually found treasure but because we could feel the immanence of treasure at every seashore. ('There comes a time in every rightly constructed boy's life when he has a raging desire to go somewhere and dig for hidden treasure' – Mark Twain.) We fished for wishes and caught them; we swam to find mermaids and became them; and we dived for pearls and returned with a stick, a bit of litter, a coin or the makings of a joke. Pearls, in other words.

We learned about tides and chance, storms and sun, the vicissitudes of what is lost and found, flotsam and jetsam, castaway luck, islands, sea-songs, rings, riddles and pledges. We learned the sense of a clean slate in the renewal of the tide-smoothed sand. We learned the physical sense of hot, soft sand on scuffed knees, the sharp cuts of seashells, and we learned what it meant to have salt rubbed in a wound. We learned a real and wise fear of swimming near rocks. No amount of Jacques Cousteau – adore him though we did – would have been a good enough substitute for the lived adventures of that modest little strip of beach, Dumpton Gap. This part of my childhood was, I know now, a passport to the world.

At home we had an old, battered (and horribly heavy) canoe which we took to the river. This cast-off canoe seemed one of the most perfect inventions of humanity for the waters belonged to us when we paddled around on mud-chill shores, and the noisy serenity of our afternoons was reflected in the bright, wet sunlight of an English river. Quite often, if we couldn't be bothered to carry the canoe we would still go to the river to sit, soggy and happy as frogs, stirring the mud.

Like all children, we saw ourselves reflected in water. Children are always drawn to it, their thinking water-like, each word fluid to many meanings in the years when the world trickles past them, unfixed as water. Children seem allergic to dryness, as the phrase 'still wet behind the ears' suggests: they are happy sliding, slipping and getting wet, 'when the world is mud-luscious and puddle-wonderful', as ee cummings put it. Being covered in wet stuff – sauce, slime, chocolate, ice cream, or gravy – doesn't bother children. ('What is the difference between adults and children?' I once asked a friend. 'Children just don't mind having jam all over them,' he answered.)

Water represents the fluxy freedom which children – spring tides running high in their lives – thirst for. The adventures of Tom Sawyer and Huckleberry Finn, the river-journeys of *The Wind in the Willows* or *The Little Grey Men*, the lake adventures of *Swallows and Amazons* or the sea adventures of *Robinson Crusoe*, all cry freedom. It's doubtful if these books would have been written if their authors had not known their waterful childhood freedom.

As a child, Mary Shelley spent a lot of time in Scotland on the banks of the River Tay, and she describes these shores as 'the eyry of freedom', for beneath the trees or on the mountains her imagination was 'born and fostered'. Without them, who knows?

William Wordsworth would sometimes take a five-mile detour around a lake on his way to school, when the school day began at six or six thirty. Without his liberty, his greatest poetry might never have been written, for he traces its origin to his unenclosed childhood. Water is a reflecting thing, and it allows children to reflect within themselves. Wordsworth describes waking at dawn and going outside to a world of nature which took him inside to the psyche's landscapes:

> . . . *and what I saw*
> *Appeared like something in myself, a dream,*
> *A prospect in the mind.*

When artists have, as children, encountered freedom, they have also experienced an ecstatic knowledge of nature. This is not only about the freedom of the body but the freedom of the mind, for art's first demand is freedom so imagination can circumnavigate a world.

One summer evening as a child, Wordsworth writes, he found a 'little boat tied to a willow tree'. He purloined it, rowing late by moonlight towards a crag, the horizon's utmost boundary. The peak seemed to have 'purpose of its own' and for many days after that haunted him with 'unknown modes of being'. His actual childhood freedom found by water led him to his psychological and creative freedom.

Children may experience the world as water, swimming in streets where nothing is dry, nothing is literal (or indeed littoral) but all is in the process of dissolving and re-forming, mer-maid, mer-man in a mer-world, a child's mind and environment so influent that they flow within it and it within them, each porous to the other. (This vision has rarely been better expressed than in the child hero of *One Moonlit Night*, by Caradog Prichard.)

Children feel a quick affinity for people whose lives seem free: those of the travelling circus, the fairground people, pirates and sailors and, of course, gypsies. When I was a child, the Romany books by G. Bramwell Evens, 'the Romany of the BBC', magnetized me with something I knew but could not articulate. I know now. It was raw freedom which even applied to adults. (And I was a little bit in love with Raq, his dog.)

Of all gypsies, perhaps the sea-gypsies – pearl fishers – seem the most captivating to the imagination, combining as they do all the mystery and freedom of gypsies and sailors both. A few years ago, I spent a day with children of the sea-gypsies, the Bajau people who live off Sulawesi in stilt-houses set far into the water, bordered by flotillas of cigarette packets and biscuit-wrappers, among hundreds of boats and sea-grass gardens, each marked by flags torn and fluttering against the sky, like a Tibetan mountain pass. The children were swimmers and divers, boaters and paddlers, rinsed with seawater night and day till they seemed half-child, half-otter.

I asked what their childhood was like. The answer was immediate: 'Children have a happy childhood because there is a lot of freedom.' The connection is noted by others: 'Delight and liberty, the simple creed/Of Childhood,' wrote Wordsworth. When Huckleberry Finn has been taken under the protection of Widow Douglas, he bitterly misses the days when he had been 'free and happy'. If happiness is a result of freedom, then surely the unhappiness of modernity's children is caused in part by the fact that they are less free than any children in history.

For the sea-gypsy children, much of their time was spent fishing from the boats or paddling. They can cook on the boats, where a rock or piece of flat coral is set as a fire-base. If they meet with problems, they told me, they can row away, just find somewhere else. I was asked if children had this much freedom where I came from. 'No,' I said, 'not so much, and they don't seem so happy either.' I had been very struck by the obvious happiness of the Bajau children: spending the whole long afternoon with about a hundred of them, not one was crying, cross, unhappy or frustrated. I can't imagine spending an afternoon with a hundred European or American children and not once hearing a child cry – unless, of course, they're watching back-to-back early episodes of *The Simpsons*. There was a problem, though, the children said: they missed not having television on the boats.

In Europe, one country seems to have honoured the relationship between freedom and childhood happiness in a way which the sea-gypsy children would have understood. A waterland of lakes, seas and fjords, a country which has enshrined in law an ancient right to canoe, kayak, row, sail and swim, to walk across all land (except private gardens and tilled fields) in a freedom known as *Allemannsretten*, 'every man's right', the right to roam.

Norway's freedom is intoxicating, a go-where-you-will sense of all the wide world, open and yours. It is exhilarating, it is vitalizing, it is a relief almost shocking for those who come from Britain, with our pinched footpaths and blocked rights of way, where canoeists are told that they are 'trespassers' in the rainwater which is somehow 'private' once it reaches a river. For all those fenced out, bullied, frightened and intimidated off the land, being in Norway is like being able to breathe fully after years of semi-suffocation.

If the sea-gypsy children, Huckleberry Finn and Wordsworth are all correct in their analysis that children are happy when they are free, what of traditional Norwegian childhood? A fascinating tale emerges. In 1960, the American psychiatrist Herbert Hendin was studying suicide statistics in Scandinavia. Denmark (with Japan) had the world's highest suicide rate. Sweden's rate was almost as high, but what of Norway? Right at the bottom. Hendin was intrigued, particularly since received wisdom opined that Denmark, Sweden and Norway shared a very similar culture. What was different? What could possibly account for such a dramatic difference in suicidal unhappiness? After years of research, he concluded that reasons were established in childhood. In Denmark and Sweden, children were brought up with regimentation while, in Norway, they were free to roam. In Denmark and Sweden, children were pressured to achieve career goals until many felt they were failures while, in Norway, children were left alone more, not so much instructed but rather simply allowed to watch and participate in their own time. Instead of a sense of failure, Norwegian children grew up with a sense of self-reliance.

Danish children, the study showed, were over-protected, kept dependent on their mothers and not free to roam. For Swedish children, a common experience was that, in infancy, just when they needed closeness, what they got was separation and a sense of abandonment while, in later childhood, just when they needed freedom, what they got was far too much control. By contrast, in Norway, 'great value is placed on the individual right to move about freely,' Hendin wrote, 'a tradition that goes back to Viking days.' Norwegian children played outdoors for long hours unsupervised by adults, and a child's freedom was 'not likely to be restricted'. They had more closeness than Swedish children at an early age, but then more freedom than both Danish and Swedish children at a later age, suggesting that closeness followed by freedom is likely to produce the happiest children.

Intriguingly, Hendin also noted the difference in the stories which children were told. In Denmark and Sweden, folk tales tended to be about heroes who needed the help of some other, higher being, so the children were saved through magic, miracle and a higher power. The hero of Norwegian folk tales is the Ash Lad, and he saves himself. He wins out by his own inventiveness, his own cunning and observation. The Ash Lad was not only a folk hero, he was also a way of being, an exemplar of Norwegian childhood which had long emphasized children's freedom – but this figure barely appears in the traditions of Sweden and Denmark.

The Ash Lad is a quintessential role model for all children. He is a happy-go-lucky child, embodying delight and liberty. No one's slave and no one's master, he acts autonomously, spontaneously and freely, following his nose, living by his wits, responding to his own volition; independent. He is reminiscent of Huck Finn, Tom Sawyer, Laura Dekker, Béasse, Laurie Lee, the young Wordsworth, Philip Pullman's Lyra and Will and indeed all those for whom childhood freedom is vital. The Ash Lad's physical freedom fosters his freedom of mind and he is a free thinker, a non-conformist, eccentric and idiosyncratic. Resourceful, he has a strong sense of initiative and is quick to improvise. Curious and attentive to nature, he is open and kind to those he meets, all of whom he treats as equals. He was a beloved influence on generations of Norwegian children.

In the decades since Hendin's work, though, the story grows sad. As Norway became more centralized and urbanized, childhood altered, involving housebound computer games rather than the free roaming of earlier generations. Norwegian children now spend more time indoors in sedentary activities, such as watching television or DVDs and playing computer games, than they do outdoors. At the same time, the suicide rate has rocketed and is now one of the highest in the world.

~

In America and Europe alike, many kids today are effectively under house arrest, eighty per cent of them in the UK complaining that they have 'nowhere to go'. It's about four o'clock in the afternoon, you've got a couple of quid in your pocket but not a lot more. You've knocked off for the day and you'd quite like to be with your mates. The cheap cafés will be closed in an hour, you can't afford restaurants and you are not allowed in 'public' houses. You tell everyone who will listen that you don't want to cause trouble, you'd just like somewhere which is dry, well lit and safe, where you can hang out and chat. So you go to bus shelters and car parks and the brightly lit areas outside corner shops. You have nowhere else to go, so you find the margins, the little pockets on the edges of public spaces. And then you are driven off as if you were vermin. The UK seems to be leading the way in how not to treat children, and a few examples are in order.

A plan to erect a netball hoop on a village green in Oxfordshire was blocked 'because residents didn't want to attract children'. In West Somerset, an eight-year-old girl was stopped from cycling down her street because a neighbour complained that the wheels squeaked. In one survey, two thirds of children said they liked playing outside every day, mainly to be with friends, but eighty per cent of them have been told off for playing outdoors, fifty per cent have been shouted at for playing outside and twenty-five per cent of eleven- to sixteen-year-olds were threatened with violence by adults for . . . for what? For Playing Outdoors, Making a Noise, Being a Nuisance.

Saddest of all, it works. One in three of the children said that being told off for playing outside does successfully stop them doing it. If a puppy is caged indoors and not allowed to play outside, its owners may be prosecuted for not allowing the dog to 'express normal behaviour' according to the law. Children are merely expressing normal behaviour and wanting rights equal to dogs.

If there is one word which sums up the treatment of children today, it is enclosure. Today's children are enclosed in school and home, enclosed in cars to shuttle between them, enclosed by fear, by surveillance and poverty and enclosed in rigid schedules of time. These enclosures compound each other and make children bitterly unhappy. In 2011, UNICEF asked children what they needed to be happy, and the top three things were time (particularly with families), friendships and, yearningly, 'outdoors'. Studies show that when children are allowed unstructured play in nature, their sense of freedom, independence and inner strength all thrive, and children surrounded by nature are not only less stressed but also bounce back from stressful events more readily.

But there has been a steady reduction in available open spaces for children to play. In the USA, the home turf of children shrank by ninety per cent between 1970 and 1990. Similarly, in Britain, children have one ninth of the roaming room they had in earlier generations. Childhood is losing its commons. There has also been a reduction in available time, with less than ten per cent of children now spending time playing in woodlands, countryside or heaths, compared with forty per cent who did so a generation ago.

'The countryside – I've been there, maybe about once,' says a ten-year-old boy from Huddersfield.

Although they are themselves part of nature, children are removed from the world of moss and trees, of fur and paw. Children don't need to live in the countryside to have access to nature, and most city children, left to their own devices, can find a bare minimum of what they need in urban parks and gardens, even on the streets. But play is enclosed indoors while outside signs bark at children like Alsatian guard dogs: NO CYCLING. NO SKATEBOARDS. NO BALL GAMES. NO SWIMMING. NO TRESPASSING.

My later childhood was hollowed by cold and poverty and that depression which sets up snares in the young psyche, trapping it for life. My early childhood, though, was far happier, in large part because my brothers and I were part of the last generation which was not under house arrest. It was not a rural childhood, but we had a garden, and a few streets away a river ran by the side of the 'wreck', as we called the recreation ground. It *was* a wreck. Scruffy. Ignored. Ours. Five minutes' walk away was a park. Two hours away were those grandparents who lived by the sea. All the games we had fitted into a bench trunk about six foot by two. We were rich in library books, bicycles and outdoors.

Outdoors, we could do what we liked. Throwing sticky seeds at each other, gurgling water or chucking it all over someone. Indoors, obviously not, for indoors was where complexity began: 'mine' and 'yours' and the difficult rules of time. Outdoors was a commons of space and a commons of time, the undivided hours till dark. Outdoors could comprehend all our moods: thoughtful, playful, withdrawn or rampaging. Outdoors was the place for voices other than human. 'Stones,' one of my god-daughters says, emphatically, 'are the most interesting things in the world.' She is five.

Outdoors, no one told us to be careful about breaking, spilling or kicking things, because that's what sticks, water and leaves were for. The verbs of 'destruction' only mattered indoors. No one could ever use up all the grass by mowing it with their teeth or spoil the sun by making too many shadows. No one could ever suck all the honey from the honeysuckle. There would always be more stillness in the pond after a rock had been hurled into it; there would always be enough rocks and no river would ever run out.

Outside, spitting didn't matter – in fact it was useful glue. How much of the world of childhood gets stuck together with spit? How many twigs, leaves, bits of rubbish, bog roll, berries and labels, pieces of clothing surreptitiously scissored off? Outside was the place to build breathless towers of stuff and then, in revenge against order, to demolish them, unleashing some archaic chaos. Recently, I was playing on a dewy morning with another god-daughter. 'Look at the million rainbows in the grass,' she said, 'and I can trample on them all.' On the beach we made a fish of sand with shells for scales. 'When can we cut it in half?' she asked, with the innocent bloodthirstiness of four-year-olds.

Nature was tough enough; she was Baba Yaga-like, leaf-tangled and hair-matted, her house dancing on chicken legs. Children will chase, catch, kill or burn just about anything, smashing ice and breaking branches, happily destroying what they can reach, but nature is generally safe from children because they don't have the tools for serious damage. Generally. The unsupervised hours of my early child-hood led to physics experiments, and one of my brothers, now a professor of the subject, thought it was a good idea to try bomb-making in the back garden and got as far as matches and a hosepipe full of petrol before Baba Yaga in the form of our dad was roused to (understandable) fury.

Along with everyone I knew, from our first day at school, we walked there. I went with my brothers and friends, a little ragged string of us, taking short cuts which weren't, chatting nonsense, swap-ping things, eating sweets, making dares, sticking chewing gum on walls, doing deals, showing off, doing silly walks, shuffling, holding hands, telling secrets, getting the giggles. It was a crucial part of the whole business of childhood. We learned our home territory; we learned which shops might give us free doughnuts if we tried to look particularly hungry; we learned which hedges bloomed with which flowers and we put the flowers on the graves of road-kill squirrels; we went into cake shops to cheekily ask why they had had the same cake in the window for two years; we learned how to avoid cars and how to look out for each other; we learned which of the older boys were truly scary; we learned which of the older girls drank whisky on her way to school and, goggle-eyed, we were particularly impressed that in her insouciance she chose to drink Teacher's.

There was, of course, safety in numbers. When today so few chil-dren are out alone, the venturesome child feels vulnerable indeed. In Britain, in 1971, eighty per cent of all seven- and eight-year-olds went to school on their own. By 1990, this had dropped to nine per cent. In 2010, two children, aged eight and five, cycled to school alone and their headmaster threatened to report their parents to social services.

They should have been awarded a medal for allowing their children the freedom which we took for granted and which gave us so much.

~

Enclosure can be metaphysical. Caught on camera or trapped in the unceasing stare of CCTV, children may be unhappy partly because of the surveillance they suffer, according to Mary Bousted, general secretary of the Association of Teachers and Lecturers. In school, children are subject to constant supervision while even 'outside school they are not allowed the freedom to play and learn unwatched.'

Among animals – including children and adults – staring is a sign of aggression. Predators target their prey by staring fixedly and this is a prelude to attack. The prey can feel it, their skin prickling, their senses disturbed, and they may want to attack back. Staring at someone may thus provoke their hostility and surveillance will certainly undermine their easefulness.

Never before have children been so subject to surveillance, supervision and monitoring. As well as ubiquitous CCTV and webcams in classrooms, there is an increasing market for 'nanny cams', the secret home camera, and for non-removable watches containing GPS devices, which seventy-five per cent of British parents are in favour of their children using. Worst of all is the 'teddy cam', that perversion of children's trust, where Teddy, with nasty little spy-cameras in his eyes, stares and films the child. Without doubt, individual parents want constant surveillance of their child because they genuinely fear for their safety, but this fear is manufactured by the companies who will profit from it.

Children who are told 'It's rude to stare' are themselves stared at all the time. It's no surprise that children desire – fervently and furiously – to be unseen, with an invisibility cloak, a mask, a spell for disappearing and their hoodies. The fashion for hoodies arose at the same time as increasing surveillance, and it surely represents a highly appropriate response to it as young people shade themselves from the constant, aggressive staring of adults. Yesterday, I asked one of my favourite hoodies if that might be one reason why he liked wearing them. Emphatically, he said, *yes*. Companies, shops and malls want to ban hoodies. I would like to ban the reasons why kids feel the need to wear them.

~

Younger children may be enclosed on the grounds that adults are frightened *for* them. Older children are enclosed because adults are frightened *of* them. The latter fear is manufactured by the media in a blitz of hatred which would be illegal if it were applied to any other group.

The Samaritans say the main contributory factor in youth suicide is leaving school with a poor sense of self-worth, and yet damaging children's sense of well-being seems something of a national hobby in Britain. The United Nations Committee on the Rights of the Child refers to a 'general climate of intolerance' in Britain towards children, and stresses that the media's 'consistently negative portrayal' of young people is unacceptable. Seventy-one per cent of media stories about young people are negative and a third of articles about young people are about crime.

Imagine if seventy-one per cent of media stories about Jews were negative. So-called 'public' houses display signs saying 'No Jews unless Accompanied by a Gentile'. Jews are disproportionately subject to police 'stop and search'. There is a Sonic Jew Deterrent to stop them gathering outside the synagogue on Saturdays. Then the synagogues are closed down in government cutbacks. A curfew is brought in, specifically applied to Jews. Without committing any crime whatsoever, two or more Jews 'hanging around' may be subject to police dispersal. Leisure centres and museums may refuse people entry on the grounds that they are Jewish. The police spray bleach in places where a handful of Jews gather to talk.

You get the picture. It's really ugly. And it is the experience of kids.

In recent years, there has been 'an increase in discrimination against children as a whole', says the UK Children's Commissioners' Report. From 2001, when the Terrorism Act came into force, the police have had 'stop and search' power over anyone aged ten or older, and it is disproportionately used against children. This was one frequent reason which kids gave for their fury which erupted in the UK riots of 2011. If you're black and male and a child, you may be subject to 'stop and search' hundreds of times before you reach adulthood.

In Norfolk, police have sprayed bleach in public stairwells because its acrid smell drives children away. The town council in Rochdale, Lancashire, considered installing low-pressure sodium lights because they make teenagers' spots glow in the dark, so they will be too embarrassed to congregate. And twenty-five per cent of local authorities in the UK have used the 'Mosquito' device, the Sonic Teenager Deterrent, which emits a noise almost unbearable to children and teenagers but which is inaudible to adults. The Council of Europe's parliamentary assembly recommends that the 'Mosquito' device is banned because it discriminates against young people. Teenagers, though, have exploited the technology, using it as a mobile-phone ringtone (Teen Buzz) so teachers can't hear their phones ring in class. (You have to hand it to them, that's a fine piece of *détournement*.)

Young people are treated as if their mere presence in 'adult' space is a malicious trespass. Children are discriminated against on public transport and by public services: they are often refused entry to libraries, leisure centres, museums and art galleries, so the commons of public space is cordoned off to them. In Britain, you can find yourself on the wrong side of the law for no other reason than that you are outdoors and under sixteen, through curfew powers to stop young people being outside, unsupervised, between 9 p.m. and 6 a.m., while dispersal orders give the police power to clear two or more kids who have committed no crime whatsoever. This power may be disproportionately used against groups of children 'hanging around', says the UK Children's Commissioners' Report and 'may penalize law-abiding children with nowhere else to go'.

It is a violation of that common and ancient right, freedom of association, but where are the mass trespasses against these acts? Where is the Kinder Scout for the Kinder of today? Where is the revulsion – in this 'free' nation – against the offensive idea that children should be under house arrest for no crime other than being young outside?

Of British adults, 1.5 million say they would consider emigrating 'mainly because of young people hanging around'. Frankly, I wish they would. But where would these grumpy gits go? Somewhere which outlaws childhood altogether? Or somewhere which perhaps routinely incarcerates children? The USA and Britain already do, imprisoning more children than any other country in the West. Children as young as ten can be tried and jailed in England and Wales, and children excluded from school can be effectively subject to house arrest, forbidden from being 'present in a public place', while wholly innocent refugee children are imprisoned in detention centres. In the USA, children can be sentenced to life imprisonment, which would be in violation of the UN Convention on the Rights of the Child, except for the fact that the USA (together with Somalia) has refused to ratify it.

What does society do with its most reviled prisoners?

~ Subjects them to loud and unpleasant noise
~ Intimidates them with 'stop and search' procedures
~ Forces them to live by clockwork routines
~ Bullies them with smear campaigns in the press
~ Forbids them equal use of public space and public services
~ Denies them access to nature and the outdoors
~ Restricts them to specific exercise yards
~ Arrests them arbitrarily
~ Refuses them autonomy, independence and freedom
~ Puts them under constant surveillance
~ Isolates them in small rooms
~ Segregates them from 'ordinary' society
~ Compels them to wear special uniforms
~ Fences them in strictly, at all times

And this is what we do to the vast majority of our children.

~

Parents may of course enclose their children out of love and fear: including of so-called 'hostile nature'. Nature is not unsafe but rather becomes so when children do not have knowledge and experience of it, when they are fenced out by ignorance. Take skating. Generations of children have skated on lakes in winter and, with some basic know-how, anyone can safely skate. But over the last few decades, wild skating has become almost unheard of, because people are led to believe it is dangerous.

~

A little digression on skating . . .

I have to confess that whenever the lakes near my home freeze over I am absolutely delirious with skate fever, as the ice issues an imperative: *Carpe Diem! Get Your Skates On!* I have skated in sunlight, by starlight and lanternlight. Once with friends we skated by moonlight in full evening dress plundered from charity shops: feathers, fascinators and fake furs. Skating is a form of flying. The god Mercury was, according to Coleridge, the first maker of skates, and every skater has his wings at their feet. John Clare skated as a child, and skating in the Lake District was, said Wordsworth, 'a time of rapture'. His sister said he was a 'crack skater' and I hope this wasn't a pun.

It so saddens me that children have been frightened off skating that I thought I'd offer a quick guide. First, find some skates. You need stiff boots with sharp blades. Next, find a place to skate. Rivers and canals are both dangerous, as they freeze unpredictably. Fields that have flooded and then frozen are fun and safe. Lakes are heaven, but you need to test the depth of the ice. To do this, take a hammer and chisel or a battery-operated drill; or, if you'll be lighting a fire, take a poker, heat it in the flames and melt a hole in the ice. When you've drilled a hole, stick your hand in: the ice should be three or four inches deep. Then take a safety rope, and a broom, too, which is good for children and novice skaters to lean on for support and (unlike a stick or a well-intentioned friend) the broom will not slip on the ice. Take food and drink and musical instruments. Then fly, for, like most things in life, skating is best done open-hearted. Trust your wings.

. . . digression ends. Forgive me: I was unable to resist . . .

~

Never mind skating, even tree climbing is 'unsafe', say some teachers. Yes, indeed. 1,067 British children were hospitalized having fallen out of trees in 2006–7. More than twice as many (2,532) were hospitalized for falling out of bed. Must we ban beds? Pantomime artists are told not to throw sweets to children in case they cause injury. Children have been told to wear goggles in conker fights and at a donkey derby in Llandudno, children were not allowed to ride the donkeys. Inflatable sheep replaced children.

The risk-averse society denies the very idea of freedom's role, it stops chance throwing a wild card, it kills the free play of luck. The adventure-monitor creeps up, pouring cold water on every fire-pit, banning people from bringing home-made cakes to school fêtes. In the otherwise important UNICEF report into childhood well-being in 2007, the authors comment that health and safety 'did not feature highly in children's priorities'. Who knew?

Laura Dekker risks death or injury, yes, and this is the very meaning of adventure: that you accept a dare, that you allow the freedom of both chance *and* mischance. I remember first reading the word 'happy-go-lucky' and experiencing the idea like a peal of bells in my head. This is a crucial quality of the Ash Lad and other folk-tale heroes, combining happiness and liberty with chance – the opposite of the controlled and enclosed life. Setting out to seek one's *fortune* is the readying line of folk tales and children are only too willing to play with risk, to draw straws with hazard. It's a rare child who doesn't take to gambling like a duck to water: they shine at the luckiness of cards, dice and tossing coins, and every child I've ever known would place a bet as soon as nick a biscuit.

Primed to see luck where they can, children turn lucky moments into wishes. In the wishing lists of childhood, you can have a wish when you throw a coin into a well; when you catch a falling leaf or see a falling star; when you find an eyelash fallen on to your cheek; when the words fall out of your mouth at the same time they do from someone else's; when you accidentally put your knickers on inside out (but-only-if-you're-a-girl); when you blow out all the candles on a birthday cake; when you pick up a fallen penny and give it away. Many of these involve falling things, as if language recognizes a form of fate: this is how things 'fall out'. It 'fell this way', say stories. Meanwhile a lottery, a lucky dip, a tombola, a lucky number or a lucky day of the week all appeal to children's sense that life is riddled with luck and that freedom means doing a deal with chance, for you cannot plan luck or control it, you cannot fence it, enclose it, or store it. You can only be open to what falls out and hold on to your hope.

This is why the risk-averse attitude of modernity is not only annoying but conceptually malevolent. It works against the correct instinct children have that they must find a working relationship with chance and risk, otherwise their adventures cannot even begin and they will remain infantilized and enclosed, stuck forever indoors in the house 'hard by the great forest' with no chance of setting out on the quest through that forest. Children know life as a huge adventure, this calling dawn, the invitation of all the mornings of the world, asking chance and childhood to play. Adventure demands you accept that the roll of the dice may give you a six or a one, that you take a risk for a venture.

Luck is deeply involved in the nature of play. Luck, writes cultural historian Johan Huizinga, 'may have a sacred significance; the fall of the dice may signify and determine the divine workings . . . Indeed . . . for the human mind the ideas of happiness, luck and fate seem to lie very close to the realm of the sacred.'

Tightly constrained by the enfeebling of a risk-averse, health-and-safety-obsessed society, many children are unable to light fires, paddle canoes, make shelters, use knives or cope with darkness. Further, children are discouraged from acts of physical courage and this is more serious than it appears, for we learn with our bodies as well as our minds – or rather we learn with the mind-body – and when we see our physical selves modelling bravery, our sense of moral courage, political courage, emotional courage or intellectual courage is heightened.

Rather than learning to trust their own judgement – paying attention to the body's own knowledge that fire is hot, for example – children are taught to obey the signs of the authorities instead, so barriers are erected around a Guy Fawkes bonfire with notices warning 'STAND BACK – DANGER' as if children are to take their orders from signage, not from the fact that there is a blazing pyre melting their wellies.

My local primary school, in winter days of glorious thick snow, forbade children from playing in it for fear of litigation in the event of an accident. But this is about far more than merely living in a culture where people are ready to sue at the drop of a hat. This is about insidiously demanding that children must always seek permission for the most trivial of actions, that they must obey the commands of others at every turn. Children today are not being beaten into obedience but being eroded into it. The risk-averse society creates a docility and a loss of autonomy which has a horrible political shadow. A populace malleable. Commandable. Obedient.

I'm not arguing that children should be unsafe. It's just that I think the one thing which truly makes children safe is their own competence, their own capability, their authentic skills in meeting the asymmetry, irregularity and unpredictability of life. How do they come by their competence? Only by the practice of it. Experience made Laura Dekker 'capable', as her father said.

A Leeds primary school banned skipping ropes after a child was hurt in the playground. The health and safety authorities, here, are laming the spirit till it limps towards a risk assessment to be registered compliant. Children *need* accidents – little ones, ideally, accidents the right size, through which they learn to avoid bigger accidents later.

Maurice Arnatsiaq, an Inuit elder from Nunavut in the Canadian Arctic, speaks of one long adventure when he was about fifteen years old. He left home with a dog team and travelled alone for two weeks, from Igloolik to Crown Prince Frederick Island, then to Committee Bay and the Melville Peninsula, voyaging over hundreds of miles of Arctic ice. 'Maybe only three or four young people would be able to do that journey now,' he says. 'They don't know about the land.'

The elders say that as children they learned what they should be scared of and what they could safely ignore. They learned navigation by the stars, or by checking snowdrifts and currents and floating sea-weed. The school system taught them little which would help them on the land or sea. Theo Ikummaq, born in 1955, ran his own dog team by himself when he was fourteen, went camping and built igloos. He found schooling risible: 'Columbus, Cabot, Math, spelling' was about the sum of it. Nothing that would keep you safe and therefore nothing which would let you have any kind of adventure. Although some hunters have tried to teach land-skills in schools in the last few years, the chain of knowledge has broken down and teenagers now don't even know how to find water, says one hunter. Children get too cold to play for long outside because they no longer wear warm gear, choosing instead the kind of clothes they see on television, say Inuit elders. For Inuit people, the clash of two cultures has been grotesquely damaging for the young. I have never seen children so claustrophobically imprisoned as these, so suffocated, so unfree, because they lack the ability to be out on the land and are therefore effectively imprisoned in the communities, bored to tears, bored to death. Many Inuit children who have attempted suicide have said it was because they were bored. The rate of suicide among Inuit youth in Canada is eleven times the national average.

For Sámi children in Norway, lessons can be pragmatic and life-saving: how to survive fog, for instance, which can kill by leading people so far astray they cannot find shelter or food. Children are taught to stop, to find a stone with some kind of protecting edge and wait until the fog lifts. I saw first-hand how Sámi reindeer herders would trust their children to be wise in fog: a ten-year-old boy was sent trekking for hours with a smaller cousin and a dog, looking for lost reindeer to bring back to the herding area.

Fog we met, in those days, fog so sudden and dense that you could barely see across the corral, fog which hugged the small children who were themselves hugging a small reindeer calf, cutting a slice off its ear and yelling out its number to see who owned it. The reindeer gallop around the pen, barging the walls, and the children spin with the reindeer around the corral, one four-year-old blowing raspberries to get the fur out of his mouth, tottering after a calf, giggling with pleasure. His mother tells me the children prefer not to be in a city because they are happier out on the tundra: 'Here they are free.' Lassoing and wrangling reindeer, driving quad bikes far over the horizon, the children almost visibly grew an extra inch of independence.

In Sámi tradition, trial and error are important and failure is helpful. Children may be left alone, tackling difficulties in often quite dangerous situations. They are given knives, scissors and matches at an early age, and this is both a challenge and a trust. Sheltering children is considered unwise because it will mean they do not know how to manage for themselves.

How to keep children safe: give them not only knives, scissors and matches, but machetes, lassoes, sledges, dog teams, snowdrifts, fire and fog. Give them competence, give them appropriate fear and the knowledge to scorn false fear. Keep Away From Children only one thing: infantilism.

In the Amazon, I've seen five-year-olds wielding machetes with deftness and precision. In Igloolik in the Arctic, I've seen an eight-year-old take an *alu* (an Inuit knife) and carve up a frozen caribou, as they regularly do – without accident. In West Papua, I've known youngsters of twelve or thirteen with such physical capability and confidence that, when asked to be messengers, they completed a mountain run in six hours: a journey which had taken myself and the guides a day and a half.

This is not only a matter of physical competence: the freedom which Inuit children traditionally experienced made them into 'self-reliant, caring and self-controlled individuals', in the words of one Inuit person I met in Nunavut. It gave them courage and patience. Indigenous Australian Bob Randall speaks of his childhood and its 'non-restrictive nature, psychically and physically. I was always totally free,' and his words bask in the memory of unfenced freedom like lizards in the sun. This freedom, he suggests, meant autonomy but not licence, the freedom to be the captain of your soul.

Mark Twain, steamboat captain, gave to his boy-heroes the chance to be the captains of their own lives and to plot their course with the ebullience of adventure. 'I did not wish to take a cabin passage,' wrote Henry David Thoreau, 'but rather to go before the mast and on the deck of the world, for there I could best see the moonlight amid the mountains. I do not wish to go below now.'

Laura Dekker, sharing this bravura, eventually wrested her freedom from the hands of the authorities and succeeded, in January 2012, aged sixteen, in becoming the youngest person to circumnavigate the world solo, having demanded her right to live on the deck of the world, to be the captain of her own soul, daring to honour a fierce daydream, the right to roam for body and mind, to set sail for horizons of magnificence.

CHAPTER FIVE

Wolf Milk in the Ink

My kitten has been awarded an Anti-Social Behaviour Order. The reasons involve the toilet, three houseplants, my other cat's ear and some genetic predispositions, including the fact that his mother was an acrobat and his father was a kangaroo.

I'd been in two minds about getting a second cat but a nearby farm had kittens *de trop* and I had house guests, among them a seven-year-old boy in an off-kilter mood whose face became suddenly cloudless when I whispered the word *kitten*. Enter Otter. The two kittens, one of each species, played together for hours and the child happily strolled over the borders, belonging to the world of brimming animality as much as to human culture.

'Thou art of the Jungle and not of the Jungle,' Bagheera says to Mowgli. 'And I am only a black panther. But I love thee, Little Brother.' That children love animals is a manifest truth and they also seek love from them. So crucial are animals to children's happiness that in a significant UNICEF study of childhood well-being children specified that pets were one of the top four most important things for their happiness. 'I want a kitten . . . a puppy . . . a horse,' children clamour for years, and this is perhaps only the most audible part of their love. Children talk wordlessly to their pets, taking a dog in their arms or, upset, burying their faces in a cat's fur and crying. They whisper secrets to their pets and feel understood by them. Children want to talk with the animals, eat with them, curl up with them and think with them, for children intuitively understand that animals are guides for the mind in metaphor-making.

John Clare, a hater of all fences, made a friendship across the fences of the species, keeping a tame sparrow called Tom which would come at his call. He introduced the sparrow to his cat and taught her never to harm the bird, by hitting her when her paws got too twitchy. In time, the cat would even bring mice for the sparrow, mew to it and let it perch on her back. After three years, though, the sparrow disappeared – possibly because, Clare surmised, it had met a cat uneducated in sparrow-cherishing.

Children's authors, peopling their books with animals, know that children are fascinated by tales of crossing the species-fences, and the stories work carnally, suggesting a nuzzling sensuality, fostering a child's animal nature and answering a longing deep within children to be suckled by earthmilk, pressing their faces into the warm flank of horse, lion or wolf, breathing in the spicy, messageful air of animals, falling asleep in their paws.

Aslan. To run your fingers through his golden mane, to see 'the great, royal, solemn, overwhelming eyes', to feel that humming, purring warmth and its ferocious power; 'whether it was more like playing with a thunderstorm or playing with a kitten', the children cannot say. The writer Francis Spufford recalls a tender trespass of his childhood when he was suddenly seized with desire for Aslan and reached his face up to a poster of the lion on his bedroom wall. Stealthily, heartfeltedly, he kissed the lion's nose. From early childhood, I remember that feeling, wanting to nudge myself deep into the musk and silage, the mushroom, rust and grass of an animal's den, wanting to know with my whole body the felt world of fur and pawpads and to feel the animal world in its fullness, in yawls, hackles and green-scent, to be batted by the paws of the furred earth, my senses drunk with it, living in the whisky of animality. And to kiss the lion's nose.

There's a fox in the garden. Those words would thrill us to the core. My brothers and I would crowd to the window in pressed silence, breathless, excited and honoured that something so wild might bestow on us for a flickering moment its feral presence. Birds and animals come in to our lives as 'guests', say Mohawk tales, and people must treat them well.

One of my god-daughters set up a snail hospital in a corner of her garden, using spit to mend cracks in their shells which were invisible to the adult eye. I've sat in trees for hours with children silent as frozen leaves, trying to conjure badgers. Children's sense of delight at the animal world is as reckless as their spelling can be: at the Aigas centre in Scotland, which runs nature courses for children, one child wrote of his pleasure in learning 'that beevis have pouchis at the baof side off it's mouf,' and another said 'the bughunt was amingszing.'

Eighty per cent of the dreams of children under six are about animals, and their psyches need different creatures: rabbit, octopus, spider, frog, whale, sloth or tiger. Children today say they lack good role models, which is a truth sadder than they know, for they deserve a range of such examples beyond the human and including, for instance, the fleet sensitivity of a deer, the watchfulness of a bird or the lazy grace of a cat. First-hand knowledge may bring them the powers of different animals, the feeling of a feather for flight or strong hind legs for leaping. 'Children use animals as a gymnasium for their own emotions,' says David Attenborough.

In the Koyukon world-view, children have an especial sensitivity towards nature and it was traditionally considered wise to raise a hawk owl around them, as these birds are clean and kill things easily, and adults hoped that children would learn these virtues. Conversely, there was a taboo against keeping dogs indoors because children would copy them, behaving badly and eating dirty food.

Animal-helpers snuffle in the hedges of fairy tales and they feather the treetops with bird-advice. In the nick of time, the winged lion or the armoured bear swerve into stories. If the fairy-tale hero treats an animal kindly, it offers its skills, pecking out grain or tracking a scent beyond human guesswork.

Creatures are friends to the psyche of a child. When Henry Old Coyote, from the Crow nation, was a boy, his grandfather would wake him early to listen to the birds and encouraged the child to know the exuberant joy of this bird medicine and to keep it inside him all day. I'm told that in Tamil Nadu, India, a child suffering nightmares may be cured by walking under an elephant's belly, being blessed by Ganesh. The nightmares, knowing better than to contend with an elephant, beat a retreat. A psychotherapist in Britain once told me about a deeply disturbed boy who came to sessions with his dog. The two had such a close relationship that often the dog would sense a difference in the boy's emotional state before the therapist, so she learned to take her cues from it. Studies show that animal companionship reduces a child's sense of alienation and increases their self-esteem, self-control and autonomy. Other studies demonstrate how children treat their pets as they themselves would like to be treated and suggest that children who have pets feel more empathy towards other people.

~

'In the old days the animals and the people were very much the same . . . They thought the same way and felt the same way. They understood each other,' says Simon Tookoome, an Inuit elder, recalling a belief common to many indigenous cultures. As a child, he adopted animals, including a caribou which followed him everywhere like a dog and, at different times, five wolves. More loving than dogs, one of these was shot for its fur, and the death left Tookoome griefstruck. Once, and thrillingly, his parents brought him a very young polar bear. His parents told him never to hurt animals but 'just to play with them', for children can, of course, be both mercifully kind and mercilessly cruel. Anthropologist Jean L. Briggs describes an Inuit child who 'enjoyed killing the unwanted newborn puppies, dashing them with squeals of excited laughter against boulders or throwing them off the high knoll edge into the rapids below'.

Tookoome explains how children were taught to understand animals so that they could hunt them better. Children often enjoy snaring, poaching, chasing and trapping animals and, to succeed in this, children need to learn to imitate other creatures, disguising themselves in order to fox their prey. Cherokee childhood in the 1860s, depicted in the autobiography of James Hightower, emphasized this 'imitation work' for children over five. His diary of childhood encounters includes an escape from a dangerous situation when the children had had to imitate a panther mewing for a mate, and describes a soundworld of baying timber-wolves, chittering squirrels, calling bob-cats, hooting owls, bellowing buffaloes and howling coyotes. One girl was the best of the bunch at coyote calls, perfecting the sharp bark, finishing on a note somewhere between a bark and a jabber, which is the signal of a coyote in strange territory *calling all coyotes*. Lit with language, and these languages understood, the world is more than human: it glistens with excitement, adventure, danger, delight and knowledge. It teems with meaning and message. 'There was not an Indian over eight years old but who could tell what temper the animal was in from his whine, or his purr, or bellow, or bark. Also every bird, whether in distress or content.'

One peculiarity of modern childhood in the West is its estrangement from the animal world and the consequent silence of that world, its unmessaged, listless, speechless vacancy. Poet Gary Snyder speaks of the necessity to 'Bring up our children as part of the wildlife', but the dominant culture treats wildlife as insignificant to children's happiness which, as children themselves know, is a terrible oversight. Children's classic *Black Beauty* and Michael Morpurgo's mesmerizing *War Horse* touch the hearts of millions of children as they willingly listen to the experience of creatures other than human.

There is a weighty book, some 379 pages long, entitled *The Inner World of Childhood: A Study in Analytical Psychology*, which was first published in 1927. There is nothing about nature in it. Oh, hang on, just the one: an entry for 'Animals, fear of' in an index which itself runs to nine pages. You almost have to applaud the book for its blink-eredness, for its majestic refusal to see animals entwined in, and beloved of, childhood.

In the bleak enclosures of modernity, adults and children alike may stand by the tiger cage at the zoo, waving and hoping for a flicker of acknowledgement in the tiger's eye, getting only the dulled stare of resentment. Forlorn, caged as the tiger, we are a lonely species now. We have fenced ourselves off, though our bodies still remember the wilds in the sinews, in the fingertips, in the skin which still thrills with electric recognition as when, for example, a wild fox was filmed on the loose in the National Gallery.

'With their whole gaze,' writes Rainer Maria Rilke, 'animals behold the Open,' while children are forced to:

look backward
at the forms we create,
not outward into the Open.

Animals can teach children how to be open to the pounce of the wind and the claw of the thorn, receptive to the handshadows of trees and the earth's telluric drum.

Children cling to animals: real ones when they can, substitutes when necessary. Take teddy bears (or, in David Crystal's witty collective noun, a threadbare of teddies). How much love goes wasted on sicked-up-all-over, chewed, tatty pieces of cloth and plastic? I should know. All those of us who are faithful to our teddies know the perfect and lifelong commitment that a passionate child freely gives and a passionate adult freely honours. From the moment I was given him – a little monkey with a plastic face, huge sad green eyes and a red collar and lead, which I tore off because he looked choked – I have loved and shared my pillow with Charlie, my protector and my comforter. I named him after Charlie Chaplin, who never made me laugh but whose sadness touched me to the core. (I wanted to rescue him.) Charlie was once sent in misdirected baggage to Dubai but his most frightening moment came just recently, when my ASBO kitten started chewing him and he lost a paw and a lot of stuffing.

Teddies are touchstones by which children read the minds of adults. When the poet John Burnside was six, his father put his son's teddy bear, Sooty, on the fire. A child 'will gauge our intentions not so much by what we say, not even by what is implied in the gift we bring him, but from the way we spontaneously treat his teddy bear', writes psychoanalyst and fairy-tale expert Bruno Bettelheim. In Kabul under Taliban rule, a Taliban speaker said teddy bears were banned. 'No,' said a BBC correspondent well versed in the list of banned items and activities, 'actually teddy bears aren't banned.' 'Well, from tonight, they are,' thundered the furious voice.

Peter Prideaux-Brune, heir to the manor house Prideaux Place, had a teddy called Me Too, and the devotion lasted beyond childhood, as he took the teddy to Oxford and it sat finals with him. A friend of mine in her forties and not given to sentimentality saw her teddy disintegrating into sawdust and rabbit fur. She was utterly unable to put it in the bin because of all it meant to her, so she gave it a burial. Almost magically alive to a child, teddies are talismanic. 'My little, lovely Bobo, my hero, my lover, my friend,' wrote my brother to his teddy. As a child, when his dreams turned to nightmares, he would 'call in Bobo. Bobo was a sort of personification of my will, when my imagined world was frightening. Thus some nasty drowning dream would be made safe because when I was underwater Bobo could grab me and draw me up to the surface. Most of my nightmares could be turned around with this semi-external benign presence.'

More than a toy, a teddy is something of a guardian angel, keeper of wishes, witness to tears, holder of the keys of sleep, infinitely kind. But this fiercely loving relationship tells of a terrible loss. Infants are given soft toys as comforters, to console them in their grief at being separated from the physical warmth and presence of humans and other animals. The very love children bestow is a measure of their need for real fur and paws, real animal or human characters.

~

One day in 1996 when he was four, Ivan Mishukov left his flat in Moscow and walked out on to the streets alone. Uncared for at home, he begged food and shared it with a pack of dogs. In return, the dogs protected him from theft and abuse and, in the frozen Moscow winters, they saved his life by including him in the warmth of their lair. Over time, the dogs came to treat Ivan, this child who could be part-dog and part-child, as their pack leader and when humans tried to 'rescue' him, he ran away with the dogs. Eventually, after two years and three attempts, the police separated the child from his pack and he was returned to human lairs.

Eva Hornung turned this true story into an extraordinary work of fiction, *Dog Boy*, which describes how the dogs reared Romochka, the fictional Ivan. A bitch offers the child her teats to suckle so he drinks the milk of animal kindness. It's the stuff of legend: feral children, raised by wild creatures, fed on animal milk. So Mowgli drinks wolf milk, the abandoned Paris is suckled by a bear and Romulus and Remus are wolf-suckled. There are real-life examples of animal suckling when, in the villages of sixteenth-century France, for instance, it was common for a child to drink from the teats of a goat when its human mother could give no milk; and, as Michel de Montaigne commented, the goat would come running at the cry of that one particular baby and for no other child, while the child would suckle from no other goat.

My kitten Otter, much to the human kitten's delight, began suckling my other cat, Tom, even though he was male, wholly unrelated and they had only been introduced the day before. The fact of Otter's kittenhood seemed to trigger a tenderness in the older cat, who licked the little one into a purring-circle. This tenderness trespasses over the borders. A human baby can evoke a maternal instinct in other species, be they dogs, cats or wolves. The milk can flow both ways. Artemis, goddess of the wild woods, suckled the young of wild creatures, and Huaorani women in the Amazon may suckle a baby monkey as well as a child, as highland Papuan women may suckle a piglet.

There is a twofold reaction to stories of feral children: pity for the child as a stunted human *déclassé* and also envy for the child having been a cub in the nestling earth, kindled with hot, rank, animal-kind. The phenomenon reflects the twofoldness within the Western tradition which divides the world into either human or animal; culture or nature; civilized or wild; the city or the wilderness. Many of the children of legend abandoned in the wilds grew up to be founders of cities, as if to be fully cultural (represented by cities), the human being must also be fully natural (represented by the animals), suggesting that culture knows it is rooted in nature. The root of the word 'culture' is the Latin *cultus*, concerning the rituals of cultivation of plants – of nature.

Semiramis, adopted by birds, founded Babylon. The abandoned Amphion and Zethos rebuilt the walls of Thebes. Romochka in *Dog Boy* builds a pretend city (made of toys) in the dogs' lair. His namesake, the wolf-suckled Romulus, together with Remus, founded Rome. Tellingly for these stories of twofoldness, many of the legends of children abandoned in nature involve twins: Amphion and Zethos, twins deserted on Mount Cithaeron; Valentine and Orson, the twins lost in the woods; Neleus and Pelias, twins abandoned on a mountain; and, most famously, Romulus and Remus, cared for by a wolf and fed by a woodpecker.

Interestingly, the Ancient Romans loathed the transgressive aspect of their city's legend, that the founding fathers had suckled on the milk of a wolf, so the poet-historian Ennius decided that *lupa* (she-wolf) should be taken to mean *lupa*, a prostitute. Nice try, this, to take the wolf out of the story, to wipe wild nature out of civilization's history, to remove the wolf milk from the ink. It failed, though, for wildness will out, in its howl of tender ferocity.

Probably the most famous true-life feral child was Victor, the 'wild child of Aveyron' found in France in 1800, who is thought to have

lived in the forests from the ages of five to twelve, when he was captured and then cared for by a doctor, Jean Marc Gaspard Itard. Victor's
story was made into the haunting film *L'Enfant Sauvage*, by François
Truffaut.

The doctor tries to teach the boy to speak, but 'milk' is the only
word he learns and he never uses another. The symbolism is striking, for milk is an emblem of our shared animality: intimate, raw,
uncultured – if you'll excuse the pun. Itard regarded his work with
the child as a failure because he could not create a relationship of
empathy with the boy, the empathy which socializes children into
culture. But, reading Itard's notebooks, it doesn't seem to me as if
there was a failure of language or of empathy, for the boy does com-
municate, he pays rapt attention and he expresses himself in a duet of
devotion – to the natural world.

'If, at any time, a boisterous wind arose; if the sun, concealed
behind a cloud, suddenly burst forth, brilliantly illuminating the surrounding atmosphere, he expressed an almost convulsive joy by
thundering peals of laughter,' wrote Dr Itard. After a snowfall, the
child 'escaped half-dressed into the garden. There he exhibited the
utmost emotions of pleasure; he ran, rolled himself in the snow, and
taking it up by handfuls, devoured it with an incredible avidity.'

Watching water, 'his face . . . took the well-defined character of
sorrow, or melancholy reverie.' On moonlit nights Victor would wake
and stare out of the window, 'carried away in a sort of contemplative
extacy [sic], the silence of which was interrupted only by deep-drawn
inspirations, after considerable intervals, and which were always accompanied with a feeble and plaintive sound.' The boy's story struck a deep
chord with Coleridge who, in his notebooks, wrote of Victor's 'restless
joy and blind conjunction of his Being with natural Scenery'.

If Itard was saddened by the child's refusal to speak and inability to join human society, he missed the fact that the child had already been socialized – by nature, within nature – and was already expressing empathy with every kind of voice, in every language he owned, resonant with the society of the moon and the forest and in sympathy with them.

~

A four-year-old boy became a dog in my kitchen. He licked the floor, he growled and barked, he wagged his bum and wanted his food thrown down to him. Bewitched by animals, children want to play with them but also to play them, to *be* them. Because they already are. Wholly engrossed, the boy was being watched by his father, an intellectual, an edgy, very witty and highly cultured man, with an expression as mixed, as self-contradictory, as torn as the human face can be. Amused, disturbed, impressed and revolted, he was staring over the fence as bewildered as his son was not.

There was a spring day in my childhood when I felt I was at the fence myself. I was about twelve, at the border of adolescence. It was a day of conscious liminality for me, and I was aware of the immense peer pressure which dictated that I should spend Saturday mornings making clumsy forays into eye-shadow or trying on clothes in front of mirrors. I didn't have a mirror or eye-shadow and the only clothes I wore, beyond my school uniform, were a pair of jeans, one brown T-shirt and one brown sweatshirt. I was, to be blunt, a total failure as a girl.

What I also felt, though, beyond the peer pressure, was the familiar tug of the green world, and I realized quite lucidly that I was being taught that to grow up meant eschewing animals and staring at mirrors, while to be a child was to grab a fishing net and a jam jar, fetch my bike and head for the ponds. That is what I did and, that morning, although it was spring and I was in my own springtime, I felt sadder than I ever had in my life, for it was valedictory, it was autumn in April, it was twilight at dawn. The bewitched time when as a child I had so unselfconsciously and easily slipped between the railings and run to the woods, and had equally easily slipped between the worlds of human and animal, was overing. Not absolutely over, but drawing to a close. I sat, crying, watching a water boatman, itself a liminal creature, rowing his oars across the whole pond-ocean with a meniscus for a boat. And I, at the tadpole stage myself but turning into a teenage frog, was entranced by his metaphor.

An eighteen-year-old recently told me of a very similar moment when he was about fifteen. He had an indistinct sense that as he grew older he was supposed to leave nature behind as 'childish'. He was meant to put on The Suit and go to The Office, and he was sadly and unwillingly trying to resign himself to this. Then, courtesy of one wise teacher, he read Wordsworth and it turned his life around because, he said, it gave him a sense of permission, that he could live his life within nature, where he felt he belonged.

Western society has adamantly insisted on The Fence between human and animal worlds. We speak and They do not. We conceive of a past and future and They do not. We use tools and They do not. We make jokes and They do not. These are uncertain issues, particularly when it comes to tool-using chimps, the intricate communications of birds and, especially, the liquid intelligence of whales and dolphins. Yes, though, we make fire and fences and fictions. We are metaphor-makers. But the qualities which humans share with animals are overwhelming: the senses, motion, life, language, belonging, loyalty, closeness and – dare I say it – love.

In childhood, the boundary is quivering because children are liminal. The door is ajar; it opens easily on its hinges. The world creeps in through the portals of our senses, there is a paw scraping at the gate and our transgression is not a sin but an act of kinetic accomplishment. At the ravenous edge of the pack, a hunger stalks our species now, the howl is in the lungs, ready to tear the throat as it roars for raw belonging. Children are not howl-proof or animal-proof. The hoof is there inside the shoe. The fins are discernible at the shoreline: starfish, dogfish, childfish. Artist Paula Rego, in *Night Stories*, etches the storytelling girl whose shadow stretches into wolf-shadow, telling a toothed story. An anarchic cat plays the fiddle with a hungry grin; animals smoke pipes, fuck and do headstands. Both children and animals are off the leash – untamed, disobedient compadres in sardonic, sometimes sexual, mischief. The demarcation between animal and human is grittily transgressed: *trespassers all*.

~

Animals matter to children as companions, as consolers, as comprehenders. A child's psyche leans to the animal world, and tales of children brought up by animals exert an uncanny fascination. Animals, though, are important to children in a further sense: they are guides to thought. They lead children to leaps of imagination. Wondering what a wasp is thinking or what a tree might feel in the wind is part of the mind's development, practising the quick spring of empathy. Children ascribe meaning, intent and emotion to animals. Faithful to anthropomorphism until they are ridiculed out of it, children nurture a relationship with the animal world whereby they become party to extra sensitivities, to other stories and a diversity of viewpoints.

Our minds are suckled by wolves. There is wolf milk mixed in the ink and no Roman historian can remove it.

It is only literalists who hate anthropomorphism, because they take it literally. (And, in this, they are really the only ones who literally believe in it.) The rest of us – virtually all cultures across history and certainly all children, Romantics fluent in the language of metaphor and far more intelligent than Utilitarians ancient and modern – appreciate that it is a way of coming into the knowledge of a creature; it opens a dialogue with nature which poetry understands, as Shelley addressed the West Wind as the 'comrade' of his boyhood.

Many children think the moon is following them. When I was a child, I thought I was the moon's daughter because it seemed that she watched over me and understood me; she was where I was from. I've heard from children that a stone might need to be moved to the other side of the stream because it was stuck where it was; that a cloud is cold; a tree is lonely; and a snail needs a trail of Tippex to find its way home. Children see the world as soul-porous. To a child, everything is lit with intent, following its storypath, coursing with will. Ascribing a liveliness to the world brings the child's imagination alive; it refuses to allow either the world or the mind to be inert. 'Sometimes he was a panther lying lazily in his den,' writes John Joseph Mathews (born 1894) of the Osage nation, describing a boyhood melting across boundaries. 'Sometimes real pain would be the result of these dream-world metamorphoses; pain caused by the desire to fly . . . Unhappiness would descend on him as he lay on his back in the prairie grass, watching the graceful spirals of the redtail.'

Every animal suggests different characteristics to children, various moods or qualities. Each is a possible costume-change in the theatre of childhood, a shift of shape. In the electrifying transformations of the children's daemons in Philip Pullman's work or in the metamorphosis of Taliesin – hare, fish, otter, bird – or the shapeshifting fight between Merlyn and Madame Mim in *The Sword in the Stone* – dragon, field mouse, cat, dog, oak, blue tit, snake, bird, gnat – you can hear the rustling in the costume box behind the scenes, the proliferating, shifting possibilities for the child's still-unfixed shape, this subtle shimmer of animal-influence.

Mowgli's story is also a tale of metamorphosis as the child is adopted by the wolf, taught by the bear and intoxicated by the monkeys in the unfenced world, the jungles of transformation. The reader can tell how Kipling relishes metamorphosis, yet just when he creeps towards acknowledging the deeper meaning of it, he recoils in horror. Metamorphosis doffs its cap towards *shapeshifting*.

In Kipling's hands, shapeshifting is part of the murky superstition of the bludgeoningly stupid villagers. Mowgli's human parents are accused of having brought a demon wolf-child into the world and must, of course, seek salvation *with the British*! Ding! rings the school bell, and we know we're back in the decent, sensible and colourless world of teatime, fact, punctuality and fences.

In much of the world, finding one's 'power animals', using a wild epistemology of metaphor, was considered a wise part of a young person's spiritual growth. The idea of something half human and half animal can be seen, for example, in the concept of the Inuit seal-woman; the wer-jaguar of the Amazon; and the mer-maid, half fish of *la mer* and half maid of the land. Within the classical tradition, metamorphosis is part of the forest allure so Dionysus, god of wildness, shapeshifts into lion, panther, snake or forest satyr. The werewolf of Europe, though, was demonized and, from the fifteenth to the seventeenth century (influenced by the literalizing Reformation with its loathing of metaphor), there were 'werewolf trials' in which thousands of men and women were charged with the crime of being a werewolf and killed for it.

A metaphor shifts into metamorphosis, which melts into shapeshifting – trespassing wisely and well across the fences of species.

Angela Carter's version of 'Little Red Riding Hood', translated into the film *The Company of Wolves*, is full of boundary-crossing between dream and reality, childhood and adulthood, fiction and fact, past and present. 'Do you live in our world or theirs?' Red Riding Hood asks the wolf as a little silver cross glints at her neck. 'I come and go between them,' the handsome huntsman-wolf answers with Gallic insouciance, Gauloise smoke coming from his lupine ears. But even as the question is asked, it is hard to know whether 'our' world means human or wolf. *Do you live in our world of wolves?* she could have meant, as she herself chooses to cross over, in the shining transgressional moment of the film, when a silky, strong, female wolf, with a little silver cross around her neck, bounds out of the windows of the grandmother's house, making a break for freedom.

Shapeshifting is an epistemology, a way for people to increase their sensitivities, to perceive the world with an imaginative leap, to feel through the body of another, metaphorically. Pueblo Indian children, from three years old, transform themselves into antelope and deer, they don fox skins, deer hooves or parrot feathers. In rituals and dances, through lyrics, choreography and costume, the child embodies earth-knowledge – of corn and cloud, of sun and lightning, of buffalo and skunk – and steps through the looking glass. Animal nature is another side of human nature, a mirror, by twilight, by twolight, where the twinnedness of those myths is reflected.

In the mirage of mirrors, *it is as if* . . . As if man-cub is wolf-cub and we can all move between worlds at will, can come and go, transgress and cross the river, our fingers unfurling into flight feathers, our arms wings. Through a relationship with animals, we humans add to the repertoire of our senses the beady alertness of a bird, the scent-subtlety of a mole, the smooth-swum escape of the fish. This is the apprenticeship which children gleefully follow, given half a chance.

Language follows the same path: first the mind's metamorphosis, then language's metaphor. As lazy as a coyote, as tricky as a fox, as wise as an owl. It is a way of 'reading' the world, of translating between nature and human nature which children's minds need, to be able to somersault and leap, to catch the branches of a simile. The mind climbs trees and performs its first aerial acrobatics. To jump is a need of the young mind as much as a need of the young body.

In the forests, our ancestor-primates needed to learn to leap from tree to tree, judging distance, space, branch width and branch strength, comparing and holding many bits of information all at once and then making a judgement which links them all. The mind does exactly this when it reaches for a metaphor, bringing all kinds of knowledge together in a sudden moment, a leap of thought.

The mind, a monkey in the branches, is a meta-forester, a *metaphorista*, champion of the forests. ('Forest' comes from *foris*, meaning outside, far out.) Metaphor is a play on words and a play on worlds. *Meta-foris*. Right outside the enclosure into the leaping, laughing forests. Far out.

Playing different roles by pretending to be different animals, children are nurturing their own animated selves. They are also practising the realization that there are other minds. The transformation in shapeshifting links with this: it is the *ur*-metaphor, the primal drama of the human mind. The force of the human sense of metaphor and art must surely come originally from our ability to step into the bodies of other animals. In this, children are then truly practising culture when they are most open to nature, learning how to be artists. Free to be fictitious, free to crack jokes, free to invent, free to lie, free to translate.

Eva Hornung writes of Romochka that the dogs cannot lie, whereas the boy can: and he may be useless as a dog, but he can pretend, including 'pretending' to be a boy. He tries to make the other puppies listen to a story and is described by the scientist as 'a master of passing' between the world of dogs and the world of humans. He could translate. He could transgress. He could 'cross . . . over'.

This is metaphor, from *meta* (across) and *phor* (to bear or carry). To carry across. Metaphors are prowling round the mind. The water boatman bore metaphor in his name, carrying meaning across the little pond; each tiny foot was an oar in the water as I watched him in grief. But what comforted me that day was the incredible beauty of this metaphor. An insect-sized boater, with six oars, each making its miniature dent in the water. I too yearned to row across waters, in the mind's psychic fluidity, with those tiny oars.

Watch the yearning: for wanting to move out of the human world and into the animal world is exactly the same pattern as wanting to step out of literal speech into metaphoric speech. Wanting to be free of the prosaic single-reference of factual speech and wanting the sheer adventure, the glee, of the unfenced world of metaphor, where things are set free of their single meanings, to fly like birds, to skiff like a water boatman. This is part of the answer to the riddle of childhood unhappiness: their minds need, and deserve, a whole world of utterly unfenceable freedom where everything has othering, everything is radiant with the possibilities of elseness.

There is ink in our milk.

CHAPTER SIX

A Ludic Revolution (and a doodle)

In which is related how the king of France's cock went up and down like a
drawbridge; who padlocked the swings; who plays guardian angel to
reverie and why play matters to the arts – because a child of six could do it.

~

You never need to teach a child to play. Made out of cogs, kazoos and
wagglesticks, play is the undeniable instinct of childhood. Children
have a sixth sense for the ludic and under their gaze lounge furniture
is no longer there simply to house books and ornaments but trans-
mogrifies into the elastic game of getting round the room without
touching the ground. Enter an adult, and the room shrivels back to
its single meaning: the Lion, the Witch and the . . . IKEA flat-pack
furniture, furnishing one-dimensional meanings.

Play is life-jazz. It relies on a sense of swing. It dances with the
moment when the moment is calling for a dance. Deep play involves
rhythm and openness, it is collaborative; jazzers or children catching
each other's glances, holding hands with their eyes to sustain the blue
note. Unscored, unscheduled, spontaneous, this ludic life-jazz improvises. Because when it comes to the living of one's life, there is no dress

rehearsal. It is all ad-libbed, extemporized. Play is the jamming of the psyche, how the child practises the greatest art of all, the art of life.

When to play, when to be silent, when to suggest a comic duet, when to judder a too-easy melody, how to send an arpeggio one step beyond, dicing on the top-notes, why to wait for the drums and how to let the flute fly solo to the stars when it is winged for the flight. *Just say yes.*

'All animals, except man, know that the principal business of life is to enjoy it,' wrote Samuel Butler. But play, like so much which is natural to childhood, is under threat. The National Association of Head Teachers has accused the UK government of killing fun and play in primary schools. Children, forced to be 'productive', are discouraged from exactly the free play which scientists say is vital to their development. Children's play is commodified as never before: there is profit to be made – at the expense of childhood. Puritans ancient and modern threaten the ludic life.

Exiled from nature, children barely play outdoors. Where I live, in rural Wales, I have canoed many rivers uncanoed by children. I have noted the uneaten blackberries and the unclimbed rocks. I can see the bit of air where a treehouse should be. Although they still get conkers from the conker tree (which mysteriously has always been known as 'the bamboo tree' to the town's children) and, in seasons of snow, the snowmen are not shy nor lacking in carrots, yet there is a sad absence of children playing outdoors, for a landscape like this should be riddled with children like rabbits in a summer dawn.

Play on the urban commons, the street, has today 'mostly disappeared', says one academic study. Even though the school playground is crucial to the continuance of aspects of children's culture, quite horribly, schools are now being built without playgrounds.

The leader of Wandsworth Council in London could afford to visit his local playground 96,000 times a year if he spent all his pocket money. (Nearly a quarter of a million pounds.) But plenty of Wandsworth's children cannot go there once, as the council is charging children £2.50 per visit. The spirit of enclosures is alive and well, fencing off the swings and roundabouts, privatizing common play for profit.

Meanwhile, at the other end of the country, heavy black letters in a stentorian voice stencil out these words:

PLEASE DO NOT USE THIS PLAYGROUND ON SUNDAYS

The chill rain palls the playground but nothing is colder than the spirit of this sign, on Raasay, one of the Western Isles of Scotland. The swings are chained up on Sundays, too, in Stornoway on the Isle of Lewis, in case the jazzy swing of childhood play had its way with the saturnine orders of the stony kirk. Swings seem particularly loathed by the Church. In Harris, the swings in a school playground are locked so children cannot play on Sundays; perhaps the Church knows that in pagan history swings were used to encourage crops to grow, in a form of sympathetic magic. Or perhaps the Kirk can sniff something of children's self-tantalizing sensuality in their ready love of swinging in the jazz of the body. The grim padlock, like a rusty heraldic shield on a gravestone-rampant, would forbid starlight if it could and would, with ruthless meanness, imprison all the generosity of play till childhood died in the dungeons of Sundays.

Unlock the gates, for heaven's sake. Let in the divine, smelling of peat and heather. For if we adults can learn anything from children, it is this: how to play generously, live with a sense of swing and always, always risk the high notes.

~

I remember the scruffy bawdiness of the playgrounds of my childhood, the source-untraceable tingling when play tiptoed towards the forbidden, and the contraband value of sexual vocabulary. ('Bum' scored round about one; 'dick' was a solid seven; 'fuck' hit ten; while 'cunt' was right off the scale.)

Gil Scott-Heron, in the lyrics of 'Sex Education: Ghetto Style', went one up on us, commenting on his boyhood, aged eight or nine or ten: 'I had never heard of Sigmund Freud, but hell I was doin' it then.' And Louis XIII of France – no ghetto kid he – outdid us all, boasting when he was not yet four that 'my cock is like a drawbridge; see how it goes up and down.'

Children's play is inherently – gloriously – embodied. The willing sexual play of children is ubiquitous. Mischievous and sometimes funny, it is also risky; it can have an edge of real distress. Nisa, a !Kung San woman from the edges of the Kalahari, related the core purpose of the 'work' of childhood: 'Most of the time we played the play of children, that of having sex with one another. We all did that. That was our work.' The boys, she relates, were keener than the girls: 'Little boys are the first ones to know its sweetness.' For girls it was complicated: sometimes they would refuse to play with the boys, sometimes they would agree and other times the boys would take a little girl by herself and 'she cries and cries.'

Children perceive – and experience – the dark side of the matter: the untenderness which tears the cloth. They treasure their autonomy, distraught if that is trampled, and try to protect themselves, fiercely and furiously, from adults pushing sexual behaviour on to them. But it seems that if there is one thing children have never particularly treasured, it is their sexual innocence. They badger away at the knowledge, they push to explore; they play at this, doggedly and cunningly, with themselves and each other.

The vocabulary of the body is important to them, including the thesaurus of funny walks: lolling, bumping, stretching, yawing, sailing, and doing it four-legged, no-legged or half-legged. Children want to know which bits of one's body are fit for which purpose: teeth as bottle-openers when fingers don't work; fingernails for screwdrivers; elbows and knees handy, if you'd excuse the pun, as extra leverage in climbing. Practising on the world, children play within their bodies, with toes, nose and thumbs – the whole kaboodle. 'My body was my adventure and my name,' wrote Dylan Thomas.

How many peanuts can you get up one nostril? For how long can the heel of your hand be used as a hammer before it hurts (too much)? In an anti-Cartesian simplicity – 'I am therefore I am' – as blunt as a banana, children delight in their embodiment and fit it snug to the world, even when all they are doing is waiting, for there are as many ways to wait as ways to walk, and as many reasons. Scared-waiting, bored-waiting, hiding-waiting, excited-waiting, or waiting to pounce on someone: much like a kitten practising hunting and being hunted. A perennial game of childhood is working out ways to lift other children, together with the benchmark moment when a kid can lift an adult, stealing their power at a stroke. (One of my brothers, fed up with being told off, once lifted up our mother and triumphantly dropped her in a different room. To her credit, she laughed.) Making a knot out of two arms and two legs, with perhaps one leg looped behind the head and a tongue or a toe stuck somewhere unexpected, just for fun, is a game any child knows. For some Inuit children, one particular delight was yanking each other naked out of bed, on to the icy igloo floor, while other games included sliding on fresh ice, pulling each other on sleds, stalking lemming and ermine or playing hide and seek, that childhood game enjoyed the world over.

While sport is structured, play is not. It is curly and impurposive, rudely anarchic. 'Ah, football,' said a Papuan man to me. 'One aim was to score goals, the other was to break the opponents' *kotekas*, their penis gourds.'

The play of the body encourages the play of the mind: 'If a child doesn't understand a see-saw, it's hard to understand an equation,' says physics professor Dr Matthew Griffiths. And I can verify that the professor did his research as a six-year-old, with me, his smaller and lighter sister, pinged into the air.

In the course of history, certain movements have damaged children's play. The Industrial Revolution (the clue is in the title) threatened what was ludic. Puritanism grimly opposed plays and players. The Enclosures, as an earlier chapter illustrated, robbed children of carnival.

Children cling to any festival they can still get their sticky little fingers on, from Pancake Day to Easter, April Fool's, Hallowe'en, Bonfire Night, Thanksgiving and, of course, Christmas. At school, my brothers laid claim to April Fool's Day as if they had invented it, with toy turds and mischief-making, reversing anything which could move and much that wasn't supposed to. Poor, poor Mrs O'Leary, did she ever forgive them?

To me, one of the saddest losses to childhood is May Day, or Beltane, the stonking celebration of sexuality which seeded the festival year with its naughtiest symbols, the phallic maypole plunged into the warmly receptive 'mother' earth, while the Green Man, the Wild Man, cavorted in leaves carrying a huge horn. Teenagers engaged in horniness of their own would sneak off to the woods while, for younger children, May Day was a gentle amble into sexuality until they grew old enough themselves to be the teenagers in a heap of mucky fornication in the bushes.

Then came the Puritans. Enemies of the erotic, of childhood and of play, in 1644 they banned the maypole and opposed carnival and in 1647 outlawed Christmas. In 1642, they had closed the playhouses. Shakespeare (1564–1616) had lived just in time. In love with theatre and the playful days of cakes and ale, he had been able to grab a fool and a lute and escape on to the commons, not a moment too soon.

Over the next two hundred years, the meanness of Puritanism and the ideology of Enclosures which robbed children of their playscape on the commons and their carnival times was underscored by po-faced Victorian morality and the ethos of the Industrial Revolution. It is hard for people today to appreciate quite what a difference these elements, combined, made to the fabric of fun in public life. Together, they severely repressed the free spirit of play. 'If a company of strolling players make their appearance in a village,' said a Parliamentary Register report in 1800, 'they are hunted immediately from it as a nuisance.' A child's experience of life was duller, quieter and far less fun. By Dickens's time, children were about to be, for the first time ever, in a word, *bored*.

Boredom is something inflicted on a person by another. The dominion of the bore – the state of boredom, the odium of tedium – was so novel that the very word 'boredom' had to be invented, by Charles Dickens, in 1852.

The word 'bored' (as ennui) appeared only after 1750, and the experience of being bored has been linked to the rise of capitalism. The word has overtones of a machine, holding something captive so it can have holes bored through it. A child, for instance. Boredom wedges the child, like a piece of wood in a vice. Boredom mechanically bores holes in the mind so the child is bored by a drill. In drilled learning, boredom gradually grinds the spirit away. Dickens's Gradgrind is the godfather of boredom and gradgrindery is the crushing of childhood imagination by the mechanical education of the 'industrial schools', as the first elementary schools were called. 'No little Gradgrind had ever seen a face in the moon . . . No little Gradgrind had ever known wonder on the subject.'

Thomas Gradgrind is a fictionalized version of the man who devised an education system designed to schedule and control the lives of children, to mould them until they are machines themselves so they may the more easily labour in factories. His name was Thomas Wedgwood: his very name a vice to wedge the wood and bore it.

Wordsworth, of all people, was proposed as a possible superintendent of Wedgwood's system. So furious was his refusal that he immortalized in poetry his dislike of those men who:

> . . . *to the very road*
> *Which they have fashion'd would confine us down*
> *Like engines.*

Children were manacled into the workforce of the *Industrial* Revolution, but they were natural freedom fighters for a *ludic* revolution. Metaphorically speaking, they were at the barricades without hesitation because the play ethic, they knew, is more ethical than the work ethic. And it's got more pompoms.

Girl Number Twenty is what Gradgrind calls the circus child, Sissy Jupe. In *Hard Times*, the circus people represent the pre-industrial age of lively, funny, whimsical, irregular humanity, and they magnetize the children of the novel. To Gradgrind's fury, his young daughter, 'his own metallurgical Louisa', steals a peek at the circus, and he sneers that she is 'childish'. (It's telling that calling someone 'childish' is still an acceptable insult today. The fact that it is not widely recognized as offensive only demonstrates the low regard in which children are routinely held.) Louisa grows up to reproach her father with the fact that his factory-theories of education had cost her the experience of childhood. Not only circus performers but also travelling players and Punch and Judy actors represented for Dickens – as the funfair would later represent for Truffaut – the unfenced life of the imagination, which sets up a temporary big top in a child's mind.

Children need circuses as they need bread. When people have taken a circus to children in Iraq and Kosovo, it has revived the children, even though in Kosovo the only place to perform that wasn't snared with landmines was a graveyard, full of fresh children's graves after the conflict. The circus of life, though, defeats the graveness of death, and an old man in the middle of it all sat crying: 'Thank you for bringing my grandchildren back. I never thought I'd see them laugh again.'

Riveted by acrobats, enthralled by stilt-walkers, enticed by sequins and glitter, bewitched by the stripy, spangly world of bananas and swizzle sticks, children loathe puritanism and they flock to those who bust the fences of convention: they are spellbound by the unrestricted adults, the dotty aunts, the foul-mouthed uncles, the public farters and the mischievous godmothers. My own outrageous, shameless and adored Nanna would gleefully announce "e'd 'ave me' or 'I'd 'ave 'im,' as she eyed up another widower walking down the cobbled streets. (She was a Pankhurst. That was her excuse.)

Children love the feckless, the spenders of life, not the savers; those who are rich in the gift economy if poor in the bank account; the charismatic, not the mercantile; the ludic, not the industrial; the circusive, not the linear; the connoisseurs of the futilitarian and the ludicrously – extravagantly – pointless; the unenclosed who play a fanfare for the circus of life which lies beyond the fence; those who do the accounts backwards: if there is a punishment for exploding cowpats with fireworks, that is really the 'price' of one ticket to the burlesque circus; children, along with the undying Romantics who so understood them, loathe Utilitarians.

~

When John Keats was a child, he played a game with other boys in the school playground. They re-created the solar system, with a sun and planets circling it and moons on faster cycles, with comets thrown in just for fun: a universe without cost in their heads and in their hands.

Children's toys were all but unknown before 1600, because children had access to a magic toyshop, both priceless and free, in themselves and in nature. John Clare recalls making cockades of corn poppies, pretending mallow seeds were cheese, listening to corn crackle in the sun, watching a grasshopper bounce, playing Harlequin and, of course, skating.

Generations of children have imitated animals, playing Leapfrog, Sardines, Piggyback, Chicken, Hare and Hounds, Gecko Gecko (an Australian tag game), Lynx and Rabbit, Fox-is-the-Warner, Dead Ant Tag, Fox Hunts Squirrel and Camouflaged Worms.

Until very recently, play has been an activity rather than a product and it has been free, free as a fox cub sneezing in the foxgloves: physically free, imaginatively free, free of schedule, free of rules and free of money. In free play, all are commoners. No one can buy a snowball; neither a whale-shaped cloud nor the blue streak of excitement in a seashore child is for sale. The bird feather, the burr and the sticky-grass have no price tag.

But then, on 3 October 1955, the Mattel toy company began advertising a gun called the Thunder Burp. It was the first time that an advert for a toy had appeared on TV outside the Christmas season, and it marked a turning point in the story of play. Play was to become an industry. Today, children in the USA aged twelve to nineteen spend an average of $101 each, every week, playing. These commercialized play-products lead to the awful playground aristocracy based on some children's ability to buy the most expensive toys.

In play, children make-believe. Stop a moment on that, for the creation of belief in the human psyche is no small thing. Turquoise fish can swim right through you in the make-believe world. Not only is make-believe an extraordinary phenomenon, but it is also crucial to children's well-being, for when children play imaginatively in make-believe worlds they learn something vital to their development – the ability to self-regulate, to control their emotions and behaviour – which is self-evidently important, intellectually and socially. This happens because in imaginative play they talk to themselves in what psychologists call 'private speech', planning and thinking aloud. In structured play, this private speech declines. But increasingly today, free play is cut short: teachers, instead of allowing children the invaluable free play of imagination, are 'starting earlier and earlier to drill the kids', says Yale psychological researcher Dorothy Singer.

The young Keats and his pals had the wealth of the cosmos within them. They, like all children playing, had an inner abundance. By contrast, children reared on toys and products provided by corporations are learning a terrible lesson: they are learning that they have a *scarcity* within, that they cannot provide for their own play, or rely on their own imagination, that they are impoverished beggars of the entertainment industry.

If the free play of the mind is a requisite for the individual child, it is also essential to art. Playfully taking a line for a walk or playing on words, photographing the play of light or playing a violin, playing with an idea or writing a play, the playfulness within the artistic process is unquestionable. Creativity is a *jeu d'esprit*, born of play's abundance which children know. The grace notes of music are superfluity made aural; a simile is superfluous to strict meaning but vital to literature's sense of abundance.

It is no surprise that the Romantics perceived how the abundance of play is related to creativity. Tagore speaks of the Angel of Surplus from which comes art. The superfluity of play, its resplendent excess, is accented by joy, and the Angel of Surplus speaks one word, and this word is 'Rejoice!' The child, like the bird, is 'born for joy', wrote Blake.

In the fecundity of Blake's delight, the creativity of Tagore's *ananda* (rapture, bliss) and the fertility of Wordsworth's joy, play has been laughing down the centuries of art. Montaigne played with his thoughts (and with his cat), while Erasmus's profound comedy of humanism doodled in the margins of joy. Dylan Thomas remembered his childhood in the woods where he 'whispered the truth of his joy/ To the trees', the 'true/Joy' of the child.

Play is light-hearted; in the spirit of levity, it depicts the lightness in the margins of life. Radiant, lit by its own light till it shines like illuminated manuscripts, it is tinted with the curvilinear glint of quintessential creativity in the margins. (The ludic spirit delights in *iota*, the literal letter 'i', like giggling will if you tickle it a little bit.)

Creativity in thinking mirrors the creative play of divine thought in the Hindu tradition and play is the impetus of life itself. In the beginning is līlā or play: free, spontaneous activity is the deepest energy in creation. So Lalita, the player, is the mother of all: she who plays and whose play is world-play.

In Sanskrit, writes Johan Huizinga, in a piece of etymology which recalls the swings of jazz, the swings in the locked playgrounds, the swinging of imagination in the free leap of metaphor, the sense of swing so beloved of children, 'the noun *līlā*, with its denominative verb *līlayati* (the primary sense of which is probably rocking, swinging), expresses all the light, aerial, frivolous, effortless and insignificant sides of playing. Over and above this, however, *līlā* is used in the sense of "as if", to denote "seeming", "imitation", the "appearance" of things, as in the English "like", "likeness". . .' The mind at play makes metaphor.

Wild play, then, is characterized by abundance and superfluity. Egalitarian and generous, it generates variations, it teems with suggestion, it spawns enigma. Without the generosity of play, how can a child discover the mind's own originality, or the vital combination of mischief, trickery, energy and light which is the chlorophyll in the tree of childhood?

This is not just child's play. The sense of abundance which free play provides, all that is surplus to requirements, motivates the experience of all the arts in their serious play.

Huizinga wrote that culture itself 'arises in the form of play'. Jung was to remark that 'Civilizations at their most complete moments always brought out in man his instinct to play and made it more inventive.'

Dare to err and dream;
A higher meaning often lies in childish play.

— Schiller

It is the first art. A child of six could do it. And *must*.

~

Play is the great doodle, *le grand griffonnage* in the wide margins of childhood, and the ludic doodle is a digression on digression, a diversion on the diverting, the pen's peregrination of purposeless possibility, the elastic escape of attention, the mind at monkey-shines. The word 'doodle', the idler's delight, is thought to have emerged from 'dawdle'.

Rabindranath Tagore, as a child, was a great doodler and he explains how his early training in rhythm had an unexpected result in his being almost unable to leave a page undoodled, for 'when the scratches in my manuscript cried, like sinners, for salvation, and assailed my eyes with the ugliness of their irrelevance, I often took more time in rescuing them into a merciful finality of rhythm than carrying on what was my obvious task.'

Tagore was in excellent company: other famous doodlers, those with the Ludic Gene Dominant, include Erasmus who drew comical faces in the margins of his manuscripts, and John Keats who drew flowers and faces in his notebooks during medical lectures, while Ralph Waldo Emerson, who hitched his wagon to a star, doodled with the enthusiasm he so valued, and Stanislaw Ulam discovered the Ulam spiral while doodling. By the way, one Internet site on doodling comes complete with a 'Disclaimer: This information is offered for your amusement only, and is not to be used for psychological assessment in any form.'

Both doodling and digressions are emblems of plenty, the barns of the human mind full to bursting with harvest, spilling out over the threshold (the holding of the thresh), pouring over the boundaries of Erasmus's margins, and both are examples of the abundance at the heart of play: the importance of all that is surplus to requirements. In gusto, in exuberance, in health and high spirits, play is abundance: play is superfluous and therefore absolutely necessary. Children thirst for the superfluity of free play, drinking all that brims over the lip of the cup. I never trust those who use 'superfluous' as an insult. It's like not liking garlic. 'Superfluous': the word is liquid and lovely and overflowing, extravagant and superb. Here is where the uncorked festival begins, the superfluous plumage of the bird of paradise, the revelrebel, the cap and bells of the jester.

Doodling, like many forms of art and play, arises from fallow times.

I well remember fallow. The ennui. The tedium setting in like Welsh rain. I don't mean we were bored, as no one was boring us. We were fallow. Waiting for something to happen.

We grew up almost entirely without television, so there was not the option automatically to fill our fallow hours with it. To be precise on this point, we were allowed to watch absolutely anything provided we could tell our mother what the programme was called, what time it started, what time it ended, what channel it was on, and why we wanted to watch it. The research involved was prodigious for a child, the assignment more like homework. Most of the time we didn't bother, though the house rules meant that we did end up watching the schoolboy revolution film *If* when we were knee-high to the cocks.

So, in terms of entertainment, we were on our own: it was all up to us. The funny thing is that when I remember the fallow hours, I remember immediately the outrageous, exorbitant, flamboyant stalks which grew from that quiet earth. It would go like this. I would be stuck for something to do. Both my brothers would be stuck. Our friends would be stuck. The pendulum would swing to its furthest extent, a yawn wide enough to swallow the world, and then, like the yin and yang of Chinese philosophy, the extremity of one feeling would create a ferocious need to create the opposite and one of us, their face cracking into a dangerous grin, a truly scary grin, a grin which could chew steel, a grin which could depopulate a wedding, would growl, '*I know* . . .' and we would hatch a plan: to spy through the neighbours' letterboxes; to climb on to the roof; to have a yodelling competition; to bet on how many cardboard boxes it would take to cover the car or how many peanut-butter sandwiches we could get someone else to eat without them being sick. (I think it was Matthew. I think it was fourteen.) What you can do with the sharp end of a peanut includes bursting a balloon full of water or, very unexpectedly, popping a pool of water trapped in ceiling plaster, bringing half the kitchen down with it and spending the rest of the day hiding from the parents.

After ennui, then, jubilation. Exultation. A creative thrill: we did this! When the soil was fallow enough for long enough, a beanstalk grew, tall as our dad, green with tall tales, fictions and fibs, a whopper big as God on a space hopper.

Earth, left fallow, experiences an inner-thriving, a self-fertilization. So too, a childhood with fallow hours thrives by its own independence, the fertility from within, the inner fecundity of life. But if soil is never left fallow, if it is force-fed with artificial chemical fertilizers, coerced into an unrelenting schedule of productivity, it will lead ultimately to crop failure and soil exhaustion. So too, with children: when their lives are enclosed, when they are subjected to endless 'inputs' and the relentless demands that every hour be productive, they experience a sense of failure, depression, low self-esteem, a sense of inner collapse and the withering of strength from within: childhood's equivalents of crop failure and exhaustion. Before the Acts of Enclosure, land was allowed its fallow times whereas afterwards it was forced into productive schedules – much like childhood, suffering its own acts of enclosure today.

How did it look, this fallowness? We were just mucking around, we said, when we were about eight: the muck and mud matters, for mucking around in the fallow soil creates the potential for creativity, ideas or rebellion. Wonder is what happens in the gaps, wonder is welcomed in dawdling and doodling. But wonder is prohibited by speed, punctuality and overscheduling. When we were about fourteen, we said we were doing sweet fuck-all. And sweet fuck-all is sweet.

Where Did You Go? Out. What Did You Do? Nothing. Written in the fifties, the book lives up to the nonchalant swagger of the title and is a manifesto for childhood's simple nothing-doing. What are the kids going to do with themselves all summer? the author, Robert Paul Smith, asks himself. 'Well, it would be nice, I think, if they spent an afternoon kicking a can. It might be a good thing if they dug a hole. No, no, no. Not a foundation, or a well, or a mother symbol. Just a hole. For no reason. Just to dig a hole. After a while, they could fill it with water, if they liked . . . They might find a penny. Or a very antique nail. Or a bone. A saber-tooth tiger's kneecap . . .'

The guardian angel of reverie is the French philosopher and twentieth-century Romantic Gaston Bachelard. 'In our childhood, reverie gave us freedom . . . we still dream of liberty as we dreamed of it when we were children,' he writes. 'Those original solitudes, the childhood solitudes leave indelible marks on certain souls. Their entire life is sensitized for poetic reverie, for a reverie which knows the price of solitude.' The Romantics championed childhood reverie, knowing that it was threatened by the Gradgrindery of the Industrial Revolution and in this, as in so many ways, they demonstrated how close was their philosophy to the nature of childhood.

The moon, said Wordsworth, was dear to him:

For I would dream away my purposes,
Standing to gaze upon her.

But the daydream police have never really gone off-duty. In the fifties, some educational psychologists warned that daydreaming could cause neurosis and psychosis. Today, parents and teachers are exhorted to watch for 'daydreaming indicators' which include blank expressions or wandering eyes. Daydreaming children are encouraged to use their time 'constructively', to join 'structured' and 'productive' clubs. Adults should 'diminish the duration' of daydreams with interruptions, should 'limit' and 'reduce the time spent per daydream' using a 'timer for planned fantasy periods'. Note the language of enclosure: planning, timing, limiting, reducing, diminishing duration for the profit counted in constructive, structured, productive output.

Parents may even be encouraged to send daydreaming children to psychotherapists and counsellors. In the classroom, daydreaming is regarded as undisciplined laziness and schools may suggest that children are tested for Attention Deficit Disorder.

'A dreamer is one who can only find his way by moonlight, and his punishment is that he sees the dawn before the rest of the world,' wrote Oscar Wilde, who would shiver at the newly coined terms 'daydreaming disorder' and 'maladaptive daydreaming'.

I cannot imagine Jesus Christ as anything other than a daydream believer and a protector of the reveries of all children, but some of his followers do not agree. Daydreaming makes you live apart from Jesus, says one Internet preacher, and not abiding in Jesus means you will be 'thrown into the fire and burned'. Go straight to hell. Do Not Pass Go.

I once watched a child going straight to hell. In a thirteen-year-old's daydream, his mother was teasing him for doing nothing. But he wasn't doing nothing, he was thinking on the inside, sailing lovely, fluent and superfluous seas of thought as the vague wave of daydream washed over his face which was vacant only on the outside. And, though he was far too lost in oceanic reverie to notice, an armada of scientists was kindly protecting him, offering safe passage to him and to all of us whose childhoods were silvered with the particular moon-light of daydreams. In daydreams, which can occupy a third of our waking state, the brain becomes highly active in exactly those areas associated with complex problem-solving, because in daydreaming the mind roams freely, broadly and profoundly across one's life. Day-dreaming nurtures creativity, as any artist could tell you without an MRI scan, and those given to mind-wandering score higher on tests of creativity than those whose minds are less nomadic. 'For creativity, you need your mind to wander,' says daydream expert Dr Schoolen of the University of British Columbia.

Scientists tell us that there are three modes of thought, the first the instantaneous reflex, snatching a hand from a flame; the second, the diligent, rational mind. But the third is the mind of insight, meditation and reverie. A hush surrounds the daydreaming child, a different kind of air; as if the nearby air of the ordinary had evaporated into the air which the soul breathes, which animates the spirit, self-mesmerizing in an inner dreamtime where the mind's wingtips are angled to the softest sirocco of reverie. The daydreaming child is, on the sudden, a voyager in an enormous and Other galaxy, an innate cosmos as far beyond as it is deep within. 'To aspire' and 'to be inspired' are verbs based on breath (like 'respire'), and these things are impossible if a child's psyche is not allowed to breathe that Other air, when the child is breathlessly entranced, taking almost no physical breaths so that the spirit can breathe. Stopping a child from daydreaming is like suf-focating a Psyche, a breath denied not just this Wednesday morning but for the rest of that child's life. Children are such stuff as daydreams are made of – it is intrinsic to their nature to play, both physically and in reverie – but modernity still puts childhood in the Puritan vice, still insists on productivity and industry, and wonders why children, expe-riencing play-poverty, are suffering. Part of the answer to the riddle of childhood unhappiness lies in allowing children all forms of play, from physical space to mental freedom. It is essential for the psyche.

Argon, the third most common gas in the Earth's atmosphere, is the chemical element of reverie, inert and named after idleness itself, *argos* in Greek. It is soul-oxygen, this argon, made of particles of elsewhere and elsewhen. And sometimes a breath from that Other air, breathed deeply in childhood, inheld perhaps for decades, may be breathed out, only now, in the line of a poem, the sweep of a brush, or one sung note, low, perfect and timeless.

CHAPTER SEVEN

A Clockwork Child

You cannot schedule a daydream.

It is impossible to make an appointment with an epiphany.

Reverie brings punctuality to a full stop.

Children in those moments live in an ecstasy of now-ness, when the present moment is open to eternity.

Epiphanies in childhood can be guides for life, these moments when the psyche, tender to the truths of its world, glimpses something of enduring significance and feels the breath of inspiration by which it lives. Children need wild, unlimited hours but this unenclosed time is in short supply for many, who are diarized into wall-to-wall activities, scheduled from the moment they wake until the minute they sleep, every hour accounted for by parents whose actions are prompted by the fear that their child may fall behind in the rat-race which begins in the nursery. Loving their child, not wanting them to be lifelong losers, parents push children to achieve through effective time-use. Society instils a fear of the future which can only be appeased by sacrificing present play and idleness, and children feel the effects in stress and depression.

'Shall I venture to state, at this point, the most important, the most useful rule of all education? It is not to gain time, but to lose it,' wrote

Jean-Jacques Rousseau in *Émile*. For children today, the focus is on the productive use of time, never to lose an hour or waste a moment.

Of course timetables can matter, and schedules and clocks are useful for planning events, for dovetailing activities and for bringing groups together. But these advantages are so obvious, they need no rehearsal. The question which does need to be asked is: at what cost? What are the elements of childhood time which are crushed by Gradgrind's deadly statistical clock 'which measured every second with a beat like a rap upon a coffin lid'?

A clockwork child loses a metaphysical freedom, the sense of autonomy and the inner sovereignty of the hours. Such a child no longer knows the feeling of owning one's own hours, as intact and as certain as owning one's own breath; an unstifled sense of time-freedom. Seen this way, punctuality can be theft and timetables the record of larceny. Forcing children into a routine which they don't want can be seen as a treason against their majesty of time. Children, though they appreciate a sense of continuity and may well enjoy a diurnal regularity, often rebel against the tight limits of exact punctuality and the stressor of speed which it demands. The psyche cannot breathe easily in that suffocating enclosure of the hours.

One child I know, eight years old, declared she wanted to go to a friend's house. 'Later, darling, later,' said her mother, overstretched, overstressed, feeling the familiar and wholly understandable adult need to schedule her hours tightly. There was a sudden – torrential – storm of tears and the child cried in utter fury: 'I hate *later* – why can't it be *now*?' She wanted her desire coherent with her moment but also, with the unconscious brilliance of children, she was demanding that the present be allowed to have presence, not reduced to later, as a pre-planned booking.

Children today are exhausted by long school hours and after-school curricula, overworked and overscheduled. In Japan, in 2004, one exhausted student dozed in class and his teacher forced him to write an apology in blood. So acceptable did this seem that neither the student nor his parents complained. Forty per cent of elementary schools in the USA eliminated breaktime between 1984 and 2004 in order that children's time should be more 'productive' and structured. The hours are tight, caged lines drawn across the vista of the day.

Imagine time as a landscape: long hills of open afternoons, unfenced horizons of hours, the vast and immaculate freedom of time which, until so very recently, all of humanity knew. But foreshorten the horizons, fence the days, restrict the hours, erect deadlines, add punctuality, alarm clocks and speed – enclose the commons of time, in other words – and people will feel pressured, even if they know how to live in a clock-driven world. It is far harder for children, as they are yet to learn how to do this. They feel the stress painfully and their furious objections to being corralled into those enclosures of time are testament to their innate sense of owning their own time.

So these time-stressed children experience their daydreams surrounded by barbed wire. An electric fence cuts right across the meadow of their thought. A concrete dam blocks a river of imagination and a mountainside of wonder is padlocked. Controlling children's time is a powerful way of controlling their spirits, overruling their will, which a later chapter will explore. At school, both time and childhood must stick to the rules of the clock. A flitting bird of poetry is caught between the walls of the timetable; history is caged by class schedules, although the curious mind learns best unenclosed. Children, asked to describe their ideal school, frequently describe their hatred of timetables which cut them off mid-thought, just when they are immersed in something interesting to them.

Some time ago, in Nunavut, the Inuit state of Canada, I spent a long evening with the (white) headmaster of an Inuit school. He was a notably sensitive man, wise to the stealthy inroads of cultural domination, a teacher good enough to know how to learn from his students. But he had one cultural blindspot: time. Traditional Inuit childhood was unclockworked. 'We ate when we were hungry, slept when we were tired, came and went with the weather,' recalled Inuit woman Minnie Aodla Freeman. In Nunavut, children and parents alike were perfectly happy with children choosing their own hours.

The headmaster could not accept that in the summer the children would play in the midnight sun, up till all hours while the wild light shines, and then be unable to wake up for school in the morning. He fussed, he fretted, he chivvied: all to no avail. 'They don't have any alarm clocks,' he lamented, appalled at the children's lateness and, more than that, at their blithe imperviousness to even the idea of punctuality. So he ordered up caseloads of alarm clocks from the South, box after box of horrible, jarring dream-deniers. By doing so, he was erecting more fences by which time is enclosed, time which, to the Inuit children, had been as unenclosed, as common, free and open as the windswept Arctic tundra. Learning to obey the clock is possibly the most fundamental lesson of all schools: children and staff alike are under the dominion of punctuality, timetables and schedules. This headmaster, for all his genuine and profound cultural awareness, could not for the life of him see that he was riding roughshod over a fundamental part of Inuit culture. He saw only an absence of clocks. He did not see the presence of time.

One Inuit hunter had been talking to me about the beauty of time on the land. Then, with a kind of rueful honesty, he showed me the alarm clock he was giving as a present to his son who was leaving for college. The boy was crossing into a different world of enclosed time and his father, understandably, did not want him to be at a disadvantage in that world.

Since the Industrial Revolution (and aided and abetted by Methodism's strict timetabling for children and the beating of those who wouldn't comply), children's time has been stolen and they have been given clocks instead. When UNICEF asked children what most contributed to their well-being, one of their top three needs, they said, was *time*. Simple, inexhaustible, priceless.

In many traditional cultures, children are held to be the best judges of their own needs, including how they spend their time. John Clare describes his boyhood days wandering until 'the hedge cricket whisper[ed] the hour of waking spirits.' Similarly, in West Papua, one man told me that as children, 'We would go hunting and fishing and just come home when we heard the crickets,' and all over the world there seems a conjunction of crickets, children and suppertime. In the children's tipi where part-Cherokee man James Hightower spent so many hours of his childhood, games might be played until four in the morning. 'The Indian is not like civilized children, having a certain time to eat and sleep.' (In his mouth the term 'civilized' is not a compliment.)

'No regimen or hard routine is laid upon them. When they are sleepy, they sleep. When they are hungry, they may always eat, if there is food. If they wish to play, no one will halt them,' writes author and conservationist Farley Mowat, describing the Ihalmiut people.

'When we're working, we just don't have time to be bothering the kids,' Margrethe Vars, a Sámi reindeer herder, told me. She broke off to drag deep on her cigarette, so her words, imitating European parents, literally came out smoking: *'Have you washed your hands? Now you must eat.'* She pulled a face: to her, children's freedom was not only a right but a relief all round. As the summer stretched out in one long day, the Sámi children would be up all 'night', sometimes until six in the morning, and no one minded because every parent shared the same view that children were in charge of their own time. So the early hours – bright with midsummer sun – would see the children revving up quad bikes, binocularing the reindeer, tickling each other or falling asleep.

'Here we sleep when we are tired, eat when we are hungry,' says Vars, 'but for other societies, children are very much organized, timing is everything, when to eat and sleep, making appointments to visit friends.' She winced at the thought of the micro-management that would entail, visualizing the nuisance of the thing, understanding perfectly how the clock causes repeated and bitter fights, daily, even hourly, for families, how the strict school bell requires strict bedtimes the night before and strict timetabling of homework before that. The Sámi way produced powerfully positive results, not only in the sharp reduction of petty conflict but also in something intangible and vital because, Sámi people say, children would grow up more self-reliant, less obedient to outside pressure, less malleable, less biddable – captains of their own hours, not captive to someone else's clock.

Bells, whistles, gongs and clappers speak of 'order, authority, discipline, efficiency, system, organization, schedule, regimentation', writes Basil Johnston, an Ojibwa man remembering the clock-time of boarding school which the authorities forced many Native American children to attend. They also symbolize 'obedience, conformity, dependence, subservience, uniformity, docility, surrender'. And where there is repression there will be revolt, somehow, somewhere. He describes the boys waiting. Sort of. For 'though they may have appeared to be waiting, the boys were in reality exercising a form of quiet disobedience directed against bells, priests, school and, in the abstract, all authority, civil and religious. Since the boys could not openly defy authority either by walking out of the school and marching north or south on Highway 17 or by flatly refusing to follow an order, they turned to the only means available to them: passive resistance, which took the form of dawdling.'

Huckleberry Finn, whose wild, self-willed time had been spontaneous and unfenced, complains about the clockworked life of Widow Douglas which would enclose him: 'The widder eats by a bell; she goes to bed by a bell; she gits up by a bell – everything's so awful reg'lar a body can't stand it . . . I can't stand it. It's awful to be tied up so.'

In the same power-struggle today, one Internet blog (well intentioned and far from rare) discusses the 'problem' of 'lazy' and 'dawdling' children. The 'solutions' include waking children with an alarm clock, dressing them by a stopwatch, making them eat by a timer and hurrying them to the ticking off of a metronome, as well as getting them to do tasks accompanied by 'fast marching music'.

Children and punctuality have never been the best of friends and they have always preferred to wend their own way through their own wild hours, in sincere and universal protest, because they do not like Chronos, the god of measured clock-time, but rather they hold a candle for Kairos, the god of timing, of chance and mischance, the god of the special moment, the colourful, variegated time of the psyche.

Children know time in so many guises: the split second of a kingfisher flash, the reckless suddenness of a toboggan run, the slow hush of thinking whether or not to drink a puddle just because your brother has dared you to do it. Time can crawl slowly as a sloth sleeping off an over-energetic yawn, or run speedy as a cub raccoon ricocheting off a tree-trunk which it lassoed with its own tail, by mistake. Sometimes it can disappear altogether. Tamed clock-time does not offer a child's soul what it needs: the swings of morning, the embers of evening and the difference of all the hours in between.

My kitten was named Otter because he arrived on 12 August which, according to the French Revolutionary Calendar, is the day of the Otter. In that calendar, to each day was assigned an animal, a plant, mineral or tool, as if the spirit of Apricot presided over one day and another day's deity was the Wheelbarrow. Clay, Slate, Sandstone, Rabbit and Flint begin the year, while Ladder, Watermelon and Fennel comprise a late-August list. The months were named after the seasons: 'snowy', 'rainy' and 'windy' months, followed by 'sprouting', 'flowering' and the 'meadow' month. The Revolutionaries overthrew the Emperor months of Julius and Augustus and replaced them with 'harvest' and 'heat'. September to December, with their lifeless numerical order, were renamed with the vitality of 'fruit', 'vintage', 'foggy' and 'frosty'. Children, sensitive to place and moment, also experience their time like this, so one day may be coloured by slate or conker or the taste of pear, while for them a month is far more fully expressed by 'foggy' than 'October'. On one day, the watering can is the hero of the moment, and another day may be spent under the auspices of licorice.

By the clock, each hour is numerical and standardized. Time itself, however, is variegated, embedded in both nature and in the psyche where different moments, hours and seasons are coloured and characterized diversely. Children live happily in this wild time, untameable, full of character, full of difference. And in this way, time has codes for the child's psyche.

Dawn, wide open, when time stretches untrapped, can nurture a child's sense of dawn within, when the mind can bask extravagantly in an open moment. Broadening sunrise, lighting on all it can see, suggests how curiosity and breadth of interest lights everything the psyche can reach. The straightforward, robust afternoon hours illustrate the mind's ruddy, tough confidence. A child who knows dusk

directly can better know the psyche's own twilight-mindedness, mesmerized by ambiguity, dwelling with dilemma and unsimple truths.

As with the hours of the day, so with the seasons of the year: the child learns aspects of the psyche itself. Nine o'clock will never teach a child anything except obedience, nor will 12/8 educate a child beyond the border. Modernity's banal sameness of time will never give a child the lifelong codes for the spirit.

But the seasons will.

A child's psyche which knows the year's seasons as reality, not as pictures on calendars, can nurture its own seasonality. To such a mind, spring may suggest soul-values of expectation, a need to begin, to conceive, the wound-up spring set to be sprung, the sense of possibility and exploration.

A psyche which knows the stretch of summer may know how its soul-analogy is pleasure, how to be fully engaged, engrossed in play. 'Time is a child playing,' said Heraclitus, and I can only see this image saturated with summer.

A psyche which knows the fruits of autumn may know the soul's harvest of generosity, open-handed and open-hearted. Death is autumnal and may shock a child less if it is already understood in falling leaves.

A psyche which knows the bite of winter may learn how to endure, how to resist the frosts, how to survive in style, defiantly burning the candles all the brighter in the midwinter festival.

These generations, exiled from the natural world, lose yet another dimension of nature: wild time, with all its seasons of significance. And Otter is better than 12/8 as a name for a day. And for a kitten.

CHAPTER EIGHT

The Will of the Wild

As if they had cider bubbling through their veins, the kids fizz with curiosity. Rain gleams on them, then, on a sudden, the sun rampages through the trees, chucking gold on the ground, the solar millionaire. A belly-burping chorus of frogs pumps out of the forest while under-foot, as children and adults congregate on one house, the mud belches, plops and gurgles. Someone is giggling; someone has fallen asleep; someone is lighting a bonfire – a *bon feu*, a good fire – for fun and the ancestors.

Greedy for life, tough as wild plants, children are crawling, twist-ing, hopping, gurning, staring, gulping, shouting, shoving and crowding their faces at the window to see what is going on. One little boy, six years old and barely more than eye-level to his dad's curly penis gourd (with a special feather tucked in the tip and a wad of tobacco by his balls), is thinking hard. His eyes are bright as a spar-row's and serious as an owl's.

Inside the house, a Dutch doctor works with the anthropologist Leopold Pospisil to inoculate the Kamu Kapauku people of West Papua against the appalling disease yaws. Yaws causes ugly, swollen lesions, eats away the face and is occasionally fatal. Children aged between six and ten are especially vulnerable to infection.

Loathing and fearing this disease, people turn up with alacrity, thronging the house, going in to see the doctor one by one. The six-year-old and his father step forward, and the man is given the injection. The boy, though, shakes his head. He refuses. He is adamant. The doctor tries to manhandle the child, overruling him. Abruptly, the father stops the doctor. 'You heard the boy, he said no!' Though everyone, including the father, knows the threat of the disease and is fully aware that the injection may be life-saving, yet in this culture there is something else which might be still more essential to that boy's life and well-being than the inoculation could ever be: his autonomy; his freedom to decide – his *will*.

According to Pospisil, the Kapauku people of West Papua believe that 'the essence of life is a free cooperation of the body and the soul. Any interference in this cooperation endangers the life of the individual.'

Will is a life force for children and without its energy something vital in them dies. What sap is to the plant, will is to the human being. Will is vitality, the iridescent juice which makes one's spirit shine. Will urges the child to its blood-and-silver path. Will flings a nine-year-old opinion in the face of a fifty-nine-year-old teacher. Twice. Will tensions the wings, lifts the flight feathers into the storm to generate its own power in the unsteady sky and to wait, hovering, holding a moment of betweenness, after flight and before pitch, between horizon and air, between inbreath and outbreath, to decide in its own moment to swoop or to soar. It is will that makes the eagle's flight radiant; in wildness is its integrity for only when it is self-willed can it be true to itself. Will animates, intoxicates, energizes; will is the rebel angel mesmerized by earth and air; it improvises, riffing where it lists.

The word 'will' is connected to the word 'wild'. In early Teutonic and Norse languages the root of 'wild' is in 'will': what is self-willed, wilful or uncontrollable. Children need to be self-willed, autonomous, ruling themselves, and when children recognize the call of the wild without, they echo it with the voice of the wild within, their own will seeking expression, establishing itself as of right: a law of nature and of human nature. It is a primal politics.

The Dutch doctor wanted the small Papuan boy to be well. The child wanted to be well too, but he saw his wellness in other terms. Wait a while on the word 'well'. To do something well is, through its etymology, to do something *at will*. The stem of 'well' is identical to that of the verb 'will'.

All shall be will and all manner of things shall be will.

In language, then, it is as if wellness and will come from the same source, an underground spring, another well, where will is as clear as water, as vital and as benign, aligned with the gentle velleities of mind welling up into life.

Without self-will, children's well-being may be affected. Without wildness, they can go crazy. Bury it though you may, wildness will explode out of the earth and out of the child. Suppressed wildness (and repressed will) take their revenge later in self-destructive madness, drugged oblivion or self-harm.

It is not only the moon, or an apple thrown into the air, which will experience the gravitational pull of the wild earth. Children, too, feel the tug of it, the psyche drawn to ocean, woods and mountains, the attraction of the wild circus of life, from laughing kookaburra to badger, from mercurial pine marten to centipede. Children need wildness – their own and the land's – they hear the voice which speaks in turquoise and topaz, they respond with fascinated attention, in a state of utter stillness on the outside and racing mobility on the inside. With a facility for the language of wildness, children can hear the verbs in the stone-running rapids; they understand the nouns of 'fox' and 'cave' and 'speedwell'; they can translate perfectly those canny, eternal abstract nouns of 'presence', of 'this-ness', of 'encounter', as the child meets a deer in the coolness of an evening wood. And they also know the rampage, wanting to startle the deer, to go Bacchic, to go bananas, to dance the tango of reckless licence with a world let off the leash. Kindled in earth, of a kind with all animals, kin to kittens, cubs and chicks, children are not aliens to wildness but akin to it, wild at the raw core. Their original fire is sparked by the embers of a world flame which also lights the peacock and the stars. Intimates of wildness, all of them.

This is not to say that children are therefore alien to culture in poetry, art and the play of metaphor, for wildness is not the opposite of culture. Rather, wildness is the opposite of capture, and that is what children are alien to: the force of anti-nature and the anti-wild, the spirit of enclosure.

Fence-jumpers and limit-loathers, children want to roam, inside themselves in imagination and outside themselves, out of bounds. Children want to know the world where the paths themselves go astray, the world lit by moonlight, where midnight-blue illuminates the world otherwise, where all is not accustomed, predictable and regular, where some wild music demands a response in the same key, for children are tuned to the pitch of a wild songline. Hungry for starlight and for falling asleep by a fire, hearing stories from the dreamtime of all cultures which work like spells on the psyche, children want to escape from the drilled mechanisms of the anti-wild.

Around the world, there are therapeutic projects working with children who have suffered abuse and whose wildness has turned violent. The schemes, including one in South Africa, take the children out into the wilds to sleep under the stars and, informed by the intangible heritage of myth and ritual, use wildness as medicine. I met Quentin Fredericks, who spent his teenage years in Soweto's gangland culture. By seventeen, he was in jail and on his release he decided to work taking young people out bush for 'purposeful and constructive rituals'. There is, says Fredericks, a 'dislocation of wilderness' because of the destruction of wild lands and the displacement of indigenous cultures. 'The wildness within young men needs a container, but without the actual wilderness, the wildness in young men is unencumbered.' The project's rituals focus on the psyche's wildness and rhyme it with wild nature. In the wilderness, Fredericks says, you can 'fly like an eagle and look skywards where your destiny lies, not in the dust. It restores dignity and self-respect.' Storms without and storms within are elemental and related, twinned stories in the twin worlds, outside and inside the psyche.

When I was researching *Wild*, I found people talking of the dangerous wildness of young people wherever there had been a sudden and dramatic clash of indigenous culture meeting non-indigenous, and the solution, people told me, was the land. Wilderness therapy is enormously effective for disturbed adolescents for, out on the land, young people can feel contained, held within something larger than themselves, a higher authority, if you like, not the petty authority of police or parents, but the ineluctable, absolute authority of mountain, ice, forest or desert. The land is tougher than the kids. In Nunavut, there are programmes to take young offenders out on to the land. One man explained it thus: 'They get rid of their anger there where it's safe. It works. There are kids who behave badly in town, but if you take them out on to the land, they behave perfectly and really come alive.'

Studies from across the world show that wilderness therapy produces positive outcomes for teenagers, it is seen to lessen distress both within themselves and in their relationships with others, and seems to offer helpful, effective treatment for problematic – difficult – adolescents. In the wilds, self-awareness and communication with other people are enhanced. What is known as adventure therapy improves young people's self-conception and sense of self-control as well as guiding them towards better social skills.

My own childhood had many freedoms, yet it lacked wildness, which I knew at first only by the thirst for it. In my teens I went climbing in Snowdonia in the deep snow of midwinter and I drank and drank the wild hills and the snow-swept, shining mountains, feeling an ancient need to leave the village, to roam the wilds. For almost all of human history, this feeling has been honoured, letting children loose in a world whose wildness becomes them. Culture, growing from the honouring of nature, is not opposed to this wild way of being but sinks its tap root deep into the hot and dreaming earth. This is how childhood thrives, cheek to cheek with the kind and thriving wildness, not in the modified and lustreless indoor life which would sterilize every drop of water and suffocate the air itself.

~

!Kung children of the Kalahari were customarily not forced into obedience and if they strongly refused to do something, the choice was considered to be theirs to make. Among the Yequana people of Venezuela, coercion was traditionally absent and deciding what anyone else should do, regardless of how young they may be, was antipathetic to their philosophy. With no sense of the hierarchy of adults over children and no assumption whatever that an adult may consider themselves superior to a child, Huaorani childhood in Ecuador shines with independence, and relations between adults and children have no stain of authoritarianism. Anthropologist Laura Rival refers to a pan-Amazonian 'political project of personal autonomy', an ethos highly developed among the Huaorani. 'In Huaorani land, no one can be coerced in any way. No one can force or order another person to do something. It is also understood that one should not force oneself either,' she writes. While 'coercion brings about illness, danger, or evil spirits', to be well and to do things well, by contrast, is to do them at will and the Huaorani portray freedom and autonomy in metaphors of birds in flight.

'Who's boss for you?' a group of Indigenous Australian women in a community north of Alice Springs asked a four-year-old girl. 'No one,' she responded instantly. 'I'm boss for meself.' It would have made Susanna Wesley (mother of Methodist John Wesley) turn in her grave, but the women laughed, delighted at the child's robust self-will. By tradition, a child should be self-directed, acting by their 'own idea', according to Pintupi people. Autonomy is not granted to a child but rather is considered their birthright. For Indigenous Australian societies, among many others, domination of any sort in terms of species, individuals, communities or nations is regarded as being against the law of nature. Pintupi philosophy rejected domination, and the quality of traditional everyday life was free, unrestricted and verging on the anarchic in its true sense, being governed by oneself and nature.

In Iroquois social philosophies, which influenced both the US Constitution and the Bill of Rights, women were held in high regard and children were not dominated. Native American cultures insisted on respecting the will of every individual, regardless of age, because autonomy and self-expression were important even for very young children and coercion was a last resort. When Native American societies cherished a child's will, certain qualities would be encouraged – strength of mind, independence and potency.

All the witnesses agree: the minds of small children 'have imbibed this prejudice, that no one whatever has a right to force them to do anything,' writes Pierre de Charlevoix, eighteenth-century Jesuit missionary in the Great Lakes area of Canada, with a kind of appalled bewilderment. Iroquois children were encouraged to be independent, not to submit to authoritarian behaviour, so like hordes of Huck Finns, they went their own way, acted by their own lights and 'have entirely their own will and never do anything by compulsion', wrote David Zeisberger, missionizing among them in the 1740s. They may be prevented from harming others, for sure, but not punished for it, only spoken to 'with gentle words'. Custom among the Laguna Pueblo of New Mexico forbids forcing children to do something against their will. Among the Navajo, traditionally, a child would not be made to do anything which they adamantly refused to do, even if it was otherwise considered good for the child, because, as with the experience of the small boy in West Papua, the integrity of the will was more important.

When an Inuit carver is sculpting ivory, he does not impose his will on the material but rather allows the ivory to suggest to him the form it may take. It speaks and the sculptor listens. This is similar to the attitude of Inuit parents to children, allowing the incipient character of the child to express its will in a kind of co-carving to release the work of art which is the child's spirit.

For the Wintu people of California, so deep is their traditional respect for the autonomy of the will that it suffuses the language itself. In English, if you 'take a baby' somewhere, there is a sense of implicit coercion. Wintu language cannot say that, it must phrase it as 'I went with the baby.' 'I watched the child' would be 'I watched with the child'; and 'I fed the child' would be 'I participated in my child's eating.' The Wintu people couldn't coerce someone even if they wanted to: language won't let them. No one 'permits' a child to do anything – because no one can give a child something which is already theirs by right: the prerogative of the child to decide. When a Wintu child asks 'Can I . . . ?' they are emphatically not asking for permission from an individual parent but rather for clarification about whether wider laws allow it, so a child does not feel at the mercy of the will of a single adult with rules which can seem capricious and arbitrary.

Take a step back for a moment. *Letting children have their own way? Doing just what they like? Wouldn't that be a total disaster?* Yes, if parents perform only the first half of the trick. In the cultural lexicon of modernity, self-will is often banally understood as brattish, selfish behaviour, children acting like spoilt gods, terrible infant-divinities. Will does not mean selfishness, and autonomy over oneself is not a synonym for nastiness towards others – in fact, quite the reverse.

For often, when indigenous people have elaborated on the importance of a child following their own will, they stress wider social subtleties. Ngarinyin children in Australia traditionally grew up uncommanded and uncoerced but from a young age they learned socialization, encouraged to pay attention to knowledge within themselves and inherent in the laws of nature. That is the second half of the trick. Children are socialized into awareness and respect for the will and autonomy of others, acknowledging that there is a plurality of wills and a diversity of selves so, when necessary as they grow, they will learn to hold their own will in check in order to maintain good relations. For a community to function well, an individual may on occasion need to rein in his or her *own* will, but, crucially, not be compelled to do so by someone else.

In contrast to the antisocial behaviour of spoilt children, both the individual and society benefit from an understanding that everyone's will matters. It seems to be the case that the more a child's will is respected, the better she or he will be at respecting the will of others. Indigenous philosophy often examines the tension between the individual and the community, and it seems that the more autonomy a child is given, the better the child becomes at valuing both individuality and community. The Huaorani, for example, treasure the communality of their longhouses but also enormously appreciate the unique and idiosyncratic characteristics of diverse individuals.

While there is evidence of children having great freedom, there isn't a society on earth that doesn't socialize its children. In India, a child is 'twice born', first as an individual baby and, secondly, between five and ten, as a social human being. Children grow towards reason, mind or thought which the Utkuhikhalingmiut people of the Canadian North-west call *ihuma*. Acquiring *ihuma* includes recognizing people, remembering, understanding and learning restraint. *Ihuma* grows from within and needs to reveal itself before it can be instructed by others; it chooses its own timing. The concept of *niwa* among the Lohorung Rai of East Nepal seems similar, referring to mind or reason as something slowly acquired. Modern scientific analysis would agree that cognitive processes and brain development come slowly and bide their own time.

Will is a child's motive force: it *impels* a child from within, whereas obedience *compels* a child from without. Those who would overrule a child's will take 'obedience' as their watchword, as they fear disobedience and disorder and believe that if a child is not controlled, there will be chaos. But these are false opposites. The true opposite of obedience is not disobedience but independence. The true opposite of order is not disorder but freedom. The true opposite of control is not chaos but self-control.

When children are allowed their will *and* encouraged to control themselves, community is well served, and Indigenous societies have typically given enormous attention to the development of self-control in children. Pierre de Charlevoix approved the results among Indigenous children, saying that they became, from a young age, 'masters of themselves'. Among Inuit and Sámi people, there is an explicit need for children to learn self-regulation. Adults don't mither their children but keep a reticent and tactful distance. A child 'is learning on his own' is a common Sámi expression. Sámi children are trained to control anger, sensitivity, aggression and shame. Inuit people stress that children must learn self-control – with careful emphasis. The child should not be controlled by another, with their will overruled, but needs to learn to steer herself or himself. Jean L. Briggs describes the mildly spoken but relentless demand for self-control in Inuit children: by the time they were ten, their self-control was 'almost infallible'.

Anthropologists in the Amazon have long commented that Amazonian myths place huge importance on self-restraint and self-discipline. In Bruno Bettelheim's beautiful analysis of how fairy tales educate children, his conclusion is very similar, for at the end of fairy tales the child has 'become an autocrat in the best sense of the word – a self-ruler . . . not a person who rules over others'.

Most fairy tales seem to agree with typical indigenous ideas – that through a freedom of will, self-regulation may be strengthened. This is exactly the kind of self-regulation which children learn in free play, in unscheduled time. It's not just fairy tales which are in accord: the Proceedings of the National Academy of Sciences of the United States of America (no less) recently published a study which demonstrates that when people had low self-control as children, this would result in poorer health, more financial problems and criminal convictions in adulthood than those with high self-control in childhood. The importance of this for both the individual and for society is underlined as the study states: 'individuals' self-control is a key ingredient in health, wealth, and public safety.'

~

The fact that so many indigenous cultures respect the will of children does not mean that their childhoods have always been easy. Beyond aspects of training and immediate care, some cultural traditions are, without question, brutal, while environmental limits have had direct and fatal results for children. Traditionally, San Bushmen would kill a baby if it was born deformed, or if the mother was unable to support it. For Inuit children, the very land could evince a calculus of cold, a bitter and terrible maths by which, if the group as a whole were to survive, a devastating subtraction must be made, which demanded the deaths of the least necessary, the very old and the very young. Since it was the men, as hunters, who were most vital for the life of all, it was not uncommon for baby girls to be killed at birth when times were hard and, in the early twentieth century, Danish explorer Knud Rasmussen noted that in one village there had been ninety-six births and of the children born thirty-eight girls were killed.

Similarly in Britain in 1712, *The Spectator* commented on the 'multitudes of infants' who were either killed or abandoned by their parents, left to die of semi-deliberate exposure or starvation when the parents were simply unable to care for them. The London Foundling Hospital was established in 1741 and, in its first four years, fifteen thousand children were left there. Ten thousand of them died. In some nineteenth-century European cities, a third or even half of all children born were abandoned.

In feudal Japan, as part of the training of young Samurai, boys were sent on tasks which seem psychologically cruel, including watching public beheadings and later returning to the site at night to leave a token of their visit on the decapitated head. In Europe and America, children would be subjected to psychological terror, taken to hangings as a way of teaching them to fear hell.

Inuit girls, indulged as children, would find that when childhood melted into womanhood a wholly different treatment awaited them, as their free will was often denied them just when it mattered the most. In language terse with repugnance, Roger P. Buliard writes: 'At seven, and eight, she is already a servant . . . At twelve she is a plaything, lent or abused, and at fourteen she is married . . . As to her personal preference, the Eskimo girl is never consulted.' Some interviews with Inuit people can read like accounts of socially sanctioned rape for, as so many testify, a girl had little choice over who she married. At four-teen, remembers Rosie Iqalliyuq, 'I was taken away in the spring time . . . I ran away . . . I was a fast runner . . . they came after me by dog team . . . they took me away again and this time they tied me down to the sled. They took me away even though I was crying and they didn't pay any attention to my crying . . . the man I didn't want was my first experience.' A lacuna surrounds that sentence. A young girl broken with shock, her will over-ridden as if she were nothing more than pack ice offering momentary resistance to the sledge run-ners: the dogs drag the sledge over her and are gone. Her selfhood is stunned, the advent of an ice age cracks her apart from within.

'Long ago, girls were forced to marry their husbands . . . if a girl left her husband, her hair was shaved right off. They were outcasts in the tribe,' says Dorothy Sanvidge, a Mowachaht woman. 'Anyone could take them and do what they liked with them and once they did that the tribe had no more use for them.'

In West Papua (where boys were told they had to get out of bed before dawn, otherwise their grandfathers would light a fire and the boys, sleeping up in the tops of the huts, would get an eyeful of smoke) children suffered acutely after a death in the family. In mourning rituals, a boy might have an ear sliced off and little girls aged perhaps three or four were chosen to take on the grief of the family and would have a finger cut off. I saw many old women whose hands were crippled, stumps where fingers should be. It was a repulsive practice, one which seldom occurs today. If people were to do it now, I was told, they would be fined a pig.

And then, as if in a category of cruelty all its own, is 'the cutting time' when girls are subjected to genital mutilation. Halima Bashir, from the Darfur region of Sudan, describes the moment it happened to her: 'I was a terrified child with all the adults in the world that I trusted causing me unspeakable pain. The shock of the betrayal was beyond imagining.'

~

Few societies have wanted to overrule completely the self-willedness of children, but the Puritans were one such society. Their demand to overcome the will of children parallels that other great Puritan project; to subdue the will of nature. Wildness, in land or child, must be eradicated, pulled up by the roots. (The converse holds: societies which honour the will of the land also seem to honour the will of the child.) So extreme was this Puritan attitude towards children that in the early 1600s Massachusetts brought in the Stubborn Child Act, by which parents were allowed to kill a child who was rebellious and disobedient.

John Wesley's teachings about the will of children were highly influential both in Britain and in America, which he visited in the 1730s, encouraging parents 'to break the will of your child, to bring his will into subjection to yours, that it may be afterward subject to the will of God'. Instead of the integrity and wisdom of wildness, in the tradition of Puritanism and branches of Protestantism a child is a hobbled bear shuffling dance-steps which its owner will more applaud the more its magnificence is broken.

John Wesley, it has to be said, had a bit of help from his mum. The will of a child, wrote Susanna Wesley in 1732, should be 'totally subdued . . . no willful transgression ought ever to be forgiven children, without chastisement . . . I insist on conquering the will of children,' as 'self-will is the root of all sin and misery.'

The attitude poisoned European society for generations such that, for example, in 1858, the influential German physician and writer on child-rearing, Dr Daniel Gottlieb Moritz Schreber, wrote that a child's 'first appearance of willfulness' should meet a forceful response, including beatings.

John Wesley had argued that the will should be vanquished in order to fight the 'natural Atheism' of children. 'It is quite natural for the child's soul to want to have a will of its own,' wrote German authority J. Sulzer in 1748, advocating the crushing of this will in early childhood. 'If their wills can be broken at this time, they will never remember afterwards that they had a will.' Most indigenous cultures would agree that will is *natural* to the child. The difference was that, whereas indigenous cultures typically consider human nature to be good, the Puritans and fundamentalist Protestants thought it evil.

'They are not too little to die, not too little to go to hell,' wrote the seventeenth-century English Puritan minister James Janeway in his tract *A Token for Children* (1671–2), said to have been the most influential English book on childcare in its time. Human nature was naturally evil, heir to Original Sin, according to the Evangelical Revivalists in Britain and America in the eighteenth and nineteenth centuries. In 1799, the British *Evangelical Magazine* advised parents to teach their children that they are 'sinful polluted creatures', while Hannah More, Evangelical founder of the Sunday School movement in England, wrote of children as 'beings who bring into the world a corrupt nature and evil dispositions'.

Nature itself – the self-willed comedic Earth, cunning in its chthonic knowing – was considered evil and corrupt. Christianity turned Pan, the great god of nature, into the devil. Children, with their great affinity to animals, their self-willedness hatched alongside the will of the wild, are thus in their nature ever closer to the 'evil' of the natural world. Babies were 'Filthy, guilty, odious, abominable . . . both by nature and practice,' said the American Puritan the Reverend Benjamin Wadsworth (1670–1737).

'Hold childhood in reverence!' was the clarion call of Jean-Jacques Rousseau. Against the background of his age, his defiance resounds like a silver trumpet in the bleak silence. Given the prevalent belief in the evil of nature and the child's nature, Rousseau's attitude was shocking, brilliant and vital. 'Let us lay it down as an incontrovertible rule that the first impulses of nature are always right; there is no original sin in the human heart; the how and why of the entrance of every vice can be traced.' Championing the will of children and the wildness of nature, Rousseau won the hearts of half of Europe for the sheer relief of the thing. Let it be said, though, that Rousseau's ideas on freedom didn't extend to girls, who 'should also be early subjected to restraint . . . that they may the more readily submit to the will of others'. It's vile, that line. Rousseau also suggested that boys should be so subtly manipulated into doing the will of the tutor that the child would be unaware of the devious engineering.

Rousseau chose metaphors which a reader today may barely remark. A child is like a wild plant, to be cultivated 'from nature itself'. The metaphor has come to seem, well, *natural*. Wordsworth would choose the image of a seed: 'Fair seed-time had my soul,' he wrote of his infancy. In Rousseau's time, it was an act of courage to select a natural metaphor to represent goodness; in a society that argued the iniquity of nature and the sinfulness of children, Rousseau argued for the benignity of both. The childhood he described was one which almost any culture would have recognized, rooted in earth but inquisitive to sky, spontaneous, tendrilled, green and growing. In no other society and in no other age would Rousseau's ideas seem so radical.

For across the ages children have been held in reverence, closer to the divine than to the devil. Lakota shaman Hehaka Sapa or Black Elk writes of babies as 'holy'. To Huaorani people, babies are considered a marvel. Among Gypsies, where there is a strong concept of pollution, babies are considered the exact opposite, as sources of purification.

In Hinduism, the child Krishna is considered a god and divinity is child-like. The Western tradition does, of course, have the image of the divine child in the baby Jesus, but there is a crucial difference. The iconography of the Christ child portrays the godhead while it happens to be an infant. It does not portray childhood itself as a state of divinity. By contrast, the scampering antics of the child Krishna (butter-stealer, milk-spiller, whey-sprayer) are not only indulged but admired, as they represent the divine nature of the child's playfulness: free, spontaneous, audacious, self-delighting, intense, vivacious, passionate and mercurial. These qualities are considered divine and to be welcomed in adulthood as well as childhood.

While Western society has stealthily portrayed play as puerile and even evil (the devil finds work for idle hands), Indian culture can see play as both funny and holy. In the juice, the sap and the chirrup, god is a child playing. Medieval Bhakti poetry of India wholly reverses the Western view so that God-the-father is replaced by God-the-child, and a naughty one. As a mother is to a child, so is the poet to (a radiant) god. 'And the brilliance of millions of bits of the universe in his infancy he obscures,' wrote Sūrdās. The god in small people is openly, utterly, besottedly adored and when Indian parents wish for their children to have 'a touch of Krishna', shining with mischief and vitality, they are welcoming the divinity of childhood.

In the Bhakti tradition, creativity is centred around childhood. The Romantics, with their genius for cherishing childhood creativity, would agree. As would the great Gaston Bachelard, writing: 'An excess of childhood is the germ of the poem.' But the pram in the hallway is the enemy of promise, of good art, in Cyril Connolly's odiously over-influential view, which prompted George Szirtes to write in a riposte-poem: 'Dear enemies of promise, how beautiful you are.'

Far from seeing will as evil, as the Puritans and Protestants did, many earth-based belief systems use will and wildness, from childhood onwards, as a way to spiritual insight, through individual dreams and visions in wild lands and seeing wild creatures as messengers of vital import. Shamanism, that ur-religion of earth, fathoms wisdom and the divine in what is most self-willed, wild and free. Shamanic creatures are overwhelmingly the wildest within any region – bear, jaguar, wolf or eagle – because intensity is theirs, and mystery. It is in wildness that children hear the voices of wild divinity, written in leaves, seas and feathers. To find their wisdom, a young person goes alone among ice or mountain, desert or shore. Theirs to know the kinetic trajectory of wild thought. Theirs to feel the canny pounce of the bear or the grave patience of a spider. Theirs to live in a world which growls with insight, which shapeshifts and alights, where a raven caws caution to a running child or lightning cracks open a dream like a nut, where a paw print is a text from a world electric with significance, where everything jumps with meaning and anyone can stretch a finger like the flight feather of an eagle's wing to the hot brilliance of laughing divinity always and only just – just – the other side of the ordinary.

~

Today, some in the States still attempt to break a child's will, still view this will as devilish. The far-right fundamentalist childcare authors Michael and Debi Pearl write of 'the evil that a self-willed spirit will eventually bring' and compare parenting with army training 'designed to teach and reinforce submission of the will', referring to a small child's 'diabolic will to dominate'. James Dobson, fundamentalist author of *The New Strong-Willed Child*, writes: 'Self-will is the essence of original sin.' He considers will as a sickness to be treated by physical beatings. Their philosophy is so far from the wisdom of language which connects 'will' with 'wellness' that it has reached the opposite conclusion, as did John Wesley, asking 'What can we do to cure their self-will?' To *cure* will. Wellness is seen as disease and vitality is pathologized. It is a far cry from Augustine, who advised: 'Love, and do what you will.'

If Rousseau was a champion for children in his age, Philip Pullman is in ours, writing the song of vehement and beautiful will, opposing the literalist evangelicalism of our day as Rousseau opposed the evangelical revival of his. Pullman's boy-hero in *His Dark Materials* is Will: will by name, will by nature. He is independent, proud, free and – importantly – enormously self-controlled. He embodies the idea of 'will' as positive, in a way which traditional cultures would have well understood, recalling the prized qualities of autonomy, flexibility, passion and potency.

Will is the keeper of the 'subtle knife' of the book title. 'With the knife he can enter and leave any world at will . . . Will is his name.' The knife is a symbol for the will of the mind, something of enormous strength and yet subtle, fine and delicate. The mind, at will, curious and independent, cuts its way into worlds unknown and opposes the brutal ignorance imposed by Authority and the Magisterium. 'Every little increase in human freedom has been fought over ferociously between those who want us to know more and be wiser and stronger, and those who want us to obey and be humble and submit,' writes Pullman. While the Bible begins in a paradise garden destroyed by will and curiosity, and ends in an abstract heaven and a destroyed earth, Pullman begins with the prisons of obedience and ends by locating heaven on the earth itself, being sung into being by imagination, love and sheer will.

Lyra and Will want no part in a kingdom of heaven. Not that they are against heaven, mind you, but they are emphatically against the hierarchy of any kingdom, so they set out to build 'the republic of heaven on earth' (six of the most beautiful words of divinity ever written). They pledge themselves to this, rooting their will in the wild earth.

Solving the riddle of childhood unhappiness must include honouring a child's will: for the well-being of childhood needs something of the wild at the core of nature and human nature. Obedience is deadly, will is divine and the vital wildness of the human spirit is purring, over there, like a cat-shadow in the beetroot patch.

CHAPTER NINE

The Fractal Politics of Childhood

History seldom documents that the sky was blue, nor that gentleness is the common sky of childhood. It is easy for historians to portray the trenchant diktat of majesty or the register of state decree but much of childhood is undocumentable. Yet in all traditions – Western, Eastern, indigenous and non-indigenous – you can, if you listen carefully, hear the whispers of cherishing which have held the childhoods of the world as a breath holds a story, the underheard voices of the precious ordinary, for, almost wherever – and whenever – you look, people seem to have treated children with kind tolerance and clever tenderness.

According to Sherpas, the two great sins are picking wild flowers and threatening children. Gypsy children were traditionally treated with notable indulgence and freedom. !Kung children almost never received physical punishment. 'A wean could be forgiven almost any-thing. A wean couldn't help himself,' writes Ian Niall in *A Galloway Childhood*. Among the Scottish peasantry in the nineteenth century, when children were quarrelsome, mothers would sing to make the children dance until they were 'seven times tired'. A naughty child would be warned that the Tylwyth Teg, the fair folk, in Wales, or the piskies in Cornwall would steal them. Admonishment for misbehaving children seems often to have been subtle and indirect, an adult perhaps telling a story chosen to mirror a child's misdemeanour without publicly shaming them.

In Indigenous Australia, people say they are careful not to offend the dignity of a child, pocket-sized though it may be, so children are very seldom slapped, while a parent who leaves a child to cry may be criticized by others. In traditional Maori culture children were almost never beaten but, if it did happen, the child's relations, aggrieved, might threaten revenge on those who had hurt the child. When Maori children were punished in white or Pakeha schools in the nineteenth century, the Maoris, shocked, called this treatment cruel, excessive, strange and tyrannical.

Many commentators present history as a line of continuous improvement, as if the past was always a bad place to be a child, bruised by pervasive violence and cruelty, as if reform gradually took place and the present, imperfect though it may be, is wholly preferable. There's some truth in this, certainly, because if one is looking at some aspects of childhood in Europe after the Middle Ages, and at early American settler society, then it is legitimate to argue that childhood was often savage and has improved. In Europe and America today children are less likely to be beaten and more likely to receive education and healthcare, but a big misperception still exists.

It is just not true that childhood in the past was universally brutal. In many cultures, the reverse seems the case.

Among the First Nations of the Great Lakes area, a mother might reproach her daughter by saying she had dishonoured her and, remarks Pierre de Charlevoix, the reproof was almost always effective. In common with some Indigenous Australian peoples, children among the Laguna Pueblo in New Mexico were reprimanded by a family member but not the parents, in order to protect the emotional sanctuary of parental love. For many Native Americans, the dreamcatcher (one of the most beautiful idea-symbols ever created, woven like a web which would catch bad dreams in its net and protect a child from nightmares) was sacred to that parent–child relationship.

'For an elder person in the Lakota tribe to strike or punish a young person was an unthinkable brutality . . . any Lakota caught flogging a child would have been considered unspeakably low,' wrote Luther Standing Bear. There was no word for punishment in the Native American Mojave language and even if a child was being obnoxious they would be tolerated. According to the Kiowa from the Great Plains, adults never whipped children but would seek to earn a child's respect: having done so, they would never need to use coercion, let alone violence. In Bolivia in the mid-twentieth century, one missionary told the author Norman Lewis that in all his years of missionary work he had never heard of a single instance of 'an Indian' punishing a child, a matter he regarded as almost a genetic defect which he could begin to remedy: as he spoke he was preparing to thrash an Ayoreo child.

In the 1740s, David Zeisberger recalled that Iroquois children were attentive, respectful and courteous as a result of their upbringing, and parents were careful not to beat their children because it produced 'bitterness, hatred and contempt' and a child may grow up to 'return the indignity'. Native Americans believed that physical punishment would make children timid and submissive, in contrast to the sought after characteristics of pride, independence and bravery.

Children will treat others as they themselves are treated, indigenous philosophy suggests. (Many in the dominant culture would agree.) A child granted respect will accord it to others, but if parents acted with anger Inuit people considered the child would do so too. Bolstering a child's self-esteem, giving it unconditional love and never raising one's voice to it are all behaviours emphasized by Inuit elders. The voice is the carrier of loving-songs, *aqausiit*, and each child has their own songs which people sing to them. Different people might have different songs for that particular child and such songs would form their identity, almost their name, a person's sense of self was warm with a sung love. Of course it sometimes happened that parents would lose their tempers and slap a child, but this was perceived as a weakness and a mistake and small children were saturated with affection, 'snuffed, cuddled, cooed at, talked to, and played with endlessly, the men as demonstrative as the women', writes Jean Briggs. If a child misbehaved, it 'never earned her more than a passing titter or a moo of disapproval'.

'Words like "don't", "no" and "move" were how we would talk to a dog. My culture tells me that the word "no" leads to disobedient children who become very hard to handle later on,' writes Minnie Aodla Freeman, contrasting her Inuit upbringing with what she experienced of mid-twentieth-century white domestic life.

Fridtjof Nansen (the Norwegian explorer who crossed Greenland in 1888, using the groundsheet of his tent as a sail) wrote that children were 'seldom, if ever, punished, and I have never even heard an Eskimo speak harshly to his child . . . I cannot remember to have met with more than one ill-disposed child, and that was in a home that was really more European than Eskimo.'

Farley Mowat, spending time among the Ihalmiut, the inland Inuit, wrote: 'In the camps of the People the child is King, for childhood is short and tragedy often comes after . . .' An Ihalmiut man asks: 'Who but a madman would, in his man's strength, stoop to strike against the weakness of a child?' The result of this upbringing, according to G. F. Lyon, joining William Parry's Arctic voyage of 1821–3, was that Inuit children grew up happy, affectionate and independent after a child-hood of devoted fondness.

Amazed by the rarity of hearing Native American children cry, early conservationist John Muir was to write: 'In all my travels, I never heard a cross, fault-finding word, or anything like scolding inflicted on an Indian child, or ever witnessed a single case of spanking, so common in civilized communities.'

I know that feeling well. In the cacophony of childhood – the playing, scuffling, giggling and fighting – one sound is almost always missing in indigenous communities: the humiliated, angry crying of a beaten child. Many anthropologists have emphasized similar observations. I spent nearly six weeks in the villages of West Papua, where parents don't consider it acceptable to hit a child, and I heard that sound only once. The child was perhaps three years old, on a bus with his mother, who was poking him, shouting aggressively, pulling and pushing him, slapping his head. I realized I was staring. I looked around and saw everyone else on the bus was appalled, watching her steadily and warily as if she were quite mad. In Europe or North America, the mother's behaviour would not have been unusual, but I had become acclimatized to a pervasive gentleness and I was shocked.

In his exquisite analysis of Indian childhood published in 1981, Sudhir Kakar argues that as a result of being caressed with cherishing, children believe the world benign, assuming that it is 'natural both to take care of others . . . and to expect to be cared for'. *Natural*. That word of such difficult simplicity. The evidence across cultures and over time is that human nature naturally chooses to nurture childhood in tenderness. It also seems that cultures which are themselves tender to nature are tender to children, themselves part of nature.

The startling exception to the widespread law of tenderness is the tradition of brutality which advocated the flogging and beating of children that arose in Europe from roughly the fifteenth century, was exported to Puritan America, and which is still evident today.

~

When the Puritan attitude to children met the Native American view, there was shock on both sides, etched into account after account. Children of the colonists were often harshly disciplined by corporal punishment in a way that was loathsome to a Native American sensibility – and indeed to a child's.

The amazed Jesuit Father Le Jeune, among the Montagnais in Canada in 1630, wrote: 'These Barbarians cannot bear to have their children punished, even scolded, not being able to refuse anything to a crying child.' More revolted than amazed, his fellow Jesuit, Father Lewis Hennepin, in 1699, described Native American children coming home: 'As soon as they enter a Cabin (or tent), they fall a smoking. If they find a Pot covered, they make no difficulty to take off the Lid to see what's in it . . . They are perpetually belching.'

It was in Puritan New England that one of the most extraordinary psychodramas in the history of childhood took place. Colonist children who were captured by Native Americans would repeatedly, adamantly, refuse to be 'rescued' by their Puritan families. One such was Eunice Williams.

In 1704, Eunice, the seven-year-old daughter of a Puritan minister, was taken prisoner with over a hundred colonists by a coalition of Abenaki, Mohawk and French soldiers. They were set on a long march and those who could not keep up (including Eunice's mother) were killed. Reaching a Kahnawake Mohawk village, Eunice was adopted by a Mohawk woman, and some three years went by, during which the child dressed and spoke as a Mohawk. Then her father tried to take her back but was told that the people 'would as soon part with their hearts as the child'. Eunice herself dug her heels in and would not leave. 'She is obstinately resolved to live and dye [sic] here, and will not so much as give me one pleasant look,' wrote her father.

Another ex-captive, Titus King, noted that many children made the same decision to stay with their Native American 'captors'. 'In Six months time they Forsake Father and mother, Forgit thir own Land, Refuess to Speak there own toungue and Seeminly be Holley Swollowed up with the Indians.'

Time after time the settler children refused to return. One, James McCullough, who had been taken captive by Native Americans when he was six, was 'rescued' by colonists when they came for him eight years later. They dragged him away, tying his legs together under his horse's belly and his arms behind his back. So ferocious was his desire to escape that he shucked off the fetters and ran back to his Native American people.

In 1763, Colonel Henry Bouquet (infamous for his part in the attempt to deliberately infect Native Americans by giving them blankets infested with smallpox) defeated a group of Native Americans at Bushy Run, Ohio, and sought to retake their white captives. Most of them, especially the children, had to be bound hand and foot to be taken back to white society by force.

But surely, one may argue, it was because children adapt, they forget, and they can re-create bonds of love with replacement parents. History offers examples of the reverse situation, where Native American children were captured by colonists, but here the children did not form similar attachments and would leave at the first opportunity, returning to their own people 'with great signs of joy'.

As Benjamin Franklin reported in 1753:

When an Indian Child has been brought up among us, taught our language and habituated to our Customs, yet if he goes to see his relations and makes one Indian Ramble there is no perswading him ever to return and that this is not natural to them merely as Indians, but as men, is plain from this, that when white persons of either sex have been taken prisoners young by the Indians, and lived awhile among them, tho' ransomed by their Friends, and treated with all imaginable tenderness to prevail with them to stay among the English, yet in a Short time they become disgusted with our manner of life, and the care and pains that are necessary to support it, and take the first good Opportunity of escaping again into the woods, from whence there is no reclaiming them. One instance I remember to have heard, where the person was brought home to possess a good Estate; but finding some care necessary to keep it together, he relinquished it to a younger Brother, reserving to himself nothing but a gun and a match-Coat, with which he took his way again to the Wilderness.

The terms tell their own story, the 'one Indian Ramble . . . no perswading [sic] him . . . escaping again into the woods . . . took his way again to the Wilderness' is 'natural' to all human beings, Franklin suggests. If the children saw freedom on one side, they saw enclosure on the other and a harshness so frightening that when children were 'rescued' by the Puritans, they often 'cried as if they should die when they were presented to us'.

Native Americans could of course be cruel in their turn. In Comanche raids, for example, men were killed, women gang-raped and often killed; but young children were frequently adopted. Once taken in like this, they were treated as one of the tribe. This is what happened to Cynthia Ann Parker, whose story inspired John Ford's *The Searchers*. Parker's family had been killed on the Texas frontier in 1836 and as a very young girl she was taken and brought up as one of the Comanche. She never wanted to leave them. When she was thirty-four, she was 'rescued' against her will by the Texas Rangers. Miserable among her colonist family, she spent a decade trying to escape back to the Comanche.

~

There is a space around a child where even the air seems sensitive – the cusp, the place where childhood, liquid and lovely, brims over into the world. But in European history, this was to be the site of floggings, splinters of raw ugliness jangling with blood and fury.

One of the early reports of corporal punishment comes from the lovely humanist Michel de Montaigne. Born in 1533, he was sent at six years old to the College of Gujenne, where he recalled with disgust 'the cries of tortured children' in the flogging years. In England, corporal punishment increased from the end of the fourteenth to the fifteenth century. The sixteenth to eighteenth centuries were stained with sadism. The Romantics, as ever on the side of children both as adults and as children themselves, loathed it, and in the late eighteenth century the young poet Robert Southey was expelled from school for writing an attack on corporal punishment. As we've seen, public opinion was beginning to turn against flogging and other forms of cruelty from about 1830, but in previous centuries, children's suffering was untold. Until 1780, in Britain, children could be convicted of more than two hundred crimes that could lead to a death sentence: in Norwich, a seven-year-old girl stole a petticoat and was hanged for it. After the Gordon Riots of 1780, several children were hanged. 'I never saw boys cry so much,' wrote contemporary observer George Selwyn.

Search for references to corporal punishment in Europe before the late fourteenth century, comments the great historian of childhood Philippe Ariès, and you will find very few. Importantly, in those rare examples, humiliation plays no part, for punishment was religious: an aspect of monastic austerity or the self-flagellation of the saints. It is from the fifteenth century onwards, says Ariès, that 'the whip takes on a degrading, brutal character and becomes increasingly common.'

I remember exactly where I was when I first heard the word 'humiliate'. I was at my grandparents' house, at the sink, washing up. My parents and grandparents were ranged around the kitchen and someone had decided that I needed to be hit for some reason or other which I cannot for the life of me recall. 'It won't hurt,' I muttered with a miserable defiance. My grandmother heard: 'It's not meant to hurt. It's meant to humiliate you,' she said. Without knowing the word previously, I knew from her face at that moment exactly what it meant, and I felt revulsion and contempt for all the adults involved actively or passively in the threat. Humiliation seems one of the most sinister of cruelties and the word heaves like nausea in anyone who has experienced it.

Church schools brought in what Ariès calls 'a humiliating disciplinary system' to be imposed on children, and the birch was 'the symbol of the subjection' of the child. It was a matter of degradation, domination and submission. It was also deliberate and systematic – not the occasional smack which an exhausted mother cat, at the end of her tether, metes out to an annoying kitten, the kind of slap which I think children more easily accept and forgive and which was far more typical in our household than a deliberated punishment.

According to the principles of the Great Chain of Being, expounded from the Middle Ages, the father is the ruler of the family. Ariès shows that at the end of the Middle Ages, children's education became increasingly hierarchical and authoritarian and he links this to the establishment of monarchical absolutism. If the king was at the top, children were at the bottom rung of the ladder. In seventeenth-century Europe, children were made to kneel at their parents' feet in the posture of submission to a sovereign. Although this politics was briefly reversed in the French Revolution ('when the Republic cut off the head of Louis XVI, it cut off the head of all fathers,' wrote Honoré de Balzac), when Napoleon declared himself emperor he drove imperialism into the territory of childhood, seeking to re-impose subordination in schools. Goethe, meanwhile, who adored children, had his alter ego, Werther, say: 'we treat them as our subjects, these children who are our equals and whom we ought to consider as models.'

A man who sires a child may still demand to be called 'Sir' – that related word. In Han China, the word for slave was derived from the word for child. Similarly, 'family' is from *familia*, the slaves of a Roman household, the belongings of one man who ruled over the wife, the children and the servants, exercising his dominion over them. 'Dominion' too is an interesting word. Its core is the Latin *domus* – home. From this comes *dominus*, the master of the house. It ripples out, the verbal *domino*-effect, into 'domination' and 'domineering', one of the ugliest of characteristics. The ripples spread wider into the 'dominions' and domination spread from the home, the *domus*, to the furthest reaches of the state's dominions. Or was it the other way round? Was the practice of political domination so infectious that it contaminated the intimacy of the home?

This is what I call fractal politics. The political pattern in the smallest unit, the family, is replicated in the larger, the same shape repeated at different scales, so the shape of domination in the home is mirrored at the larger scale of class hierarchy, the monarchy and the empire, right up to the scale of god.

The fractal politics which rhymed the family with the state seethes through the imagery of the Puritans: 'The familie is a little Church, and a little common-wealth . . . it is as a schoole wherein the first principles and grounds of government and subjection are learned,' wrote English Puritan William Gouge in 1622. By contrast, John Lilburne (1615–57) organized the first democratic movement, the Levellers – by name and by nature – whose goal was 'the right, freedome, safety, and well-being of every particular man, woman, and child in England'.

In the 1860s in the States, when there was a stirring of revulsion against corporal punishment, one school committee claimed that this kinder attitude to children would have terrible consequences at the largest scales because: 'Its spirit carried out in society would work the destruction of all civil government and inaugurate universal lawlessness.'

~

There are telling examples of fractal politics in this era too. George Bush Senior and his brother were brought up by a physically violent father, the US senator Prescott Bush, as the brother relates: 'If we acted disrespectfully, if we did not observe the niceties of etiquette, he took us over his knee and whopped us with his belt. He had a strong arm, and boy, did we feel it.' The niceties of adult etiquette included brutalizing children at home while, abroad, the ethics of etiquette included being the director of the Union Banking Corporation, a firm involved with the financial architects of Nazism. George Bush Senior grew up to strong-arm entire nations, invading Panama and spearheading the North American Free Trade Agreement (NAFTA).

'Child rearing is an invasive procedure. You are invading the soul of a developing human being,' say fundamentalists Michael and Debi

Pearl. Invasion is, for the domineering parent, just part of the job, as much as invading nations is part of the job of being British prime minister or American president.

James Dobson has had an enormous influence on the Bush dynasty, and CNN used Dobson to bolster support for the invasion of Iraq. When he writes of children, the politics of domination bleeds through every page. 'When you have been challenged, it is time for you to take charge – to defend your right to lead . . . spanking is the discipline of choice for a hot-tempered child between twenty months and ten years of age,' he says, ignoring the fact that you cannot 'discipline' a baby or teach it self-control because the brain capacity to do so simply doesn't exist at that age. But the child will, I suppose, be left in shock and awe.

Michael and Debi Pearl write of a child having 'an innate need to be governed', and they advise beating a child until he is 'totally broken'. After a flogging, they say, when a child's crying 'turns to a true, wounded, submissive whimper, you have conquered'. 'Hold the resisting child in a helpless position for several minutes, or until he is totally surrendered. Accept no conditions for surrender – no compromise. You are to rule over him as a benevolent sovereign.'

There are those who see the politics of domination from the other side. François Truffaut never forgot what it feels like to be a child and his films glow with the rushlight of his childhood's spirit, hurt by bullying, disdain, beatings or neglect. 'Of all mankind's injustices,' says a character in Truffaut's *L'Argent de Poche* (*Small Change*), 'child abuse is the most unjust, the most revolting, the most unbearable . . . Children's rights are forgotten . . . Why? *Because children can't vote.*'

Marlon Brando once said: 'The lack of rights that apply to *children* are the ones that appal me.' Dr Benjamin Spock (whose book, which was shelved at child's eye-height on the most prominent bookshelf in our house, for ease of self-referral I suppose, was the bible of my mother's mothering) at first accepted mild corporal punishment. However, he came to oppose it wholeheartedly precisely because of wider social and state violence, citing not only domestic violence but also the government's pursuit of nuclear arms and aggressive foreign policy, all of which he thought was encouraged by the generalized acceptance of physical punishment for children.

If ever there was an example of the fractal politics by which totalitarian childhoods are mirrored in a totalitarian state, it must be Nazi Germany. Psychologist Alice Miller terms the domination and subjection of children 'poisonous pedagogy' and shows how it had been building up for generations. In a 1752 book on child-rearing, J. G. Krüger wrote that a child should be 'vanquished' to 'total obedience' being 'a faithful subject of his parents'. Beating your child, advised German physician Dr Schreber, means 'you will be master of the child forever.' So fanatical was he in forcing obedience that he invented a series of devices to control children's physical movements, including harnesses to stop sleeping children turning over in bed. His son, Daniel Paul, went mad as a result of his upbringing while another son committed suicide.

All the leading figures of the Third Reich were trained in obedience from childhood, reports Alice Miller. For them, the family was 'the prototype of a totalitarian regime. Its sole, undisputed, often brutal ruler is the father. The wife and children are totally subservient to his will, his moods, and his whims; they must accept humiliation and injustice unquestioningly and gratefully. Obedience is their primary rule of conduct.' Generations of Germans had grown up robbed of independent will and therefore needing to be commanded – the psyche of a nation in search of its Führer-father. 'Servile, uncritical, and almost infantile' was the attitude of Hitler's followers towards him, writes Miller.

What happened to the conscience of the German nation in the Holocaust? the world asked. How could such evil have been allowed to happen? It is thought that prolonged physical abuse in childhood can interfere with an individual's sense of conscience; the inner voice may be overruled: obedience had poisoned the domestic life of generations of Germans.

'We want this people to be obedient and you must practise obedience,' said Hitler in a speech to young people in 1934. Leni Riefenstahl's documentary on Hitler's rise to power is aptly titled *The Triumph of the Will*. (Not the plurality of wills but the ruler's mono-will.) Within the Hitler Youth, young people were forced to demonstrate absolute obedience, including being flogged without complaining. 'I want a brutal, domineering, fearless, cruel youth,' Hitler said in 1933. And he already had in the palm of his hand those who could begin the programme, for when the Nazis came to power in 1933 the most common occupation, in the Party's core of professionals and middle classes, was that of elementary-school teacher. The wild, diverse and plural wills of children would be crushed into obedience to authority for its own sake, leading to the triumph of the fascist will.

It was constantly impressed upon me in forceful terms that I must obey promptly the wishes and commands of my parents, teachers, and priests, and indeed of all grown-up people, including servants, and that nothing must distract me from this duty. Whatever they said was always right. These basic principles by which I was brought up became second nature to me. – Rudolf Höss, Commandant at Auschwitz.

~

Emerging from a long and bitter winter, blinking with surprise and relief at the gentle restitution of May, human nature seems in the ascendance in Euro-American society. Children, says the United Nations Convention on the Rights of the Child, should be protected 'from all forms of physical or mental violence, injury or abuse'. If the nineteenth century introduced the voice of the working class and the twentieth century the voice of women, says historian Theodore Zeldin, the twenty-first century is listening to the voice of children. In the USA, the number of adults in favour of physical punishment fell from ninety-four per cent in the 1960s to seventy-one per cent by 2004.

Beaten children, it is now understood, may become more defiant and aggressive, more likely to suffer anxiety and depression and to misuse alcohol and drugs. Even low rates of physical punishment predict psychological distress in ten- to sixteen-year-olds and, unsurprisingly, a worsening of the parent–child relationship. Fear, anger, hate, a sense of apathy, a lack of empathy towards the suffering of others, obsessiveness, paranoia and extreme dissociation can result from physical punishment. An overwhelming proportion of violent criminals were victims of violence as children. Also, physical punishment doesn't work. It damages a child's executive function, their ability to self-regulate, their sense of self-control.

And yet there is a spike against this kinder trend. As a political or theological strategy, a vociferous minority encourages the beating of children. In the UK, some libertarian fundamentalists, who think that child pornography should be legal, contribute to the politics of cruelty, demanding the 'right' of parents to beat their children – but not the right of children to be free of violence. In the USA, where far-right religious fundamentalists strongly favour corporal punishment, their key text is Proverbs 23:14: 'Thou shalt beat him with the rod/And shalt deliver his soul from hell.' 'A child can be turned back from the road to hell through proper spankings,' write Michael and Debi Pearl, who have sold some 400,000 copies of their book *To Train Up a Child*.

Lydia Schatz was a Liberian girl, adopted aged four by Kevin and Elizabeth Schatz and taken to their home in Paradise, California. Paradise it was not. She was brutally beaten, as were the couple's other children, and when she was seven she was killed. The parents were committed to the writings of the Pearls, who recommend beating babies with a branch, or a one-foot ruler or paddle, while an older child should be flogged with a cutting from a shrub. Among the cruel and stupid bric-à-brac of abuse, the Pearls, on their website, suggest lengths of quarter-inch plumbing pipe. Lydia's parents beat her repeatedly with exactly that weapon. Early in February 2010, she was held down and flogged for hours. The flogging was so severe that her vital organs could no longer function and she died. Kevin Schatz received a sentence of twenty-two years for torture and murder, while Elizabeth Schatz was sentenced to thirteen years for manslaughter.

What had Lydia done? She had mispronounced a word, thought to be the word 'pulled' (a word which quite possibly, given the linguistic background of her first years, she simply *could* not pronounce) in a home-school reading lesson. This is literalist Christianity, obsessed with the letter of the law, the word of their god but none of the grace.

The Pearls describe a child who cries at nap time and won't lie down but, they say, he can be trained to learn that 'to get up is to be in the firing line and get switched back down. It will become as easy as putting a rag doll to bed.' A rag doll, puppet of its parents, is the Pearls' metaphor. Philosopher John Locke chose a *tabula rasa*, the blank slate, the wax tablet waiting, passively, to be written on by the will of others, a child void of meaning until adults impose the imprint of their text. It was an ideal metaphor for literalist Christianity. Lydia Schatz, her body imprinted with the switches of punishment for not pronouncing the exact text her parents demanded, became a *tabula rasa* in the wax of death.

~

The fractal politics of childhood were played out cruelly in the years when indigenous societies wished so fervently that we Europeans had stayed at home, tended our broad beans and been nicer to our children, rather than stealing theirs.

Generations of indigenous children were removed from their homes and sent to residential schools, including not only Indigenous Australians but Sámi people in Northern Europe and Inuit and Native Americans. In America it was federal policy after 1879, and children were taken sometimes over a thousand miles from their homes. For many, this experience was like a childhood spent in prison and, as a result, said Clyde Warrior (Ponca) in 1967: 'Very few ever became more than very confused, ambivalent, and immobilized individuals.'

The Stolen Generations of Australia are the most infamous, and when the child-snatchers came, whole communities went on red alert, sending children off out bush, hiding them, sometimes rubbing their faces with charcoal and animal fat to blacken them. The paler they were, the more likely it was that they would be taken. The rationale was to 'breed out' Indigenous Australians by removing children and forcing their integration into white society.

With seconds to spare, children were scooped up and bundled into sacks of flour. *Be quiet in there, don't move*, implored the parents. Hot in the prickly sacks, fearful and wriggly at the same time, the children would try to stay still. *Don't sneeze*, their parents cried, *don't sneeze*. One only-half-smothered explosion of a sneeze might be all it took, and a child might lose her family for ever. Or one little toe peeping out of a rolled-up swag might betray a boy, stealing him from his land and community. So the authorities took up to 100,000 Indigenous Australian children between about 1909 and 1969 in the scandal of the Stolen Generations, a public policy which has been called genocidal by the Human Rights Commission Inquiry.

Each stolen child left an inconsolable hollow behind. One woman said that after she had been seized as a child, 'every morning as the sun came up the whole family wailed. They did this for thirty-two years until they saw me again.'

'We were treated as slaves,' says Wadjularbinna, of the Gungalidda people, who was stolen by the Plymouth Brethren when she was three or four. Snatched from her grandmother's arms, she remembered the wailing of the old woman all her life, although she never saw her again. She refers to her incarceration as a 'concentration camp'. Girls who tried to escape were chained to trees and flogged. Brutality was common: in a collection of life stories from the Stolen Generations, one person remembered, 'We used to get whipped with a wet ironing cord and sometimes had to hold other children (naked) while they were whipped, and if we didn't hold them we got another whipping. To wake us up in the morning we were sprayed up the backside with an old-fashioned pump fly spray. If we complained we got more. Hurt and humiliation was a part of our everyday life.' One in five stolen children was sexually abused in care. And a (white) school textbook published in 1952 stated: 'We are civilized today and they are not.'

Among the Inuit, too, countless cases of sexual abuse took place, leading to lifelong trauma. It was 'the bitterness which never leaves you', one Inuit man told me quietly. His anguish and fury seemed all the greater for being spoken so softly. 'I wish that I and the other abused children had tortured the priests to death.' These words were spoken as a statement of fairness, because the children had been tortured to the point where something in their spirits died. Their bodies often could not survive the soul-murder of residential-school abuse and many indigenous people describe how this experience leads to alcohol and drug abuse, often resulting in criminal activity, followed by prison. From there, many walk out through the only open door: suicide.

Indigenous children all over the world were dislocated from their culture's sense of significance. What was taught at the residential schools was held to be superior to their indigenous cultural education: ceremony, ritual, stories, land, philosophies, languages and inherited ways of knowing.

Sámi shaman and musician Nils-Aslak Valkeapää (1943–2001) wrote scathingly of his boarding-school education: 'so small Sámi children learn to have a nose for money, to think of time in terms of money, of land as money, learn to strive for honour, position and status. Learn that one must have idols . . . have new toys like machine guns and Hunter jets. That's education, that is.'

As a twelve-year-old boy, the nineteenth-century Native American Assiniboine chief Dan Kennedy (Ochankugahe) was lassoed, roped and taken to a government school. In keeping with the school's promise to 'civilize the little pagan', he says, his braids were cut off. It was a common practice. The stolen children were taught that indigenous people were 'evil and wicked' and the 'spawn of the devil'.

The authorities also cut off children's indigenous language, telling them it was the tongue of the devil and forcing them to wash their mouths with soap as if their language was dirty. (Dirty – of the dirty, lovely dirt of earth, rooted in the bright and living dust – dirty it was, and precious. All land-saturated languages hold earth in their hands, words intimate with everything belonging to country, language linking everything on the land.) Without their language, the children were quite literally lost for words. 'The very last vestiges of native language were eradicated from the minds of the children,' says Douglas George-Kanentiio (Mohawk-Iroquois). 'If there was one act initiated by the United States and Canada that was meant to finally eradicate native people by destroying their spirit that was it.'

'Eradicated': the word comes from *radix*, in Latin, meaning root, and 'eradicated' means torn up by the roots. Across the world, stolen children were bereft of their land. In Australia, children had been rooted in the Dreaming civilization of Lightning Spirits and Rainbow Snakes, of stories, song and Law – the Dreaming which lit a land with vitality just as the sacred waterholes and freshwater lagoons were bright with the immanent life force, where the spirits of children waited like giggly seeds jumping to be born. All this was as nothing. Instead, argued the Catholic Bishop of Australia in 1845, 'They might be encouraged to have little gardens, and be gradually brought into habits of civilization.'

The Walkabout – that practice which profoundly associated young people with their kith, their country – was specifically targeted. 'It is impossible to persuade the men to give up their wandering life,' except 'by taking the children from them very young,' according to the authorities in 1845. If children were 'at liberty to roam about without employment until sixteen they would be useless afterwards'.

Instead of belonging to the land, Indigenous Australian children would be owned by the white authorities: in 1936, the state authorities of Western Australia took guardianship rights over all Aboriginal people up to the age of twenty-one.

Today, children in Indigenous communities in Australia are ambushed by the physical results of poverty and the psychological results of the land-dispossession and despair which surrounds them.

In Adelaide, I met a Ngarrindjeri woman who had been stolen as a baby, and she told me how it continues to devastate her life for, without any experience of parents, she struggled to mother her own children.

For all the obvious warmth, love and tenderness towards children, Indigenous communities are often suffocatingly overcrowded, blistered with violence, feverish with the effects of racism and stigmatization. Suffering accidents and plagued with 'payback', entire communities are unwell, with poor diet, trachoma, alcohol abuse, renal dysfunction and untreated diabetes all rampant. And, as it always has been, the longest, deepest, most heartfelt need is for the land, the wellspring of health. (Studies show that traditional connections to the land can have preventative effects on suicidality.)

Punyu is a term in the Ngarinman language, used by the Yarralin people, which means happy, strong, healthy, knowledgeable and socially responsible; being fully alive. The term is used for land as much as for people and, widely, the relationship is considered reciprocal as the land looks after people who look after land, a double helix of tending. Strength, will and wellness jump up from the land, and children should be rooted, ineradicably, in the deep red earth, energized by the philosophy of the Dreaming.

CHAPTER TEN

Who Owns a Child?

The scene is a schoolroom in Sardinia, shortly after the Second World War. A six-year-old boy, Gavino, is at his desk when suddenly the door bursts open and his father cannons in, grabs the child and removes him from school, for ever. Gavino does not want to leave but has no voice in the matter: the father is the master of the child's fate, the *owner* of the boy.

In the bleak mountains, Gavino must tend sheep under his father's brutal tuition, and over the years the child suffers fear, loneliness, humiliation and such violence that after one beating the father thinks he has killed the boy. This, by the way, is a true story. Bitterly isolated, the relationship between father and son crescendoes to a dangerous and tragic intensity. The fury of a slave is in the child's heart, a serf's acid sense of injustice in his eyes, the hatred of a bonded labourer for his owner.

Later, Gavino joins the army where, knowing only the Sardinian dialect, he is humiliated for not being able to speak 'proper' Italian. A fellow soldier helps him learn – 'Think in Latin,' he advises – and Gavino immerses himself in words and the relationships between them, for words have genealogies, fathers and sons, as much as humans do. At one point, he intones the words related to 'father': *padre, patriarca, padrino, padrone, Padre Eterno'* – father, patriarch, godfather, master, God – as an image of his own father haunts him in all these roles.

Gavino leaves the army and returns to Sardinia but refuses to work for his father, whose demand to dominate his son is unabated: 'I am the master here, and your father,' he says, which offers itself as the title of Gavino Ledda's 1975 autobiography, and later the film *Padre Padrone* (*My Father, My Master*), directed by Paolo and Vittorio Taviani.

'Patriarchs like you only do two things in life,' Gavino furiously tells his father. 'First they obey. Then they command . . . Obedience is the air you breathe.' The fractal politics of this familial domination and the wider political analogies, in a nation which had been dominated by the fascist Mussolini, are clear. Just as one shepherd can be tyrant to one child, so one Il Duce can tyrannize a nation.

One morning, Gavino is listening to music on the radio. His father orders him to turn it off. Gavino instantly turns up the volume. The father silences the radio, plunging it into a sink of water. Almost without interruption, though, the melody continues; Gavino is whistling it. They fight and eventually the father withdraws to his bedroom, sitting motionless on the bed. Gavino, who wants to leave home for good, needs to get his suitcase out from under his father's bed and as he kneels down to reach for it, he briefly puts his head on his father's knee, a semi-automatic gesture of obedience, of submission and of supplication to a father, a master and a god. His father almost rests his hand on the son's head in blessing, but at the last moment snatches it away. The father has been a dictator to the son and it has been a malediction, but the child has still looked for a benediction. In the end, he has learned his *own* diction, to speak for himself, not as a possession of his father. As an adult, Gavino becomes a professional linguist.

Gavino's father thought he owned the boy; as if the child were his property to do with as he willed. It is an extreme example of a common enough belief that a child is a possession, that a parent can own a child as they would a fridge, a car or a dog, and that this ownership is 'natural'. It is not a human universal, though: many societies do not think parents 'own' their children.

In the empire of the family, it has been too easy for adults to see a child as *Terra Parentis*, a dominion, a region of territorial expansion for the parent. In Rome, in the days of empire, a father had *patria potestas*: absolute power of life and death over his children. This sense of proprietorship persisted so children 'are in most absolute subjection to their parents', wrote seventeenth-century Enlightenment philosopher Thomas Hobbes, and parents may sell children or give them in 'servitude to others; or may pawn them for hostages, kill them for rebellion, or sacrifice them for peace'.

'No mother doubts at the bottom of her heart that in her child she has given birth to a piece of property,' wrote Nietzsche, 'and no father disputes his right to be allowed to subjugate his child to his concepts and judgements. Indeed, it used to be considered proper (it was true of the old Germans) for fathers to determine the life or death of a newborn as they saw fit.'

~

Some societies believe that a child carries the soul of an elder. Among Sotho communities in Africa, for example, children could represent dead ancestors, and one effect of this was that children, treated as if they were that person, could be revered. Native American children may be referred to as 'little grammas and little grampas', giving them a sense of their future stature and also acknowledging that, although they are young, they have their wisdom.

If time is viewed as linear and is allied to an idea of progress where 'later' is automatically considered 'better', then childhood is philosophically disadvantaged, with every child intrinsically inferior to all adults. But any idea of superiority and hierarchy simply as a result of age is impossible to contemplate if a two-year-old is 'older' than its father.

Maori children could be given the name of an ancestor and, in instances when those children were subject to beatings in white schools, the Maori families sometimes withdrew their children not only in disgust at the practice of hurting children, but also because the act was interpreted as hitting the ancestor themself, damaging the ancestor's *mana*, their spiritual power.

One of the reasons why Inuit children were traditionally given so much freedom and were so indulged was because of the belief that the soul of an elder resides within the child. This soul, as well as the child's, expresses its will, and to deny the child is to deny the elder, while to punish a child would be an insult to the elder within. As a grandmother may be given the best food and certainly never chided or scolded, so the child is accorded the shelter of her name. Focusing close up, you see the child of today but, refocusing into long sight, you see the elder of yesterday; thus the Inuit child as namesake links the present and the past. Cultures which honour this belief can find that it deepens not only the family's relationship with that child, but also their relationship with their ancestors.

The kin terms of the Kunjen people of Australia go down from one generation to another. So a grandmother might call her great granddaughter 'Little Auntie'. The child is not the property of the parents, rather the whole family is an intertwining, an interownership, an inter-belonging between the past, the present and the future as natural as gentle genetic spirals. The belief that the soul of the elder passes to a child could be read as a subtle metaphor for genetic inheritance, as there is a widespread belief among the Inuit that, together with the name, the child inherits the skills and characteristics of their namesake.

Simon Tookoome's granddaughter was named after his deceased sister: 'Her spirit moves through her. She speaks and acts like my sister. To me, my granddaughter is my sister. I do things for her as if my sister was asking.' The child arrives pre-loved, cherished both for her own sake and for her name's sake in an augmentation of love.

As the namesake is honoured, the child is partly identified with the elder, as if the child is a new narrator for the story of that name. The name may be thought to possess a cumulative wisdom, snow of one life piled on the snowdrifts of earlier lives, so the experience of the *atiq* – the elder after whom a child is named – can have a powerful narrative voice in the child's life. If a child's *atiq* drowned, for example, they may be scared of playing by water and, through the name, this cautioning fear is passed on.

Sometimes a parent may dream that an elder wishes to have a child named after them. In other cases, before an elder dies they may notice that a particular child needs some of their own qualities: perhaps there is a child who is too easily intimidated, so a stronger-armoured elder may ask for their name to be given to the child, hoping that it will work like a spell for the child, giving them new courage.

~

There are societies which do not consider anyone – child or adult – to be a possession of another. Among the Yequana, even the idea of owning another person is absent; the concept of 'my child' is non-existent. In Australia, the idea of ownership does not exist in Ngarinyin life, because it would be destructive to think that way. 'Your children are not your children,' as Kahlil Gibran wrote.

In Europe in the Middle Ages, as soon as a child was out of infancy 'he belonged to adult society,' writes Philippe Ariès, rather than the private family. Life was convivial: the child belonged to the throng, to the commons, to the village, to the street. Intimacy was not narrowed into the family home but extensive and widespread. Many teenagers did not live with their parents but moved to other households as apprentices or servants.

Over the years, both adults and children have suffered a loss of this public world – the street, the commons – and of unfenced belonging. Both land and childhood have been privatized and enclosed. Children who once belonged to a wide adult society became increasingly the private possessions of their parents, the father in particular, as the idea of the family gathered strength. Ariès examines the weakening of the position of wives and children from the fourteenth century and shows how in the eighteenth century the idea of the family spread among all classes and 'imposed itself tyrannically on people's consciousness'.

The importance of happy family relationships is obvious, but the cost of the specifically *nuclear* family has been terrible and is rarely examined. It includes the loss of sociability – for when the modern family prioritized private family life at the expense of relationships with colleagues, neighbours and friends, it ushered in the Age of Loneliness, the isolation which shrieks in the ears of single parents, which tears at the heart of a divorced man losing his children or an unwillingly childless woman, the isolation which weeps in the empty laps of lonely grandmothers living alone, the isolation unit like a prison cell when no crime has been committed. Parents have come to fear what used to be an ordinary experience: that their child may belong to the street or the commons as much as to the home. They dread that heartbreaking reaving of intimacy precisely because the nuclear family has become almost the sole site of that intimacy.

As well as isolation, a further price is exacted by the nuclear family: the over-intensity of the parent–child relationship. When there is no ease of the village, no margin of the street, no relief of the extended family, when a child 'belongs' only to its parents, when an entire childhood depends on just one or two relationships, the psychological stresses are bound to be appalling – more than kin and less than kind, for both parents and children. There is a torque of anger and sadness between so many parents and children, the fault of neither, but arising because society as a whole has created a tension of grief-ire which twists the parent–child relationship into a psychological high-wire act. Everything depends on that one thread. There are no other ropes and no safety net either. The relationship becomes hot, tense and dangerously insular. '*Odi et amo*,' the poet Catullus wrote: I hate and I love. Love and loathing fighting each other to the death, as Gavino, at the end of *Padre Padrone*, suggests.

I had a birthday party once and invited a friend, a mother of young children. We lived miles apart and I hadn't seen her in years. She bounded into my house with a beautiful Labrador leaping at her side. 'Oh, *Kate*, you've got a *dog*!' I said with delight. 'Jay,' she said, an octave below her normal speaking voice: 'I've got a husband, two kids and a dog, and, frankly, if I had got the dog first, I'd have stopped there.' The vehemence and candour of her words made a pool of quiet around us. 'That didn't sound very good, did it?' she said. 'It's okay,' said another mother of two small children, in a rueful voice: 'I've thought about infanticide.' 'Haven't we all?' said a third mother, quietly. It shouldn't be like this.

Motherhood, for too many women, is stressful, boring, exhausting and utterly, appallingly, killingly *relentless*. All over the world, by contrast, traditions show how the upbringing of children was not just the responsibility of the mother but of the wider family and indeed the whole community.

Among Inuit people (and many others), grandmothers have a special niche in childhood. Uqsuralik Ottokie, an elder from South Baffin Island, recalls a frequent practice of a child sharing a bed with her grandmother, which created a bond. The warmth was literal as well as metaphoric, as she remembered how her grandmother would always help her warm her feet when they were cold. Midwives, too, had an enduring role in a child's life and, as a boy grew up, he would give his first kill to his midwife; a girl would give her the first thing she had sewn.

The grandmother is the source of an infinity of lullabies, say the Boora people of the Peruvian Amazon, and grandparents among the !Kung people have a particular closeness with their grandchildren, so children may discuss things with their grandparents which they couldn't talk about with their parents, while grandparents might well act as advocates for a grandchild's interests. Children would readily and happily move to live with grandparents, aunts or other close relatives if they didn't get on with their parents.

In Indigenous Australia, typically, each child was surrounded by relatives and no single adult had the full-time care of any child. Grandparents, or any elder taking a grandparental role for an Indigenous Australian child, were by turns guardians, teachers, entertainers, healers, storytellers, singers, jesters, comforters and clowns. In Euro-American culture today, parents are expected to play all those roles, and to do so from dawn till dusk. Support, generosity, familiarity and warmth were crucial qualities of Pintupi childhood, as any parent would agree, but, importantly, Pintupi children received these gifts from multiple sources. Many people 'grow up' a child, say Pintupi people, and adulthood itself is defined by the ability to take care of others. For the Ngarinyin people, everyone is responsible for a baby born to the community.

Children in traditional Welsh villages used to be considered 'village property' and, in Africa, there is one famous saying that 'It takes a village to raise a child' and another that 'Every child is my child.' In traditional African societies, one person may call many people father, mother or brother, regardless of the actual genetic relationship, and these terms pledge people to take responsibility for each other.

Nigerian poet Wole Soyinka's writings on his childhood overflow with a sheer abundance of adults, including the police who look after him when he gets lost and the bookseller's wife who treats him as if he were one of her own children. The child in a nuclear family knows well only a tiny number of adult personalities, but a well-villaged child will meet, identify with, reject or learn from a multitude: the wily, the funny, the sad, the dreamless, the storied, the austere, the august, the silly, the sexy, the mean, the easy, the awkward, the nasty, the gentle, the torn, the transparent, the formidable, the drunk, the helpless, the manipulative, the fond.

'Thou hast no sense. You French people love only your own children, but we love all the children of the tribe,' said a Naskapi Native American to a Jesuit missionary in the eighteenth century. In traditional Dakota life, all the adults looked after all the children, and two effects for a child were said to be a sense of great security and self-assurance. Born into an extended family, a Mohawk-Iroquois child traditionally learned from the elders. When such a connection is broken, people experience internal trauma.

I spent some time with a Salish friend, Julie Cajune, in Montana where children, traditionally, belonged to the whole community. Today, I was told, this happens less and their unbelonging is 'destructive'. The whole community once marked the stages of a child's life, said Cajune, who has worked on education and children's issues: when a boy caught his first big game, for instance, he gave the meat away to everyone. 'As a child, you feel that so many people are watching and paying attention to you.'

What was the best thing about growing up in a community like this, I asked her. 'Everyone knew you,' she replied instantly. What was the worst? She pulled a face and laughed: 'Everyone knew you. You couldn't get away with *a-ny*-thing. You feel a sense of social control. If you're stingy or lazy or dishonest, people pay attention and you'd be shamed. Shaming was a powerful thing.'

One Salish man born in 1942 told me how he was brought up by his great-grandparents, who themselves remembered what their grandparents had taught them: he could, he said, hear the voices which had spoken in 1870. Another Salish man told me of his teacher, a generation ago, Basil Left Hand. He was, he said, three hundred years old, because he could remember his great-grandparents, who could remember theirs: the extended family, extended over centuries.

So collectively orientated can some societies be towards children that among the Oglala people of South Dakota a breastfeeding infant would reach into the blouse of any nursing mother, for such milk was common property. Among the Huaorani, a woman may breastfeed her child, a sister's child and a grandchild. It is a poignant, intimate example of the villaging which children have long known, a right to roam in and out of other lives. Wole Soyinka remembers his household full of guests, relations, visitors and waifs, while Luther Standing Bear recalled that for every child, 'no matter where it strayed when it was able to walk, it was at home, for everyone in the band claimed relationship. Mother told me that I was often carried round the village from tipi to tipi and that sometimes she saw me only now and then during the day.'

Older people in Britain, particularly those from working-class neighbourhoods, may recall something similar: the permeable nature of anyone else's house on the street, which children could visit without especial invitation or particular supervision.

All this is not to say that traditional societies are or were cloyingly, annoyingly, perfect, for every community on earth has its envies, dislikes and cruelties. It is, though, worth demonstrating how peculiar (and recent) is the idea that children must live as claustrophobic possessions of their parents, giving rise to the intense difficulties of the parent–child relationship, the loneliness of so many old people and the isolated, over-burdened experience of being a parent, all things which are part of the same problem: the nuclear family. ('Nuclear' here not just as in nucleus but as in bomb.)

Most parents in the dominant culture cannot give their children the full run of an extended family or the experience of being villaged – here using the idea as a process, an experience, a verb: to village. So kids today are segregated out of public life, out of the convivial, messy, difficult, mischievous commons of the street, spending less time with other age-groups and as a result becoming less capable than they are when they can learn from older children and diverse adults.

'Now my children do not learn my thoughts or my stories. We do not talk as we would have on the land, in the igloo. It is because of the walls. Everyone goes to a different room. We do not talk all together any more,' writes Inuit elder Simon Tookoome.

The unwalled vitality of an unsegregated household is portrayed by D. J. Williams, describing his late-nineteenth-century Welsh childhood, where children were fully involved in the life around them:

animals, farming, music, firesides, neighbours, illness, funerals, fairs, auctions, the *eisteddfod* and the merry-young-uncle-in-search-of-a-wife. It is a far cry from the isolation of a child of today playing alone with a machine, spied on by a teddy-cam and texting his or her friends.

~

It is hard to imagine an otter cub with low self-esteem, an anxious kitten or an unhappy puppy who doesn't know how to play outside: the buoyancy of their sprung energy makes these things seem against nature. But in the UK at the beginning of the twenty-first century, one in ten children aged five to sixteen has clinically significant mental health difficulties. Britain ranks lowest of twenty-one industrialized nations for childhood well-being. A 2007 Cambridge University study of primary-school children showed that they suffered from consumerism, materialism, the cult of celebrity and saturation TV, creating a 'loss of childhood'. Kids are becoming the 'products' of a global industry which is coming to possess childhood.

Children once felt they belonged to their kith, their land. They also belonged with (but were not necessarily owned by) their kin, the wide extended family. In the last few hundred years in the West, they have been treated as possessions of their parents who 'own' them. Now, in a peculiarly stealthy way, children may be the possessions of their possessions.

Exiled out of their kith, kids are seduced indoors, addicted to Play-Stations, chat rooms and Xboxes. Given pre-packaged, processed entertainment, some children say they 'do not know how to play outside'. By the age of eighteen, the average American has spent two years being possessed by television. The evidence is very clear that too much television is unhealthy: the amount of television which children watch correlates with measures of body fat; seeing violence on television increases children's aggression; children who watch more television when they are four are more likely to tease and bully classmates at the ages of six to eleven. The more children are exposed to the media (television and the Internet), the more difficulties they will have in their relationship with their parents and the more mental health problems they will experience, according to the brilliant American social scientist Juliet Schor, who shows not only how television encourages children to value possessions, money, brands and products and induces discontent, but also how consumerism in childhood creates depression, anxiety and low self-esteem.

'Do you know the surest way to make your child miserable?' asked Rousseau in *Émile*. 'Let him have everything he wants . . . toys of all kinds and prices – what useless and pernicious furniture!'

It has to be said that children *like* useless and pernicious furniture: gizmos, gadgets and junk. But a lot of children also quite like seeing traffic accidents, and it doesn't mean that parents should lay on a car crash for the kids every time they go to visit Granny. Moreover, children like what they know, and children who do not know the natural world will of course veer towards staying indoors with the gizmos. Today, fifty-two per cent of American children go shopping each week, while only seventeen per cent play outdoors.

In Britain, the pressure to buy 'stuff' is more acutely felt in poorer households: one reason is a desire to protect children from the appearance of poverty, while another is the long working hours needed to pay rent and mortgages, so parents, unable to spend time with their children (which is what children expressly want) spend money on them instead. Overmortgaged, overworked, overspent. Consumerism: three. Kids: nil. If you want to see the tragedy of this aspect of contemporary childhood in eighty-five minutes, watch *Last Train Home*, directed by Lixin Fan. The documentary follows a Chinese family experiencing the cutting edge of capitalism as the parents, fleeing rural poverty, join the 130 million migrant workers of China, taking work in inhuman conditions in the garment factories of the industrial centres. They can go home to see their children – for whom they are making this sacrifice – only once a year.

When a child is born among the Turkana people of Kenya, it is held to its mother's breast while the names of surrounding nature are called out. The baby is understood to choose its own name, indicating its choice by beginning to suckle; at this point, the last name to have been spoken is the name given to the child. One Turkana person commented that it felt like an honour to be named after something utterly precious. Their name was Rain.

Traditions of naming children after nature run deep in all cultures: Heather, Rose or Violet, for example, or the children of the sixties onwards named River or Star. Today, children in the USA may be named after cars and brands, and hundreds of children have been called Lexus and Armani while other names include Porsche, Chivas Regal, Fanta, Pepsi, Nike and Chanel: so the child is branded for life. Meanwhile, in Argentina a few years ago, the civil registry removed people's indigenous names, replacing their birth certificates with names including Chevroleta, Ford, Twenty-Seven, Eight and Thirteen. In mockery of their indigenous roots, some were re-named Domingo Faustino Sarmiento, after the nineteenth-century president.

Children learn what they need to survive in the cultures they are born to, and what they learn – or fail to learn – faithfully echoes wider cultural values. So today, children learn the protocol of ownership, they read price tags and understand money even while they do not know the words for varieties of trees or birds and cannot read the landscape. I was out camping with friends once when the full moon rose behind the trees and an eleven-year-old boy looked up, bewildered, saying, 'Oh, there's the sun.' In the USA, three-year-olds can recognize an average of one hundred logos. Only half of British children can identify an oak leaf and thirty-eight per cent of children aged nine to eleven cannot identify a frog. If you cannot identify something, how can you identify with it? Why would you ever want to protect it?

Children's naturally animistic imaginations are being wrested away from animals to brands, from living things to lifeless plastic, from the free charisma of nature to the priced mercantilism of the mall. In schools, where children should find their horizons broadening, their minds expanding, children may find the meaning of the world shrunk to commercial transactions, as they are taught to crack the codes of consumerism, to read adverts and to value money. The young are being moulded into an 'economic category', says American author Neil Postman, 'whose purpose is to fuel a market economy'. Not only are children subject to thousands of adverts per day, but schools themselves are funded by corporate advertisers. Children, imprisoned in schools, are a captive audience. They have been called consumers in training and their development of brand loyalty may last a lifetime. Better versed in their consumer identity than in their artistic identity, more skilful in reading the subtexts of consumerism than in reading the woods for their words, schools are educating children into a feeling for profit which is their loss; a notion of business which is none of their business and an ideology of consumerism which consumes their childhoods.

Advertising and marketing present themselves as the fantasia, the harlequinade, the masquerading mystique of growing up. The common dreams of children are by nature jewelled with the glamour of imagination, misted with reverie, enticing the child with the ever-just-out-of-reach allure of the eternally tantalizing, the never nameable, the *je ne sais quoi*. Consumerism puts a price tag on the mysterious domain and sticks a (brand) name to reverie. It works because of children's enchantability. It works because children know how to dream. It works because they are reckless Romantics, susceptible, temptable, bewitchable – the collective opposite of the cynical predators who prey on them. The manipulative corporations – Disney, McDonald's, Mattel, the makers of Barbie – are privatizers of the commons of dream, forcing their way into the child's mind, whose capacity for self-enchantment is as vulnerable as it is precious.

Sleepover parties – for sale at $17,500 – are booked solid, reports Schor. I have to admit to incredulity here: how is it *possible* for anyone to pay this much money for a fluffy bunch of pyjamas, noise, sweets and nonsense, giggling, spillages, nasty remarks, tears, jokes and affection: pandemonium on a stick? Why on earth would anyone need anything other than toffee, gin and earplugs to organize a sleepover party? But glee is for sale, products are seen as markers of children's status and corporations are trespassing into that sacred part of childhood, the trust of friends, using small children as 'brand ambassadors', bribing them with free samples or money. A child, confiding in another about her new toy, pretending friendship, may really have her eye on the commission and bonuses she'll get if she sends a marketing company photographic evidence. The 'Girls Intelligence Agency' has operated in the USA from 2002, with a network of some 40,000 girls from the ages of eight to eighteen who act as 'agents', to give out product samples and hold slumber parties then offer feedback of their friends' responses to the GIA.

Grooming children into certain roles; slithering into their bedrooms at night; inveigling themselves into children's affections with free gifts; wanting films of children privately manipulating their mates;

isolating children from their friendships by encouraging them to betray trust and treat friends as objects; stealthily invading their dreams at night: consumerism for children is a form of cultural paedophilia.

The contemporary hysteria about paedophilia is intrinsically related to consumerism. As never before, people in the West are subjected to a media-driven frenzy of fear about stranger-danger, depicting a world where the woods are thick with 'peedos', every bush camouflages at least a couple, every playground fence is peppered with them, the riverbanks crawling and every street corner a lurking place. The media gives 'a totally unbalanced impression of the risks which children face from strangers', says the UK's Children's Society. But the fear is devastating: I share it when, looking after my tribe of godchildren and nephews, anxiety wrenches me if a child is out of sight for a millisecond. My fear is irrational: I know that I have been hoodwinked, but it works. The media sets up a false proximity so what happens far away can have the semblance of local importance, and its reiteration of one single abduction gives the appearance of a pandemic of paedophilia.

At least ninety per cent of child sexual abuse happens courtesy of a family member or family friend. That is where the vast, terrible and lifelong damage is done. The real threats to children – the family car, parked with the motor running in the drive, causing accidents and climate change, and the dodgy uncle, parked on the sofa with his motor running and patting the cushion next to him – are dramatically underplayed in the media.

The media profits from stranger-danger because fear sells. But who else gains? Far more insidiously than the media moguls, it is the toy, gadget and entertainment industries which profit. Children, enclosed indoors through false fears of paedophiles, are a captive market, imprisoned and bored. The corporations are the real predators, grooming the children, spying on them, brainwashing them, isolating them, addicting them and possessing them for the whole of their lives.

The increasingly widespread idea that children could be privately owned by their parents seems to have gathered pace along with the rise of capitalism. While (non-capitalist) traditional and indigenous cultures have often refused to see a child as a possession of its parents but rather as a self-owning autonomous person, capitalist societies seem to have decided that children should not own themselves or belong on the commons but be the possessions of their parents. Contemporary consumerism trumps even that parental role, steering itself remorselessly into the role of ownership, possessions possessing childhood.

CHAPTER ELEVEN

The Tribe of Children

Some years ago, I was walking in the highlands of West Papua as part of my research for *Wild*. Late one afternoon, approaching a village with the guide barely thirty paces ahead of me, my path was suddenly cut off and I was caught alone. Bristling with bows and arrows, a tribe of fifteen people had blocked my way in a swift, deft ambush. They demanded a ransom for my release: I paid it and they let me pass, grinning. The ransom was sweets. The bows and arrows were miniature. None of the ambushers was over ten (all of them with childhood's obligatory trails of stiff, sniffed snot). For the next couple of days, this tribe of children followed me wherever I went. They chased me when I went for a pee, they thronged the riverbank when I went to wash, they pursued me, spied on me, teased and giggled when I pulled ridiculous faces for them, or played the handflute and pantomime games. They treated me like a strange frog just hopped out of a forest pool and they hovered between excitement, kindness and potential cruelty.

All across the world, children congregate in gangs, ever on the lookout for excitement like sailors looking for a puff of wind to stave off the doldrums. Any breeze will do: ambush, hunting, poetry or pickaxes, spite, spit or sanctity. Among themselves, they toss out suggestions for activities, careless and rich with ideas, with a run-it-up-the-flagpole-and-see-who-salutes-it enthusiasm.

'We lived in our own tribe, among its ideas, its loves and wars; and the tribes of other children,' wrote Joyce Cary of his late-nineteenth-century Irish childhood in *A House of Children*. 'New ideas sprang up among us every moment, as unexpected and rousing as partridges out of turnips.' Happily self-maddening, with crazes for wheelbarrows or tongue-twisters, Chinese burns, clapping games, intimidation or impromptu performances, the easy conviviality of a tribe of children is like a school of fish: mercurial, responsive, electric with enthusiasms, swimming in its self-influencing miniature eco-system, self-swayed with its own momentum, stirring, swelling, cresting until it spends itself to bubbly nothings on a pebble shore.

The strict age segregation which contemporary children experience is very unusual, as, for most of human history, children have roamed in packs, playing together. Part of the riddle of childhood today begs the question of how children may need this typical sense of living in their own tribe. Belonging to each other, they express the fact that they are not owned by their parents. In their tribes, they can escape from the adult empire which can rule children as if they were diminutive dominions; they can set up their own republic free from adults and practise shifting equality and fraternity with each other.

The tribe of children can be as brutal as a lynch mob, as imaginative as jazz, or as beautiful as altruism. It is a scaled-down version of the adult world, with its adventures, enemies and crises. Religious manias sweep through it like wildfire; it has markets, banks and businesses, laws and law enforcement. The tribe of children has art, plays, shows and dances: it has tortures and decrees of exile. It has ranks and hierarchies, up-endable though they may be through an impromptu coup d'état. It has an intelligentsia and its loathed informants. It has smut, braggadocio, bullshit and bullshit detectors, it has dialects, secrets and nonsense, it has language: fertile, furtive, funny and rude.

Legislative terms are vital to children's tribal culture – protocol, process, obligation, right and permission – and children need to learn their tribe's Code of Hammurabi. According to the great authorities on the culture of childhood, Iona and Peter Opie, a schoolchild has 'affidavits, promissory notes, claims, deeds of conveyance, receipts, and notices of resignation'. They are verbal and 'sealed by the utterance of ancient words which are recognized and considered binding by the whole community'. They include affirmations (for example, swearing, spitting or making crosses); testing truthfulness; placing bets; making bargains ('No going back on it'); swapping, giving, gaining possession by 'bagging' or 'finders keepers'; claiming precedence; avoiding; vows of keeping secrets; and, importantly, a truce term for gaining temporary respite in a game in order to go to the toilet, to put a shoe back on or to catch their breath. Among truce terms, the Opies mention kings, cruses, scinch, exsie, vains, fains, faynights, scrucies, pax, barley, screws and scrases. These terms are localized and the Opies draw a map of Britain showing swathes of territory marked by different truce terms. These words have belonged to their localities for centuries, they say, and children new to an area must learn them fast.

In a paragraph which applies precisely to children, Kenneth Grahame in *The Wind in the Willows* writes that there are things which a small animal has to understand before it goes into the Wild Wood: 'pass-words, and signs, and sayings which have power and effect, and plants you carry in your pocket, and verses you repeat, and dodges and tricks you practise; all simple enough when you know them, but they've got to be known if you're small, or you'll find yourself in trouble'.

There is a tough etiquette at play, a rule-of-thumb morality and a fistful of blunt justice. The tribe's codes may passingly resemble the codes of adults, so while a pen may be summarily appropriated – finders keepers – a mobile phone so collected will be seen as theft by all adults and most children.

Nonsense rhymes, tangletalk and tales-which-never-end are all part of the subculture. Having-the-last-word, and made-you-look, saying-the-same-thing-at-the-same-time, are all coded into communication. The eternally popular taboos of farting, pissing, shitting, screwing and dying are honoured: my brothers and I would snort with reckless dirty laughter at rhymes which combined as many of these as possible.

> *There was a man from Brazil*
> *Who ate a dynamite pill.*
> *His heart retired,*
> *His bum backfired*
> *And his willy shot over the hill.*

Nothing, absolutely nothing, was funnier than reciting this within the hearing of a grumpy grown-up.

A recent study into childhood lore and play headed by Professor Andrew Burn admitted the project had found rather less filth than the Opies had found in their work in the fifties: 'In the changed geography of childhood, the street as a place for play has drastically diminished; while playgrounds tend to be more scrupulously overseen by teachers, learning assistants and playworkers. Either children produce less rude rhymes in these circumstances; or they keep it more carefully hidden.'

A parody of disease, too, lurks in this culture, as many games of catch or tag or tig suggest. The fingertip of the chaser can 'poison' or 'kill' the chased. In my childhood, the moment a child was caught, we said they had 'got the lurgy' and while I'll probably never know if, as I suspect, this is a corruption of the written word 'allergy', it certainly suggests that preoccupation with swift transmission which is part of childhood messaging, fizzing with rapidity like a germ on speed. Its irreverence is infectious, its ribaldry contagious and its dirtiness catching. (*Doctor, doctor, I need a new bum. Why? Mine's got a crack in it.*)

The tribal culture of childhood can puncture adult pomposity, can sometimes see that the emperor has no WMD faster than the general mass of the populace. While the debate raged about whether or not to invade Iraq, and only very few – and very brave – adults were speaking publicly about the ulterior motives of the UK and the US, two children spoke to me about it in a mock-stern voice: 'We are *not* having a war against Iraq because of the oil . . .' Pause. Hiss: *'It's for the petrol.'*

Like any subculture, the underclass of children has its own lingo, inventive, parodic, rude and frank. It mocks songs, carols, adverts, football chants: anything it can get its thieving little fingers on. It grabs all the resources at its disposal, undermining, subverting, mixing, mashing whatever it can.

While Burn's report discovered that some games have declined in these media-dominated generations, yet the traditional lore of the playground is alive and well, co-opting material from television, musicals, pop songs and adverts as happily as children, borrowers all, have always done, taking what they want from adult culture. When we were small, our tribe at school had its own version of the carol 'While Shepherds Watched':

While shepherds watched T V by night
They watched on IT V.
The angel of the Lord came down
And switched to BBC.

Somehow the tribe saw that the established Church and the establishment BBC were singing from the same hymn sheet and we laughed at them both.

Some parts of the cultural collage may be contemporary – particular TV shows re-enacted in a thousand playgrounds – but the essence of childhood tribal culture is ancient. The earliest clapping game in Europe was first documented in 1698, and they are still going strong. The basic lore and language of childhood persists today in rhymes and songs which have come down the years, and the tribe of children is a keeper of tradition today just as much as when the Opies in 1959 wrote: 'Boys continue to crack jokes that Swift collected from his friends in Queen Anne's time; they play tricks which lads used to play on each other in the heyday of Beau Brummel; they ask riddles which were posed when Henry VIII was a boy.'

Children themselves don't realize the antiquity of their culture. You may know the situation: a child asks you a joke question which they have just heard, something which is, to them, a fabulous novelty. Dredging your memory, you come up with the answer from your own childhood. The child is absolutely incredulous that you, so 'old' in your thirties or forties, could possibly know something so 'new'.

To the tribe of children, Public Enemy Number One is usually the adults. They don't laugh at farts. When civility and table manners became more popular throughout society, when loud belching and laughing at farts began to be frowned on, the distance between children and adults grew greater, suggests fairy-tale expert Jack Zipes.

(The remote-controlled fart machine is probably the best present I've ever given a kid.)

'It was our theory that the grownup was the natural enemy of the child,' writes American author Robert Paul Smith, because 'what they wanted us to do was to be like them.' C. S. Lewis and his brother established a bond which excluded adults: 'We stood foursquare against the common enemy.' As children, Edward Elgar and his siblings staged a play about their fantasy world and adults were banned. He wrote music for this, as a child, reworking it decades later into *The Wand of Youth*.

In his films, Truffaut's staunchly remembered tribes of children blank out much of the adult world, finding their rapport with each other and with art. Joyce Cary says he doesn't remember any adults 'above the knee' until he was about seven. 'We were a crowd of children in our own world, which is as different from the grownup world as that of dogs or cats or birds.' Recalling a child's perspective, Kenneth Grahame refers to adults as the Olympians who possessed the licence of the gods to indulge in all the pleasures of life including climbing trees and buying gunpowder, yet who never took advantage of the freedom which children hankered for. We 'could have told them what real life was. We had just left it outside, and were all on fire to get back to it.'

Children in the company of adults (no matter how kind) feel their impotence, and it hurts them. They have few rights and little money, power, acknowledgement, autonomy, freedom or status. No wonder they want to live from time to time in the independent free state of childhood which they know within their tribes, so, when they can, they subvert the *status quo* as carnival does, the topsy-turvy reversal of sense into nonsense, the small people overthrowing the big people, the lowerarchy overturning the higherarchy.

In their own tribe, children can be the right size, but in the adult world they are miniatures, toys. Adults love the smallness of children: the very thing which most children, most of the time, most want to get away from. They don't want to be miniature and they are not toys so, in their own tribe, with their personhood fuller, they can be themselves at the scale they choose, epic and enormous.

There can, of course, be a very brutal edge to the tribes of children. In Leicestershire, there is a street called Bardon Road. A few years ago, the street sign had been altered to read 'Bordom Road'. It was indeed a sign for anyone who could read, and one local teenager said tellingly that local kids were bored to death. 'There's nothing to do other than get pissed or take drugs.' So, over time, a tribe of children gathered, some as young as ten, and they mocked and bullied a mother, Fiona Pilkington, and her disabled daughter and son. The gang pelted the house with eggs and stones, shouted taunts and abuse and attacked the son at knifepoint. The hate crimes continued over a ten-year period. The kids were bored to *a* death, to be specific. The abuse got so bad that in 2007, when Fiona Pilkington was thirty-eight, she was driven to kill herself and her daughter. For a tribe of children can be vicious when dizzied by its own rhetoric: the microtribe in howlback can behave, like any crowd, far worse in its throng than any individual would behave alone.

The press fell over itself to damn the children involved, quoting *Lord of the Flies* as if it were prophecy, although, as this chapter will tell, in the one known real-life *Lord of the Flies* castaway situation, the outcome was the exact reverse of Golding's bleak vision. The media took scant interest in the reasons why children may be so cruel, but there were two signs: one was Bordom Road, the other was a statement in the House of Commons, no less, when research was quoted which analysed the reasons why children may become abusive: the main one was being unloved. When children are not loved enough in very early childhood, they are not able to empathize with others or to appreciate the effects of their behaviour on others.

~

My guide in West Papua, who was very amused by the ambush on the footpath, told me that by the time he was eight or nine, part of his 'job in life' was to look after younger children. 'As children, we all looked after each other,' said Sure-yani Poroso of the Leco people in Bolivia. 'It was a tribe of children, independent of adults.' In Ghana, according to journalist Ryszard Kapuściński, 'children take care of children, so that adults can devote themselves to their affairs,' and older children take care of younger children: a six-year-old looking after a four-year-old who has full authority over a two-year-old. One of the commonest sights in traditional villages from the hill tribes of Thailand to the forests of South America is the tribe of children of all ages, looking after each other.

In a nuclear family, children occupy the constant position of underling, unless they resort to some magnificent and decibel-defying tantrumming, which is, of course, what many children are forced to do in order to seize just a little power back. In their own tribe, though, they swim between being cop and being robber, playing different parts in the full fetch of the wave. Yes, some children dominate their tribe and, yes, some will bully, but one of the virtues of the mixed-age tribe of children is that fluidity is built in because, as children grow older, so younger children turn up. Typically, children are looked after, bossed around or protected by older children and then themselves take that role towards those who are younger.

Joyce Cary noted the pattern for his tribe, aged between four and fourteen. 'Whoever was the eldest girl present, assumed the manner of a governess, and abused us. Delia, who, when she was not the eldest, led the mischief; in charge, was the most severe of all.' One Sardinian woman told me how she, as a child, had felt more surrounded, influenced and affected by the tribe of children than the tribe of adults. There was a custom among Lakota people, says Luther Standing Bear, whereby 'an older boy voluntarily adopted as a special charge some younger boy. The older one appointed himself as guardian and helpmate to the younger, the obligation to last throughout life.' Younger boys would tag along after the elder boys and, he writes: 'The nice thing about it was that the older boys never seemed to regard the younger ones as nuisances. They took time to look after us and, in fact, all seemed proud to share in this responsibility.' Children can learn that they are the protectors as well as the protected, responsible for each other.

Little girls, writes Jean Liedloff, will 'behave instinctively' towards infants, giving them exactly what they need and she reports how, among the Yequana, girls from the age of just three or four would take full charge of babies. 'To give the profound maternal urge in little girls no quarter, to channel it off to dolls when there are real infants about, is among other things a serious disservice to the children of the little girl when she grows up.'

If you're a child, it is a privilege – an honour – to be allowed to tend a baby. But there is more. If children look after each other, they will learn that they are not only recipients of care but *providers* of care. They will learn that they themselves are not just sinks but *sources* of protection, love and help. Their own qualities of kindness, empathy and responsiveness will be developed, and they will experience, as both givers and receivers, the elastic, multi-directional, diverse security of their tribe.

By contrast, if children are looked after only by adults, they will learn a tense dependence on the top-down protection of a parent, the vertical politics of hierarchy. If children experience care as something which comes only from adults, they may relinquish responsibility for each other. They may not get much practice in the horizontal politics of equality, the skills of cooperation and mutuality which recognize the common good, and will not be in the habit of initiating imaginative ways to achieve that joint-stock merrymaking.

Lord of the Flies is a portrait of children indoctrinated by hierarchy, authority and racism. As soon as the boys arrive, they look at the island with the colonizing gaze: they 'savored the right of domination'. In an odiously racist text, the boys who become the cruel killers are described as becoming a 'tribe', hunting, dancing, chanting and 'garlanded', their long hair tied back: 'a pack of painted Indians'. They pursue Ralph, the good and righteous leader, who has kept his Britishness intact, and he is rescued by a uniformed naval officer disappointed to see that the boys – although British – have become 'savages'.

Apart from its shocking racism, one of the tragedies of the book is that it is used as a cultural shorthand for a supposed perennial truth about what Golding, after Conrad, calls the 'darkness of man's heart' deep within the child. It is as if, without the 'civilizing' effects of adult influence, children will become the vicious little monsters which many adults secretly fear they are. It is a maligning of childhood as much as of indigenous cultures. Generations of children are made to read the book and are inculcated with a nasty and untrue piece of political propaganda against their own childhood selves, a message created by those who hold such dominion over them: the adults.

Stuck in a pattern of individual need (especially when those needs are unmet) and dependent on a hierarchy of power of adults over children, deprived of closeness and love in infancy, young people may learn to behave to other children like the kids in Bordom Road; they may begin to act like Golding's Jack or Roger. But given a background of love enough and freedom enough, and given the practice of caring for each other in their own tribes, the results may be quite the reverse. For there has actually been a real-life *Lord of the Flies* situation and the children's behaviour was the opposite of that depicted by Golding.

Tonga is the only island nation in that region of the South Pacific that was not subject to formal colonialism. It was once known as the 'Friendly Islands', apparently because Captain Cook was kindly received there (although this is disputed by some who say the only reason he was well treated was because people couldn't agree on how to kill him). One day in 1977, six boys, all friends, from the Friendly Islands, set out on a fishing trip. On this azure day, the turquoise of the South Pacific called them out, out of sight of the palm trees of their known shore, and the boys rowed the boat out into the ocean. The nets were curled at the bottom of the wooden boat, a couple of boys curled around the nets, a siesta snoozing through their afternoon. Sometimes fishing over the side of the boat and sometimes swimming lazy and happy as dolphins beside the boat all this long moment, their present was perfected in an eternal afternoon of childhood. And then the dot of the future appeared, a tight wad of fear packed into one thundercloud, tiny at first on the horizon.

A stillness suddenly surrounds the boat. A stillness within the boys. They are too far out at sea to return home before the storm. Then the wind summons a stealthy cold streak and the rain falls in drills. A gust of wind dashes the side of the boat then rain starts sheeting down, but it is the darkness which they fear the most because day-darkness is a foreteller. It prophesies, it keeps nothing unforetold, it shakes every scrap of joy, every ribbon of happiness out of the boys, and then the prophecy of darkness is upon them. It is a perfect storm. The six boys are sick, they are terrified, they sob, they pray, they fall silent. The sky, bruised, is hurling winds and torrents of rain. It does not stop. No wish, no prayer, no vow the boys make has any effect. The storm lasts for days. Through mornings and evenings and terrible long nights, the storm has the boat and its cargo of childhood in its teeth and then, in one ferocious howl, it throws them on to a reef. The boat is crushed to splinters. Weak, frightened, exhausted and trembling, the boys scramble to the beach as the palm trees thrash in the gale. The boys do not know the island. Slowly, as the storm subsides, they pick themselves up and begin to look around. The island is totally uninhabited and they are alone. What do they do, this little tribe of children? How does the story continue? Authored by Golding, the story would involve cruelty and humiliation. Authored by the children, the story involves sense and grace.

They made a pact never to quarrel, because they could see that arguing could lead to mutually assured destruction. They promised each other that wherever they went on the island they would go in twos, in case they got lost or had an accident. They agreed to have a rota of being on guard, night and day, to watch out for anything that might harm them or anything that might help. And they kept their promises, for a day which became a week, which stretched into a month. Time wore on, one month yawning into two and four and six and twelve. A year passed. Fifteen months had gone by when suddenly two boys, on watch as they had agreed, saw the dot of a new future approaching, tiny at first, a speck of a boat on the horizon. The boys were found and rescued, all of them, grace intact and promises held.

The story is reported by Susanna Agnelli, in a Report for the Independent Commission on International Humanitarian Issues, whose interpretation is as follows. The boys 'owed their survival to a shared faith; to the fact that none had any reason to exploit the other; and, especially perhaps, to a culture which gave more weight to co-operation than to competition. Modern education has gone to such lengths to subvert this principle that, faced with a similar situation, the urban youngsters of today would be unlikely to react with the same unselfishness and self-reliance.'

It is a glimpse of the fractal politics of childhood: if a society's politics is more concerned with common purpose than self-interest, children may also make the common good a priority. Where self-reliance is fostered in children by allowing them autonomy and where the independent free state of childhood is uncolonized then children may act in their own wisdom: shipwrecked perhaps but not spirit-wrecked.

CHAPTER TWELVE

On the Character Fault of Exuberance

Like the thud of a bored metronome which knows the metre but not the music, Plato's *Republic* issues edicts with its thin metal tongue. Excessive laughter is banned and so is the liquid superfluity of metaphor. Plato would rid his ideal state of anything that could arouse emotion, mischief, wildness or fun. Banning, like an Ancient Greek Taliban, mimesis, pantomime, imagination and Sicilian cooking (yes, he does), so ghastly is his *Republic* that it could be interpreted as satire. But, generally, its ambition has been taken with deadly seriousness as a founding text on the education of boys. The purpose of *The Republic* is to school its youth to be good soldiers engaged in unending war to take the resources of neighbouring lands. It is a handbook for the education of imperialists.

Brick by brick, Plato builds the walls of his citadel of control, hierarchy and obedience. His ideal republic is obsessed with rule – not only the rule of command, but the rule of measurement. It is a book in praise of ratiocination – in everything the 'rational principle' should rule – and when he writes of 'civilizing the wildness of passion', you see the heart of his vision that Apollo, god of measure, metre, civilization and, surely, god of metronomes, should keep Dionysus, god of the Romantic movement, god of wildness and nature, firmly under his thumb.

Not for Plato the creation of children through a Dionysiac shag in the woods. For him, children should be created by cold, dry Apollonian reason, not hot and wet Dionysiac passion. Forget the shimmering vitality of Aboriginal Australian conception sites and ignore Dafydd ap Gwilym's lovemaking in the green woods of Wales: fertility should be governed by maths. He spells it out, his geometrical figure controlling 'good and evil' births. (I'll type it small, so you can skip it more easily.)

The period of human birth is comprehended in a number in which first increments by involution and evolution [or squared and cubed] obtaining three intervals and four terms of like and unlike, waxing and waning numbers, make all the terms commensurable and agreeable to one another. The base of these (3) with a third added (4) when combined with five (20) and raised to the third power furnishes two harmonies; the first a square which is a hundred times as great ($400 = 4 \times 100$), and the other a figure having one side equal to the former, but oblong, consisting of a hundred numbers squared upon rational diameters of a square (i.e. omitting fractions), the side of which is five ($7 \times 7 = 49 \times 100 = 4900$), each of them being less by one (than the perfect square which includes the fractions, sc. 50) or less by two perfect squares if irrational diameters (of a square the side of which is five $= 50 + 50 = 100$); and a hundred cubes of three ($27 \times 100 = 2700 + 4900 + 400 = 8000$). Now this number represents a geometrical figure which has control over the good and evil of births.

Babies, says this founding father of our culture, should be removed early from their mother's milk and sent to segregated factories according to class. Aldous Huxley, with his alphas, betas, gammas, deltas and epsilons in *Brave New World*, was taking his cue from Plato's alphabet. Literally. Plato promotes the literal over the metaphoric, the measurable over the mysterious, so poetry was considered an unwanted elixir and poets exiled.

Plato is unwilling to admit any storytellers to his republic and has the temerity to censor Homer, but though he would strike out many passages of the ancient poet, he would, interestingly, keep these lines:

> . . . *sit still and obey my word* . . .
> *The Greeks marched breathing prowess,*
> . . . *in silent awe of their leaders.*

Silence in class! Sit still! Do what you are told! The natural will of children must be repressed into rank obedience.

Plato wanted to ban flute music from his perfect republic because it stirs the passions. It is hard for the soul to breathe in the stifled atmosphere he describes – the flute player cannot catch a breath – and in this dispirited, deanimated world, something in the spirit expires.

Many languages see a direct connection between soul or spirit and breath. *Anima*, in Latin, meaning both breath and spirit, is ultimately derived from *anemos*, wind: the wind that plays us like a flute. The first flutes were created by the woodpecker co-inspiring with the wind, according to Native American legend, as the woodpecker hammered out holes which turned the trees into flutes that the wind would play through.

The flute was the instrument of Dionysus, which was another reason for Plato banning it in *The Republic*. He knew its power, the force of wild inspiration in the respiration of breath, the *anima*, the spirit blowing free as the wind. Plato would have banished *anima*, the spirit, the breath of life, and *anemos*, the wind, if he could; the lively animating wind. And as the flute was banned from Plato's republic, so millions of whistling, hooting, bird-imitating, handfluting, owl- and cuckoo-calling, grass-harping and acorn-cup-whistling children, staunch Dionysiacs, were silenced by the rule of Plato's inheritors. (The piercing shriek you can get from whistling over the top edge of an acorn cup is my own favourite.)

If there is one fundamental text of denatured schooling, Plato's *Republic* is it. Not only the child's will but their affinity with nature should be overruled, surrendering to architectured control. The child's metaphor-making mind is to be soured into literalism. Freedom is unwelcome and the passionate soul of childhood is suffocated every time it takes a breath, crushed by the strictures of segregation in schooling like factories. And this has been taken as a model, Plato's influence on education 'all-pervasive', according to educationalist John Dewey.

~

When I think of its opposite, I see the picture in sepia at first: the solitary child at the window, gazing out through the Venetian shutters. His eyes are large. His hands hold only each other. His heart is broken. Rabindranath Tagore lost his mother when he was between eight and ten years old, and the loss shattered him. After her death, his father was frequently absent and Tagore was lonely and friendless, brought up in what he called the 'servocracy' in which the servants ruled, confining him to the family compound where the second-in-command servant sometimes drew a chalk circle around the boy and forbade him to step out of it. As an adult, Tagore wrote of his soul's 'rigorous repression during my infancy', and the tighter the restrictions, the more he longed for the green beyond.

In the house by the closed windows, behind the drawn blinds, the shuttered child sits, quiet and still on the outside. But on the inside something else is happening. I see it in green. The bathing ghat glitters with sunlight and the inner garden is shady, watered and deep green. Meanwhile, the child's eyes are drinking, liquid with love for the nature which replaced his mothering.

Then came school; a crushing experience for Tagore. One teacher would punish him by making him stand for hours in the scorching sun if he made a mistake in his lessons. For Tagore, it was the school of the dead. 'We had to sit like dead specimens of some museum whilst lessons were pelted at us from on high like hailstones on flowers.' The deadening lessons took place within 'bare white walls staring like eyeballs of the dead'. With all the life of his soul, he revolted against it. He hated school for its lifelessness and its cruelty and he began playing truant. Tagore, who would have been banished from Plato's ideal state, grew up to become a musician, a poet, a philosopher of play and the guru of Gandhi. He also founded an education system wholly opposed to the British model of imperialist schooling which he experienced.

In the history of European schooling, certain concerns echo down the centuries: hierarchy, obedience, violence and class control (pun intended). A school system was established, half factory and half prison, in order to create a passive and disciplined workforce where schooled, uniform obedience was demanded. *'Anima, anima!'* cries the stifled spirit of childhood, then and now. The overt curriculum was bad enough, but the covert curriculum has often been worse, reflecting a right-wing ethos which used school to further imperialism abroad and class division at home, while also viewing the child as a subject in the empire of the school.

~

The European school system originated in the cathedral schools of the Middle Ages, set up to recruit boys to the Church. The syllabus began with the trivium of grammar, rhetoric and dialectics, followed by the quadrivium of geometry, arithmetic, astronomy and music. (This might have been at the back of James Joyce's mind when an interviewer once asked your man: Aren't your puns a bit *trivial*, Mr Joyce? No, he replied, they are at least *quadrivial*.)

From late in the sixteenth century, boys began attending school in large numbers and the ruling classes in England and France pretended they wanted education spread across all social strata to combat poverty, laziness and immorality. More honestly, says Philippe Ariès, it was 'to make pious, serious workers out of what had been depraved adventurers'. 'Workers': a word which dogs the history of schooling.

In the eighteenth-century European Enlightenment, Voltaire (who considered the word 'education' to be a 'presumptuous neologism') and fellow members of the upper class loathed the idea of education for all: education should be a privilege for the wealthy in case the labourers got ideas above their station and stopped wanting to work. Ignorance and illiteracy would confine them to manual labour. For conservatives of the nineteenth century, education was considered dangerous because it could seed the working classes with revolutionary ideas; if they were to be schooled, it would be in the image of the factory.

Tagore described school as an 'education factory, lifeless, colour-less, dissociated from the context of the universe'. In the UK, the factory was actually a prototype for schooling, when Pitt's Bill for the Reform of the Poor Law (1796–7) urged 'Schools of Industry' for children aged five and over. These became known as 'Factory Schools' or 'Industrial Schools', and sought to instil in children the subservience that would be required in factories. 'Obedience to the Master's rule disposes to the observance of other rules human and divine,' opined Parliamentary Papers of 1847. The chief end of edu-cation, wrote nineteenth-century sociologist Benjamin Kidd, was to 'impose on the young the ideal of subordination'. Children would learn the syllabus of the Industrial Revolution: the trivium of tedium, obedience and the clock; the quadrivium of uniformity, regularity, efficiency and control.

American educator Ellwood P. Cubberley, dean of Stanford's School of Education from 1917 to 1933, wrote approvingly: 'Our schools are . . . factories in which the raw products (children) are to be shaped and fashioned into products . . . and it is the business of the school to build its pupils according to the specifications laid down.' Woodrow Wilson, in a speech to businessmen just before the First World War, said: 'We want one class to have a liberal education. We want another class, a very much larger class of necessity, to forgo the privilege of a liberal education and fit themselves to perform specific difficult manual tasks.'

In France in 1990, schoolchildren in Lyon demanded that their school was turned from an exam factory into a 'place to live in', as Theodore Zeldin reports. Anthony Seldon, the anti-Gradgrind head of Wellington College who famously introduced 'happiness lessons' for his students, gave a speech in 2010 entitled 'An End to Factory

Schools', describing contemporary education as 'the apogee of Ford-ism gone mad', where the school-factory was 'owned and operated under the strict top-down instructions of government, who decreed everything that went on'.

In that spirit, here are some instructions from the factory owners:

~ Take approximately 110cm of raw material.
~ Make a baseline assessment of the material's quality.
~ Keep the raw material away from snow and do not expose it to more than fifteen minutes of direct sunlight daily.
~ Require material to be available and registered at daily assemblies.
~ Segregate new material from classes of older material.
~ Process the material of one class with identical and uni-form treatment.
~ Ignore variables in units.
~ Reject imagination, autonomy, reverie and play.
~ Adopt standard processes and general attainment targets.
~ Inspect material regularly and subject it to product testing.
~ Quality certification will be given in Grades A descending.
~ High-quality product will be sent for further processing.
~ Defective product will be subject to product recall.
~ Non-compliant material may be treated with methylphenidate.
~ Material which is both defective and non-compliant should be warehoused.
~ Irredeemably defective non-compliant products will be subject to expulsion from further factory process, and operators will refer to prison guidelines.

The factory operators

~ Operators will be considered interchangeable.
~ Operators will be subject to regular inspection.
~ Operators will have attended training programmes set by the factory owners and will use instruction manuals produced in accordance with owners' guidelines.
~ Operators will be required to spend more time in factory administration work and less time in direct contact with material.
~ Operators' requests to use intuition, flexibility and independence will be ignored by the factory owners, as will demands for smaller factories.
~ Factory results will be listed in league tables available in all public media.

~

This is not what children want. This is also not what teachers want.

'What did you learn at school today?' a friend asked a four-year-old child on his first day. 'I learned to queue up and I learned to sit quietly on the carpet.'

When teachers ruefully refer to their work as 'crowd control', their voices carry a sad shadow – of a wish to educate, an enthusiasm for their subject and the modestly gigantic ambition of influencing the adults of the future. At my school, perhaps two teachers in twenty-five enjoyed control for its own sake (and I doubt the proportion is very different anywhere), but teachers and children alike are corralled into a system which leaves them little room for manoeuvre. Discipline has come to be considered a central issue in school.

Medieval schooling was anarchy on a stick, chaos with bells on. All ages were mixed together so, on going to school, children entered the world of adults. (Segregation by age was brought in from the late fifteenth century or so.) Ariès quotes a shocked report of the 'jumble' of a medieval school, where rooms on one side were rented out to students and on the other to prostitutes – truly a school for scandal. By the sixteenth century, this degree of licence was considered intolerable and control, repression and timetables were brought in.

Although the media may think that knife crime in school is a horrible example of modernity storming the citadel of innocence, many children in Europe used to go around wearing a sword or possessing firearms. So common was it for children to go to school armed that the Jesuits' *Ratio Studiorum* of 1599 advised that children aged five onwards should be disarmed on arrival at school, and be given receipts for their weapons, which would be returned as the children left school again. One of the reasons for this was class war: the danger of children fighting their 'masters'.

Children experienced vicious and public punishment at school. Michel de Montaigne describes the classrooms of the mid-sixteenth century as strewn 'with the bloody stumps of birch and willow', where you hear 'nothing but whipping and brawling'. One school in France, at the beginning of the eighteenth century, gave instructions on birching children: 'the child must be beaten harder if he screams.'

Hurt and humiliated, children responded with fury. There were armed revolts, violent mutinies against the masters. There was a rebellion at the Jesuit college of La Flèche, on Shrove Tuesday, 1646. This day was traditionally a carnival of youth and should have been a day of ribald glee. But some of the college's older pupils were seething with humiliation and pain having been publicly flogged, and the magistrate had added salt to their wounds by forbidding the election of a young Master of Ceremonies, a ritual Lord of Misrule. So a real mutiny began. One boy drew his sword and was captured by the masters so the other children rioted, arming themselves with sticks, swords and blackjacks, and first laid siege to the college then forced their way in to free the boy. The Jesuit Fathers armed their servants with sticks, halberds and muskets. In the fight, one of the masters was hit by a bullet in the thigh. In 1649, at one of the French Protestant academies, the boys barricaded themselves inside the college, fired pistol shots and 'fouled the rostra', as Ariès writes. They chucked the benches out of the window, tore up books and climbed out of the window.

School mutinies in England became increasingly frequent and violent in the late eighteenth and nineteenth centuries. At Winchester, the boys occupied the school for two days, running up the red flag. At Eton, the monitors seceded and left the school. In 1818, at Winchester, soldiers with bayonets were called out to put down a rebellion among the pupils. At Rugby, boys burned their books and desks, and camped on an island: again, the army was called in; it mounted an assault to retake the island. Also in 1818, Eton boys, who had been locked in, pelted their master with rotten eggs and demolished a wall to escape. The last mutiny at Eton was in 1832. To crush it, eighty boys were flogged. The last serious mutiny occurred at Marlborough in 1851.

But what of those who were not sufficiently privileged – if that is the word – to be sent to public school? In nineteenth-century Britain, the authorities were most concerned about juvenile crime, juvenile soaplessness and juvenile lack of respect. The worst juveniles were working class. They were cheeky. Grubby in mind and morals, thumbing their noses at the middle classes. They needed to be controlled, thought the authorities, who came up with the answer. 'Schools were structured as mechanisms of discipline for the children of working-class people,' writes Fiona Paterson in *Out of Place: Public Policy and the Emergence of Truancy*. 'They were predicated on the necessity of producing and sustaining hierarchical relations of authority.' From the head to the teachers, the monitors and the pupils, everyone would learn their place and learn to obey their 'superiors'.

With this, schooling introduced a lie so large it is hard to see: that hierarchy and discipline are necessary for education. Instruction, poked into a child through its earholes, could only happen when the child was pinned taxonomically into its place in the hierarchy, like Tagore's 'dead specimens'.

It was dehumanizing for teachers as well as for children. D. H. Lawrence in *The Rainbow* (1915) describes Ursula taking a teaching job with classes of fifty to sixty children. 'The prison was round her now! She looked at the walls . . . at the long rows of desks, arranged in a squadron, and dread filled her . . . she could not breathe: she must suffocate . . . they were not individual children, they were a collective, inhuman thing.' The children must be forced into 'one state of mind, or being. This state must be produced automatically, through the will of the teacher . . . imposed upon the will of the children.'

Her pupils try to rebel, as children always do. Film director Jean Vigo raised the curtain on a light-hearted aspect of this rebellion, its delirious mischief and clowning anarchy, in *Zéro de Conduite* (*Zero for Conduct*), 1933, depicting the pupils' carnivals of subversion, the tricks and pillow fights and roof-top protests. Such escapades were banned by the school authorities, and the film itself was banned by state authorities for its 'praise of indiscipline'. Both school and state sought to control the freewheeling, cartwheeling fantasy rebellion, but shortly after the film was made, the deadly seriousness of control and obedience was being played out across Europe.

Alert to uprisings of fascism in Europe, Dr Maria Montessori warned that 'the obedience which is expected of a child both at home and in the school – an obedience admitting neither of reason or of justice – prepares the man to be docile to blind forces.' From this is born 'the spirit of devotion – not to say of idolatry – to the *condottieri*, the leaders', because the child who 'has never learned to act alone, to direct his own actions, to govern his own will, grows into an adult who is easily led'. Conventional schooling can take the form of 'submissiveness, of incapacity to put up the slightest moral resistance'. Montessori teachers refused to declare loyalty to fascism in 1931, so Hitler closed down Montessori schools, Dr Montessori's books were burned and she was forced into exile.

'We educate older children . . . for either dominance or subordination,' Aldous Huxley wrote in 1937. 'The traditional education is training for life in a hierarchical, militaristic society, in which people are abjectly obedient to their superiors and inhuman to their inferiors.' As if unaware of the historical dangers of abject obedience and militarism, Britain's current Conservative education secretary is encouraging ex-military personnel to become teachers so they can inculcate discipline, hierarchy and militaristic obedience in children. (One school in Oldham, as I write, is proposing to use *only* ex-military as teachers.) Meanwhile, the UK government is ratcheting up class inequality by removing the Education Maintenance Allowance (which allowed poorer children to stay on at school until they were eighteen) and also by increasing student loans – which are known to disproportionately deter people from poorer backgrounds from getting a university education. Most societies have maintained their intellectual heritage by educating the most gifted children according to their ability, and no tribe except the tribes of modernity has demanded that those children should go into a polite form of bonded labour for it.

Students are taking to the streets in protest. One sixth-former, Rosa, had helped organize demonstrations at school and then went to join the public protests. Her head teacher was furious and, calling their actions 'truancy', he gave three-hour Saturday detentions to younger students and stripped Rosa of her honorary position as a senior pupil, in punishment. 'I was told this was due to being a truant and a bad role model and not implementing the school's voice but my own,' she told me. Of course! Wanting further education and speaking with one's own voice are terrible traits in the young. When all of nature speaks of diversity and difference, of colour, distinction and iridescent originality, Rosa's head teacher is on the side of grey uniformity.

The aim of public education, said H. L. Mencken, writing in *The American Mercury* in 1924, is not 'to fill the young of the species with knowledge and awaken their intelligence . . . Nothing could be further from the truth. The aim . . . is simply to reduce as many individuals as possible to the same safe level, to breed and train a standardized citizenry, to put down dissent and originality. That is its aim in the United States and that is its aim everywhere else.'

No part of the school uniform is more important than the school tie. But what does it mean, this dangling piece of suffocating pointlessness? Ever since people stopped wiping their noses on their cravats, the tie is one piece of attire which speaks a purely symbolic language. What it says is an unfunny pun of tying down.

It may symbolize the chain around the neck of the wage slave. It may symbolize the fetters of imperialism. It may symbolize tying the wearer to their class, to their background ('the old school tie') and tying other people out, the ties that bind. It may symbolize a quasi-military mindset – and indeed the origin of ties was the cravats worn by soldiers from Croatia in the Thirty Years' War.

I can remember first putting on a school tie: it is one of those memories where I can recall exactly where I was and how I felt. I felt like an animal on the alert in the stealthy presence of something predatory and potent. The tie was powerful precisely because it was without function and was therefore a statement. But whose? It was a piece of alien symbolism around my throat, strangling my own voice and speaking with the voice of the school.

The current Conservative education secretary, as well as seeking to draft ex-soldiers into teaching, wants schoolchildren to wear ties. He also wants to see the end of freeform classrooms which encourage cooperation and co-learning and seeks a reversion to the 'regimental format' – children sitting in rows, split apart from each other, the soldier-teacher ranking the class, the 'squadron' of D. H. Lawrence. When children have been asked what they felt about classrooms, many said they disliked the rectangularity and preferred round shapes, explicitly yearning for classrooms in the form of domes – the shape of the human head, naturally leaning to learning.

Children, strangled by ties and regimented by soldiers, are learning a covert curriculum of power relations and normalized militarism. They are learning a right-wing political ethos that hierarchy is inevitable, that obedience, discipline and control are all-important. They are being taught that competition is the basis of education and that test results indicate superiority. In age-based classes and measured by numerical marks, they are learning that classification and measurement are the most important tools of thought.

Measurement has its place, of course, in children's learning: working out how many of them could fit inside a blue whale, for example.

Scaling up from the appetite of one child to find how many cups of pasta they need for twenty. Ranking their knees in order of knobbliness. Calculating how much of the Amazon has been cut down since they were born, or attempting to measure whether the Great Barrier Reef will have been killed before they turn twenty-one.

But from Plato onwards, measurement has been given a significance it does not deserve. It was satirized by Dickens in the figure of Gradgrind, a man 'with a rule and a pair of scales, and the multiplication table always in his pocket, ready to weigh and measure any parcel of human nature, and tell you exactly what it comes to'. Pitifully little life can exist here, *anima* grows pale; the sense of scamper atrophies and the child's unmeasurable soul, wan and unwanted, withdraws.

'School initiates young children into a world where everything can be measured, including their imaginations, and, indeed, man himself,' wrote Ivan Illich in *Deschooling Society*. 'People who have been schooled down to size let unmeasured experience slip out of their hands. To them, what cannot be measured becomes secondary, threatening. They do not have to be robbed of their creativity . . . Once people have the idea schooled into them that values can be produced and measured, they tend to accept all kinds of rankings.' Part of the covert curriculum includes teaching children to notice what is measurable and ignore what is not, which is why the clock is of great importance but time is overlooked. The curriculum takes scant notice of empathy, symbols, intuition, metaphor or significance, and I have never heard of a proper lesson on Jokes.

The surveillance which so bullies today's children has close ties with school history. In France, the Regulations for Boarders at Port-Royal in 1612 stated sinisterly that 'A close watch must be kept on the children . . . this constant supervision should be exercised gently and with a certain trustfulness calculated to make them think one loves them.'

Tagore recalled his school's white walls *staring* like dead eyeballs. Children at school are 'under a cruel eye outworn', wrote Blake, with the typical Romantic sensitivity to their feelings. One horrible invention for use in schools was the Panopticon, a tool of control created by the father of utilitarianism, Jeremy Bentham, whereby all inmates were under continuous observation while the observer, in a central command viewpoint, remained invisible. Like an ancient Panopticon, Plato refers to 'our superintendence' of childhood. In the USA, a chief of education is often called the 'superintendent of schools'. In Britain, the state keeps an eye on the government inspectors who observe the heads who supervise teachers who watch the monitors and senior pupils while everyone has their sights trained on the children. Children hate the power imbalance; they perceive that its purpose is to control and intimidate and, today, the Children's Panopticon is a campaigning website which fights for children's privacy as their human right.

The Panopticon was designed for people in schools, asylums and jails. Commonly and appallingly, children feel like prisoners in school; they make calendars for 'doing time', crossing off days until the holidays and singing songs to count down the jail terms: 'Six more days of schoooool, six more days of sorrow. *Six* days *five* days *four* days *three* days *two* days *one* more day, and we'll be home tomorrow.'

Montaigne described the earliest schools as 'little else but jails for our imprisoned youth'. Monday morning for Tom Sawyer meant 'going into captivity and fetters'. In the 1880s in England, Flora Thompson wrote, 'The hamlet children hated school. It was prison to them, and from the very beginning they counted the years until they would be able to leave.'

William Blake likened school to a cage:

How can the bird that is born for joy
Sit in a cage and sing?

Tagore wrote of 'schools, where children of man are imprisoned' and said that as a child he was 'imprisoned within the stonewalls of lessons'. The walls, the walls. Children loathe their imprisonment, from Tagore to Pink Floyd's *The Wall*, which, in its prowling fury at once bleak and incandescent, was so powerful an influence on my generation.

An adult has more power over a child in a confined space than in an unconfined one, and children, senses on the *qui-vive*, know this. (As do bullying or abusive adults.) Children can bitterly resent their loss of power when they are detained, interned, enclosed indoors, and many respond to being caged as any self-respecting animal does: with a rise in aggression and a wish to escape. What crime of ebullience or offence of exuberance have children committed which is so terrible that they must be in prison? The crime of being young.

The ultimate realization of prison-schools for the young can be found in contemporary America. A Californian schoolgirl dropped some cake in the school canteen and failed to pick up the crumbs. So a school security officer arrested her, breaking her arm in the process. Police – often armed – patrol American schools, ticketing children as young as six for things including shouting. One schoolchild was arrested for throwing paper aeroplanes. In Austin, Texas, a twelve-year-old called Sarah was being bullied by classmates who taunted her, saying she smelt. Upset, she put some perfume on herself. The teacher called the police and Sarah was arrested. Also in Austin, approximately one in thirty schoolchildren was given a criminal citation in 2007–8. Poorer parents often cannot pay the ensuing fines and so, on reaching age seventeen, children are sent to jail for non-payment.

~

I want to make one thing very clear: none of what I say is anti-education. I am writing in defence of wise and deep education, against which children's vitality, self-will and curiosity does not need to mutiny. I loved my education: I did not always love my schooling.

School in the seventies and eighties included shiny squares of hard toilet paper, which worked about as well as using a sheet of glass to wipe your arse. The corridors were painted the colour of gangrene. Woodwork was either mildew-olive or decay-grey. Zest and melody languished in one prefab classroom where a little music seeped dubiously from a festering piano. For a game, as children, we tried to hold our breath driving through tunnels. At secondary school, we tried to hold our breath till we were eighteen.

The school was not without its gems, though, including the gangly, emotional Irish art teacher who told us of the Mock Turtle's education: 'Reeling and Writhing, of course, to begin with, and then the different branches of Arithmetic – Ambition, Distraction, Uglification, and Derision . . . Mystery, ancient and modern, with Seaography . . .' He would shout the entire 'Jabberwocky' and pick arguments with a god he didn't believe in while he tossed out A-grades and fails like an extremophile. My class teacher, who took my writing seriously when I was nine, won my lifelong devotion on the instant. We had a teacher who made the library bright and warm: I think I even remember flowers there, and I certainly remember the exact shelf where I first met and fell in love with Rupert Brooke, and where I was sitting when the headmistress publicly issued a report for me and some pals which said we had a 'cavalier attitude'. Oh, my chevalier, how dear was that word to me, an insult to be treasured. The instant she said it, I was on horseback, riding in the forests of my mind. I have no idea what she said after that. What she saw was disobedience. What she failed to see was a fealty to language and a love affair with literature which would last my whole life. My earlier school reports had included the comments: 'She is a distraction to herself and others,' and 'She must learn to keep her sense of humour under control.' My father, bless the man, read that line and laughed. A lot. I played truant more and more often as I got older, to read and study at home. Somebody once said the reason children don't like going to school is that it interrupts their education, and that was my feeling.

Many artists and writers are at war with formal tuition and often leave school young. Tagore, who left aged thirteen, wrote: 'I was fortunate enough to extricate myself before insensibility set in.' Today, he'd be given Ritalin. 'There is no use in education,' said William Blake. 'Thank God I never was sent to school/To be Flogd into following the Style of a Fool.' Émile Zola got zero for literature and Picasso left school when he was ten, as the only thing he would do was paint. When Eckhart Tolle was thirteen, he abruptly refused to go to school and spent his time reading widely across cultures. 'Thank goodness, my education was neglected; I was never sent to school,' wrote Beatrix Potter. 'It would have rubbed off some of the originality.'

A child may be seen as having eight intelligences: logical, linguistic, cultural, physical, social, personal, moral and spiritual. Schools, says Anthony Seldon, who has popularized this idea, have concentrated on the first two alone, and the failure to engage all the intelligences is linked to high levels of truancy. Schools should be places of 'spiritual delight', and music, arts and 'outdoor challenge' should be seen as essential. 'Soulless, desiccated education damages children for a lifetime. It diminishes their chances of living a life full of meaning, full of love, full of hope.' Without animation, without spirit, without the flute music or the poetry, without soul.

For Tagore, school meant the theft of a child's whole world. 'We rob the child of his earth to teach him Geography, of language to teach him grammar. His hunger is for the Epic, but he is supplied with chronicles of facts and dates . . . Child-nature protests against such calamity with all its power of suffering.' Soulless schooling gives children routines, uniformity and utilitarian thinking, but there are other modes of thought, where wildness dares the child, where spontaneity and unpredictability trips and surprises, where wisdom juggles with certainties.

Children are by nature thirsty to learn but they have rebelled against school for hundreds of years because school is so often antithetical to their human nature, and children say so in every language they possess. Arguably, school inhibits their maturing. Neil Postman argues influentially that the category of 'childhood' arose because of literacy: prior to the advent of the printing press, children were infants until about the age of seven when they had mastered language, and from that moment on they were effectively small adults. But after the coming of print, becoming 'adult' meant becoming competent in reeling and writhing, so schools became necessary and childhood (beyond infancy) came into existence. It has to be added, though, that children of indigenous cultures also receive a complex *oral* education which initiates them into adult society as effectively as children in the Western tradition are initiated into adult knowledge through learning to read.

In the seventeenth century, Ariès shows, there was a current of opinion which regretted the idea of school precisely because it put the brakes on children's development: before widespread schooling, children had to mature earlier, swimming with the adults. It is a point echoed by Black Elk of the Lakota: 'When we were living by the power of the circle in the way we should, boys were men at twelve or thirteen. But now it takes them very much longer to mature.'

Likewise, an 'artificial extension of childhood' is how Dr Robert Epstein describes schooling in his thesis in *Scientific American Mind*: the segregation of children from adults hinders their maturity. So teenagers, 'isolated from adults and wrongly treated like children', will be in revolt, leading to teenage antisocial behaviour. This, argues Epstein, is not normal; if it were, it would happen widely among all cultures, and it doesn't. In a review of research on teenagers in 186 pre-industrial societies, some sixty per cent of those societies had no word for adolescence and teenagers spent almost all their time in the adult world, with very little sign of disturbance and antisocial behaviour. Not only anthropologists but also historians have remarked on this generally peaceful transition to adulthood. From the 1980s, long-term studies across many cultures in work done at Harvard University suggest that Western-style teenage trouble appears soon after the impact of certain Western influences, particularly television and schooling.

Contemporary schooling may also be bad for children in three further ways. First, there is a dishonesty at its heart which tells the child the experience is about learning while in fact it is about the creation of a workforce. Second, the curriculum can so easily be used for propaganda, as children don't have the experience to sift for truths. The third and most modern of the lies is that perhaps one in ten children is told that they are sick and need drugs for the sake of their health, whereas a more honest reason is that it is a novel way to control them: the centuries-old feature of school in a new guise.

Fib the First. Schools are for education. If only it were true. In matters of schooling, Anthony Seldon (among others) identifies the primary objective of governments as 'to produce a workforce', and, noting the long connection between employers and schools, he comments: 'employers do not see schools as developing the whole child but rather as a production line turning out a trained workforce.' Tagore similarly disliked 'subjecting children to a protracted programme of unwanted learning for the sake of remote prospects of employment'.

Fib the Second. The school curriculum can be a form of propaganda both in terms of imperialist history and the corporate colonialism of today. By the time Tagore was born, a colonial system of education was in place in India, creating a class of Brits-by-proxy, brought up studying in English the subjects the British decreed. 'By increasing education and by giving jobs to more and more Indians, the British rule can be made permanent,' the British Parliament was told in 1857.

The ethos of colonialism was writ in large brushstrokes across the lives of nations and in little sharpened pencils across the lives of children. It was anathema to Gandhi, who stated that 'real freedom will come only when we free ourselves of the domination of Western education'. To impose an empire was bad enough, but to insinuate its success into the very minds of its subjugated children was an act of metaphysical arrogance. 'Soap and education are not as sudden as a massacre, but they are more deadly in the long run,' said Mark Twain.

History is the subject which propagandists most want to get their hands on. Today, in Britain, the Conservative education secretary and right-wing historians aim to implement right-wing propaganda in the teaching of history. They state that children should be taught that the 'big story' of the last five hundred years is the triumph of the Western domination of the entire world. The majority of the dominated world would agree with that but view it as a tragedy. 'What is called history at school is . . . nothing but a swindle invented by the schoolmasters,' said Hermann Hesse.

Right-wing historians present history as an inexorable rise to power of one small section of humanity: progress for the few at the expense of the many. In *Lies My Teacher Told Me: Everything Your American History Textbook Got Wrong*, James W. Loewen brilliantly exposes the process of misinformation which suggests it is somehow 'natural' for one group to dominate another, and he analyses the way Native Americans, for example, have been written out of history, even though Hitler took America's efficient extermination of Native Americans as a model for the extermination of Jews and Gypsies. No child is well served by this: neither the children of the winners nor those of the losers, whose perspective is poignantly portrayed by Native American scholar Rupert Costo: 'There is not one Indian in the whole of this country who does not cringe in anguish and frustration because of these textbooks. There is not one Indian child who has not come home in shame and tears.'

Tibetan children in Chinese schools must undergo 'patriotic re-education', in which they are ordered to vilify the Dalai Lama, taught that Tibetan traditions are bad and forced to pledge allegiance to the communist party. In Texas today, the state education board is con-trolled by far-right evangelicals who insist on promoting patriotism and demand that pupils pledge allegiance to the free enterprise system and creationism. In one curriculum amendment the Civil Rights Movement is criticized for creating 'unrealistic expectations of equal outcomes' among minorities. The slave trade is no longer called the slave trade but has been re-baptized with the innocent term the 'Atlan-tic triangular trade'. This, too, is patriotic re-education.

West Papuan children are expected to go to school in a uniform which is red and white, the colours of the flag of the invading Indonesians. They are given compulsory education in Indonesian history, but not Papuan history. If children object, saying that they have their own understanding of history, they are told they will be given a fail in their exams.

'I is for Israel, our enemy; J is for Jihad, our aim in life; K is for Kalashnikov, we will overcome,' writes Åsne Seierstad in *The Bookseller of Kabul*, describing the teaching of children in Afghanistan under the Taliban. The teaching of maths went along these lines: 'Little Omar has a Kalashnikov with three magazines. There are twenty bullets in each magazine. He uses two-thirds of the bullets and kills sixty infidels. How many infidels does he kill with each bullet?' The boys are not learning sums but significance, learning what their society values. Although this may be the starkest example, the principle is the same. History is written on the *tabula rasa* of the child's mind.

Propaganda today includes corporate colonialism. Disliking environmental awareness in schools, companies have begun what Juliet Schor calls 'an expensive propaganda effort to obscure the nature of the environmental problems facing the planet', providing schools with 'shoddy and biased materials that serve commercial interests'. Children, whose very nature is so nested in the green world, who want to protect it so furiously, whose lives ultimately depend on the health of the environment, are fed lies about its well-being.

Fib the Third. This is the lie that cuts to a child's soul, the deceit by which a child is told they are being given drugs for the sake of their health. It's a new version of a very old story: *control the children*. Through surveillance, through discipline and punishment, through prison-like schooling and factory-education, through uniformity and regimentation in classes, schooling has wanted to control the wriggliness of childhood. Children have been immobilized, their exuberance squashed.

'Exuberance' – that lovely word, robust and elastic, a word made of rubber, a word made to bounce – was once considered not just a problem but a sin. *On The Character Fault of Exuberance in Children* is the title of a book published in 1896. 'One of the traits in children that border on abnormality is exuberance,' writes its author, S. Landmann. Play, which for the Romans and Greeks was at the heart of curiosity and learning, was drummed out of childhood by the Victorians. Today, the spirited, fizzing energy bombs at a child's core are being extinguished in an altogether stealthier way: drugs.

'Don't take drugs,' society tells children. Drugs screw you up; they affect your development in unknown ways; you won't know who you really are; they can lead to severe addiction and personality change; drugs can colonize the soul. All of these statements apply to methylphenidate, whose street names include 'mph' and 'kiddie cocaine'. Prescribed for children, it is called Ritalin. Whereas Landmann asserted that exuberance was a character fault, society now calls it a medical disorder: ADHD (Attention Deficit Hyperactivity Disorder).

It is of course true that a very small proportion of children may behave so peculiarly that it would be fair to diagnose them in terms of pathology, but one could argue that children's reported behaviour today is a normal reaction to abnormal experience. Receiving insufficient closeness in infancy, bored at school, over-enclosed as older children and plugged in to dementing 'entertainment' could be designed to madden any child.

One study by the Children's Hospital and Regional Medical Center in Seattle shows that children aged one to three who watch more TV than others will have a dramatically higher incidence of ADHD by the time they are seven, and each additional hour of TV per day increases the likelihood of developing ADHD by ten per cent. Inuit elders say that hyperactivity is a result of being physically separated from mothers in infancy; due to the loss of that physical closeness which children need. Meanwhile not paying attention is a wholly appropriate response to being bored: the boredom which children have experienced in school since Gradgrind.

One could also argue that children haven't changed much but diagnosis has, so 'hyperactivity' may be nothing more than an insulting word for that exuberance, the charging-around rowdy mayhem which children naturally, gleefully, indulge in and which parents have generally dealt with by shovelling children out of the house, into the garden, the street, the park, the woods or the commons. The behaviour now called ADHD has perhaps always existed, but in the past it happened out of sight of adults. As children would be swept outdoors to go wild unsupervised, only coming back indoors when all that crackling energy had been discharged, perhaps adults prior to this generation simply never observed it. Now you see it: then you didn't.

Perhaps the contemporary enclosure of children causes ADHD as, far less free than any generation in history, caged children are bound to explode. As Richard Louv pertinently notes, nature may be useful treatment for ADHD, but: 'If it's true that nature therapy reduces the symptoms of ADHD, then the converse may also be true: ADHD may be a set of symptoms aggravated by lack of exposure to nature. By this line of thinking, many children may benefit from medications, but the real disorder is less in the child than it is in the imposed, artificial environment.'

Black children, boys and working-class children are disproportionately diagnosed. Also, given that people on benefits in the UK may receive extra money if their child is diagnosed with ADHD, it is possible that poorer families want the diagnosis out of understandable financial need. It is also, frighteningly, possible that 'ADHD' may be a grotesque misinterpretation of a child's troubled life. Family psychotherapist and author Jan Parker comments that the kinds of behaviour diagnosed as ADHD are also the kinds of behaviour which may be exhibited by children who have experienced trauma, abuse, emotional neglect or other serious difficulties in their lives. 'The dominance of the ADHD diagnosis in current thinking and practice risks pathologizing some very vulnerable children.'

The vast majority of prescriptions for Ritalin and Ritalin-equivalents are given to children, and up to nine per cent of children in the UK now 'have' ADHD. The rise in diagnosis has been correlated with the rise in marketing from drug companies supplying Ritalin and its equivalents.

But some professionals do not even acknowledge ADHD as a medical condition. Dr Gwynedd Lloyd, education expert at Edinburgh University, comments that ADHD is diagnosed by means of a behavioural checklist which includes: 'Getting out of your seat and running about'. 'Half the kids in a school could qualify under that criterion,' she says. (Only half? I thought that was a feature of being under twelve.) 'Blurting out answers to questions' is another diagnostic criterion, which might trouble anyone who remembers being bright and bored at school. 'Appearing to be on the lookout for any reason to leave their seats' is also on the checklist. This is normal behaviour for all mammals, as is another diagnostic criterion: 'turning towards movement and noise'. A dog-owner who used drugs to stop their puppy turning towards movement and noise, thus preventing it from engaging in natural behaviour, could find themselves on the wrong side of the law. Put in these terms, it is possible that we are indeed seeing an upsurge of a terrible disease – a disease called childhood – but the fact that so many children have contracted child-hood may be a cause for celebration.

Jim Wilson, a consultant systemic psychotherapist, stresses the importance of therapists attending to a child 'as a human being and not an expression of a genetic brain dysfunction. This is a political stance as much as a practical one,' and comments that when it comes to calling children 'different' or 'special', then 'the ADHD label points them towards a medical treatment that, in effect, drugs their specialness into submission instead of finding ways to accommodate, support and humanize practice with them.'

Ritalin is prescribed for fidgeting, yet brain science shows how hand movements are related to thinking and talking; gestures help constitute thought and restricting hand gestures impacts negatively on speech. Babies and young children point while they babble and the child points to name things. We grapple, wrestle and tussle with intellectual problems, we point out truths, grab at straws, grasp ideas and get hold of concepts. Words involving thought processes include 'comprehend' and 'apprehend', from *prehendere*, to catch hold of, seize, while the thought-related words 'intend', 'contend', 'attend' and 'pretend' all stem from the Latin *tendere*, to reach with the hand. The mind handles the world with tender attention, and that word 'tender' shares an Indo-European root with *tendere*.

With four hundred years of sorrow in the words, Loris Malaguzzi, Italy's most brilliant educationalist, wrote:

> *The child has a hundred languages*
> *a hundred hands*
> *a hundred thoughts . . .*
> *. . . but they steal ninety-nine.*
> *The school and the culture*

separate the head from the body.
They tell the child to think without hands.

— *'The Hundred Languages of Children'*

Children, whose linguistic skills have co-evolved with hand-pointing, are told, 'It's rude to point' and they are given Ritalin for something which is part of a child's learning process: fidgeting and pointing, touching the world and being touched by it, feeling and handling it, tickling the world so that it will laugh within the child for the rest of its life.

Philosopher and educator A. N. Whitehead stressed the importance of embodiedness, and the connection of intellect and body which is, he says 'focussed in the eyes, the ears, the voice, and the hands. There is a co-ordination of senses and thought, and also a reciprocal influence between brain activity and material creative activity. In this reaction the hands are peculiarly important. It is a moot point whether the human hand created the human brain, or the brain created the hand.'

And I wasn't joking when I said that today Tagore would be given Ritalin: when he was eleven, he underwent a coming-of-age ritual with his brothers in which, shaved and sent into retreat, they were supposed to chant and meditate. Instead, Rabindranath 'rollicked, beating drums and pulling his brothers' ears'. No one seemed to mind.

There are no reliable figures for how many children under six have been given Ritalin. None. Society, so keen to watch every wretched child picking his nose and saying 'fuck' in front of a fucking CCTV camera, cannot be bothered to record or supervise children being given personality-changing drugs by the state's health service, often at the behest of schools. There are, though, reliable reports of children in nursery and pre-school being prescribed unnecessary Ritalin, often because parents or schools pressurize GPs. The *Guardian* reports the case of a five-year-old receiving a double dose of Ritalin although his school insists he is 'among the best-behaved children in his class'. The medication is prescribed 'to help mum at home'. The educational psychologist on the case said these 'strong psychotropic drugs' were being handed out to children 'like sweets'.

Side effects can include sleeplessness, appetite loss and reduced growth rates, but most worrying is precisely that Ritalin is a psychotropic drug; it turns the spirit – from *tropos*, turn, in Greek, and *psyche*, the Greek word for soul. The drug twists the soul's freewheeling flow, its exuberant abundance, the animated effervescence of the *anima*, the spirit. Some children say it affects their personality. Some say that they feel unreal on medication: the 'real me' is the 'me' not taking drugs. One thirteen-year-old boy drew his life's timeline with a psychotherapist. His graph marked all the years of his life, and the line he drew moved up and down in great detail (some bits good, some bad), except for one part, where it flatlined between the ages of nine and twelve. He called these his 'felt nothing, can't remember much' years, when he was on Ritalin-equivalent medication.

Another boy was six when his school told his mother that he must either take Ritalin or face expulsion. Neither he nor his mother wanted him to take it, but his mother was frightened by the idea of expulsion. They were bullied into it. Now thirteen, he is still on drugs. 'I hate taking it,' he says. 'You just don't feel yourself, you feel so drained out. It makes you feel disgusted and down. Like you've got no soul or something.'

A hollowed child. An unhallowed act. The animating, inspiring breath is gone. It is a kind of soul-theft.

CHAPTER THIRTEEN

Mirrors of the Mind

The train stands stationary at the platform, fresh water gushing from the toilet-tank. In this fountain, the train's cleaner – a grubby little sweep small enough to crawl under the seats and between legs who had, on the train, briefly touched my bare ankle, the 'Mind the Gap' between trousers and sandals, and flashed me a huge white-teeth smile – is taking advantage of the unforeseen shower and is washing uproari-ously in the 'Mind the Gap' between the train and the platform.

Just outside, in the road near Santiniketan, India, a little girl, frilly to the nines in a pink, fluffy dress, rides her father's enormous black Enfield bicycle like a dragonfly piloting a paddle-steamer.

Santiniketan. I have wanted to come here, to this school (and, later, university) campus founded in 1901 by Rabindranath Tagore, since I first heard about it twenty years ago. In direct opposition to the mono-cultural colonial educational system, Santiniketan opened its doors to the cultures of the world. If conventional schooling denied the garden to the child, Tagore made the garden itself the school. If his own schooling had been a deadly experience, he held life as the core of his vision here in the liveliness of the child, the vitality of nature, the living arts and the art of living. As he had felt his boyhood school to be a prison, here at Santiniketan his watchword was freedom.

Freedom glints in many guises in Tagore's writings on education: freedom of language, freedom of imagination, freedom of soul, freedom of personality, freedom of emotions, physical freedom and freedom in time. Tagore's vision would trample all the fences: he was a wreaker of transcendental havoc against the forces of control.

But in this freedom-founded place, which used to be an open complex, there are now twenty-five kilometres of fencing in a one-kilometre area. Barbed wire and angle-fences cut across the grounds. 'It's constricting, binding and against nature,' said one teacher, Rati Basu. The asserted reason for the fences is 'for security' after Tagore's Nobel prize was stolen from the museum. But the prize can't be stolen twice and anyway, in a symbolic sense, it is the Fences which are stealing the real Prize – the priceless freedom Tagore advocated. The object of education, he wrote, is 'freedom of mind, freedom of heart and freedom of will'.

Other thinkers have associated education with freedom, Montaigne for example recalling that 'My father had been advised to make me relish knowledge and duty of my own free will and desire, and to educate me in all gentleness and liberty.' (So sweet-hearted was his father that he would never have the child woken suddenly but only ever by the sound of a musical instrument, 'and always kept a man on hand to render me this service'.) Campaigning journalist William Cobbett gave his children no formal education but left books lying around for them to pick up at will.

I remember classrooms with high windows to block out reverie. As a committed daydreamer, Tagore knew that children need gazing horizons, so the mind can saunter. He didn't make the windows larger: he got rid of the walls. Initiating outdoor classrooms, he also sited buildings around a playground in ways which would encourage conversation as a mutually co-influencing dialogue. In direct protest against the power-positioning of the class in rows under the command of the teacher, Tagore instituted lessons in circles. Remembering the deadliness of his own schooling, Tagore wanted a school where life would flow and be seen to flow, so a student could encounter a cook preparing potatoes, a muralist halfway up a wall, or a philosopher and a scholar in hot debate. You couldn't move for meeting someone.

The physical design reflected Tagore's inclusive philosophy of education. A place 'where the world makes its home in a single nest' is the motto of one of Tagore's institutions, Visva-Bharati, the bird of the world dovetailing with the flight feathers of the mind. He loathed narrowness, be it in narrow classrooms, with narrow windows on narrow horizons, or the narrow corridors of narrow-mindedness. True education happens 'where the world has not been broken up into fragments by narrow domestic walls'.

A. N. Whitehead, a contemporary of Tagore's, sought 'to eradicate the fatal disconnection of subjects which kills the vitality of our modern curriculum. There is only one subject-matter for education, and that is Life in all its manifestations.'

Tagore wrote poetry and songs for his students, many of them honouring the passage of time through the day or the year. Time: not the Clock. For Tagore, deep time was stung to shallowness, nettled by the clock. But today, just as the physical freedom of Santiniketan is fenced and enclosed, so too is its freedom of time: now, there are tightly set timetables, everything is 'confined', says one teacher, to finish *strictly on time*.

Tagore wanted children to mix freely with teachers, learning by being with them. Students were encouraged to read out their own writings on special literary evenings, invited to illustrate and publish magazines, to be close to the many visiting artists and writers, and they had access to the room where Tagore read out his new work.

When a teacher's enthusiasm is transmitted like this, it is impossible to forget. Tagore believed that his true education began after he left school, when he was immersed in the cultural life of his family of mathematicians, novelists, musicians, artists and scientists. In his adolescence, as he writes with lovely liquidity, a 'cascade of musical emotion' flowed through them. 'We wrote, we sang, we acted, we poured ourselves out on every side.'

Art was integral to Tagore's educational philosophy because for him the aesthetic senses needed development as much as the intellect. The word 'art' has roots in the body, linked to *artus* in Latin, meaning the joints and connecting parts, the wrists, elbows, knees and ankles. Art joins and connects ('Only connect! . . . Only connect the prose and the passion, and both will be exalted,' wrote E. M. Forster), and schools which are 'mellowed with the touch of art' will lose their 'rigid discordance with life', wrote Tagore. Art asks differences to speak to each other, it leaps across the Mind the Gap between two concepts, in metaphor, in the carrying-across of an idea. Tagore used a beautiful metaphor for Santiniketan, calling it his tangible poem, the boat which carried the best cargo of his life.

The art teacher, Rati, is deeply in accord with Tagore's vision, teaching her students not only art but a way of life in how she dresses, how she chooses flowers for the classroom. Even in the smallest detail (when they are making collages, she encourages students to tear paper with their fingers rather than to cut it with scissors, because it makes edges softer and more interesting) she encourages the students to be sensitive to the body's senses.

Tagore loathed the puritanism of his schooling, which painted the rainbow in black and white. It was joyless and therefore unnatural. By contrast, young creatures – child, cub or kitten – learn by pleasure. 'The natural mode by which living organisms are excited towards suitable self-development is enjoyment,' wrote Whitehead. Tagore thought of joy as a serious thing, a touchstone for judging whether an experience or an activity was truly worthwhile. This is not about some easy pleasure or jokey levity, but a profound response from the soul.

For Tagore, joy in education was both natural and divine, in tune with the Hindu idea of the world-creator's play of creation, dancing and zestful, with which the playful words for school, *ludus* and *skhole*, share a happy affinity. *Ludus*, the root of 'ludic', means play, and, shocking to Gradgrinds ancient and modern, *ludus* also means school. The word 'school' itself comes from the Greek *skhole*, which means 'leisure', illustrating that, for the Ancient Greeks, anyone with any leisure-time would be eager to learn, to let the mind wander along curiosity-paths. Curiosity behaves like play, taking risks, self-directing, following its nose. The mind at play, the mind at riddle, the mind at jest, is how we learn. The mind is a gleeful acrobat of the abstract noun, a tightrope walker of edgy ideas, a juggler of questions in the circus of the brain. Gradgrind, we recall, forbade his children to go to either circus: the real circus or the circus of the mind.

Children want to learn, but they very sensibly add a rider. They dearly want not to be bored. Teachers have made vast improvements to schooling in Europe and America in the last decades, heroically attempting to give children more interesting and relevant lessons, but some of the reasons for today's widespread discontent among young people – the riddle of this book – must be sought in the role which school plays in their lives.

Schools stress children with exams and tests – including for children under five, in Britain – and by giving them targets and assessments. Too often, mainstream schooling insufficiently acknowledges the themes of child-nature: a freedom of movement, a sense of deep time, reverie, play, self-will and independence. There are, though, philosophies in the margins, including Italy's pioneering Reggio Emilia approach and those of indigenous cultures which emphasize the education of the heart, the world of the senses and of feeling, the ways that the mind learns naturally – in story and metaphor – and the role of nature in education.

~

Nature was at the heart of Tagore's vision. For an entrance hall at Santiniketan, Tagore had an arbour of madhabi creepers; to the east, a grove of mangoes; to the west, palm and jambolen. Trees everywhere. The children's education was as rooted in nature as the trees – which they were free to climb – were rooted in the earth. 'Children have their active sub-conscious mind which, like a tree, has the power to gather its food from the surrounding atmosphere,' wrote Tagore. Nature was part of the below-ground curriculum: what children absorb from their surroundings without overt instruction. Nature was part of the above-ground curriculum, as, down to the tiniest insect, nothing in nature was undeserving of a child's attention.

The Romantic philosophy, which so perfectly comprehended childhood, championed the role of nature in children's education: as Blake depicted the reading child learning in an arbour, so Wordsworth wrote of the knowledge which comes from nature. Tagore made the relationship as real as leaves and as solid as tree-trunks while he also resonated with the transcendentalist aspect of Romanticism, the feeling of oneness with nature which is at the heart of human nature. Children, given half a chance, learn about nature as kin to themselves, unfurling their love outwards into the world.

Both exams and commerce were anathema to Tagore's vision.

When the school expanded into a university in 1921, he declared there would be no exams or conferring of degrees. Today, it is government-funded and exam-based. 'He who pays the piper,' says one man teaching here, tight-lipped. Tagore disliked the promotion of rigid exam-based syllabuses with their eye on commercial viability and he urged not financial commerce but 'a world-wide commerce of heart and mind, sympathy and understanding'.

Sympathy is an important word for Tagore, who also wrote: 'We may become powerful by knowledge, but we attain fullness by sympathy.' But – and his fury singes the page – 'we find that this education of sympathy is not only systematically ignored in schools, but it is severely repressed . . . our life is weaned away from nature and our mind and the world are set in opposition from the beginning of our days.'

When Don C. Talayesva, as a Hopi boy, attended a Western school at the beginning of the twentieth century, he remarked: 'I knew how to sleep on a bed, pray to Jesus, comb my hair . . . I had learned that the world is round instead of flat, that it is indecent to go naked in the presence of girls, and to eat the testes of sheep or goats. I had also learned that a person thinks with his head instead of his heart.' The elliptical sadness of that line tells of a child made lonely in a world of feeling.

In Tagore's philosophy, meaning comes heartfelt, mindfelt, hand-felt. The connection between the hands and the brain noted in the previous chapter is only one aspect of the body's role in intelligence. Only connect the mind and the body and both shall be exalted. A Kiowa child's learning 'is begun only after becoming aware of the mystery of all that is around him, strictly from a feeling point of view', says Kiowa spokesperson Allen Quetone. This is common to all children: to learn feelingly, the mind and the body walking hand in hand. We say 'it makes sense,' meaning that a thought is coherent, as language itself remembers that mind is inheld in the body, skeined into an intricate kinship with the body which is itself catscradled in nature. Thoughts are interlinked in feeling. For feeling is not only a sense of touch but a form of knowing, the psyche dispersed, sensitive in skin, muscle and gut, perceiving the messages of a speaking world: the mind sensitive as the strings of a harp struck softly by an unlying wind, an Aeolian harp with a quality of ceaseless potential music sung into sound with breath, the lightest inspiration of a million, million messages.

As the mind-body sends messages within itself, so the human body is a message-system in a messaging world for earth, too, is lit with mind, mercurial in its myriad inter-relationships; nerve-quickened and fleet. Call it animism, call it the spirit of Mercury or Hermes, call them the angel messengers if you will; to me it is a matter of the embodied truth of metaphor. That we are messengers all, quick to the animated world, electric with meaning and our mercury runs quick-silver in the messagescape.

There is a 'conversation between the world and one's creaturely body', writes David Abram in *Becoming Animal*. He gives permission – politically radical – not only to inhabit and cherish but to *think with* one's body and to appreciate intelligence in the natural world. To small children, he says, awareness is a ubiquitous quality of the world but they are too often taught that this is not true: 'the conviviality between the child and the animate earth is soon severed.'

'Let nature be your first teacher,' said St Bernard of Clairvaux (1090–1153).

My school the earth
My teachers,
The sky, the clouds, the sun, the moon

wrote seventeen-year-old Darrel Daniel St Clair of the Tlingit people.

Tatanga Mani, of the Nakoda or Stoney Nation, writes of 'nature's university, the forests, the rivers, the mountains, and the animals which include us'. Amazonian shamans refer to learning from 'plant teachers'. A plant may be an 'adviser', says Gypsy shaman Patrick Jasper Lee, and Gypsy children are taught to respect plants, for some herbs may advise a person on how best to use other herbs. There are only two teachers of art, said Austrian maverick genius Friedensreich Hundertwasser: 'one is your own childhood, your own self; the other is nature.'

But to take it as far as having outdoor classrooms? There's the rub. I'm one of those people who can feel cold with four thermal vests, two jumpers and a coat, indoors in May. So when I heard about Tagore setting up outdoor classrooms in India, I thought he was lucky with the climate, but you couldn't get away with it in Wales. But then I heard about Tolstoy, who set up outdoor schools in Russia, by Jove – *Russia*.

In the open air, according to Tolstoy, relationships between students and teachers would be 'freer, simpler and more trustful'. Being taught in nature affected children's personalities, thought Tagore, including giving them a greater degree of naturalness, gentleness, grace, self-confidence, poise, self-delight and independent judgement.

'It is necessary to be outside for our brains to be stimulated from the flow of sound, light, shapes and colours that nature provides,' writes David Ingvar, professor of neurophysiology, 'especially between the ages of three and six.' Europe now has Forest Schools, set up in Scandinavian countries from the 1950s. In Denmark, about one in ten schools for three- to seven-year-olds is a Forest School. The children learn about the seasons, including how to stay warm in snow; how to build a snowman; how to identify plants, trees, animals and birds. They learn to respect nature and to be part of it, climbing trees, chattering like birds in the branches.

Studies show that the impacts of Forest Schools on young children include greater self-confidence, independence and self-belief as a result of freedom in time and space. Their awareness is increased and their social skills are improved through sharing and cooperation. A Forest School education leads to more sophisticated written and spoken language and helps children to focus and concentrate, encouraging a positive attitude towards learning. The experience fosters physical stamina and coordination and leads to a respect for the environment and a greater sense of observance and insight into nature. Outdoor education leads to improved cognitive outcomes and long-term gains in terms of attitudes, self-perceptions, interpersonal skills and memory.

What's not to like? And yet in Britain there is no legal obligation for nurseries to have any outdoor play area whatsoever.

In Danish, a Forest School is called a *skovbo*, which means a home in the forest – a nest in the woods. Educating children in nature gives them their deepest dwelling in the nest of the world. Uneducated in nature, though, children are metaphysically homeless, unnested. As adults, we are all teachers for children, with an ecological role to tend the deep nest, the home of the world and the home of the educated mind for, intertwined with the world of fur, feather and twig is the world of metaphor where mind makes its nests.

~

At Santiniketan, Rati Basu's life was split in two when her husband died, very young and very suddenly. The children surrounded her, brought her armfuls of flowers, giving her the shelter of their utterly unprompted – instinctive, spontaneous – love. She has tears in her eyes now as she tells me how much it meant to her, while a student cycles past with a sculpture of a metal person cadging a lift on the back of his bicycle. The affection is clear. Visibly free with their teachers and open-hearted, the children are magnetized towards her, like little fish drawn into warm pools of sunlit water where they bask awhile then melt away.

A good teacher, argued Tagore, becomes one with his students and learns more from them than he teaches. 'A true teacher regards himself as a student of his students.' It seems to me that teachers should be paid more than any other profession (except kite designers, conscientious reporters, artists and musicians of light, human rights lawyers and wise mind-doctors) for teaching is work which demands a genius of rapport. One of France's most successful documentary films, *Être et Avoir* (*To Be and to Have*; 2002), is about a primary-school teacher who embodies all that it means to be a true teacher. In a one-room school in Auvergne, teaching ages four to eleven or so, Georges Lopez is counsellor, referee and architect; parent, audience and cook; nurse, tease and judge; coach, witness, beloved and clown. As a child, Lopez lived in an ordinary village and went to an ordinary school. Then something amazing happened – a destiny fell out of the sky. He knew immediately that he wanted to be a teacher and stayed faithful to that calling. He is a *passeur*, a guide through the mountainous regions of childhood, leading the children out into the world, while he also educes from the children their own intelligence.

There is a happy quarrel to be had over the roots of the word 'education'. Derived from Latin *educare*, to bring up, to rear, with the idea of bringing a child out into the world (the '*e*' suggesting 'from', 'out of'), it is also connected to *e* and *ducere*, to lead, so *educere* is to educe, to draw out, to lead out. Why choose? Why can't they both play nicely together? For good education both leads a child out into the world and educes from the child its own wisdom.

One of my favourite images of education comes from an almost unknown book written by Archbishop Richard Trench, *On the Study of Words*, published in 1864. What is education? the archbishop asks. 'Is the process of education the filling of the child's mind, as a cistern is filled with waters brought in buckets from some other source, or the opening up of its own fountains? . . . Education must educe . . . draw out what is in the child, the immortal spirit which is there, this is the end of education.'

There is a scene in *Être et Avoir* where one small boy, Jojo (who spends much of the film with a finger up his nose educing a delicate thread of snot), is being helped to count. Ten, twenty, fifty, a *hundred*, he gets to triumphantly. Pause. 'And one,' says the teacher, gently. Jojo's face breaks open. 'A hundred and two, a hundred and three . . . a hundred and ten . . . twenty . . . fifty . . . two hundred, five hundred . . . a *thousand*!' Again the triumph. Again the pause. 'And one,' whispers the teacher. Jojo's got it. He can count to infinity and beyond and his eyes are shining. A good teacher is a child-whisperer and like a *Pi* Piper the teacher has drawn out from the child infinity . . . *plus one*.

Education should be 'to educe, to call forth', wrote Coleridge, 'as the blossom is educed from the bud'. When Coleridge wanted an image of education, he chose flowers: for Tagore it was a tree. 'Man is Born like a Garden ready Planted and Sown,' wrote Blake. Metaphors matter: a kindergarten, a child-*garden* or a *nursery* school are sweetly natural, evoking both a nursing mother and plant nurseries where Rousseau's plant, Tagore's tree and Blake's and Coleridge's flowers may all grow. Other terms, though, are odious: think of '*pre*-schools' and '*pre*-paratory schools', suggesting that what matters is what comes later, as if the main characteristic of children is their failure to be older. The framework for under-fives often includes 'school readiness' targets which suggest that the stage they are at is less important than the stage they will reach.

'What are you going to be when you grow up?' adults ask children, as if they are not beings now, as if their childhood is merely a state of insufficient progress to maturity, a lack of adulthood. (So a ten-year-old is an unfinished twenty-year-old. But you could equally argue that the twenty-year-old is an imperfect forty-year-old who is an incomplete eighty-year-old who is an unfinished corpse.) It is what philosopher Gareth B. Matthews, specialist in the philosophy of children, has called a 'deficit conception' of childhood, their simple failure to be older. Rather, he argues, children are better at learning languages than adults, they make art which is more worthwhile and are more likely to have philosophically interesting thoughts than they are as adults.

~

It is spring, 1945. Reggio Emilia in Italy is a town 'rich only in mourning and poverty', says Loris Malaguzzi, he of 'a hundred languages'. People want to make a school for their children and all they have is an army tank, six horses, three trucks and a politics of kindness. Out of these, they create not only a school but, with Malaguzzi's vision, an educational philosophy which has inspired the world.

The Reggio Emilia system is rooted in traditions of civic community and participatory democracy, with children seen as the collective responsibility of the local community in that region of Italy. Unlike the traditional European schools historically modelled on prisons, factories and militarization, Reggio Emilia schools are like extended families, humane communities where children have rights. At one school, a group of five-year-olds articulated some of their rights including children's right to friendship, the right to make mistakes and the right 'to think about flying, to dream'.

Children in the Reggio Emilia system frequently use project-work, often choosing subjects close to home, asking perhaps how pipes work under the city streets, or the process of the grape harvest. The reason for the proximity of the subject matter is that if children study something near to them, they may also be contributors of knowledge and information and, driven by their ideas, enthusiasms and curiosities, children may explore anywhere in the world by starting right where they are. I well remember starting where I wasn't. My first school project was 'France'. I remember a bit of cheese, the Italian flag, some glue which stuck the pages together and feeling very, very lonely. It took about a hundred years.

The Reggio Emilia system encourages a hundred (and one) ways for children to express themselves and children learn through listening, seeing and touching, that hand-craft which the brain cherishes and reflects. Reflection is everywhere, and this is partly literal, with mirrors scattered on floors, ceilings and walls, because the mirrors prompt experimentation, inviting children to take new roles at any moment, to go through a looking glass into other worlds. Partly, though, the sense of reflection is metaphoric, as the teachers reflect back the children's own dialogues and observations to them while, on the walls, children see their work reflected, kept, documented in photographs, pictures and words. Not only does this demonstrate that their work is respected, it also allows them to spiral around their knowledge, becoming familiar with what is new – and coming newly on the familiar – observing and re-observing, representing and re-representing.

The physical environment, which the Reggio Emilia system calls the child's 'third teacher', is washed in light, green with indoor plants and vines. The classrooms open out on to a central courtyard. Each classroom has a door which leads outside, there are windows the size of walls, and openness of communication is the key to the design: classrooms are connected by telephones, passageways and windows. With this interconnecting architecture, luminous, engaging, mirroring, messaging itself, spiralling its knowledge in complex, changing forms, the schools look like the way the mind works best.

A piratical conspiracy links the Reggio Emilia teacher to the children as collaborator. The teachers believe that children want to learn whatever is relevant, interesting and worthy of their attention and that children have the right and duty to speak from their own perspective. Tantrums are not interpreted as anything other than a cry for help; self-understanding is part of the core curriculum. No drugs are given and if certain children are more active than others, their need is accommodated.

One teacher describes the role as being a 'dispenser of occasions'. A teacher may also be a provocateur who complicates a situation, resisting simplicity, temporarily confounding the predictable, ensuring creative confusion so that children can supply the delirious plurality of possible answers. Miss-takes are well-come as they throw open possibilities for better results. Luck, serendipity and opportunity are invited to play. 'To be with children is to work one third with certainty and two thirds with uncertainty and the new,' says Loris Malaguzzi. Teachers allow conflicts between children over ideas and methods, so a group can take stock of its collective wisdom. There is, for children, real delight in planning a complex game, caring little for executing the plan because the planning is itself the game. I know the adult temptation to step in, telling children, 'If you spend so much time *planning* the game you won't have any time to actually *play* it,' forgetting what I knew perfectly well at seven, that being the architect of the game can be more satisfying than laying a single brick.

Give children the outline of a leaf and watch what they turn it into, suggest the teachers. Transformation is all. 'Children have the privilege of not being excessively attached to their own ideas, which they construct and reinvent continuously. They are apt to explore, make discoveries, change their points of view, and fall in love with forms and meanings that transform themselves,' says Malaguzzi. They get fizzy with thought, problem-solving, improvising, symbolizing, and the Reggio Emilia system respects that universal truth of education: children like thinking.

~

Her business card says Camila Batmanghelidjh Suitably Titleless. Her costume is extraordinary. Multi-patterned, multicoloured, every bit of her which could be bedecked is. Around her neck are green and blue scarves and her wrists are wreathed in yellow, orange and pink and she wears a dragon dress of fluorescent yellow, gold, orange, blue, green, everything – trumped by a flowery pink and turquoise turban. She is circus, crazy fireworks and birthday cake all in one. She is carnival and carousel. She is a fairground attraction and she stops you in your tracks. Her get-up announces you have just gone through a portal and entered a world where all the rules change.

Batmanghelidjh is the founder of Kids Company, which aims to improve the lives of thousands of London children who are traumatized, neglected and abused. Kids Company reaches some fourteen thousand children, with a drop-in centre used by almost a thousand kids, eighty per cent of whom have a history of drug use, crime, school exclusion, homelessness and mental or emotional troubles.

At one of the centres there is a sentinel box at the gate, with SECUR-ITY written in coloured buttons. There are flowers painted everywhere and images of nature abound: cherries, a peacock, trees, birds and bluebells. Kids Company has nurses and social workers, people able to deal with issues of housing and immigration, and therapists of many varieties. (Great attention is also paid to the bathrooms, and in one centre there is a room which the kids call the 'Princess Bathroom' where, in a way which abused children will understand, they can practise regarding themselves as beautiful, can try to love their bodies.)

Education is at the heart of the project – education about the brain, about how the mind can be damaged but can learn to heal. A child's brain develops because of the care the child receives, and when a small child is exposed to terror, the brain is damaged, leading to impulsive hyper-vigilance and a damaged sense of self-regulation. This leads to trouble. Jo, now twenty, tells me candidly that when she first came to Kids Company she could be 'a shit – a designer shit'; she'd been imprisoned three times before she was eighteen. At Kids Company, she says, simply, 'I was cared for, no matter what I did.'

Another girl, aged fourteen, says one of the best things about Kids Company is that it encourages the children to get educated. She is a hurt child with a deep kindness about her which shines in spite of both her pain and her shyness. She tells me she wants to become a paediatrician so as to help other kids.

One of the centres has the words 'Education is the key' written on the wall. There are pictures of the brain everywhere and children learn how it works. The carers don't keep clinical records private, says Batmanghelidjh. Everything is shared with the child so that 'they develop psychological thinking and a language. Normally, these children are too traumatized to think.' This is about the restitution of stolen property: the children's minds, stolen from them, are given back through the deep wisdoms of the psyche. They are educated in the subject of themselves.

~

'Every son was taught to be generous to the point of sacrifice, truthful no matter what the cost, and brave to the point of death,' wrote Luther Standing Bear.

At the core of an ideal education are kindness, sensitivity, wisdom, truthfulness, generosity, self-control, self-confidence and physical and moral courage. You'd be hard put to find a parent in the world who wouldn't want that for their child and yet, in formal schooling in Europe, these qualities have long been overlooked. When in 1781 Henry Home (Lord Kames) wrote *Loose Hints upon Education, chiefly concerning the culture of the heart*, he stated that this culture of the heart in childhood should be 'the chief branch of education' specifically because he considered that it was ignored by most writers on the subject.

Many cultures have long held that spirituality and physical prowess are each important, and that courage and courtesy are core to the curriculum of the *cœur*, the heart.

In 1744, commissioners from Maryland and Virginia invited Native Americans from the Six Nations to send boys to William and Mary College. The invitation was declined, thus:

> But you, who are wise, must know that different Nations have differ-
> ent Conceptions of things and you will therefore not take it amiss, if
> our Ideas of this kind of Education happen not to be the same as
> yours. We have had some Experience of it. Several of our young
> People were formerly brought up at the Colleges of the Northern

Provinces: they were instructed in all your Sciences; but, when they came back to us, they were bad Runners, ignorant of every means of living in the woods . . . neither fit for Hunters, Warriors, nor Counsellors, they were totally good for nothing. We are, however, not the less oblig'd by your kind Offer, tho' we decline accepting it; and, to show our grateful Sense of it, if the Gentlemen of Virginia will send us a Dozen of their Sons, we will take Care of their Education, instruct them in all we know, and make Men of them.

Indigenous cultures obviously don't educate children in exactly the same ways, yet it seems there are widespread common attitudes which acknowledge the importance of nature, the strength of the body and the education of the heart, often through story. Living close to nature, children may well need to be on speaking terms with endurance. Many Native American memoirs include descriptions of deliberately contrived inflictions of pain, not to humiliate or to punish a child but to encourage bravery and fortitude. Aspects of education were 'harsh and hard to take', says a Nitinaht man, John Thomas, recalling being hit with a switch and thrown into a cold river, instructed never to cry out no matter the pain. His uncle taught him the prayers which would accompany those river plunges, secret prayers kept within families which were intended to 'purify our bodies and minds at the same time'.

In many societies, boys have been told stories of heroism till the words shone, Homeric and golden. The courage of their ancestors, the glory, the honour and the rewards of bravery were held up to them until 'the youth take fire at these recitals, and sigh for an opportunity of imitating what they have thus been made to admire,' wrote Pierre de Charlevoix.

Every society seems to use stories for the education of the heart. Each story is a store of ripened knowledge in the oldest barns of human culture. Myths, ripened in October, are the apples of the mind, carefully laid out to preserve their meanings. In the soft darkness of the storehouses, close your ordinary eyes to the ordinary world and open your extraordinary eyes to the extraordinary world, best illuminated by the grandparent voice in the autumn years telling tales in the dark, the dark of evening and the fertile dark of the mind. There, in potent story-warmth, the subconscious breathes in the texture, significance and meaning of the story like quietness steeped in the smell of apples.

It is the role of older Ngarinyin men in Australia to educate through stories, through dance, body-painting and ceremony, introducing the child to that potent imaginative world. In the Amazon, people told me how stories would encode spiritual, ethical, historical, political and ecological information. In Montana, Salish educator Julie Cajune spoke of stories as teaching survival skills: physical, social and emotional, adding that the skills of how to be a good human being were more important now than ever.

The word 'listen' is often used to begin a story. Every story needs a storyteller and a story-listener, because while the one offers the necessary words, the other gives the necessary silence. Children were traditionally taught to pay similar attention to the land, 'to listen intently when all seemingly was quiet', in the words of Luther Standing Bear. Listening lets the outer world be re-created within you. Listening means being willing to let one's borders be porous. Listening does what light does for a seed, asking it to swing upwards into life and giving it a reason to do so. 'Listen, and you will hear the patterns of life. Are they the same, or is there a change in the sounds?' is how the Ojibwa storyteller Ignatia Broker describes an early lesson for a child, adding that children were encouraged to listen to an older person before they spoke themselves. Inuit people were happier with children who took their time learning to talk because listening was the skill which children needed to learn fast: speaking could wait.

To get the attention of a child, you can shout 'Shut up!' or you can say 'Listen!' When children want other children to hear them, they normally say 'Listen!' And it normally works. Moreover, there is a different quality of attention given in response: 'Shut up!' may provoke resentful attention while 'Listen!' may invite an unguarded curiosity. Demanding someone's silence is one thing: offering your own is another. I remember disliking – to the point of fury – silence being imposed on us, but being spellbound by self-willed silence, breathing in silver air, mirrored as water.

'Silence, love, reverence – this is the trinity of first lessons,' says Charles Eastman, on the trivium of the Native American Ohiyesa people. Silence is 'the sign of a perfect equilibrium. Silence is the absolute poise or balance of body, mind and spirit.'

If silence is revered, words are honoured. From the moment children begin to speak, they are taught to respect speech, 'how to use the word and how not to use it,' says Henry Old Coyote (Crow.) 'The word is all-powerful, because it can build a man up, but it can also tear him down. That's how powerful it is. So a child is taught to use words tenderly and never against anyone.'

I would draw no particular distinctions between any cultures in the implicit wish that children learn tenderness and truthfulness, these hand-held words on which the human heart relies. There have been, though, differences in the explicit aims of different educations: indigenous cultures overtly emphasize the importance of helpfulness and consideration while formal education in the dominant culture has too readily ignored those aims.

Since both giving and grasping seem to come easily to children, part of an indigenous child's education involves generosity. Inuit children were taught not to be stingy about anything, especially food. 'As a child I understood how to give; I have forgotten that grace since I became civilized,' wrote Charles Eastman (Ohiyesa). 'It was our belief that the love of possessions is a weakness to be overcome . . . it will in time disturb the spiritual balance of the man. Therefore the child must early learn the beauty of generosity . . . If a child is inclined to be grasping . . . legends are related to him, telling of the contempt and disgrace falling upon the ungenerous and mean man.'

Lakota children, told that nothing is too good to give away and encouraged to share, would often invite passers-by into their family tipi, whereupon their mother would have to prepare food for the guest immediately, because 'to ignore the child's courtesy would be unpardonable', writes Luther Standing Bear. Children of the South Dakotans, even from poor families, were encouraged to make ceremonial gifts, in order to build up a sense of their ideal selves, their truest identity, practising honour. Adults would repeatedly single out selfishness and competitiveness as misbehaviour.

In the dominant culture, something odd happens. Children are told that winning isn't everything, that it's wrong to be selfish and greedy and that it is good to give. Yet at the same time, wider society encourages competition, materialism and unshared wealth. Children aren't stupid: they get the message that society is hypocritical and that much of what adults say about the supposed wrongness of selfishness and greed is just vapid nonsense so they ignore it and ratchet up their demand for more pocket money.

Here are some things you never need to teach a child. Number one: it's not fair. The concept of fairness would be devilishly tricky to teach a child if a child did not have a ready sense of justice. There are many more. You never need to teach a child what magic means and you never need – and cannot – teach a child to daydream or to giggle.

You never need to teach a child metaphor – and I'll be coming back to that. Intriguingly, it seems, you never need to teach a child empathy for, from early infancy, children replay other people's actions and re-feel emotions through mirror neurons, so they can only be *untaught* empathy. And you never need to teach a child a ready love of nature.

'The old Lakota was wise. He knew that man's heart away from nature becomes hard; he knew that lack of respect for growing, living things soon led to lack of respect for humans too. So he kept his youth close to its softening influence,' wrote Luther Standing Bear, who was born in 1868 and died in 1939. Across the ocean, and in a lifespan almost exactly the same (1867–1935), the Irish mystic 'A. E.' wrote of the Celts, the indigenous British, for whom: 'legends and faery tales have connected his soul with the inner lives of air and water and earth, and they in turn have kept his heart sweet with hidden influence.'

Courtesy towards nature is part of the curriculum for many cultures and so, for example, children among the Nitinaht people may learn the spiritual lesson of how to speak to a tree before cutting it down, treating it 'like a person coming home'. Inuit people would teach children never to abuse or mistreat an animal, because those who did so would start to lose their ability to hear birds. *Qaqiliktuq* is the word. That there exists a word especially for 'losing the ability to hear birds' is an exquisite thing. Perhaps if an entire culture routinely mistreats nature, it may lose its collective ability to hear the birds. For such a society, a silent spring.

Part of children's education, in virtually every culture in the world, has been to allow them to feel reverence for an endlessly reverable world, to perceive the transcendence, the immanent divinity every-where, be it an idea of God or the Dreaming or the Great Mystery or the Great Mother or the incipient spiritedness of animism. When Anthony Seldon drew attention to the education of a child's spiritual intelligence you could feel the rarity today of this ancient wisdom: the shock of the old.

Pray while walking, George Louis, an Ahousaht man from British Columbia, was told by his grandmother. Go alone and unseen, maybe for four days or eight days. And then, she said (and at this point I imagine a little smile of spiritual thrift playing around her face), stay home for a while and don't go into other homes, 'because if you did, all your blessings went to the other person's house and you lost that.'

Amazonian children may well take ayahuasca, one of the 'plant teachers', for the health of body and spirit. It is part of their education, the plant itself a metaphoric teacher, understood to guide the mind from within to find its own wisest intuitions. But the Peruvian state is sending into the forest an army of literal teachers, believers in lit-eralist fundamentalism, wholly opposed to that metaphoric world. The teachers tell the children not to take ayahuasca and embarrass them until they grow ashamed of their beliefs and practices and move into an emptier, harder, shallower and more brittle world. When these literalist Christian teachers mock the traditional religion, the children find their rituals undermined. One Ashaninka man, Jaime, from the Peruvian Amazon, says they teach children that their visions are 'something to be feared', and although in the past children were not frightened by the experience, now they become so. It is a widespread policy: Theodore Zeldin notes how missionaries use children, sys-tematically turning them against their parents' beliefs and humiliating the fathers in front of the children.

Attending to metaphor, to the spirit, the body and the arts are all important in a child's education. So too (and I hope this is obvious) is literacy. I've never heard a finer description of its magic than that reported by Assiniboine chief Dan Kennedy (Ochankugahe) describ-ing an elder talking of 'the magic art of writing . . . Without the aid of a spoken word our children will transmit their thoughts on a piece of paper, and that talking paper may be carried to distant parts of the country and convey your thoughts to your friends. Why even the medicine men of our tribe cannot perform such miracles!'

Of all educations I have come across, the most extraordinary is the training of the *Mamas*, the spiritual leaders of the Kogi people in Colombia. As an infant, a specially chosen boy is taken from his mother, shut in a cave in the dark, alone, with just enough light to avoid blindness and just enough food to live. For nine years, as film-maker Alan Ereira reports, the child lives in the dark and is informed about the world, the sky, the birds – but does not see them. For nine years, he lives only in a world of imagination for, in his work as a *Mama*, he will work in the world visible only in the mind. The Kogi, profoundly spiritual, see their role as the 'Elder Brothers', with the white race the reckless 'Younger Brothers'. The job of the Kogi *Mamas* is to care for and sustain the world through their spirituality. Nothing less.

It is hard from a Western perspective not to view the treatment of these Kogi boys with ambivalence, because that individual child must pay a great price in coins of loneliness and hardship. It is easy to see – with the literal mind – what the boy does not have: play, companionship, mothering and sunshine. It is harder to see what he does have: the entire world of metaphor, meaning and spirit which is illuminated in the darkness of the cave, the shadow-side which matters to the world beyond compare.

The Kogi child in the cave is encouraged to live in the fertile dark of the mind, the brain cave where imagination shines brighter than reality. He lives in the twilight world of intuition, shadow-languaged. His mind dwells at the edge of night and meaning, where he hears the voice of metaphor alone, resonant, shapeshifting, in a nine-year-long witching hour. Alone, his mind creates worlds in the dark, as the mind of the Great Mother did, in creating Earth. There are two worlds: the actual world and the world of the mind, and he is a voyager in the second, a discoverer of worlds within worlds. Told of a world he doesn't see, he 'sees' through language and imagination, a seer in the invisible world. Imagination becomes his primary reality and actuality comes second. So from nothing he creates in his mind a microcosm of the whole world. All that there is, to begin with, is a black sea shuddering in its depths, waiting for sunlight. If Wordsworth was right that children come into the world trailing clouds of glory, then for the young Kogi boy, in the dark of the cave, the radiance of mind shines ever brighter, a chiaroscuro of reversal, until he is brought out into the world, dazzled by the mind of the Great Mother so surpassing his own guesses and dreams that he is awestruck for ever.

Children are willingly mesmerized fascinatees. They want to be 'e-ducated', led out into the world by the Pied Pipers of the mind, and many of the things which appeal to children are in fact mirrors of the mind. A pirate plundering a ship's chest, a clown making mistakes, an explorer going into the unknown, a detective, a spy, a firework-maker or a lock-picker are all metaphors for learning. Children delight in following threads and pieces of string, tying and untying knots, gluing and ungluing, investigating, experimenting, acting, disguising, masking, dressing up, transforming, firelighting, tending seeds, drawing, wriggling, catching things thrown to them and dreaming of flying. Again, all of these are images of the thinking mind.

'Let's pretend!', 'I've got an idea', 'I remember', 'I know' and 'Did you know?' swell with children's intoxication at thought itself. Children are galvanized by curiosity – Why? is the question which really appeals to them, although it is a subtler, deeper question than its cohorts. Children are metaphysicians of why before they are pragmatists of how? what? where? and when? Why? is the ultramarine question, it comes from across the sea. Why? And the why? before that. (A friend of mine, comically exasperated by a child's unstoppable whys, eventually came to his final answer and said with an angelic smile: 'The Big Bang.')

Children relish both rituals and surprises, both short cuts and digressions (their own more than other people's). They are captivated by paths through forests; journeys and voyages; spirals, labyrinths, mazes and being amazed. They are gleestruck by the mind-leaps of jokes; spells, stories, secrets, clues and riddles. They cherish keys and passwords, things which shine with significance. They love wit and serendipitous findings. Games of hide and seek, treasure hunts, questions and quests all enrapture them, because they are on a quest themselves.

CHAPTER FOURTEEN

The Woods and the Quest

Zurrumurru – whisper, in the Basque language – *hush!* Step from the ordinary noise of the tilled fields or the busy streets into the quiet of the woods. Step across the boundary and the trespass of story will begin. The forest takes a deep breath and through its whispering leaves an incipient adventure unfurls. The quest.

In the lull – not the drowsy lull of a lullaby but the *sotto voce* of a woodland clearing, scented with story as it is with wild garlic – this is the moment of beginning, the pause on the threshold before the journey. So many tales begin here, hard by a great forest.

Gypsy fairy tales are located in the enchanted woodlands, 'the place where all the fairy-tale spirits reside, where the imagination is respected, where there is no prejudice, no ownership, no geography and no time,' writes Patrick Jasper Lee. It is possible that our fairy tales are the codes of Gypsy shamanism coming, as many of the stories did, from India and Persia to Europe, and adding their magic to the already enchanted woodland of Britain. It is certain that the Gypsies, ever on the road, have contributed to the long cultural memory of the quest. One king of the Gypsies in Wales was said to be Abram Wood who, wooded by name and wooded by nature, told stories of the forests, now retold to the children of Wales by the breathtaking storyteller Daniel Morden.

Children go to the woods when they need to think about their own stories in their own lives. Tom Sawyer, upset after a quarrel, 'entered a dense wood, picked his pathless way to the centre of it, and sat down on a mossy spot under a spreading oak', with that instinct children have about thinking under – or in – oak trees. American author Howard Thurman describes a 'unique relationship' he had with an oak tree as a child: 'I could reach down in the quiet places of my spirit, take out my bruises and my joys, unfold them and talk about them. I could talk aloud to the oak tree and know that I was understood.'

In his often very unhappy childhood, the poet John Burnside would spend hours in the woods looking for angels. There, 'another life began . . . when the perfect moment came, it would take hold of your spirit.'

As a child, Jean Liedloff found a glade and walked 'as though into a magical or holy place, to the center'. There she lay with her cheek on moss. 'It Is here,' she thought. 'I felt I had discovered the missing center of things, the key to rightness itself.'

Children need the woods for their spirits to thrive. A woodland gives children a trustworthy tranquillity; it 'calms' the mind, in John Clare's term. Like many children, Clare had an emotional attachment to certain trees. 'We felt thy kind protection like a friend,' he wrote to an elm which was later felled for the Enclosures, in which fell act, he writes, 'our friendship was betrayed.'

A friend of mine was asked, together with his classmates, to plant a tree each in the schoolyard, and though he did not love the school, the tree was like a friend and he tended it for two years. Suddenly, without warning, the school ripped out the trees and tarmacked over the ground for a car park. He was upset, bitterly betrayed.

Tagore, as a child, befriended a banyan tree, his eyes drawn to the shadow-play in its aerial roots coiling and stretching in green leaf-light which played on the child's imagination: 'It seemed as if into this mysterious region . . . some old-world dream-land had escaped the divine vigilance and lingered on.' Tagore's friendship with the tree endured. He kept a tryst with the tree all his life, writing to it when he was an adult. Children trust the trees which they befriend and find in trees something as solid, enduring, as rooted as truth. Trees stand for the deep truths of the psyche which language knows. The words 'tree', 'endure', 'tryst', 'trust' and 'truth' are all related, sharing a common root in Indo-European languages.

Many spiritual traditions have long known that trees are good to think with. The Buddha meditated under a tree and there are many cultural versions of the 'tree of knowledge'. Children have instinctively gone to the woods to reflect, to mull things over, yet many children today are denied that solid witness of trees which children attest helps them psychologically. So common is a child's love for trees, so common a memory in later life, so common the friendship, the consolation and the calm, that its absence is shocking. In the nineties, at a woodland project for children in London, forty children aged seven and eight arrived one morning for a visit. Only two out of the forty had ever been to a woodland before. There should be a word for this lack – a woodless child, as one speaks of a fatherless child, a homeless or a friendless child. They may live too far from a woodland to get there easily, they may be literally fenced out in woodland privatization, they may be scared off by bogus bogeyman tales, they may worry that they wouldn't know what to do without artificial toys and, so often, they don't have the time, those long aerial afternoons of coiling hours and stretching days which, like Tagore's banyan tree, escape the benign vigilance of parents and linger on.

Whatever the reasons, an unwooded childhood is bleak. This, to me, is another part of an answer to the riddle of childhood today.

Children are being given medication for the sorrows of the psyche in greatly increasing numbers and yet at the same time they are denied the soul medicine which has always cared for children's spirits: the woods.

When utilitarian capitalism looks at the forests, it sees the raw material of timber. But there are raw materials of a child's soul, including reverie, magic, time, transformation, destiny and identity, and the greenwood is a dreamwood for the mind at play. In T. H. White's novel *The Sword in the Stone* the child King Arthur is educated by Athene (wisdom) into the time of the forest and he dreams the thoughts and conversations of trees. The raw material of time grows here as the Wild Wood of the British imagination grew at the end of the Ice Age. It is ancient and long gone yet it is evergreen in memory. In the forests there is an abeyance of clock-time, a freedom outside time. Elsewhere in the lucky literature of childhood, wood is the raw material of magic, so the wardrobe through which the children reach Narnia is made from wood from an apple tree which itself grew out of an apple pip from Narnia.

In the woods is the raw material of transformation so necessary to the quest. The questing heroes of medieval romances, including Tristan and Lancelot, became outlaws, wild men of the woods, before they transformed again into knights of the castle.

Children often find things in the woods which become talismanic, augmented by the forest's ability to magnify meaning. Perhaps the most important thing for them to find is their own destinies, and children, in fairy-tale terms, begin the quest hard by a great forest, in imagination if not reality.

T. H. White's Arthur is sent to the forest to seek his identity; many children find woodlands the right place to go to talk to themselves, to dream themselves into a different being, to effect their changeling masquerades away from the eyes of adults. For under the gaze of others, a child can be forced to hold one form, to keep a single identity, but in woodshade and tree-shadow, a child's spirit can stretch, alter and change: it is always easier to change your self in the dark.

Children may also identify with trees and sometimes this identification is embodied in rituals like that of the Karen people in Northern Thailand and Burma, who leave a newborn baby's placenta in the crook of a tree branch, symbolizing how the child's well-being is intimately related to that of the tree. When the child can walk, the father introduces the child to their 'life tree' to teach the child to care for it and, by extension, to respect the forests. There are widespread traditions of planting a tree at the birth of a child, from Native American to Pacific Islander to European custom, with the hope that as the tree grows strong so will the child. One of my brothers, as if in an unconscious understanding of this, planted an acorn when he was young and for several years raced against the sapling in height. The tree still grows, I think, in his mind.

In the forest, the child. Inside the child, the forest. Dwelling well within themselves, children can right wrong turns, can find the clarity of a clearing in the woods. Breathe deeply enough the scents of pine, mushroom, moss and beech mast and they will stay with you: listen to the forest attentively enough in childhood and the blackbird will still be singing seventy years on.

To be 'grounded' and 'well rooted', to be able to 'stand firm' or 'stand one's ground' and also to 'branch out' and to be as resilient as the willow's lovely sprung strength: terms of psychological health can seem like descriptions of trees. (The word 'resilient' is related to the Latin word for willow, *salix*.) The woods are the place for the unfolding of mind in a child, like a fiddlehead fern unfurling in spring, a green mind sprung with resilience, curiosity and story.

The woods, where the stories start, may be profoundly ambivalent and, like many children, I found them magnetic, fearsome and unpredictable. It was like being within another mind, a green and changeable psyche where delight could turn quicksilver into fear as one flick of wind turns aspen leaves around, from the green happy-side-up to the grey dark-side-out. The forest is a sleight-of-hand magician and, with a myriad tricks of the light, things appear and disappear. In a lilac-scented twilight, it can be impossible to locate the flowers. Woodcalls of the animals are hard to pinpoint. Everything jumps from jewelled presence to camouflaged absence in a flash. Everything is in on the act of trickery, both to protect itself from predators and to help it hunt its prey.

When trees writhe into life before night or storm, when they howl and stretch, when their branches twist into arms and their twigs turn into claws, when their stumps become yawning hollows like lurking skulls, children know what Mole felt: the 'Terror of the Wild Wood'. There was nothing to alarm him at first. Then the funguses began to resemble caricatures. 'Then the faces began . . . then the whistling began . . . then the pattering began . . . in panic he began to run too.'

'Panic' is *le mot juste*. In its root it refers to the feral fear of Pan, but it also suggests something of the thrill of danger which children court and the awe, also, of the woods. What is familiar becomes unfamiliar. What might pass as ordinary elsewhere can become potent in the woods. Encounters in the woods are polarized – the kindness of an animal-helper, or the deceitfulness of a troll. But if a child has adult company, the magic of the woodlands is reduced because adults can lessen both the depth of mystery and the need for courage, for one of the lessons of the forest is how to journey through it alone, lonely, perhaps, but learning to rely on oneself and leaning on the friendship of trees. Hansel and Gretel, whose father is a poor woodcutter living 'hard by a great forest', are abandoned deep in the woods and, in a theme common to fairy tales, must use their own ingenuity to survive.

Folk tales (mirroring the experience of the psyche) often begin with a child abandoned in the woods because the parents are too poor, or too mean, to feed them. This has a metaphorical truth for all children, suggesting that no parents are in themselves enough to feed the mind of a child, who must learn to drink from other wells, whose mind must be fed by a wider world, travelling far and farther than far to do so.

The forests represent lostness and confusion, and when the Ash Lad, the Norwegian folk hero, was in the deep forest, he 'did not know where he was nor where he was going . . . and thought the forest would never come to an end'. The forests, however, also suggest that lostness can be positive, that bewilderment can be fertile, that even in lostness there are threads of possible paths, implicit promises of plurality. Being lost in a great forest is 'an ancient symbol for the need to find oneself', remarks Bruno Bettelheim. Being lost opens a person to the need to see things differently, to make new connections, to seek directions, both physical and psychological.

When the Ash Lad is lost in the forest on his search for Soria Moria Castle, he needs to ask his way, so he finds a poor old couple. ('Their hair looked like grey moss, and the woman's nose was so long that she sat by the hearth and used it to rake the coals with.') They do not know the way, but the old woman asks the Moon and the West Wind who take the boy there. Being lost in your thoughts allows you to enter the mind's forests, the story suggests, where the West Wind within can blow you somewhere sought and as yet unfound. Just at the point where you are lost in the thickest thickets, tongue-twisted ivy in snagging brambles tangling around you, the path can open – inside. The way out can be the way within. The child not only enters the forest but *is entered by* the forest. Moreover, she or he is also entered by the different ways of knowing which the forest contains: the advice of the old couple, the help of the Moon or the West Wind.

In confusion, shadow-language can speak. Opaqueness can also be dense with opportunity, shining all the brighter in the dark like a bird leaving a turquoise feather on the path. In the uncertainty, a child's observation is sharpened: *Notice the feather!* the stories say; *Stay alert!* For lostness is itself a kind of latency, holding within it many possibilities. The dark woods rustle with immanence. All the oak-to-be is compressed within the acorn; all the autumn already inheld in spring. Children, too, elastic with incipience, share the latency of leaves in spring, drinking sunlight till they are ready to roll out the barrels of summer.

Maturing – whether of whisky or child – is not an act but a process. It needs the extensive time of the woods. The journey will be elliptical and enigmatic, with as many differences of meaning as there are wood-shades of green or children to count them, but the quest is one of psyche-survival above all: in transformation, change and disguise, in order to find one's path through life.

~

When John Clare's elm, befriended in his childhood, was felled for enclosure, the tree speaks a 'Language of pity and the force of wrong'; it 'speaks home to truth', writes Clare, as if tree and truth were not only etymologically but ethically related. When a tree is cut down for private profit, children can be griefstricken, feeling that an immoral act has taken place. Many of the anti-road protesters in the 1990s in Britain, living in treehouses to protect woodlands, recalled a sense of outrage and distress when, as children, they saw trees destroyed. Recently, a nine-year-old boy, Felix Finkbeiner, began a tree-planting project and took his campaign to the United Nations, reproaching adults for their treatment of the world's forest commons.

Star witness in the ethical courts of childhood is Robin Hood, associated with the Greenwood and with Sherwood Forest. John Clare wrote Robin Hood into the very landscape as someone who stood, a moral outlaw like the trees themselves, opposed to Enclosure. I have never met a child who disputes Robin Hood's morality: he is 'noble', as Tom Sawyer says. Robbing the rich to give to the poor is his most famous policy, but he also personifies one of the most important social codes: the idea of the forest commons. It is possible that there was a historical Robin Hood who dwelled in the forests at the time of two charters: the Magna Carta and the lesser-known Charter of the Forests, which laid out the rights of commoning, including grazing and gleaning. It is certain, though, that whether or not there was any historical figure, Robin Hood symbolized the commoners' rights, and in his honour the Robin Hood games were held on Whitsunday, taking place wherever the woodlands provided commoning rights.

The Romantics, including Keats, Scott and Thomas Love Peacock (what a name with which to strut life's stage!), in a further example of their uncannily precise mirroring of children's values, were drawn to Robin Hood, appreciating, as children do, his mixture of the revolutionary and the reactionary. Icon of today's Romantics, Subcomandante Marcos, heroic freedom fighter in the Fourth World War – for humans against money – writes to children and to 'the child we all have inside' because he appeals to the justice of liberty, equality and fraternity which children readily feel. A real-life Robin Hood, he is also hooded in a ski-mask; no one knows his true identity, only that he fights for indigenous rights, for the defence of nature and childhood.

I remember when I first came across Robin Hood, in my elder brother's bedroom, when I picked up a book he was reading. I felt unmistakeably that I already knew Robin Hood, had in fact always known him but had only been waiting to be introduced. Puck, too, or the Green Man, seem to mirror the spirit of the woods so well that a child may only have to know the woods to know the characters. They survive in the wild dreamwood of childhood. Without the woods, they cannot. Rudyard Kipling's Puck, in *Puck of Pook's Hill*, says that he came to Old England with the trees 'with Oak, Ash and Thorn' and he will only leave with them. The flip side of that is he *will* leave *when* they are felled. Cut down the trees and lose the imagination of a nation. Somehow these characters – Puck, Robin Hood, the Green Man, the Wild Man of the Woods – all have a forest ethic surrounding them, to protect the woodlands.

Kipling also offered children a glimpse of a jungle ethic, just when it was being destroyed. In India, the British initiated the first Forest Act of 1865, which aimed at the 'extinction of customary rights', i.e. commoning. The Forest Act of 1878 then managed to destroy the forest commons. So terrible were the effects for forest commoners of India that the indigenous Dang people felt that time itself had been split apart, axed like a tree by these acts into two epochs. After the acts was the time of tax collectors, land demarcation and forest guards. The time before that, though, was characterized by freedom, by rights of hunting, gleaning and gathering. This time was called *moglai*.

Mowgli.

It was the inspiration for *The Jungle Book*, published in magazines in 1893–4, illustrating the ecocratic world where animals were prismatic in their differences but quintessentially free, the wolfpack describing itself as the 'Free People', while all the creatures honour the 'law of the jungle', a law of sharing which was opposed to accumulation and meanness, a forest ethic based on the jungle commons where children can draw on the food of the pack. Kipling seemed to honour the forest ethic which children instinctively support, even as he was himself part of the imperialist process which destroyed that ethic and brought the age of *moglai* to an end. In a similar way, in mid-nineteenth-century Europe, the Brothers Grimm were immortalizing the psychological importance of the forest to a child's mind at the very moment when access and commoning rights were forbidden.

Collecting kindling was one of the traditional rights of the commons, and gleaning another, as people picked up what they could after the harvest. Children have gleaners' rights in the woodlands of the psyche, finding in real woods kindling for the kind of metaphorical fire from which a phoenix can arise. For their inner world can have the intense immensity of trees, and when that immensity is mirrored in real woods in childhood it is easier for the psyche to understand its own interior forests.

With today's forest privatizations and the enclosures of indoor entertainment, what happens to the customary and common rights of children to go to the forest to collect stories, to find destinies, to discover ways through their own thickets? Children are robbed of woods without and worlds within. Denied their role as part of the wildlife, TRESPASSERS WILL hangs over the stories of childhood and, without those woods, something in the psyche goes awry.

Adventures in the forests are cloaked in disguise, hooded in a canopy of leaves, like Robin Hood – a hoodie – who is hooded by name and hooded for disguise. 'Robin' means a little robe, and he is robed in green, not to be seen. Children need the woods to hide in, disguised and pretending to be who they secretly know they are. If children can't pretend, they are condemned to someone else's reality.

Like many seedlings and saplings, children need shade, hoods and canopies. Denied it, they will reformulate their own. Thus hoodies in shades, stalking the out-of-bounds and adopting disguises in their unwillingness to be identified, seem to re-create something to answer their need, covering their heads and disguising themselves – in hoodies and sunglasses – from the glare of too much sun, from too much surveillance and the glares of disapproving adults.

Language suggests young people's perennial need for forests. A hood is a gangster, and a hoodie is the cub version. In the hooded and hidden way that the human psyche works, young people with no access to the hooded, shaded woods, no opportunity to play at being Robin Hood, no chance to shelter in the green canopies, disguising and pretending, may end up fighting *turf* wars, in the urban *jungle*, in *outlaw* activity. The encounters of the woods mutate into the aggressive encounters engineered by street gangs. While children can initiate themselves in the real woods and, crucially, return to their community, gang rituals offer rites of initiation, but they never end; the child seldom returns home. The attraction of both is similar and the mystique and subterfuge of street gangs may be seen as a distorted mirror of the woodland sense of mystery and latency.

Perhaps there is a deeper shadow. If sapling teenagers cannot find the shade they need in the real woods, they may re-create that shade only too successfully, in the dark psyche, the sunless abyss of teenage depression. One teenager, in an agony of long-term depression, tells me he longs to go to the woods, sleeping in a ditch if necessary, but to go to the woods.

~

Once upon a time, there were three brothers. The eldest two set out to seek their fortune, but they refused to take the youngest with them.

He was a dreamer, they said, good for nothing except sitting around in the cinders, the ashes. This is how the Ash Lad got his name, just as *Cinder*-ella or Aschenputtel got hers. The brothers, greedy and cruel as Cinderella's step-sisters, took all the food in the house, leaving nothing but crumbs for the Ash Lad, so he collected up those crumbs and set off on his own journey. Alone.

He came to a great, wild forest. But he had his eyes open, says a crucial line, and he caught sight of something strange tied to a tree. It was an image, a painting of a beautiful princess. The Ash Lad was wonderstruck. The image of his desire hung on the tree and the shape of his destiny hung delicate in the air. Just then, an old woman approached him and asked for food. He had only the crumbs, but he willingly shared them with her and, in return for his gift, she gave him a magic ball of grey wool to show him the way. 'Just roll it along on the path in front of you,' she said and, like the rolling lines of a story, like the rolling earth, like the rolling on of a life, it will take you wherever you want to go. (We'll pick up that woollen thread later.)

His quest became clear: to find the princess and win her and half the kingdom. With the help of the old woman, a raven and a little grey donkey, he set out again and travelled far and farther than far, across many a land, over mountains and moors. Until, yes, he found his princess in the castle and 'They both lived happily ever after,' says an eight-year-old to me, with delicious malice; 'They lived happily ever after *for just one day*.'

The forest is where the quest begins. What the quest is, where it takes a child and what it demands from the child is the subject of the rest of this chapter.

The young must follow the hero's journey. Setting out on the romance of the road of life, the departure may be saturated with sunshine, blazing with happiness and drunk on excitement and hope – *As*

I Walked Out One Midsummer Morning – or more commonly the stumbling, bewildered, abandoned beginnings lost in the dark forest, but either way the departure is crucial.

The quest requires many qualities of the quester, and the Ash Lad is one of the best exemplars, representing the characteristics of intelligent childhood. He is true to himself and ruggedly irrepressible. His imagination is lit by images: the picture of the princess or the image of the castle he seeks which lies east of the sun and west of the moon. Observant and brave, he has a curved sense of morality. He holds to his path, tenacious in his quest: he is open-hearted, open-minded, canny, ingenious and generous. His quest includes discovering what all children need to know: how to behead trolls, become invisible and steer one's own course. His helpers include the man so fleet of foot that he can run to the end of the world in less than five minutes, the man whose sight is so sharp he can shoot a troll at the world's end, the man whose hearing is so keen he can hear grass grow, and the man with seven summers and fifteen winters inside him.

The Ash Lad is often treated unkindly by his brothers and unfairly by his parents who may give the older brothers the entire inheritance, leaving nothing to the Ash Lad, while the princess's father or an employer may try to cheat him – but he never gives up. The quest is all, whether it is for the castle, far, far away, shining on the horizon, or his journey to a place nine hundred miles further than the world's end.

In one story he must go to the woods 'to make a ship which goes as well on land as on water'. The meanings of this intriguing image are multiple, perhaps a metaphor for wonder or for adaptability, flexibility, resilience or the ability to travel successfully over the elements, but one thing is clear: the story must begin in the woods, finding a tree for the magic to begin. It is a rite of passage at the site of passage carved in the very material of passage as the ship's timbers hold within themselves their roots in the forest. It is an embarkation of bark, as those words themselves intimately link ship and tree.

Children, embarking on the quest of their own lives, can see in the Ash Lad something of the qualities required. Curiosity, attention, generosity – all of these the hero-child must offer; and every child is a hero of her own journey, the knight of his own quest. As Joseph Campbell illustrates, each person is on the 'Hero's Journey', which may be arduous and frightening but is ultimately worth every step: going out of the community, into the wilds or down into the depths alone but returning with the treasures of the psyche, brought out of darkness and into light.

The Ash Lad story, like 'Cinderella', begins in the ashes. Ash represents most clearly the poverty of the family's situation but also, importantly, ash is a symbol of purification. The Ash Lad suffers hunger, thirst, exhaustion and loneliness on his quest. He may have a vision, a dream or a challenge to follow. In the wilds, he pays attention to the 'ancients' and to the guides, he watches out for signs and messages from birds and animals and pays tender attention to everything he sees.

Whether or not to go on the quest? You have absolutely no choice in the matter. *How* you travel, though, is in your hands, which can share even crumbs, and in your mind, which can share even crumbs of knowledge. The quest can provide encounters between a wordless psyche and a non-verbal world which nevertheless calls, beckons, shifts, asks and offers. You may encounter a Scarecrow or a Tin Man along the way and it is the quest that has led you to the encounter.

But the one character more inviting than the Scarecrow or the Tin Man, more entreating than the Lion, more charismatic than Dorothy and more endearing than even Toto is – the road itself: *Follow the yellow brick road*. Why is it so important? Because because because because because: the road is within you. The quest is not so much the path but your readiness for it: your willingness, courage and curiosity. When you are ready, the path appears. The journey is within the child, there where the mind watches stormclouds gather, slays witches, melts horizons, casts rainbows, digs wells deep enough for wishes to swim in and stilled enough for a crazy gnat to play hopscotch on its own reflection. The quest is in the quester, folded up tight at first, a mazy path waiting to unravel itself, a catscradle cradling itself until it unspools out into the waiting world. The child, setting out far and farther than far, is actually here, and nearer than near. The quest is a profound paradox, though, for as the quest is within the child, the child is always, in the end, both at home *and* on the road. 'There's no place like home,' Dorothy says as she wakes from her dream at the end of *The Wizard of Oz*: she was there all along.

Mind how you go, the quest tells the child because the quest is the metaphor of mind, and how the mind makes its journeys will influence how one's life will turn out. The qualities demanded of the questing heroes are the qualities of thought, for the thinking mind is an inquisitive, questing thing, asking questions – that related word. It is alert, it gives and takes, it feels with its perceptions outering on the edges of oneself. It thinks with the ethics of the senses so it is touched, touching and tactful; it listens and gives audience; it is observant and insightful; it tastes and absorbs; it scents things and sniffs out a trail to follow.

East of the sun and west of the moon, the questing mind knows ambiguity like the boat which goes as well on land as on water; the questing mind lets paradox fill its sails. It appreciates enigma: the Ash Lad's enigmatic ball of grey wool is like the brain, that sphere of grey matter which will take you wherever you want to go. The questing mind is alert to the unusual, to uniqueness and to quiddity. It takes its questions to the woods and the wilds, off the map, off the beaten track of the ordinary world, off the habituated pathways to where things must be seen newly. Unaccustomed as it is to public highways, the questing mind is unusual, unfamiliar even to itself, eccentric and idio-syncratic. The qualities of the Ash Lad are the qualities of a thinking mind. Generous, it generates ideas. Kind, it sees kinnedness every-where, making connections. Alert, it walks the paths of metaphor where thoughts move in leaps and bounds.

I've seen pictures of brain imaging where the brain is coloured turquoise, green and gold. It is like looking at the mind as a wild world, turquoise like oceans ringing with the communiqués of whales, green like forests with the tree-talk of a cerebral canopy, golden as deserts lettered with footprints. The brain sends rumours through its pheromones, mysteries in the hormones and enigma in its chemistry: *Pssss, pass it on*. The questing mind must be quick to signs, signals and clues, running with, flickering with, lit with wit until paths of the mind work like paths of the land – they lead, they join up things of signifi-cance, they lay down patterns, they invite, they hold memory.

What is it, this quest? If I try to look at it directly, in broad daylight and straight ahead of me, it is not exactly there. But if I look away, I can see it clearly from the corner of my eye: twilight sight at the margins.

The quest is an enfolded way in the holloways of the mind; it is a path made deep by being trodden for generations until it has sunk below the level of the ordinary fields and we are walking the ancient thoroughfares, now, dug by footsteps down into the reach of tree roots. The quest is both eternal and present, both intimate and uni-versal, both earthed and electrifying, all at once. It is the absolute opposite of an enclosed childhood.

What matters is not the destination but the journey. The comic brevity of the end-lines ('They got married and lived happily ever after full stop') demonstrates the unimportance of the arrival. The drawing-near is what matters.

It is not about the finding so much as the seeking: the search matters more than the object of the search. It is the path from the actual present to the as yet unrealized future. The quest is about potential, incipience and becoming, yearning, longing, wishing and praying: the quest is betweenness. It is about stepping near, moving towards, reaching out. In Latin, the word *tendere* (which, as previously noted, has influenced many words for thought) is like one of the ancients on the path; this word is an old, old woman whispering her advice down the centuries. *Tendere* means to reach out, to direct one's course, to strive for something. The quest is there, in that quality of *tender* attention; the quest is a *tendency*, a way of *tending* to one's path, as *tendrils* of vines are *attentive* to the branches and stems where they might twist their spirals. The *tension* of the storyline shows how the quest *tends*, *extending* itself towards the *tenses* of the future.

The quest is not the same as a child's daemon, which, as a later chapter will explore, has a remarkably explicit vision for itself. The quest is implicit, its vision hidden in dreams and in tree-trunks, in woods and in wells, in mountains and rivers, its meaning steeped in metaphor.

The quest is the converse of the memoir. The memoir pounces on precise scenes, saying, '*This* is what happened,' and wanting to etch it exactly in the sharpest silver. Its pain is nostalgic; it longs backwards, for home in the past. The memoir is the literature of the old while the quest is the literature of the young. The quest has vision but not precision. It has a hundred impulses of longing; it says, 'Anything might happen,' and its yearning is inchoate. Its colour is not silver but green.

Its ache is the sense of being magnetized towards the very idea of *onwards!* itself, drawn as the tides are for the moon, longing forward, for home in the future.

The child must go alone, on a quest for vision, for insight, finding their own path. Many quest tales emphasize this by describing the child as an orphan, and even societies which, like the Hopi of the American South-West, have no orphans (because at the death of mother and father the wider family become parents to the child), still tell stories of orphans abandoned in the wilderness.

The family in fairy tales is often absent because it is necessary for the young psyche to go alone, hearing with its own ears, responding with its own heart, going out into the wilds to reach beyond the known limits of the village into a different presence.

There are fascinating parallels between some of the features of folk tales and the idea of the vision quest. Isolation, fasting and prayer were features of the traditional vision quest of Native Americans, mirroring the lonely, hungry but wishful hero or heroine of folk tales. The vision quest often began with 'purification ceremonies . . . in the sacred lodge', according to Nakoda or Stoney Chief John Snow, as they begin in the purifying ashes of the hearth for the Ash Lad and Aschenputtel or Cinderella.

After the days of ashes, the young person goes into the wilderness, living close to nature. In his childhood visions, Black Elk remarks that the natural world spoke to him, saying, 'Be careful and watch!'; as the fairy tales say, 'Pay attention!' The young person is perhaps given a special revelation, says Chief John Snow, which might come 'through a dream or a vision, through the voice of nature, or by an unusual sign. It might be that the wild animals or birds would convey the message of his calling to him.' He refers to the vision quest but what he says applies as well to the fairy-tale quest, for there are animal-helpers in fairy tales like the animal-helpers in those vision quests where 'the Great Spirit' sometimes 'spoke to us through the wild animals, the birds, the winds, the thunder, or the changing seasons'. Black Elk says: 'I could understand the birds when they sang, and they were always saying: "It is time!"'

Chief John Snow recalls the words which an old Nakoda or Stoney medicine man gave to those going on a vision quest: 'You must search and search and you will find ancient truths and wisdom that shall guide you in the future.' In West Papua, people have 'dream-shrines' on the mountain, places of textured intensity for the psyche where you go on a quest for a dream to guide you, the dream's wisdom bestowed by the Ancestors who live in the mountain. From the folk tales' deep pools of intuition, the dreams and visions well up with a similar stress on the old. The 'ancient truths' spoken of by the Nakoda or Stoney medicine man have rhymes with the West Papuan Ancestors, and also with 'the ancients', the Methuselah characters of folk tales, the old woman on the path or the ancient grandfather. Children need the wisdom of the past, the wisdom of the ancients, say all cultures, but today's children are subject to a pervasive prejudice of our age: a disdain for the past.

Vision quests and folk tales alike emphasize the gift culture of the mind: if you give the gift of attention, you will receive messages, tokens, signs and guidings. Prayers strew the path both in descriptions of the vision quest and in folk tales, where, although they are diluted into 'wishes', they are as fervent as any prayer. Contemporary Euro-American children may be less encouraged to make wishes within the concept of the gift culture than to make purchases in the mercantile world.

The quester is solitary but never truly isolated, suggest both the fairy tale and the vision quest. In the Salish tradition, young girls were sent out alone into the wilderness to learn they were never alone. To be precise, they were alone only as far as humans were concerned. The English language doesn't give us a distinction – and we need one – between being alone lacking human company and being truly alone, bereft also of birds, trees, rivers and hills. Today's children are in many ways bereft of animals and nature, isolated and lonely, and they do not have the opportunities for the learning which happens in those positive solitudes which all quest traditions emphasize.

When Lakota medicine man John Fire Lame Deer (born in 1903) was sixteen, he went on a vision quest for four days and nights. The initial test was solitude, because it was the first time he'd ever been alone and he was scared. Then he began hearing the wind, the trees, an owl hooting and then: 'Suddenly I felt an overwhelming presence. Down there with me in my cramped hole was a big bird . . . a voice was trying to tell me something. It was a bird cry, but I tell you, I began to understand some of it.' What he was told was that he was sacrificing himself there to be a medicine man. 'Then I felt the power surge through me like a flood.'

This vision quest is also part of the European tradition which used to place great store by dreams and their interpretation in many guises, from the aisling tradition to the Dream of the Rood, from the nineteenth-century Christian mystic George MacDonald's radical fairy tales to the psychoanalytic importance placed on dreams from Freud onwards.

'Each of us needs a quest, and a person without one is lost to himself' is inscribed at the end of Kevin Crossley-Holland's exquisite book telling the story of the young King Arthur, *The Seeing Stone*. If many teenagers today seem lost to themselves, in mental illness or drug and alcohol abuse, it is perhaps because young people are given no chance of a meaningful quest, no opportunity for the transitioning rites of transformation: those who have no chance to transcend may descend and never recover. For the quest is and was and will be; it is an ageless need to find one's power, one's name and one's self – a need which is part of the riddle of this book, for every child needs their time in the woods, to find their vision or their dream, and the quest traditions are universal. Yet most children today have no such rite, no way of negotiating that difficult transition into adulthood. Neither the twisted anti-heroic rituals of drug abuse and self-harm nor the bland grades and measured assessments of driving tests and A-levels fits the bill.

But just when the thread is thinnest, just when Euro-American culture seems to have let the traditions die, just at the moment of maximum forgetting, there has been a resurgence of attention to that threshold in various brave commitments to help young people to make meaning of their lives. Through the work of, for example, Steven Foster and Meredith Little and the beautifully named School of Lost Borders, and so many others who also deserve mention, young people may discover how to lose their child self and find their adult self, to understand their medicine and to know their gift. So those who have the chance of such rites can write their lives as mythic stories, paying attention to the delicate play of their own intuition interpreting the world, for, tucked right in the heart of the questing child's imagin-ation, right at the core, the heartwood of the child, divinity can be found, a sense of faërie, of otherwise-sight, right in the middle of the child's path like a turquoise feather, deep in the dark woods.

CHAPTER FIFTEEN

The Ship That Goes as Well on Land as on Water

Vasalisa the Wise has a doll in her pocket which can always tell her what she must do. This Russian story suggests that children have a small core of intuition, a gut feeling on which they can depend. When I told the story to two girls aged six and seven they were enraptured because they were just beginning to know and to trust their own instincts in life and the story validated this opaque knowing in the pocket of the mind. The Vasalisa wisdom wasn't pre-packaged and literalized for them in any Disney screen-version but could speak to their twilight-minded imagination.

'Look, raspberries! I love this Earth. It's the only one with magic,' says the young daughter of the American poet Kim Stafford. 'The other Earth by Japan and Disneyland doesn't have magic. Would you like some magic? Here, put it in your pocket so it won't fly away. I love this one Earth. Can we live here forever?'

Disney, for all its seductive appeal, blocks the holloways of the idiosyncratic mind's eye. NO THROUGH ROAD for metaphor. No right of way to one's own inner vision. Disney sells literal and predefined images to children until, in time, the child's own pathways to the metaphoric realm are overgrown with nettles and brambles. It is another form of enclosure, albeit an utterly charming one.

Fairy tales do not speak of enclosure but of the quest. Children are invited to take the intimate footpaths which journey into the boundless, unenclosed and mysterious realm of their own metaphor-making minds. Children scent the quest at the start of the story, knowing they have already embarked on the ship which goes as well on land as on water, the ineluctable, perplexing and magnificent quest to grow into adulthood, aided by the enigmatic authority of fairy tales. Ours is in many ways an age of literalism, but children dwell in the imagination – and need to. That is the world which fairy tales nurture – the glancing magic of the mind's metaphors.

Fairy tales are good medicine. I once met a 'story doctor', an Indigenous Australian woman in Alice Springs, who would listen to someone's situation and 'prescribe' them a story that would help. In traditional Hindu medicine, someone who was psychically disoriented would be given a fairy tale whose meaning paralleled the difficulty they faced, a story which might give the psyche ways to survive. Sufi stories can work in a similar way.

A culture's collection of folk tales is like a Swiss Army penknife for the psyche to use in life's tests, a toolkit in the pocket of the mind. One time, a person might need a magnifying glass to pay attention to the details; another time, scissors to cut the ties that bind, or a hoof-pick to aid the animal-helpers, a knife to slice a way into another world or a saw to hack through thickets.

Who are they who know a child's mind so well that they can fashion such stories to suit it? Children. Fairy tales are co-created by them: children are the *ur*-authors, writing in that invisible original font, the arche-type. Countless small and unnamed Homers would have listened to a story, reacted in certain ways, thrilled by some bits, frightened by others, indifferent now and then. Before the stories were written down, they were endlessly alterable and were changed subtly along the way. Question after question: the child's perennial why? and how? would have affected the adults' telling of the story, causing them to refine it more and more carefully to fit the shape of childhood's psyche. Goethe's mother was a renowned storyteller and she recalled the fairy tales she crafted together with her young son. If the fate of one of the characters didn't seem to be going as he wished, he would be angry or tearful and would suggest a different outcome, 'so my imagination often was replaced by his,' said his mother, and she adjusted the storyline to accord with him. When she did so, 'he was all excited, and one could see his heart beating.'

So, like tiny ship-builders in the port, children began the carpentry to craft the mind's boats in which they could sail away from safe harbour and across the difficult seas. Whittling the story back to only what is necessary or beautiful or funny, the little carpenters would plane the wood down here, add a carved detail there, thoughtfully working on the mindcraft until wood joins word, until story fits psyche and it can float. Then they added sails made of that priceless silk: a child's refusal to see things merely as they appear. Over the oceans the ships travelled, the words arriving true for other children later, for the best stories do come true. Like wishes.

Some of the earliest written stories were about the quest, that core image of the earliest romances. In these stories, so popular in the Middle Ages, the hero, knight-errant and adventurer, sets out to seek his fortune, and children, knights-errant all, are drawn to the role. The early stories were called *roman* (a novel, in today's French), a word which combines the romance of the troubadour stories, those gleeful strolling minstrels, and the romance of roaming adventure as the third son or youngest daughter sets out to seek their fortune, no matter how uncertain it may be.

In the French novel *Le Grand Meaulnes*, written by Alain-Fournier in 1912, the imaginative quest for an elusive, mysterious domain is described so the angle of its longing hurts its characters, willingly, dangerously, mesmerizingly. With all the passion of adolescence, the quest becomes a matter of life and death. It opens as Meaulnes stumbles on a fancy-dress party while in search of something else, in pure serendipity. Everyone is disguised and transformed, so anyone may be anyone else. (It is not unlike the appeal of festivals for adolescents today, the hazy masquerade where none of the usual rules apply.) Ever after, Meaulnes seeks the masquerade – the domain with no name – again. His search is contagious and his friend, the book's narrator, catches it. 'For the first time I too am on the path of adventure . . . I am looking for something still more mysterious: for the path you read about in books, the old lane choked with undergrowth whose entrance the weary prince could not discover.' What is it, this mysterious domain? What is it? *Later, later,* the story says: *I'll tell you later.*

As the narrator grows up out of mystery, he enters the ordinary world. Meaulnes, though, persists with 'the role he insisted on playing . . . the young hero of romance'. He plays the part of knight-errant with chivalry coursing in his veins and, his heart on fire, he kneels in devotion to the idea of his lady Yvonne, the subject of his quest 'so ardently sought, so deeply loved'.

When he is not on horseback, smoking a pipe, a tilter at windmills and the world's most beloved freedom fighter, Subcomandante Marcos is a children's writer. He tells the story of a small beetle who has stolen some of his tobacco. 'I followed to see where the tobacco thread was going, and to see who the hell had taken it and spilled it. A few meters away, behind a rock, I found a beetle sitting at a little desk, reading some papers and smoking a tiny pipe . . . I asked him what he was studying. "I'm studying neoliberalism and its strategy of domination for Latin America," he answered . . .' This is Don Durito of the Lacandon, a medieval knight-errant with the gift of the gab. Small, funny, sometimes cross, sometimes bossy, but always devoted to chivalry and valour, he is a beetle with an instinct for the ethics of the quest. 'This little beetle has traveled the roads of the world, righting wrongs, rescuing damsels in distress, healing the sick, aiding the weak, instructing the ignorant, humbling the mighty, and exalting the humble. The greatest knight-errant the world has ever seen, Don Durito of the Lacandon lives, still amazing the stars that find him back in the jungle's night,' writes Marcos.

He sees life from the underside, both politically and literally, and children are quick to appreciate his beetle-eye viewpoint. Like Don Durito, children have an easy understanding of chivalry: they idolize those they love, they want to rescue animals in distress and to poke fun at pompous, powerful people. They are sensitive to honour and dishonour. They don't particularly want to 'be good' if all that it entails is obedience. They do, though, want to be heroic, tough, funny and brave: the knight-errant. Kenneth Grahame's story 'The Roman Road' suggests how the child (and the artist) are both knights on a quest to find the ambiguous Golden City, following those who, like Lancelot, have taken the road before them.

Clearly the idea of the quest as the path from childhood to adulthood predated the quest stories of the Middle Ages and obviously it has been part of the cultural imagination of the whole world but, in European terms, the Middle Ages seems to exert a particular fascination both for children and children's writers.

As a child, when I pictured the Middle Ages I could see who

everyone was: a woodcutter with his axe, a merchant selling satins, a farmer or a weaver. People's activities and their trades were graspable, visible and knowable, unlike careers in finance, project management, or consultancy, which are incomprehensible to children. Where there were unknowns, in the Middle Ages, they were known unknowns, the secret magic of witch, healer, seer and wizard. (I realize I'm sailing close to Donald Rumsfeld, whose life redeemed itself, just the once, in his extraordinary rendition of human unknowing, but I won't let that stop me.) In terms of landscape, the Middle Ages told me of a finite, knowable village and an infinite and knownly unknowable beyond, and both glimmered with appeal. No plastic. Things were handmade and crafted, unprocessed and unfactoried. Everything was itself and was knowably makeable, findable, buildable. Everything came from the known earth around: leather, wood, wax, honey and apples. Things known, in this sense, shade into being close, intimate and beloved: this is not about information but relationship. Like most children, I wanted to understand things, I wanted objects to speak their names, and it seemed as if in the Middle Ages everything carried its own weight in its own hand, the hand-held heft of the thing, so a child would touch the earth directly in everything they touched.

Children's writer of genius Ursula Le Guin sets much of her work in a medieval world. She writes from the intuition that real magic lies in knowing the true names of things. In that true name, everything keeps its quiddity tight as a conker in its shell; language, tucked right into the kernel of the thing it refers to, is incarnate truth. Thus word would embody world and would do so with such galvanizing power that by knowing the words one could change the world – by spells. The primary power of a child's mind comes when they can make their first spells of utterance, outerance, putting out into the world what is within their heart. The mind conceives, the mouth expresses and *hey presto!* a word creates a thing in the mind of another. A two-year-old Prospero can begin the conjuring: apple, boat, no, yes, story. Language, no more and no less, and if that is not magic, I don't know what is.

Other children's writers return to the medieval period again and again. C. S. Lewis's academic work was a chivalric defence of the Middle Ages; Michael Rosen writes of the mischievous tricks of the medieval character Till Owlyglass; Michael Morpurgo tells the medieval quest tale of Gawain and the Green Knight. Angela Carter's work is backlit by the Middle Ages, and the girl's dream in *The Company of Wolves* is set in a medieval village. Robin Hood is a medieval character; Tolkien was a medievalist and Middle Earth is steeped in the Middle Ages. *The Sword in the Stone* and other tales of King Arthur so popular in the Middle Ages retain their bewitchment today and author Kevin Crossley-Holland finds roots of beauty there. Rima Staines, the best illustrator of the realm of faërie, oak-smoked, sad-strung but vital, that I have ever seen, says she was born a Londoner in the twentieth century but 'has always had one foot in Early Medieval Europe'.

~

Fairy tales have certain themes, including the inherent importance of nature and animals, a respect for words, promises and spells and a high regard for thinking. Fairy tales care about heroism in childhood, although girls have been cheated of their heroic inheritance for a few hundred years. These tales advise their listeners to bestow significance on signs, to fight injustice and to love someone in spite of appearances – the lesson of 'Beauty and the Beast'. Take everyone you meet along with you is the message of one Ash Lad story, because you will need them all later.

Of these ethics of faërie, one of the commonest is the demand to treat nature well. Animals and birds chissick, scamper, howl and hoot through the tales, but this is more than a storytelling detail. Fairy tales are a cultural reminder of a fact of first importance: that humans need to be on speaking terms at least with the natural world, and preferably on gift-giving terms, so that children may receive their gifts in turn and learn from animals how to rescue themselves, when to seize the advantage, or become their ideal selves. The fairy-tale mind insists that the animal world has magnificence and meaning and deserves kindness, respect and attention from those whose lives are animated by it, those in convivium with it, those nested in the same world.

Fairy tales have many qualities of nestness, and the endings of fairy tales almost always involve the 'nest' of a home. Nested within that larger idea of home are the many small details of snuggery glimpsed along the way, the round baskets filled with provisions like birds' nests full of moss and chicks, the shoemaker's wife stitching the elves their made-to-measure suits or the shoemaker making their perfectly fitting shoes.

The Little Grey Men filled me with a kind of nest-nostalgia and pleasure at the same time. The gnomes used coracles made of frog skin, carried wheat in small sacks of dock leaves and kept their wine in snail shells. Most delightful to me, they lived in oak-tree roots – the oak in British culture being the tree of knowing. The author, 'BB', describes them at night: 'the gnomes lay down, each snuggling into his moleskin sleeping bag' and after a while 'under the root, which smelt of oak smoke and kippered minnow, three tiny snores rose up like elfin horns.' I longed to be with them and so I read the book tucked into the hollow of tree roots on a riverbank over several cold afternoons one October until it was too dark to see and my fingers were too cold to turn the pages.

In folk tales, everything (moon, wind, rock, bird or child) has its own story and role, and traditional stories across the world seem to share this quality, giving significance to all the players, culture paying homage to nature, holding everything in mind, attentive to each, so the point of view of every aspect of nature is considered. What arises from this is the understanding of the inherent and necessary between-ness of things, the incalculably complex relationships of an ecology. A society which tells its children only stories with one point of view – that, for example, of humans – will be out of practice at considering ecologically diverse perspectives. Implicit in story-diversity is bio-diversity and an ethic of behaviour which in Indigenous Australian culture is called, sternly, Law.

When a young Indigenous Australian is well taught by the stories, they know that good actions resonate with – and sustain – the impetus of life while wrong actions lead to deadliness, as the tragic ending of the film *Walkabout* shows. The traditional walkabout is a quest for young Indigenous Australian men, where they must travel alone on the land and survive, physically and psychologically. In the film, the boy on his own quest stumbles on the mass graves of animals killed – just for fun – by European hunters and the idea so harrows his soul that he dances himself to death.

Charles Dickens said he'd always wanted to marry Little Red Riding Hood and I can understand his choice, especially the character from the earlier, oral versions which tell of a brave and clever girl who defends herself against attempted rape – the kind of role model girls need. But something horrible happened to her story along its path. Her tale fell among thieves and robbers. Charles Perrault, supporter of some pretty rancid politics, rewrote the story to warn girls not against predatory men but against the tender ferocity of their own sexuality and, in the altered telling, Little Red Riding Hood is punished for failing to tame her desirous nature.

Original, oral folk tales had their goddesses, matriarchs and active young princesses, but they suffered a malignant spell and were transformed into stories which were misogynist and patriarchal. The goddess became a witch. The active role of the young princess was played by a prince. The child-hero became, most often, male. If you are a princess in many fairy stories, your role is to be endangered, to be prey, to be chained up or imprisoned by ogres, beasts or nasty husbands until you are rescued by a very nice young man. These stories provoke a particularly sexual terror in girls, without giving them any advice at all on dealing with the monsters who may, in real life, be silently turning the handle of their bedroom doors.

There are still girl-questers, of course: Gretel, who saves both herself and Hansel, her brother, or Gerda, the girl who finds and rescues the boy, Kai, from the clutches of the Snow Queen. But women who are active in the stories are often evil, such as the wicked stepmother, the witch or the evil thirteenth fairy at the christening, while women who are good are often inactive. The quintessence of this passivity is Sleeping Beauty. Although Bruno Bettelheim tries his best to argue that this story has a positive purpose, that in adolescence 'both active and quiescent periods are needed . . . the long, quiet concentration on oneself,' he perhaps underrates the malevolence of this passive role model for girls in later life. It may create a listlessness in the listener which lasts a lifetime, a passive waiting for a prince who may never arrive and the writing of an awful story of loss; wan and wanting womanhood waiting uselessly in the wings to be woken by another until she is widowed by wishing and the curtain falls on a life which has never even stepped on to the stage.

In Philip Pullman's Lyra, girls have the literary role model they deserve. Fascinated by Milton's *Paradise Lost*, Pullman creates a 'second Eve' to fight for all the virtues the Authority loathes: bravery, cunning, fierceness, curiosity, pride, kinetic vitality, independence, fiction, metaphor and initiative – original spirit, not original sin. She has the curved ethics of the Ash Lad, unstricken by convention or propriety. She gives her fealty to the tough demand of what she intuits to be right. She knows the ethic of the quest, and it involves her whole being, her love and loyalty, her sharp senses and her frank opportunism. The quest requires her kindness, stubbornness, seriousness, chivalry, tenacity and implacable courage. Wild and self-willed, she doesn't aim to please, she is not malleable, she won't smile for the camera or perform on demand. Obedience disgusts her. Like a self-respecting knight-errant, she chooses her own path on her own quest. She is, in short, a hero.

~

People used to say there are times when the veil between the worlds is thin, the twilights of dawn and dusk and the twilights of the year, May Day and Hallowe'en. But there is another time when the veil is no more than gossamer and it is when the psyche crosses the threshold of enchantment. In childhood, reality may be rent for a moment, like the scene in Satyajit Ray's *Pather Panchali* (1955), when the young Apu watches the world through a torn blanket. Framed thus, he sees myth everywhere, whether he watches a folk-play performance, a train passing or his sister being beaten. Wonderlight shines gravely in his eyes. 'To enter into the fabulous times, it is necessary to be serious like a dreaming child,' says Gaston Bachelard.

There is no stillness quite like a child stilled by faërie: spellbound, captivated, transfixed; visibly motionless because the imagination is in flight. The spell is cast the moment the child crosses the delicate threshold from the outer world to the inner.

Spell, commented J. R. R. Tolkien, once meant 'both a story told, and a formula of power over living men'. The spellbound realm. Something deeper is coming into view.

Faërie is a paradoxical realm, both fleetingly glimpsed and eternally known. It is marginal and yet central to the human imagination, both delicate and robust, both shy and defiant. It works on the edge of perception, with the potency of the penumbra; it is nocturnal, unfixed and uncertain, the land of perhaps, dangerously alluring. One of artist Paula Rego's pictures illustrates this perfectly: the children stand in a circle of bright light which emanates from a book, a conversation or a game while in the shadows that surround them hover the creatures of imagination: fairy-tale characters, Scissorhands, Alice or Toad.

Outside the circle of the ordinary, faërie has a spiralling quality of difference; it redeems the idea of otherness. In that realm, the Little People live off different food for something extraordinary nourishes them. If it is summer in this world, it is winter in Narnia. People live by different rules of morality, of gravity, of fact. Faërie is dramatically opposed to the Aristotelian rules of tragedy, the unities of place, time and action. In the faërie realm, a person can travel to the ends of the world in five minutes, can appear and disappear at will and can sleep a hundred years in one night. A four-year-old girl once told me matter-of-factly that she was going to give a star to one of her friends. 'How will you reach the star?' I asked. 'With a ladder into the sky,' she replied, her imagination supplying the precise image which William Blake used, as a child gets a ladder to unhook the moon.

Faërie alters the sense of scale. When Coleridge was eight, his father took him out one evening to show him the night sky, naming the stars and telling the child how Jupiter was a thousand times the size of the earth. The child listened with 'profound delight &

admiration' but with no incredulity, for from reading fairy tales 'my mind had been *habituated to the Vast.*' The mind itself has vastness, it has ladders long enough to net the stars by moonlight and in the faërie realm, likewise, everything increases in immensity and meaning. Louder, larger and more significant, all is gigantized, so giants abound in folk tales as they do in the psyche (and not just in childhood). In all the rifts of life, when the ordinary world is rent apart, in the big changes of life, in deaths and separations and losses, the mind is a magnified world of monsters, angels and messages crying out with import. Every decision casts a long shadow, every meeting matters. Faërie understands this sense of consequence and in its narratives it multiplies the effects of actions so the Ash Lad, for example, gives the old woman a gift of crumbs because it is all he has, while in return she gives him the advice he needs to win a princess: what would be an ordinary act of kindness elsewhere recoups a dramatic reward in faërie's moral amplification.

One summer day, as I was walking along a footpath, aged about ten, I saw a dead mole. But that's not quite right. I *encountered* a dead mole. I'd seen other dead things, but this was for some reason charged with significance, the difference between seeing and encountering. The deadness was overwhelming and the mole's coat was dulled and dusty with death in summer. On the folk-tale quest, encounters matter, be they with people, animals, luck or death. What is important in the quester is the readiness to encounter, the willingness to recognize those moments when something becomes archetypal, when an apple tree which is *any* apple tree slips its moorings and becomes *the* apple tree, when a dusty little mole becomes Death itself.

I picked the mole up and took it home and treasured it, like many children and folk-tale heroes, collecting and cherishing things which others say is litter. The Ash Lad gathers up his findings (a dead magpie, an old willow hank, a broken saucer, two ram's horns, a wedge, a worn-out shoe sole), ignoring his scornful elder brothers, who call them junk. It is as if fairy tales acknowledge children's ready wish to treasure their findings, to gather what they can along the way. And this is also how the mind works, gathering what it can as it goes, collecting, recollecting, noting one's findings. This is intelligence, from *inter* and *legere*, whose primary meaning is to collect or gather – the gleaning of the mind.

~

The opposite of 'true' is not always 'false'. Sometimes, the opposite of one kind of truth is truth of a different kind, most clearly seen in the difference between literal and metaphoric truth. Fairy tales dwell in the latter world; they are true but unreal. To children, this distinction is important and they need no help in understanding it, although this is a complex idea.

Many adults know the situation, when they are telling (not reading) a story of the fairy-tale kind and the child interrupts to ask: 'Is it true?' (If the adult is reading, it is clear to the child that it is from the story world and they don't ask.)

Is it true? the adult wonders, thinking about his goblin neighbours, troll boss, and the princess he has been secretly in love with for years, and answers thoughtfully, 'Well, *yes*, it is true, *in a way*. In its own way, it is true.'

'But is it true like in *real life*?' the child persists.

'No,' the adult will say, the distinction clear. 'Not like in real life.'

The child's question is not one of disbelief, but rather comes from the important need to clarify what kind of truth it is and therefore what kind of belief to give to it.

This is a way in which shamans use language, easily speaking the language of metaphor by which the mind so kindly invites the world closer.

There are two worlds. One is the outer, visible world, known to the body's eyes – sight. The other is the inner, invisible world known to the mind's eye – vision. The world we see becomes, under this second sight, not so much transparent as translucent. The inner spirit world is true with the deep truths of metaphor, a textured depth of truth, resonant with authenticity, as if truth had harmonics and only one note in the chord was the obvious, actualized truth, while the others were sounded out by the far fetch of the brain's waves.

Far-fetched. The scornful remark of the under-imaginative, those whose minds, subdued by the merely visible realities, would dampen the imagination of children and would give them mental automata rather than magic in mind. When I was a teenager, I babysat occasionally for a small boy whose parents were dogmatic literalists. Robin Hood was far-fetched. Father Christmas didn't exist. Nor did the Tooth Fairy, Snow White or any other creature of faërie. The boy was told that these characters were not 'logical', 'rational' or 'real', those words which can be boots to give imagination a good kicking. He followed their line, declaring his unfaith with an anger at once smug and bitterly bereft.

The world of faërie is metaphorically true – true to the psyche. Ask someone who has been there. Italo Calvino describes the time he spent editing his book of Italian folk tales: 'For two years I have lived in woodlands and enchanted castles . . . having to choose between the cloak of invisibility or the magical foot, feather, or claw that could metamorphose me into an animal. And during these two years the world about me gradually took on the attributes of fairyland, where everything that happened was a spell or metamorphosis,' he writes.

Predestined loves, bewitchment, disappearances and 'paths bristling with obstacles leading to a happiness held captive by dragons . . . this was not a hallucination, a sort of professional malady, but the confirmation of something I knew from the start. My singular conviction that impelled me on my quest among the fairy tales was this,' he writes: '*le fiabe sono vere*: fairy tales are true.' He describes a way of looking, seeing right through reality to the truths beyond. He is one of the beyonders, those wise enough and willing enough to yearn to dwell tenderly in the metaphoric world.

John Clare as a child was passionate about fairy tales, and G. K. Chesterton in 'The Ethics of Elfland' writes: 'My first and last philosophy, that which I believe in with unbroken certainty, I learned in the nursery . . . The things I believed most then, the things I believe most now, are the things called fairy tales.' Fairy tales founded in him the belief that the world was a 'wild and startling place' and that 'life is not only a pleasure but a kind of eccentric privilege.'

Anthropologist and writer W. Y. Evans-Wentz points out that 'In the fairy-faith lie the germs of much of our European religions and philosophies, customs, and institutions.' He refers to an idea that fairies are a folk-memory of an earlier race who were driven into the mountains and wildernesses by the Celts. No matter the truths of these assertions, what children persistently feel has the quality of *recognition*. They recognize this faërie world as if recognizing the truths of their own imaginations, stories *re*told to them, not told for the first time. They are always tales of an earlier time, the once upon a time, some time ago, because they locate themselves in the earliest thinking of children. In their first years, children dwell more in the right hemisphere of the brain, the part where metaphor matters.

Children, in their *re*-cognition of this world, have an immediate, untutored understanding of things which accord with the faërie vision and things which do not. What belongs is the *largesse* of metaphoric meaning but not the meanness of literalization.

Gifts but not payslips.
Promises but not contracts.
Vows but not certificates.
Justice but not prison sentences.
Debts but not bills.
Wishes but not prayer books.
Numbers but not equations.
Beliefs but not dogmas.
Barters and bargains but not currency exchange.
Timing but not clocks.

Signs and significance but not a single signifier, not one postcard, not even a little Post-it note of a postmodernist signifying nothing, because postmodernism's only meaning is its meanness and it can frankly, solipsistically and self-referentially post itself back, return to sender, *largesse* unknown.

We do not *see* paintings as much as see *according to* them, said philosopher Maurice Merleau-Ponty. Fairy tales are extraordinary works of public art and we can see *according to* them with the vision of twilight mind in shadow-knowing, in a mirror of the mind's twofold processes.

Mirrors matter in fairy tales, so Alice goes through into the looking-glass world, or the fairy-tale queen seeks answers from the mirror on the wall. What you see in the mirror is true but unreal and this is the status of fairy-tale truth: it mirrors the world, allusive and evocative, as dreams mirror daylight, in the darkness.

~

Say 'fairies' to most adults and they – quite understandably – may feel slightly nauseated at the image of little tinsel-winged creatures in a world of twinkly nonsense. In the great scheme of things, that picture is quite recent. It seems to have arisen from early in the seventeenth century, and Tolkien (who vastly preferred the older and weightier term 'faërie') would write of fairies: 'I suspect that this flower-and-butterfly minuteness was also a product of "rationalization", which transforms the glamour of Elfland into mere finesse. It seems to become fashionable soon after the great voyages had begun to make the world seem too narrow to hold both men and elves . . .'

Rationalization. When things had to be either real and visibly true, or unreal and false. Either or. Nothing else.

Tolkien dated the belittling and intolerant attitude towards faërie to the voyages of 'discovery', to the reign of Queen Elizabeth I. Shakespeare seems to give voice – allusive, implicit and enreveried though it is – to a nostalgia for that way of perceiving the world which was ending as he was writing. Shakespeare's work – *A Midsummer Night's Dream*, in particular – holds the faërie inheritance of a kingdom, a culture's imagination, preserving it just when metaphor and imagination were under attack from the Reformation, ushering in literalism and exiling metaphoric truths.

When the Protestants were out to smash the art of the churches and of the imagination and the Puritan project would close not only the theatres of the land but also the theatres of the mind, Shakespeare kept faith with an older vision. According to that beautiful Shakespeare scholar A. D. Nuttall: 'the fairies are old England and old England was a world of friars and chapels and holy rites'; Shakespeare writes 'as if the Reformation hasn't even happened – and we are all friends'. It is possible that Shakespeare was himself a Catholic and it is certain that he sensed that something of the faërie imagination was banished by Protestantism.

Richard Corbett, Bishop of Norwich (1582–1635), writing 'The Faryes Farewell' in idiosyncratic spelling, overtly associated the fairy-faith with Catholicism:

> . . . *the Faries*
> *Were of the old Profession;*
> *They're Songs were Ave Maryes,*
> *They're Daunces were Procession.*

With their 'rings and roundelays', wrote the bishop, their merriment was rooted in the Catholicism of Queen Mary, and it was the Reformation which banished them.

A matter of faith, maybe. 'Fairy' and 'faërie' find roots in Latin *fata*, the fates, and it seems a word which dances its own roundelays, shimmering with recusancy, refusing to be pinned down. Near to where I live in Wales, there is a little wooden gazebo in a wooded valley. In the visitors' book, a couple of young girls wrote that they had gone out looking 'for feres'. The girls, looking for ancient beliefs newly found in themselves, were looking for a faith always just out of reach of the literal letters.

In Kipling's *Puck of Pook's Hill*, Puck is lured out of the hill by children enacting Shakespeare's *Midsummer Night's Dream* on midsummer evening. One of the children remembers a verse from Bishop Corbett's 'Farewell' and says sadly to Puck: 'When I was little it always made me feel unhappy in my inside.' Inside. These are the truths of the inner world – not that the fairies were *actually* Catholics but that faërie represented a mindset which was imaginative and metaphoric, full of inner meaning, whereas the mindset which drove them out was outer-directed and literalist, carrying within it seeds of the later Enlightenment and Utilitarianism.

'In a utilitarian age, of all other times, it is a matter of grave importance that fairy tales should be respected,' wrote Dickens. He was quick to see that faërie was a way of imaginative thinking which was exiled by the brutality of mere literalism and utilitarianism. Poet Kathleen Raine, sharing Dickens's intuition, writes: 'In all times and places, with the sole exception of our own machine-made world, the universe is held to be living . . . Of this world-wide animism the fairy-faith is an expression.'

'If you want your children to be intelligent, read them fairy tales. If you want them to be more intelligent, read them more fairy tales,' said Einstein. Metaphor is how we think. 'All is metaphor,' said Goethe, that great Romantic poet and scientist, so enraptured by fairy tales as a child.

Tolkien wrote: 'it was in fairy-stories that I first divined the potency of the words, and the wonder of the things, such as stone, and wood, and iron; tree and grass; house and fire; bread and wine.' The literal facts were given the depth and texture which is the poet's vision and, says Tolkien, '*Faërie* itself may perhaps most nearly be translated by Magic – but it is magic of a peculiar mood and power, at the furthest pole from the vulgar devices of the laborious, scientific magician.'

The intelligent mind can unite a *conte de faits* (a tale of facts) and a *conte de fées* (a fairy tale), finding the *image* of *imagination* in the *magus* language, that of the wise man or woman, the only true *magic*, as all those cognate words understand. Sheer, steep wisdom.

Words happen upon children in a lyrical delirium, as if felt by the body as warmth, fear, roughness or water. If there are primary colours, might there not also be primary words, the ones which children experience with their minds inextricably embodied both in the physicality of the world and of their own bodies? 'Water', 'fire', 'sun', 'sky', 'boat'. There is no boat which is not a pure miracle: it floats and carries its cargo of meaning from shore to shore. Words are alive to children as fizzy, vital, living things. Words have lives, biographies, relationships with other words and with certain people. Words are potent as spells, sweet as lullabies, scary as ghosts. First met, they have a 'bigness' which I remember without hesitation: the word 'roof', for example, well fitted, its meaning tucked in tight like the blankets around me when I slept. 'Sunshine' was bright water; 'bath' a rolling word wet and round in the mouth as 'mouth' itself. 'Brother' was a word of good wood, three little blocks like a set of wooden toys.

I've just stopped writing. Something happened in the last paragraph which I hadn't seen coming. Now, when I re-read these descriptions, I realize that I have defined them all 'as if'. I have described each – 'roof', 'sunshine', 'bath' and 'brother' – in terms of something else. That was how I learned, or rather experienced, these words: metaphor was there at the beginning and these words are my demonstration to myself.

Children are musicians of thought: they transpose from the key of *fact* to the key of *magic*. How? Through metaphor. Children understand metaphor instinctively – and this is a breathtaking idea. If they didn't, imagine how difficult it would be to explain it to them. As it is, I know (because I've done it) that you can put an empty Heinz baked-bean tin on a rug with a child who has barely learned to speak and tell the child the rug is the sea and the bean tin is a boat and lo! there it is in his mind. A boat carrying its cargo across to the other side, just as the word 'metaphor' itself does, as we've seen from *meta*, 'across', and *phor*, 'carry'. There is a metaphor within the very word itself.

On meeting something new, children carry its meaning across from something they already know. They express themselves in metaphor. They think, play and live by metaphor. That empty Heinz baked-bean tin on the rug is a boat on the sea. It is not *like* a boat, it *is* a boat, carrying its cargo across seas of thought.

Many people who work with young children dislike giving them literal toys which denote only one object, for example a toy duck, which will only ever be a duck. Instead, they say, when children use non-literal toys (an empty bean tin, a cardboard box, leaves and stones), they vivify them to become, metaphorically, absolutely anything.

Faërie sees the world Otherwise. Its insights are on the outside. The double-sight, the mysterious domain, refer to the same thing: metaphor. This is why the deadly intellectual paralysis of literalism is both stupid and unkind. For wisdom and curiosity are nurtured in metaphor, and so is empathy. Empathy, another little boat, carries its cargo across the seas between us, the seas which threaten to keep us apart for ever. The boat of empathy keeps chugging across, bearing one person's feelings over to another. Kindness (to humans and to the natural world) is also ferried in the same boat, carrying across one experience into another's understanding.

When the Ash Lad searches for the castle east of the sun and west of the moon, it is as if he has been given the coordinates of the imagination, and this is the treasure which children must find within their own psyche, where they must travel far, and farther than far, crossing threshold after threshold until reality is transformed by the magic in the heart of thinking, of science, of music, of poetry and all the arts, and then faërie is recognized for what it truly is: a metaphor for metaphor, humanity's collective reverie, a metaphor, simply and deeply, for imagination itself.

CHAPTER SIXTEEN

The Secret World of a Child's Soul

The story begins in the dark. Mary Lennox is first a neglected child and then an orphaned one. It is winter both outside and within her; lonely and lightless, she is sent to live at the estate of her uncle, a melancholic man of black moods. So begins *The Secret Garden*, Frances Hodgson Burnett's classic story of the intimate journey of a child's spirit.

In a moment both bleak and hopeful, Mary talks to a robin. 'I'm lonely,' she admits to the bird and the confession itself invites a transformation from unwanted loneliness to sought-after privacy. The distinction is important. She needs a secure and secret space and she is told of a walled garden which her uncle's wife had cherished. But after her death, ten years previously, Mary's griefstruck uncle had locked the door to the garden and buried the key. The robin, though, points the way, first to the key and then to the door, long hidden behind overgrown ivy. It is the portal.

'There is always one moment in childhood when the door opens and lets the future in,' wrote Graham Greene. Reach your hand out to a book, your thumb halfway down the cover, to open it where the door knob would be, if this were a door. And, of course, it is: it swings wide open on its hinges and you cross the threshold, through the portal to a different world. Within these book-worlds there are more and more portals, to galaxies of otherness which you can reach with Pullman's subtle knife, down Alice's rabbit-hole or through the wardrobe.

'Does there exist a single dreamer of words who does not respond to the word "wardrobe"?' asks that angel of reverie Gaston Bachelard. It is a wordrobe for dressing up thoughts and a guardword for spells, the place of lions and witches where Lucy finds herself touching frozen branches instead of fur coats. Ambiguous, hidden in the ivy, easily overlooked, these portals are gateways to the extraordinary, but they are always tucked side by side with the absolutely ordinary, suggesting that their magic is democratic, available to everyone. With the opening words 'as if', they unlock the door to the other side, while the sadder words 'if only' lead the mind back, recalling the reader to the ordinary world and closing the wordroad door.

Frida Kahlo tells how, aged six, she drew a door and went through it to a world of her own creation. How to make worlds: go through the secret door, alone. 'The Secret Garden was what Mary called it . . . She liked the name, and she liked still more the feeling that when its beautiful old walls shut her in no one knew where she was.' Thus children step through their portals and doorways, into the secret gardens where their spirits may be nurtured.

Children sometimes need to shy away from adult attention, seeking solitude and private dens where they can tend their souls unseen. Given the chance, these places are in the natural world, child-nature needing nature for its world-making, soul-making work, yet children today – for the first time ever – are being denied the outdoor space and the privacy which combine to give them a place of becoming.

Mary doesn't tell the adults about her discovery of the secret garden, in a desire for secrecy common to children. Reticent about many of their privacies, children may be unwilling to tell adults their deepest findings and observations because they can be vulnerable to nothing harsher than the wrong kind of stare, a cynical remark or spirit-vandalizing pragmatism.

'Children stop talking when grown-ups draw nigh,' writes Jean Cocteau in *Les Enfants Terribles*, for they live in 'the true world of childhood . . . whose momentous, heroic, mysterious quality is fed on airy nothings, whose substance is so ill-fitted to withstand the brutal touch of adult inquisition'.

In sculpting their personalities, children fight for the right to keep secrets from their parents. They know myriad privacies, including a privacy of language in secret codes, a privacy of emotions and a privacy of play. Psychologists report that the most profound, creative and imaginative play stops when parents arrive on the scene because the privacy of the fantasy is crucial. I was once on holiday with a friend and two small children and the little girls played with us – games of chance and daring – but they also, separately, played mesmerized games of make-believe. When they moved into this register of deep play, we were neither invited nor expected to play, because children know that adults rarely suspend disbelief. We may crouch and squeeze ourselves into Wendy houses but we are self-conscious players and that spoils it. We are pretending to pretend. They are not. That said, there have been times as an adult, playing with a child, when I have become as bewitched as them, as utterly lost to the real world in the metaphors of make-believe and children have a sixth sense for noticing the moment when an adult has crossed that threshold. Then, they let us play.

Adults often don't like this privacy in children. Wole Soyinka recalls parents taking their children to 'native doctors' to cure 'brooding'. The thoughtfully withdrawn self-intimate child of Britain or the

United States may find him- or herself taken to a child psychologist for the same reason.

The most precious gift adults can give children is social space, argue the Opies: 'the necessary space – or privacy – in which to become human beings'. Needing privacy, children are today given its opposite – surveillance, and this damages children's soul-moments. Picture a child, playing alone, weaving a nest of thoughts for her own self to nestle in. Her refuge shelters her self-definition and here is where she can begin the song of herself for, unsupervised, she dwells unselfconsciously in the mysterious domain of becoming; each moment is potent with the possibility of transformation. From this nest she may fly, for imagination is a winged creature. Her unwatched time is metaphysical, she may slip away from watch-time into the commons of reverie and, unstared at, she may achieve that dream of childhood and become invisible. Her nestled psyche is at its most vulnerable: the tiniest snapping of a twig would disturb it. Suddenly she realizes that, far from being invisible, she is being watched. Her bird-psyche is instantly on the alert. Immediately she becomes self-conscious, for watching a child will make her watch herself. The integrity of her seclusion is stained. She may be troubled with an unsourceable guilt, as surveillance provokes guilt in even the most innocent. Under surveillance, the mind can neither nest nor fly.

When I was a child, I drew a large imaginary island with all the things I wanted: mountains, fountains, trees, swings, tents, flowers, a thatched cottage, pools of water, a fairground and a sailing boat. I have it in my hand now, that scrappy bit of pale-blue paper which was my treasured island. I would go there to be alone. From *Treasure Island* to *Coral Island* to the island of *Swallows and Amazons* or that of *Lord of the Flies*, islands fascinate children. *Robinson Crusoe* would not appeal to children half so much if the island weren't a major character.

The contours of that island were so important to the young Rudyard Kipling that he would repeatedly play at being Crusoe, with a coconut shell, red cord, tin trunk and a bit of packing-case, writing: 'The magic, you see, lies in the ring or fence that you take refuge in.'

These literary islands each contain two islands, the island *in* the book and the island *of* the book, the refuge which reading grants to a child. Not only in reading but in writing, children seek solitude in coded messages and tiny scripts designed to be beneath the notice of adults, as the Brontës and Beatrix Potter did. Secret writing symbolizes privacy, but it also enacts a powerful metaphor: children are themselves both the author and the book of themselves. They are both the artist and the art and their task is to create themselves.

They are conscious, however, that they are works-in-progress, incomplete. Many writers loathe being required to give a synopsis of a book before it is written, because the glare of other eyes is brutal and inappropriate to something so delicate. Such writers may fiercely protect their unfinished writing from the eyes of others, knowing that in privacy transformation can occur. Children, self-authoring, do not want to be called to account to give a précis of their true selves before their own inner book is written. They want a room of their own as much as Virginia Woolf did, they want to write themselves in secret tiny code, they want not to be disturbed in those moments when they are silently concentrating on their inner book of twilight beginningness. These are the rites and rights of privacy: the rites of lines drawn, secrets kept, drawers closed, the right to the walled solitude of your own mind as to a secret garden of your own.

Wanting their secret places, children make dens from the age of about six, building forts and constructing treehouses in a worldwide habit of childhood. You no more have to teach a child to make a den than give a mouse training in burrowing. One of my dens was a small clearing under the rhododendron bushes in a friend's garden, with a low branch for a perch; it was a nest for the small animals we were, in the shaded cool green where something was always about to happen. (My friend's staggering, hyperbolic, magnificent lies, the rotten stairwell, the tramp in the woods, the wall as high as a house – all were always on the point of breaking into story.)

As they grow older, particularly around the ages of nine to eleven, these are places of profound privacy. Children often don't want anyone to see them entering their dens and they go there sometimes just to sit alone, sometimes to read, to be secluded, often in silence, to hide treasure and keep secrets. The imagination wants its solitudes, its hideaways of intimacy for self-invention, self-discovery and self-making, so a den, dug on the borders of adult notice, is not a matter of ownership but of self-ownership.

A scruffy bit of land, preferably with a stream, but a puddle will do, preferably with trees, but stones, bushes, dirt, sticks and rocks are enough. Children making dens are not copying adult houses but rather translating into the vernacular architecture of childhood all the dwelling which the human animal needs: refuge, lookout, water, shade and soul-shelter. I remember one den I made with friends. 'We need somewhere to hide so we can see them coming,' someone said. I was young enough to know we needed this, but old enough suddenly to want to know – *who?* 'Just enemies,' said the oldest girl, and we settled for that. According to some psychologists, children make nests with lookouts because they are genetically programmed to do so.

There is a tatterdemalion commonness to children's places; they choose the field-margins, the waste, the ungardened bits where all things run to seed, tangly and weed-strewn. This is where children den up, among the riff-raff. While the wood-haunts of rural children are often the areas disdained by adults, in urban areas children make holts in the rough patches among dumped mattresses, soggy card-board boxes, mangy cats and the condoms which very small children think are bubblegum. In a palace, Charles Baudelaire says, there is no place for intimacy. Children don't want palaces, they want to be kings and queens of the tatty bits, and they seek the unwanted spaces, the unironed, untidy parts messy enough to mess about in.

Children head for the neglected areas, derelict, forgotten and over-looked. It is common knowledge that children want to be noticed, but they *also* want their times of being ignored. For their dens, they seek gap-toothed edges, the holes, borders and between-places, the under-neaths, arounds, aboves and behinds. In rural places they want weeds and wilderness while in urban places they want rubble and rubbish, not because they like garbage but because it is more likely they will be left alone. Children need the unlimited, undefined, untamed places precisely because they reflect their own undefined and unowned selves. When Mary finds the secret garden, it is 'a world all her own'. But she clarifies this possession: 'It isn't mine. It isn't anybody's. Nobody wants it, nobody cares for it.'

In the acute rhymes of childhood, a child will often make a den on a building site because the child is similarly 'under construction'. Set in the Glasgow tenements in the 1970s, during the national garbage strike, Lynne Ramsay's film *Ratcatcher* catches the childhood hunger for dens, as the boy-hero finds a half-built housing development between urban sprawl and the fields. Materially poor, part of the human garbage of a class-ridden society, he co-opts one of the half-constructed houses (his ownership includes pissing into an unplumbed-in toilet) and he builds his dream, a place to shelter his 'self'.

Children take possession of things apparently unpossessed and when they are excluded from their sites and excavations, or when their dens are torn down by awful adult municipal tidiness, when adults insist on owning every last scrap of space, when councils harangue families into getting planning permission for treehouses and when neighbours moan that den constructions are unsafe, children may be heartbroken, because their daydreams have been repossessed and they have no territory for their interiority.

Scavenge it, nick it, break a bit off something else, use 'umm, borrowed' materials, as children euphemistically put it, the engineering handbook for dennery recommends all these. Dens are unplanned and unplannable; the only permit they need is the licence of childhood imagination. They are not meant to be physically safe but places of far more urgent psychological safety, and when children have access to the woods, they don't need to 'umm, borrow' their timber. It is true that free tarp remains an unsolvable problem, but bin bags, corrugated plastic and pretending-to-be-dry all work to keep the rain off.

The instinct for dens comes to the fore during the unformed and provisional time in children's lives, and this is represented in their appreciation of these untidy, unfinished and messy places. Mary's secret garden is beautiful to her because it is unkempt; the plants ramble overgrown and the roses hang in a 'hazy tangle from tree to tree'. 'It's nicer like this with things runnin' wild,' Dickon says. 'Don't let us make it tidy,' Mary responds: 'It wouldn't seem like a secret garden if it was tidy.'

Although Mary and her cousin Colin belong to the wealthy family of the estate, the real treasures of life all belong to the peasant-child Dickon, who has animal-companions, freedom, music, knowledge and the commonwealth of the commons. He enlivens their world with a fox, crow, squirrels and a lamb, he enchants it with wildness, waking the garden. At the core of his charisma is the trust which he wins from birds, people and animals, earning their confidence by his attention to, and love for, their vulnerability. Mary instinctively confides in Dickon the secret of her garden. 'Whatever happens, you – you would never tell?' she asks, sheltering her own fragile, nestling self. The tenderness of his response is heartbreaking. He keeps secrets all the time, he says, about the dens, holes and nests of animals and birds. 'If tha' was a missel thrush an' showed me where thy nest was, does tha' think I'd tell anyone? Not me,' he said. 'Tha' art as safe as a missel thrush.'

What a dove-cote is for a dove, a dream-cote is for a child's soul. Mary's great wish is to tend the garden and plant seeds and, in a kind reflection, the garden is also tending to her and the seeds of her own future self are planted here. The garden dovetails with her soul. Like her, the garden is at first dark and wintry, and both bulbs and child need the darkness first, protected in the minding earth. For Mary, the garden is a cocoon, as dens, forts, treehouses or secret hideaways are for all children, places where they spin their own silk, weave their own refuges for their transformations, the metamorphosis intimate with reverie and innerness. Giving children ready-made treehouses or prefab tipis just isn't the point, well intentioned though it is, because children need to make their own places rather than have them ready-provided. This is a soul-matter: a den is a self-spun cocoon for the child's vulnerable psyche and myth itself is on the child's side. The Greek goddess Psyche is represented as a moth or butterfly, and the psyche needs its cocoons *before* it can fly and *in order to* fly. Wordsworth called the butterfly the 'Historian of my infancy'.

Like moths and butterflies, children need to direct their own timing, emerging when their time is ripe. Moments of emergence can impress a child like bright sunshine after cloud and one man recalls a startling sense of emergence when he was twelve: 'Suddenly for a single moment I had the overwhelming impression of having just emerged from a dense cloud. I knew all at once: now I am myself! It was as if a wall of mist were at my back, and behind that wall there was not yet an "I". But at this moment I came upon myself.' A 'wall of mist' is like this psyche-silk; soft, intangible but real. The emergence is a transformation no psyche can forget, and Carl Gustav never did, for it is he, as an adult, writing about the young Jung.

I have a memory of stepping across the threshold between our lawn and a patio behind our house one day. Nothing happened on the outside. But on the inside, quite suddenly and with total clarity, I thought 'I am,' and it felt like a momentous, mysterious emergence.

Many children want a fire in their den, at the heart of the hearth of themselves. From about the age of eight, Jung was drawn to the 'caves' in the walls of an enclosed garden, writing: 'I used to tend a little fire in one of these caves . . . a fire that had to burn forever . . . No one but myself was allowed to tend this fire . . . My fire alone was living and had an unmistakable aura of sanctity.' The fire of the mind was sacred, and children, whatever their reticence, whatever their vocabulary at the time or later, know the seriousness of their spirits. This isn't to say their fire antics are necessarily sombre: my brothers and I once made a den with an old sheet wrapped around the bamboo wigwam set up for the runner beans. Then the inevitable fire. The whole thing – beans, bamboo, sheet and all – went up in flames, and three small, singed children spent the afternoon hiding the evidence.

As well as fire, children want water for their special places. Given the choice, and enough 'outside' to play in, children seek out dens by flowing water, echoing their own fluid transformations as, in the waters of the mind, children voyage through liquid horizons. Children also take food to their dens, symbolizing how these places are sustenance for them, while food also seems like an offering, a libation to the divinity, to the goddess Psyche, within each child. The presence of these things nourishes the child, animates the place and vitalizes the time, for food, fire and water are primal ways to create a sacred space, a *temenos*.

Between the ages of eight and fifteen, the American writer Kim Stafford spent all his free time in the woods making shelters for his psyche. His adult description of it illustrates the significance of those dens, and his intense recall of his fire-affirmed identity reveals something of how children kindle their souls:

> In the woods by myself, fire was the heart of it all. In my secret den, or in some refuge off the trail . . . this was the repeated prelude to my identity . . . Here was my private version of civilization, my separate hearth . . . I would take any platform or den that got me above, under, or around the corner from the everyday. There I pledged allegiance to what I knew, as opposed to what was common . . . My separate hearth had to be invented by me, kindled, sustained, and held secret by my own soul as a rehearsal for departure.

Some origin-fire, some moment of flame, draws children from within. The 'fire' tended both actually and symbolically is the fire to dry their wings by, as the butterfly needs to dry its wings in the warmth of sunfire.

When the adult butterfly emerges, it is called an imago – the butterfly of Psyche is imagination incarnate. Jung was to develop his theory of the imago as a presence left in the psyche created from the absence of something: a 'revenant', a 'trace', something situated in the beyond. 'Imago' is related to both 'imagination' and 'magic', and in *The Secret Garden*, spring warms the garden until 'it seemed as if Magicians were passing through it drawing loveliness out of the earth.' Imagination makes things not larger than life but deeper, wider and more vivid.

Childhood is itself a walled garden within the adult estate and our childhood is not behind us but within us. For many writers, artists and musicians – those who are compelled to live by the imagination – the secret den persists and they are often fiendish protectors of their adult dens; their studies, studios, desks and sheds and their hours of privacy. Why the protection? Why the fortification of the 'forts' of childhood? Because we are, both as children and as adults, vulnerable when we think. Lost in thought and alive to the world of the imagination, we are dead to the world of reality and we need shelter because, our attention focused elsewhere, we are easy prey. Adults may concoct varieties of defences – 'boundaries', rituals and habits; children actualize their symbols and build forts, while their very selves need a sense of condensed shelter.

~

No one has entered the secret garden in ten years, Mary is told, though the grumpy old gardener has nipped over the wall to prune the roses. This reinforces the parallel between the garden and Mary's psyche, as she too is ten years old and just as neglected, though the gardener has nipped over the walls of her defences with symbolic secateurs a couple of times, giving her some sharp advice.

When Mary and the garden thrive, they grow together, fertile, rich and kind, the inner world of the child and the outer world of the garden reflecting each other. As the garden emerges from its winter cocoon into spring, the child steps out from her cocoon into imagination, the wonder of her own mind, as well as the wonder of the garden. At this threshold in her life, she is at a radiant mirror-moment, not just experiencing the world but experiencing the ecstasy of having a mind with which to do it.

In her quality of attention, she conjures, like a magician, the flowers and skies within herself, and this experience is common to children, even if it is delicate as silk and subtle as mist, this moment when the world makes you gasp twice at exactly the same time, once for it, a breathless wonderstruck gasp, and once for the mind, the gasp chasing breath inwards, in a consonance of self and world. Transactions of intensity take place at the reflecting border and there is depth behind depth of reverberating significance as children make their quests outwards into landscapes and inwards into mindscapes, voyagers in two directions at once.

Imagination, the imago of the butterfly, takes wing, and all the arts of the world can trace their beginnings here. One of my godchildren, aged eight, fell asleep with a little black exercise book of poems, her own poems, open on her nose like a butterfly drying its wings before it flies. 'Without poetry our world would be locked within itself,' says an eleven-year-old child, in an observation treasured by author and teacher Richard Lewis. Children's first relationship to language, Lewis says, 'is a poetic one, reaching far beyond utilitarian speech'.

In one study of how creative thinkers recall childhood memories, a shared theme emerges: each of them experienced a strong feeling of their individuality as a child and, at the same time, a sense of profound immersion in the world.

The American writer Dolores LaChapelle describes lying in grass as a young girl, watching the sky and feeling as if there were no separation between herself and the world. Art critic Bernard Berenson recalls: 'I felt suddenly immersed in Itness. I did not call it by that name. I had no need for words. It and I were one. Surely most children are like that.'

The paradox of emerging individuality and deep immersion in

nature can perhaps be resolved by love, for there seems an inherent attractive force between child and world, a force of gravity in the psyche. Gravity used to be called Eros in homage to this magnetic attraction which the earth asks of all who dwell here.

'Our Dickon can make a flower grow out of a brick wall,' says the boy's sister. 'Mother says he just whispers things out o' th' ground.' Children are world-whisperers, whistling a universe into being in a tryst of cosmopoeisis, or world-making. And the world in turn is a child-whisperer, drawing them out, calling them out into their flowering selves.

Whatever you call it – an aesthetic, a poetic, a spirituality, a cosmopoesis – one thing is clear: issues of the soul really matter to children. They want to know if you believe in a god or ghosts or spirits. They ask what happens after death. They are searchers after significance; they take it seriously; they care about the soul. One woman told me that when her grandson was three, he addressed his very first question to her, and it was this: 'Is my soul in my head or in my heart?' A large proportion of children's questions are about cosmogony – the big questions, the creation of worlds – and they perceive a divinity in nature.

Children can be mavericks of malice. They can be vengeful, grittily nasty, dishonest, cruel and manipulative. Children bite and cheat and bully. Yes. But they are seekers as well as scamps; pilgrims as well as thieves.

One of my godchildren, aged six, constructed a prayer-game: we would all write wishes, asking 'the giant' to make them come true. 'We need to pick flowers for the giant,' she said, 'and tie them with the wishes on to a tree.' She asked the giant to grant the wishes and as she did so she touched them with a 'wand' dipped in clean, cold water. (She is adamant that 'good giants like clean, cold water, while bad giants like hot, dirty water.') If the note is gone in the morning, 'it means that the giant has read it and the wishes will come true.' She was inventing a rite – the prayer, the devotional offering, the purification of water, the wand to release the magic and the hope that divinity will give some proof of itself.

C. S. Lewis's autobiography, *Surprised by Joy*, describes poignant moments in his childhood spirituality. In one such moment he was troubled by 'what I can only describe as the Idea of Autumn . . . the experience was one of intense desire' as well as a 'sense of incalculable importance'. Years later, reading of the twilight of the gods, 'there arose at once, almost like heartbreak, the memory of Joy itself . . . a single unendurable sense of desire and loss, which . . . had eluded me at the very moment when I could first say *It is*.' This sense of yearning, of inchoate desire and longing, is more than the story of one individual child's psyche. It is right at the heart of Romanticism, and that is no coincidence. Romanticism expresses truths of childhood which are both deep and enduring (as the last chapter will explore), and children are unimpeachable Romantics, born with a longing for something beyond, whether that is nature, or divinity, or spirit. Something ultimate.

Children need little help recognizing the divinity of the natural world, and in children's literature it often appears as Pan, god of nature. In *The Little Grey Men*, Pan's mysterious call is heard and it seems to contain birdsong and windsong and insects and trees, the voices of streams and seas. At Dickon's first appearance in *The Secret Garden*, he is sitting with his back against a tree, playing a low little call on a wooden pipe, surrounded by rabbits and a squirrel. Like Pan, he charms animals and birds till they draw close to listen, and he talks to the animals. 'He could speak robin,' writes the author.

When one of my godchildren was six, she repeatedly took my

ocarina, saying she was 'whistling for Pan'. The previous midsummer night, her mother and I had read to her 'The Piper at the Gates of Dawn', the Pan chapter from *The Wind in the Willows*, which is situated right in the middle of the book. Rat and Mole are rowing their boat, looking for a little otter which has gone missing, and they find not only the otter but also Pan. The scene takes place at midsummer, the centre of the year, and in the middle of the midsummer night, on an island in the middle of the river. At the heart of everything is Pan. (Sadly, this core chapter is excised in some editions of the book.)

Rat, entranced, hears the pipes just on the threshold of hearing. The music rouses 'a longing in me that is pain'. As they arrive at the island, Rat knows it with the unequivocal recognition of finding oneself at the heart of things: 'This is the place of my song-dream, the place the music played to me . . . This time, at last, it is the real, the unmistakable thing, simple – passionate – perfect'.

Pan grants the animals a necessary forgetfulness so they are not later haunted by a nostalgia they cannot bear. It is as if Grahame is writing of the necessary forgetfulness which adulthood demands, that we forget some of the simple, passionate, perfect knowledge we had as children, dwellers under a different sky.

~

Children have a grandeur of soul which adults can often overlook. 'I think children love dignity,' writes Joyce Cary. 'In all their eagerness to learn, they are seeking some glory and honour, some beauty.' Children deliberately call other children 'people', quietly insistent on their seriousness. Gravitas becomes them, pride as wide as the rings of Saturn, and they understand heroism, valour and glory. This isn't to say children want to be pious or good or obedient, but rather they want to hear the codes of the soul which wills the world to be worthy of their devotion.

'We grownups are always around pumping our kids full of what we laughingly call facts,' says Robert Paul Smith. 'They don't want science. They want magic. They don't want hypotheses, they want immutable truth.'

In the early 1960s, a North Carolina girl of eight spoke about the newly desegregated schools in the American South. She was walking to school alone, with segregationists screaming around her, 'and suddenly I saw God smiling, and I smiled.' A woman was standing near the school door, shouting at the child: ' "Hey, you little nigger, what you smiling at?" I looked right at her face, and I said, "At God." Then she looked up at the sky, and then she looked at me, and she didn't call me any more names.'

The timbre of the spirit needs echoes of its own tones, when its abstract nouns are of fealty, courage and splendour. In traditional Dakota life, a young boy coming through initiation tests was given an ash wand so he would be resilient, a cup to symbolize hospitality, a wolf tail as the warrior's symbol, and crow feathers to represent unerring flight. This kind of thing can be irresistible to the young. Tom Sawyer's eyes are alight with it, my childhood self recognizes this language and kids in gangs may well understand it faster than any. For if children cannot find powerful and positive glory-stories, they will find powerful and negative ones. Gangs offer children security, protection, a substitute family-life and, crucially, the kind of momentous significance which children yearn for.

Kidulthood, directed by Menhaj Huda, is an extraordinary film which exposes urban gang culture in all its ugliness and violence, but it also hints at its appeal. The moment comes when the film's hero, Trife, aged fifteen, is given a gun. Time shudders. It pulses, ricocheting between the airwaves: this time, this place is suddenly sundered into a gigantic otherness. The gun is talisman, trophy, taboo and totem. Refused glory – talismans which guide the spirit, trophies which honour it, taboos which protect it and totems to which the spirit can pledge its allegiance – refused their inheritance, kids will look elsewhere for it.

The soul-splendour is ambiguous, of course, for children are rarely religiose and, even at their most spiritual, they are often only half a step away from a comedic, rude pragmatism and are delighted by gore as much as glory. Most children, if they were honest, would quite enjoy seeing a house on fire; when we were small, a nearby house burned to cinders, and all the children on the street piled down to get front-row seats. It was awesome, it was enormous, it was unforgettable: it was the best entertainment we'd ever seen.

Perhaps one of the reasons for the enduring appeal of Tom Sawyer is that Twain conveys these ambivalent truths of childhood glory. Tom is curious about Huckleberry Finn's escapade 'because it was a grand adventure, and mysterious, and so it hit him where he lived'. Tom lives a lot of the time in the irreal world of oaths, incantations, melodrama and the laws of the Gothic. He has the idea that he and Huck should attend their own funerals, and when they return to school, they are much admired by the other children, particularly when they get out their pipes and smoke. Then 'the very summit of glory was reached. Tom decided that he could be independent of Becky Thatcher now. Glory was sufficient. He would live for glory.' At one point, he considers disappearing from his ordinary world and becoming a clown, but the indignity of the frivolity, jokes and spotted tights 'were an offence when they intruded themselves upon a spirit that was exalted into the vague, august realm of the romantic'. He considers becoming a soldier or joining the Indians or becoming a pirate. 'That was it! *Now* his future lay plain before him, and glowing with unimaginable splendour.'

His glory is 'glowing' to his mind. When people think the boys have drowned, their notoriety is 'dazzling', and the grandeur-cum-trouble they are creating is 'illustrious'. Glory lights up a child's mind with words of radiance.

Light is the great presence in the inner childscape. There is, it seems to children, some luminous core to life which they recognize in every age and culture. 'Something that "shone" at the heart of Matter,' priest-philosopher Pierre Teilhard de Chardin calls it. Aged only three, Hildegaard of Bingen was overwhelmed by a vision of 'heavenly light'. To the seventeenth-century poet Thomas Traherne, in childhood, 'Eternity was manifest in the Light of the Day, and something infinite behind everything appeared.' Alice Walker's earliest memory was of dust motes in sunlight, 'glinting beautifully, mysteriously', which she came to think of as 'an early imprint on my psyche of the cosmos, which I so love'.

The child-god Krishna's mouth is full of starlight. 'I am Aengus; men call me the Young. I am the sunlight in the heart, the moonlight in the mind; I am the light at the end of every dream,' wrote 'A. E.', of a dream-vision. An eight-year-old Hopi girl dreams of flying with her dog (reports American author Robert Coles), waving to the sun and stars which, she says, give the gift of light. 'The light, the wholeness' is central to Jean Liedloff's special glade of childhood. A primal luminescence is theirs: in his novel *Runt*, Niall Griffiths's hero is a sixteen-year-old savant who describes his mind 'like a cloud with the sun bright in it'. Flora Thompson recalls stories in childhood which 'shone with a kind of moonlight radiance in her imagination'. This is where the other light is, the psychelight streaming into a child's conscious awareness.

That central chapter of *The Wind in the Willows* is lit with the reverie-light of every midsummer night's dream. When Aslan approaches Narnia, the warmth and light of spring begin to break the winter thrall. In *The Secret Garden*, giving the bulbs light enough to grow is Mary's first – instinctive – piece of gardening, just as Mary finds the sunlight she needs too, and the literal energy of all the transformations comes from the increased sunlight as the year grows towards summer, while the author comments that metaphoric healing is a result of thinking positively, which is 'as good for one as sunlight is'. In its assured affinity with childhood mind, Romanticism in general is fascinated by light, and light is a central image of Sturm und Drang.

I recently read the historian A. L. Rowse's description of a childhood moment when he sensed 'the transcendence of things'; it comes from the light of the blue sky seen through white apple blossom. I gasped, reading that, because as a child, I also had a moment in an orchard, skystruck by blue seen between the branches of an apple tree. I was transfixed. I couldn't move. It was that walled-garden-moment from which, in Persian, we get the word 'paradise'. Paradise is nothing more than a walled garden, lit with the twice-light of sun and mind. It is nothing more and nothing less either.

The English writer Richard Jefferies described his sense of wanting to 'have the inner meaning of the sun, the light, the earth, the trees and grass, translated into some growth of excellence' in himself. 'We the illuminati,' said Kenneth Grahame, of being a child, and Emily Brontë wrote, 'we wove a web in childhood, a web of sunny air', while Wordsworth describes 'the radiance which was once so bright' in childhood. Light is the literal and metaphoric illumination but, as childhood fades, so does the light: 'Whither is fled the visionary gleam? Where is it now, the glory and the dream?' When adults retain the Romantic sensibilities of childhood, those illuminations 'Are yet the fountain-light of all our day, are yet a master-light of all our seeing'.

Children have a kind of light – an otherwise-light – to see things by twolight, the invisible light of imagination, so that they may be guided by their inner lights. To think is to reflect – like a mirror, like water – light. Their dazzled moments speak of their inner sunlight, streams of bright thought, when children are backlit by sunshine of a different order.

CHAPTER SEVENTEEN

Eureka!

One summer evening when I was perhaps three years old my mother was reading to me from a children's book. She sat with the golden sunlight behind her falling on the page and through her long brown hair. I was taken by the light, as children so often are. But I was more struck by the book, a yellow hardback with red edging on the pages. I pointed at the words on the front, deciphering the code slowly, and my mother explained it was the name of the story. 'No, those *other* words?' I was perplexed. The name of the writer, she said, and my whole world staggered. That a story was not a pre-existent fact – that a person could create a book – seemed magical to me. Magical and mine. It was a moment of profound recognition.

Language had me spellbound from the beginning: my mother said I started talking well before I was one year old. Before I went to school, I learned the alphabet, replacing the baby letters (ah, buh, cuh) with their adult equivalents, and in my determination to learn I trailed around the house after my mother, so that every time I got stuck (usually on 'w'), I could ask her. Then I went back to the beginning and tried again. So I learned to talk almost before I could walk, learned to read almost before I could feed myself, such was my hunger. I read under the bedclothes, read in the car, read at parties, read up trees.

One night, when I was about five, I lay in bed, awake and desperately upset because I had read a word and couldn't remember how to spell it. I kept getting the awkward vowels mixed up in the word 'b-e-a-u-tiful'. Remembering it now, what comes sharply to mind is the seriousness of the situation, to me. I *must* learn to spell it: I felt as if my life depended on it. It was a need of total intent, something larger, older, deeper than me, as if the demand was there almost before 'I' was there. This is what I was *for*. I went over the word in my head, over and over, until the vowels slipped into place and held.

When I was about seven or eight, I missed months of school through illness. For many children, being in bed this long would have been torture. I wasn't particularly bothered because I could read everything I could find. I was so determined to read that even my failure to understand what I was reading did not deter me. I 'read' *War and Peace* when I was eight, mainly by skipping all the war, ignoring all Russian names and keeping a sharp eye on the conversations. Pierre talked a lot. When I was nine, my mother gave me a gift of enormous meaning when, one afternoon, she ushered my brothers and me into the children's library, settled the boys in a corner, then took me by the hand and suggested I started reading from the main, adult, section. This is a book you might like, she said, and pulled from the shelf a small, navy-blue hardback with thin pages like bible paper. It was a bible to me, this book which I would over the next ten years read twenty times. *Jane Eyre*.

It was my eureka moment. I had found it. When I read the book, it was a portal through which I was swept away into a world where I belonged and where, like most writers, I have dwelled ever since. To this day, I remember the precise layout of the library and, blindfolded, I could find my way there, to the exact part of the exact shelf, as if even as a child my mind foresaw the significance and made a mental map of the library like a guide to the treasure, an X marks the spot. I cannot imagine the poverty of my childhood without this particular library, which has now been threatened with closure.

At about the same age, I read *How Green Was My Valley*, and some lines in it I have never forgotten, nor my vehement sense of the injustice which the miners felt about their treatment and the necessity for unionization. My brothers and I created our own union: somewhere I may still have the minutes of our meetings. This political sense was reinforced by accidentally reading *The Ragged Trousered Philanthropists*, which I'd thought, judging by the cover and the title, might be like *The Adventures of Huckleberry Finn*.

My reading was chaotic, catholic, anarchic, untutored, bizarre, serendipitous. Like most children who are avid readers, I read anything and everything, and an early short story of my childhood was centred around the word 'monofluorophosphate', simply because I could spell it. I read Freud before I was eleven, mistaking his *Interpretation of Dreams* for a book of short stories. (I thought they were rubbish.) I remember where I was when I came across certain words and I recall the frightened seriousness I felt when I read the word 'Nazi' and an uncle gravely told me what it meant. I shared what is probably a very common childhood disappointment on discovering that the wonderful word 'picture-skew' is actually pronounced in that horribly dainty way 'picturesque'. (My nephew, hearing it without seeing it, writes it 'picture esk'.)

When I was eleven, I read 'Ariel's Song' from *The Tempest* – 'Full fathom five thy father lies' – and I was submerged in an ocean which I had not known was there, a resonance of bells and a depth of blue, a grief shot through with turquoise and treasure and all the dazed jewels of intensified passion. I cried. I knew my allegiance.

What is it, this sense of fidelity to one's own inner flame? In the

Western tradition, it is known as one's daemon, one's calling. Everyone has one, a guiding spirit – though not a fore-ordaining one. It is not the self, but the seed of purpose, the necessity of destiny inheld in earliest childhood, the child sheltering its own adult-to-be as the acorn shelters the future oak.

For Plato, the daemon was a guardian or guide of souls which belonged both to the child and to the world soul and so could 'know' the future. In Roman culture, the daemon became the 'genius' of each person, their idiosyncratic significance, the law of their own nature, as different as pine marten and snow leopard. The term 'daemon' is morally neutral but was perverted by the anti-pagan early Church from the third century to represent something of evil, and the word was written 'demon'. No lovelier an idea has been so wrenched out of true, though it has been rescued in recent years by psychologist and author James Hillman and by Philip Pullman.

'We carry within ourselves the direction our lives will take. Within ourselves burn the timeless, fateful stars,' wrote Antal Szerb in *Journey by Moonlight*. Every child is star-guided and the star which burns within yearns to shine outwardly, although for some children the patience required is a furious penance. That daemon-light flames further than the child, so a child may feel self-magnetized, drawn by something both within them and yet beyond them: the daemon throws a magnet far ahead of the child, who is then compelled to follow it.

Children, like the Romantics who so utterly understood them, seek their destiny within themselves, that destiny which will be their destination. The idea of the individual is central to the young as it is to the Romantics and, for both, the process of self-becoming is an aesthetic: the art of sculpting one's own character, carving one's unique self, 'to selve', as a verb, to shape the intrinsic person and delineate one's identity. The importance of being true to oneself, to one's own inner lights, is something children readily understand.

In Pullman's work, the daemon is illustrated by various animals. These daemons are also shapeshifters and, though they will gradually settle into a fixed identity, their early liquidity is part of the daemon's subtlety. Subtle but certain, though, because for all that the daemon or genius of a child is enigmatic, it is also adamant. It is delicate as silk, yet tough as a claw.

The relationship between the self and the daemon is a ruthless conspiracy. The daemon is implacable and when it is dissatisfied it would jettison anything and risk everything to find what it needs. It is a relationship at once hidden and yet as searingly clear as a lightning strike: a conversation inaudible and deafening. The daemon may conceal itself for safety and then reveal itself when it chooses, shifting in and out of sight, a sleight of hand in the psyche's life. The daemon may appear now as beauty, now as beast; it may be stern, kind, protective or furious. It is not rational or predictable or explicable, yet it weaves a faithful pattern; the fate, the lot in life spun out of its destiny. Entelechy, I suppose. Something potential becoming actualized.

Right in the core of a child there is a self-determining, autonomous sense of self-rule, an independence of identity, mitigated, influenced and shaped though it will be by the happenstance of life. The calling may be one of friendship or fishing, a vocation of teaching or theft, a destiny of music, engineering or rampant idleness, but whatever it is, the daemon will search for opportunities where the child may grow into their own fruition. When those opportunities arise, the psyche may see something of the shape of its destiny, and under their breath the child may begin to sing from the songline of their own soul.

The riddle of this book asks why so many children are not happy. For part of the answer, let me tell you that the Ancient Greek word for happiness is *eudaimonia*. *Eu* means good, or in this case pleased, and *daimonia* is the person's daemon. Satisfying one's daemon, fulfilling one's destiny, is so important that a life's happiness may depend on it, the pleased daemon successfully expressing itself.

The daemon has a specific dream: it seeks its originality, the specific this-ness of an individual self, carving a unique path. The daemon does not come mass-produced. But today, children's daemons have been kidnapped by the child-snatchers. Huge numbers of young people say they want to become 'celebrities', famous for being famous – factory dreams of an identikit destiny. It's the opposite of the daemon-dream, which seeks to be acknowledged for its specific gifts and its unique self.

The daemon is not the same as a child's will, but the two share, as it were, a political ethos. Both seek autonomy, the self-rule of sovereignty. Both detest being subject to the diktats of empire. Both are prepared to be revolutionaries to get what they need.

The daemon is numinous. When it makes itself felt, the child may be rapt in its presence. In a daemon-saturated moment, children may feel a sense of uncanny recognition of something they have never met with before, something apparently unfamiliar, never previously encountered, and yet something they feel they know. (So it was for me, discovering that E-N-I-D B-L-Y-T-O-N – there, I've said it – spelt the existence of The Writer and therefore my future self.) Children may give this strange thing – a violin, a lake, a book – a nod of profound recognition, inner assent to a kinship. It may not be an object at all but a gift, a skill, an art, a quality: something, though, which the soul knows itself aligned with, something akin, its inner likeness outered in the world, an inner whisper uttered into life. Those moments are unforgeable, unstageable and unforgettable – the psyche's homecoming.

Then comes trouble.

For the daemon may be hellishly demanding. To prompt the child or impel it towards its full selfhood, the daemon may force it to arrogance or shyness, to doggedness, disobedience, secrecy, eccentricity or laziness.

A creative power, said Wordsworth, in lines which perfectly describe the daemon:

> Abode with me, a forming hand, at times
> Rebellious, acting in a devious mood,
> A local spirit of his own, at war
> With general tendency . . .

It won his lifelong service: 'Hence my obeisance, my devotion hence.'

The daemon may be clandestine or furtive in its motivation and protection. 'It invents and persists with stubborn fidelity,' writes James Hillman in his beautiful book *The Soul's Code*. 'It resists compromising reasonableness and often forces deviance and oddity upon its keeper, especially when it is neglected or opposed . . . It can make the body ill.' Or make a child want to kill.

Elias Canetti was five and fascinated by writing. He was mesmerized by the words in his father's newspaper and the letters in his older cousin's notebooks as she was learning to read and write. He wanted to touch the letters, but she refused. He begged and pleaded for the writing but she held the notebooks above her head, well beyond the reach of his actual five-year-old self. But not beyond the reach of his daemon. Elias, alas, impelled with a fury and a need which the whole of his later life would fill out, walked away from her, round to the kitchen yard, his child's footsteps carrying the imprint of his adult destination, and got an axe to kill her. Raising it, he started back towards her, chanting murder: 'Now I'm going to kill Laurica! Now I'm going to kill Laurica!' Luckily for Laurica, he was overheard and disarmed.

Pablo Neruda, almost eleven, found himself suddenly daemon-wracked, destiny-tormented, 'seized by profound anxiety, a feeling I hadn't had before, a kind of anguish and sadness', and in that Orpheus moment he wrote his first poem. Later, he would recall that moment when:

something started in my soul,
fever or forgotten wings.

Before he was school-age, Wole Soyinka, pining for books and words but too young for school, dressed himself in clothes most like the school uniform, took some books from his father's study, walked to school and plonked his two-year-old bum on the bench. 'You are not old enough to learn from books,' said the teacher. With the pride and solemnity which is often a feature of the daemon-voice, the toddler replied: 'I am nearly three. Anyway, I have come to school. I have books.'

Audre Lorde's very first words were 'I want to read,' and a children's librarian granted her wish. 'That deed saved my life,' she wrote. For her daemon this was no exaggeration: it was a matter of survival.

'I write therefore I am,' says the poet Lemn Sissay, who spent much of his childhood in care homes. (He uses gigantic and sarcastic inverted commas around the word 'care'.) During these years, he says, 'a book washed upon my shore' like a treasure chest on a deserted island. It made him feel treasured himself, as if he was worth something, he says later. The book was *The Mersey Sound*, a book of poetry, and he describes it as a portal to the world.

The daemon speaks with the wisdom of *anima mundi* from the deeps of the dream-ocean. 'We meet always in the deep of the mind, whatever our work, wherever our reverie carries us, that other Will,' wrote W. B. Yeats.

Every child is both a reader and a writer of their life. Each has an uncanny skill in prolepsis, reading ahead, flicking forward several chapters in the book of their life, and also writing in childhood a sketchy outline of adulthood, the first notes towards their own testament. Aged six, William Blake sketched out a country of his imagination called Allestone. As an adult he would create his own mythological world.

When I was young, I had a recurring dream of being a child in an occupied country during the Second World War. In those dreams, I was always entrusted with the most important messages of the Resistance because, being young and female, the enemy would take no notice of me. That was the first message. A second message, though, was encoded in the first; a message from the underwater world of the subconscious, a message from my daemon saying that in my life I must receive messages (read) and I must transmit messages (write). Mercury the messenger is my favourite of the old gods, wings at his heels, and I think many writers align themselves with him. Seamus Heaney recalls a dream from his childhood: 'I dreamt I was running across fields to tell about an invasion . . . I was the only one there to raise the alarm.'

Walt Whitman's 'Out of the Cradle Endlessly Rocking' is set by the seashore, and the poem reveals the making of the poet. The boy (Whitman, the poet-to-be) had been closely watching the nesting of two mockingbirds and listening to them. He:

Listen'd long and long.
Listen'd to keep, to sing, now translating the notes.

This word 'translating' hints at Whitman's early sense of his messenger role: he was a careful listener before he spoke, a careful reader before he wrote the notes. This is a deep, deft pun, for it is only now as an adult that Whitman can translate the notes, not just the musical notes which the birds sang, but also the psyche's notes from childhood, those scraps of memory to be fully filled out – fulfilled – by the mature writer.

The bird, the ocean and the moon speak unmistakeably 'To the outsetting bard', and this is the moment of his birth as a poet when the child's soul knows the daemon call with all the vehemence of his heart:

Now in a moment I know what I am for . . .

For a thousand songs, for the bard-life, his calling as a poet. He takes his calling from a calling bird, calling for its lost love. Who is the messenger? The bird, the boy or the poet? All of them. With flooding tears and burning recognition, riven with significance, he writes:

The messenger there arous'd, the fire, the sweet hell within,
The unknown want, the destiny of me.

His songs 'awaked' from that moment:

And with them the key, the word up from the waves,
The work of the sweetest song and all songs . . .

His fidelity to that moment was his gift to the world.

~

Just a few years earlier, a young boy, John, was writing poetry in secret and hiding his papers in an empty cupboard. His mum wanted the storage space, so he tucked them into a hole in the wall instead. Spring-cleaning one day, his mother found the poems. Thinking her son was just practising his handwriting, copying things out, Mrs Clare used the poems to light fires or to protect her hands when lifting a hot kettle. So John Clare's earliest poetry, hidden in the dark like seeds before spring, are now lost for ever, but we do know one impulse of its germination: it came from his having read, aged thirteen, James Thomson's *The Seasons*. Jonathan Bate's beautiful biography of Clare tells the story of the spring-cleaning and relates that '*The Seasons* opened him to his own vocation. He never forgot the sensation – a "twitter of joy" in the heart, he called it – that he felt upon reading the first few lines of "Spring".'

Children, in the springtime of their lives, often remember a moment of germination, like a seed husk breaking open, as James Thomson's 'Spring' describes seed, song, muse and bird in ascent.

A hot seed, deep in the dark pause of earth, swelling on the cusp of the moment when all its energy, tightly compressed, is ready to spring, when the spirit, curled tight as a drum, begins to break open. Spiralling and uncurling with meaning, it bursts with the ferocious energy of inheld force, latent potential becomes potency as a seed of the soul, detonating in the kindly earth, explodes into green shoots reaching for light with its own inaudible eureka! Germination.

In childhood, the future is born. Both heroism and sorrow find their seeds there:

In the lost boyhood of Judas
Christ was betrayed

                   – '*Germinal*' by '*A. E.*', George William Russell

Judas and Jesus alike had a daemon. No one is without their genius: for fun, or food or fixing things; for tidiness, for devotion, for jokes or for fatherhood. The daemon is a democratic spirit, Coleridge referring to the 'attendant Daimon or Genius of an individual'. A child's genius may not be for a grand role, or even a socially approved one, but genius each child has, as surely as oaks have acorns and acorns oaks. Some thirty years ago, in a town near Italy's Lake Garda, there was a six-year-old boy who played truant from school to go to various building sites around town, trying to help the builders, climbing and clambering anywhere, reaching beyond his grasp. Time after time, he was told it was too dangerous and he was shooed away: time after time, he returned. His mother could do nothing to stop him, and he would barely go to school. He grew up to create a highly successful 'extreme building' company that used helicopters and climbing gear to work on buildings in almost unreachable places – now within his grasp.

The daemon within the child requires a good witness, whether that is a parent, aunt, godfather, grandparent, teacher or family friend. In its moments of self-revelation, though, the daemon is vulnerable. When I was a teenager I knew well an older boy who, at seventeen, wanted to be a primary-school teacher. He would have made a gifted guide for small children. When he mentioned it to an adult, I was with him, proud of his ambition but protective of him too, knowing he was opening his heart. Within two minutes, the idea had been decisively crushed. There was no money or status in it, plus it was a job for girls, he was told. He'd chosen the wrong witness, someone who could 'see' money and status nicely shaded with misogyny but could not see the gentle genius which was radiant in the boy. He never, to my knowledge, mentioned it again.

No adult can give a child their daemon. We can only play the retiring roles: to notice, allow, support, stand aside and witness. Reticent though those roles are, they are vital for the daemon, which needs to be acknowledged, listened to and taken seriously.

I was lucky that my mother and her mother saw my love for books and encouraged it. My grandmother was a stern woman who had not always had an easy life, and she could be short-tempered with small children but when, aged about five, I wrote my first book, sellotaped it together and gave it to her (I was living with her at the time), she received it in both her hands, gazed at me with solemnity far more than love, and told me, with a belief that left me both aghast with acknowledgement and apprehensive with the enormity, how much she looked forward to reading the first book which I would get published. She never did: she died when I was still a child, but she gave me an unshakeable belief not that she had given me the keys to the palace but that she knew with certainty that the keys were in my pocket right from the very beginning.

In the absence of witnessing adults, the child may practise a psychological DIY, appealing to their own future selves for witness. Children can dissociate not only in space but in time and sometimes in my childhood, needing an understanding adult, I would write to myself-in-the-future, someone who could comprehend the peculiarities of my psyche, its quizzical vicissitudes, stubborn curiosities and its unsatisfiable, implacable journeyage.

Sometimes there are moments of time when the daemon springs to attention, totally alert, knowing with a kind of thrilled love that this is the calling moment. Ed O'Brien of Radiohead told me of one such moment, his initial teaming-up with Thom Yorke when they were still at school. 'I was crossing the school drive, guitar in hand, and he basically said, "Do you want to play?" Together we walked down to the music school. At that stage he didn't have a band, rather it started then and there at the moment of conversation. Not a note had been played, it didn't need to be, it came from somewhere else and – or – right there. It was a filmic moment.' He knew with all his heart the significance which that question, that moment, held for the whole of his life. It was like a photograph, he says: the imaginary camera in his mind's eye was witness to the shifting of his entire world.

For François Truffaut, as a boy, the camera was witness, a future-camera in the hands of tomorrow's director – himself as an adult. He had an unhappy childhood – unwanted, begrudged at home and partly raised by his grandmother – and, in his sadness, he found escape first in books. He read children's books but secretly also read his mother's, for the daemon within the child can sometimes loathe things that are tailored for children. After books, Truffaut explored films, and watched his first two hundred films on the sly, climbing into cinemas through toilet windows or emergency exits, often with his childhood friend Robert Lachenay. The daemon will steal to get what it needs and, wanting to compile dossiers of directors, the boys would slope off at one o'clock in the morning, armed with screwdrivers, to nick movie posters and stills from cinemas, and then they would steal milk from doorsteps because they were hungry and thirsty. But the hunger of the soul came first.

'We played truant to go to the cinema, not just for fun,' said Lachenay, later. A telling phrase, that: *not just for fun*. For the daemon will angrily insist on seriousness, the severity of a lifelong commitment. Once, watching a film while two adults idly chatted through it, the boy Lachenay grew furious, turning to them and declaring: 'The cinema is a place of silence and work.' Expelled from several schools, when he was fourteen Truffaut decided to become self-taught, aiming to watch three films a day and to read three books a week. He was authoring his future self, as *auteur*.

While he was a teenager, Truffaut's mother and stepfather virtually abandoned him and he was adopted by the cinema critic André Bazin, who became guardian to the boy from fifteen years old. Bazin was a father figure (Truffaut's father was 'unknown', according to his birth register), and also a crucial witness for the child's daemon, but the ultimate witness was Truffaut himself, in the future.

'A child's eyes register fast. Later he develops the film,' wrote Jean Cocteau. The line recalls the adult Whitman 'now translating the notes' which the boy had scribbled. Truffaut translated his childhood into the semi-autobiographical film *Les Quatre Cents Coups*. If Walt Whitman's is the quintessential poem to illustrate the moment of the daemon's *eureka!* then this is the quintessential film. (The title is unfortunately translated as 'The Four Hundred Blows', entirely missing the French figure of speech: it would be better translated as 'Raising Hell'.)

The Truffaut character is Antoine Doinel, a bewildered, hurt, resourceful child. He is harshly treated by his mother and schoolteacher, though shown some warmth by his stepfather. A *truand*, daydreamer and thief, in one scene Antoine steals a typewriter as Truffaut himself had done as a boy, lifting it from the newspaper offices of *L'Illustration* to sell for pocket money and cinema tickets. It was itself an illustration: stealing what he needed to survive; the *auteur* which Truffaut would become took the tools of his trade to write the script of his own life. Antoine spends a night in a print shop: in the daemon-dream, the *auteur* sleeps within the text of the life.

At the heart of the film, Antoine is deep in reverie reading Balzac's *The Search for the Absolute*, which portrays a dying man crying '*Eureka!* I have found it.' This is for Antoine also a eureka-cry: the child's mind cuts through from the world of unhappiness into the world where his psyche belongs. Antoine sets up a shrine to Balzac

(Truffaut's own childhood hero), with a picture of the older author and a votive candle. Then Antoine pulls a curtain over the little home-made altar, suggesting how the child's daemon may be veiled and hidden from the hurtful gaze of adults though revealed to the kind witness of the camera. But children are sometimes unable to contain safely the flame within them. The psyche may catch fire too violently and in the film the curtain catches fire, the shrine becomes pyre and Antoine breaks down in tears.

The making of *Les Quatre Cents Coups* also tells an extraordinary story. Filming began on 10 November 1958, and that night André Bazin died. It was as if the witness which Truffaut's daemon needed had been transferred, with exquisite symbolic timing, from the real witness, Bazin, to the metaphoric witness, the camera. Truffaut him-self, as his guardian died, stepped into the guardian's shoes, guardian to his own boyhood self and also now mentor to a real child, Jean-Pierre Léaud, the actor playing the young Truffaut.

Both *Les Quatre Cents Coups* and Whitman's 'Out of the Cradle Endlessly Rocking' are bird-sung works, for at the end of *Les Quatre Cents Coups*, as Antoine makes a break for it, birdsong breaks into the soundtrack, wild and free, and Antoine escapes in flight to the sea. Whitman and Truffaut seem to have the minds of birds, their flight feathers unfurling for one particular current in the air. Like birds, the adults they became are winged messengers, translating the notes of childhood.

Throughout the film, Antoine feels compelled towards the cinema and the seashore, and the powerful final shot seems to cast the silver sea in the same role as the silver screen; drawing Antoine. In Whit-man's poem, the sea calls the boy to his role as writer, and it also stands as emblem of time, of life and death, repeating like a mantra: 'Death, death, death, death, death.' In Truffaut's film, Balzac's eureka is cried by a man at the point of death. Death and birth entwine further, though, for in the closing sequences, Antoine escapes from a work-camp, running to the sea. As he reaches the water's edge, he turns to face the camera in a coming-of-age moment, as childhood dies and an adult is born. At that village on the seashore, Neuilly-sur-Seine, some quarter-century later, Truffaut himself was to die. So the filming was born at the moment of a real death and ends with a metaphoric birth prefiguring Truffaut's literal death.

Children readily understand the chiaroscuro of the psyche, the brightness of flame which is seen best in darkness while in death the radiance of life shines most brilliantly. In Whitman's night, in Truffaut's cinema, in the nocturne of a child's reverie, the most brilliant and pure flames of the mind catch fire, for the daemon dwells in the realms of flame and starlight and the child knows that the only way to honour this kind of fire is to keep it alight. It's the stuff of myth, and children do live mythically, Olympians all, even as, just like the Greek gods, they may well be found with their fingers in the till, or nicking the typewriter. Theft is a language, and sometimes it is the only language available to a child to tell the adults around them what they need. (I stole a heater.)

Children live in the world of historic time and actual circumstance, yet their daemon demands to live also in the mythic time where its spirit belongs, where the child can escape into dusk and story and a different day. The daemon is a trickster with time, and children may live in both the present and the future at once, their huge mythic version of themselves reaching far ahead of what their real, small hands can grasp. A friend's child, as a toddler, inhabited a swirl of small fury, angry that he could not craft words properly, for his mind talked a blue streak long before his mouth could. His present self was enraged as if his daemon knew that his future self would find its great fulfilment in language. When he learned to read, there was a sudden and spectacular sense of release in him, though he did not so much 'learn' as suck up writing as if it were water and he were dying of thirst.

An icon of Romantic genius, Beethoven knew, from the age of four, what his daemon or muse demanded. 'Music from my fourth year has ever been my favourite pursuit. Thus early introduced to the sweet Muse, who attuned my soul to pure harmony, I loved her, and sometimes ventured to think that I was beloved by her in return. I have now attained my eleventh year, and my Muse often whispered to me in hours of inspiration, – Try to write down the harmonies in your soul . . . My Muse willed it – so I obeyed, and wrote.'

Yehudi Menuhin was once given a toy violin to play, made of metal. The maestro was furious and insulted – as one would imagine. He had a terrible tantrum, bursting into tears and throwing it on the floor. He was, after all, only three, and while the child had been given a child-sized toy, the daemon of the child knew it needed and deserved a Stradivarius; anything less was an affront to his soul. He was in fact given his Stradivarius when he was twelve, and a photograph captures the boy with the violin, daemon-sung, gazing into the middle distance. Commenting on this later, Menuhin said: 'Actually I was gazing in my usual state of being half absent in my own world and half in the present.'

When he was eight, the British violinist Daniel Hope was a student at the Yehudi Menuhin School in London and adored Mendelssohn's Violin Concerto. 'I desperately wanted to learn it, but basically wasn't good enough and wasn't allowed near it,' he recalls. 'I became so frustrated that after several months I secretly borrowed the score, but then I got caught and was frog-marched to the Director of Music's office – it was a very serious matter to be caught practising the Mendelssohn Violin Concerto without permission!'

The daemon hears early the melody which the child's fingers cannot yet play, but the calling is unmistakeable: the clarity, the certainty of knowing that they had heard the signature tune of their lives.

Becoming who you are depends in part on the prefiguring daemon drawing the outlines of the life in a space far larger than the child, with darkness enough to germinate safely, with light enough to stretch its leaves, with space sufficient to grow into the tree of oneself, fully filling out the silhouette of one's own meaning. Oona King, who, aged only twenty-nine, was to become the second black woman MP in the British House of Commons, announced, unimpeachably presidential at four years old, 'I want to be Prime Minister.'

Some years ago, a small boy, abandoned by his parents, found his way to Howrah railway station in Kolkata. In the hot and thronging crowds, he slid in and out of queues and knots of people, as sleek, quick and unseen as an otter, his hands slipping in and out of jackets, pockets and bags. He became the most successful pickpocket at the station. Some time later, he was taken in by a charity which gave him somewhere to stay, food and schooling. He grew up and began his working life at an Indian airline. Promoted up the ladder, he became the airline's security chief. His daemon – of alertness, observation, detective skills – had served him well, on both sides of legality.

From the pickpocket to the president: Barack Obama, whose life has been so affected by issues of racial identity, wrote of his early relationship to himself: 'I was trying *to raise myself* to be a black man in America'; and of Malcolm X he wrote, 'his repeated acts of *self-creation* spoke to me.' (Italics mine.) A boy 'raising himself' suggests neglect, but many parents have an uncanny sense that something else is parenting their child. Something of weird authority, intact in its vision, perhaps the only thing a child may obey, something both ancient and immediate, something amoral but with an implacable wisdom, a voice speaking from within the child. Trenchant guardian of the soul of the child, the daemon can disdain the temporary, actual, parent. Shakespeare's Coriolanus stood 'As if a man were Author of himself, And knew no other kin.' The daemon is like this.

The daemon is wiser than the child. It is a guide, the captain steering the course, always looking far ahead, reading the currents of the ocean, reacting, adjusting to the weather, navigating by lodestars of the mind so that the life of the child may sail a passage true to its own course. 'The daemon is that part of you that helps you grow towards wisdom,' writes Philip Pullman.

The sea, Shakespeare's ocean in 'full fathom five' was a significant site for me where the daemon spoke, and the sea seems to recur in the revelations of children's daemons. It is an emblem of eternity, and a child's daemon lives in that kind of time, the dreamtime of the mind. A daemon-moment for Lemn Sissay involved feeling as if the sea itself had thrown him his book of poetry. Both Whitman and Truffaut use the sea for their moments of revelation and identity.

As it is Philip Pullman who has done more than anyone to rescue the idea of the daemon, I found it irresistible to ask him about his own. He leaned immediately to the image of the sea. Telling stories as a child, he said, he never knew how they would end, but he always had a sense of trust; as if you were in an ocean, he said, and trusted the waters to carry you, to sustain the story. I asked him when he knew he wanted to be a writer. 'I've always known it, it was always there. From aged three, or four or five.' He shared a bedroom with his younger brother and he would tell stories in the dark, after the lights had been switched off.

Slightly older, and considering his future, he thought that writing would not make an income, so he toyed with other possibilities, things which he could do while writing. He wondered about being a vicar, as his grandfather had been. Or a prophet. Briefly, he wanted to be a customs officer: 'It was the Thames that did that for me – living near the river in Battersea and playing down on the mud at low tide and seeing the police boats going up and down, clearly on the track of the Black Hand Gang. But that didn't last very long.' Best, perhaps, to be a lighthouse keeper and write. He remembered feeling overwhelmed reading *Superman* and *Batman* comics, not because he wanted to be Superman or Batman but because he wanted to be that *other* superhero, the invisible one, the person who created them: the storyteller.

When he was small and learning to read, he read the 'Just So' Stories. Remembering this, he holds his hands in his lap, as you would a book, his fingers latticed together. And there was a moment, he says, 'when I could see the *meaning* through the words'. His fingers ease slightly apart, unlatticing a stretch but still holding together, his eyes refocusing no longer on his fingers but just behind them. It is an eloquent gesture, suggesting the double vision of reading: the literal letters, the signage on the page, and, behind them, the significance, the deep and true meaning. It's clear the memory of this is sharp as daylight today and it is as if, when the thought came to him as a small boy, the moment was illuminated with the daemon knowledge, the kind of sudden insight, the flash of light from a lighthouse by which the child's daemon steers the ship of their whole life.

A fourteen-year-old boy was swimming in the Thames in 1757. At the end of the day, and on the banks, alone with wildflowers gold in the evening sun, the child felt lit from within with a sudden wisdom: rather than being forced to learn Latin and Greek, 'it is surely more natural that I should be taught to know all the productions of Nature,' he thought, so Joseph Banks began teaching himself botany, visiting wise women among the Gypsies well versed in plant medicine and growing into his illustrious career as botanist and naturalist. Another fourteen-year-old boy would frequent an abandoned coastal quarry in Scotland in the 1970s, where he whiled away hours with orchids and insects, 'dreaming of a future life as a naturalist', as Callum Roberts, now author and professor of marine conservation, recalls.

The philosopher R. G. Collingwood, at eight years old, began reading Kant's *Theory of Ethics*. To begin with he was riven with excitement but then he became indignant at his inability to understand the text. Then, 'third and last, came the strangest emotion of all. I felt that the contents of this book, although I could not understand it, were somehow my business: a matter personal to myself, or rather to some future self of my own . . . I felt as if a veil had been lifted and my destiny revealed . . . a task whose nature I could not define except by saying, "I must think." '

Joseph Campbell, who so fabulously popularized comparative mythology, had his eureka moment aged nine, on a visit to the American Museum of Natural History, where he was spellbound by Native American culture.

When the Lakota shaman Black Elk was five, he first heard, through bird voices, the message that a sacred voice was calling him, and when he was nine he had a vision of the unity and holiness of the world. Joseph Campbell comments that in childhood or early youth shamans have an experience of the calling, the powerful daemon at work, and the equivalent of shamans today, he says, are poets and artists of all kinds. It seems to me this must be true: the role has never disappeared and it is both universal and common. There is far too much cultural appropriation surrounding the term 'shaman', making it hard to use in the dominant culture, but the role is there without question, the outline of the calling, fulfilled in a myriad of ways, for every society needs soul-guides, healers, charismatics and pied pipers who lead their audiences out of themselves; and in Euro-American societies the role is most often glimpsed in the work of artists, musicians, writers, poets and singers. Coleridge practised from childhood the subtle shapeshifting known to poets as well as shamans, a practice of identifying oneself so closely with another creature, object or idea that one animates it and it animates you. This co-inspiration is the very breath of poetic art, by using the imagination to comprehend another, in Coleridge's words: 'by a sort of transference and transmission of my consciousness to identify myself with the Object.' Woody Guthrie and Yehudi Menuhin alike correctly divined that their playing was a form of healing.

The healing may begin with a need to heal oneself in the frequent episodes of physical or psychological distress – or both – with which this calling so often begins. It is, says Campbell, an overwhelming psychological experience that turns young people totally inward, as if the whole unconscious has opened up and they've fallen into it, feeling as if they are on the brink of death.

It is an experience that Nikolai Fraiture, bassist with The Strokes, knows, and he told me about it in depth. When he was still a teenager, he went on what he calls an 'errant' trip through the USA, and the word is revealing: like all young people, he unconsciously knew the quality of the knight-errant, on the quest of his own life. 'I have writings in my teenage angst-y voice, just prior to leaving, saying things like: *After this trip, nothing will be the same.* There was definitely an element of irrepressible inviting, or calling,' he says. Here, as so often, it is as if the daemon can read ahead in the story of one's life. While he was on this journey, he contracted Rocky Mountain Spotted Fever, which was part physical, involving sudden weight loss, and part psychological, leading to mental confusion and hallucinations. It is fatal without treatment, and he was ill for months. When it was eventually diagnosed and treated, he recovered physically fairly fast, but the psyche takes longer. He felt the illness had split his life in two: 'In my mind, there is the "me" before then, and the "me" after. I would ask my friends if I looked different to them because I felt there was no way I was the same person.'

His girlfriend left him. He could no longer keep up with school. 'To find yourself, you must first completely lose yourself,' he wrote in that same teenage voice which as an adult he calls 'daft', but it isn't: only young. 'I could never tell if the illness triggered the breakdown or if I was headed for it anyway, but I realized that I was helpless against such a force.' The daemon can indeed be a dangerous force of nature which needs a powerful attending. He played bass, immersively: it 'became my only true solace', and he found the witness he needed. 'I met a musical instructor who taught me much more than just an instrument. Often, we talked more than we played. He was a burly African-American native New Yorker with long dreadlocks and, of all names, his was Buddy.' He was a compassionate guide, not only to music but to philosophy, introducing Nikolai to Eastern philosophy and literature. 'He took me out of myself and introduced me to the connectivity of Music.' Nikolai played himself into wellness and then, only then, could he begin to play for others, in our society's version of the shamanic role.

Nils-Aslak Valkeapää, the Sámi musician and shaman, was an elusive, bookish, dreamy child who played with animals and spoke with birds. His was a reindeer-herding family, with reindeer meat a staple of the diet, but in a defining moment of his childhood, Valkeapää found himself unable to kill a reindeer. The experience shocked him. He cried and felt alienated, but it was an event which exiled him into shamanism, art, poetry and music, and he sang the traditional Sámi *yoik*, the songs that conjure the land or object they describe. His daemon knew where it belonged; with the moon, the dream, the drum and the ocean. On the tundra of the mind, his daemon showed him his path to that other sun on the other side of reality, the world of image and evocation, of symbol called into being with the image-drum, the shaman's drum, drummed into mind with the language of wind, time, moss and stone.

As Whitman listened, 'translating the notes', so Valkeapää was a translator between worlds. People began coming to him for psychological healing, for his uncanny wisdom, trusting his vision because of his familiarity with the landscape of the mind, that shamanic skill. Valkeapää's role, glimpsed as a child and fulfilled as an adult, also included being a voice for his people, supporting their self-expression and their political liberation. His calling was to be a messenger from the spirits of the land to the human psyche, to dream things into being, on that other side.

He contrasts the nature of his knowledge on the ordinary side of life, where he feels he knows nothing, with the shamanic wisdom of dreams. When I read his work I feel as if Whitman were singing a duet with him, because they both spoke from the earth, their spirits lit by the old fire, their daemon a bird, a winged messenger of the mind.

Angellos is the Greek word for messenger, from which we derive the word 'angel'. Neruda recalled that messenger moment of his first poem, in 'fever or forgotten wings'; William Blake had a childhood vision of 'bright angelic wings'; and the daemon seems to offer the kind of wings the mind needs to stretch into its ideal flight. To Blake, childhood was winged but vulnerable to *Aged Ignorance*, the title of a picture of an old man shearing the wings of an angel child (possibly a childhood memory of a spiteful old woman with a pair of shears who rode an old grey mare to chase kite-flying boys and to cut the strings). Blake felt guided by his 'Genius or Angel', and in Romantic literature, the daemon is winged as a rebel angel, winged as Whitman's 'demon or bird', winged as Valkeapää, who describes his mind in flight like a bird, writing:

when I was a child
I wondered
why did I not have wings
like other birds

though no longer a child
I wonder still.

The little bird, a muse to him, flies through his work, calling, alerting and singing, and Valkeapää knows he must make a nest for the bird in his heart, an image of the importance not only of obeying one's daemon but also sheltering it, giving it a home, so the song of the daemon and singer are one. The shaman-flight is feathered: the messenger has wings. Something of the angels attends them.

CHAPTER EIGHTEEN

To Affinity . . . and Beyond!

Dandelions bounce out of the spring earth like chicks. Yellow. Fluffy. Gone.

The moment passing, Wordsworth's 'spots of time' or Blake's 'eternity in an hour' are features of the non-linear time which childhood knows. It is not linear, but it is not exactly cyclical either, for this time honours neither geometry nor clockwork. Children experience moments of such irrefutable now-ness and this-ness where everything is lit with its innerness so apparent, its presence so certain to the mind's eye that the body's eye may believe it sees it too. The *autrefois*, as the French call our 'once upon a time', is a time which holds the past and future as a burning penumbra around the flame of the present, a sense of time as ricocheting intensity, dwelt in by very young children and, often, yearned for ever since.

It is in that timbre of time, that sense of the present-eternal, that both childhood and Romanticism exist – a time within the mind. (In honour of the permanence of its truths, I prefer to use the present tense.) All the themes of childhood are cherished, reflected and vehemently protected by Romanticism: passion, imagination, heroism; a dislike of social convention; a sense of justice; a sense of quest and chivalry; a desire for integrity and the authentic; a will towards self-determination; a willingness to see the sublime; a concern with the particular and local; a need for freedom; an innate love of nature; intuitive creativity; a sense of inner, epiphanic, spontaneous time; an interest in the daemonic; a belief in faërie; an ability to endow the ordinary with mystery; an anti-mechanistic world-view; and a sense of wildness and the transcendent.

All of these, in contemporary society, need to be defended now by the ethos of Romanticism. Each of those themes (the chapters of this book) is a touchstone to the truth in answering the riddle of childhood unhappiness.

To sum up: children have been exiled from their kith, their square mile, a land right of the human spirit. Naturally kindled in green, they need nature, woodlands, mountains, rivers and seas both physically and emotionally, no matter how small a patch; children's spirits can survive on very little, but not on nothing. Yet woodlands are privatized; children are scared away from the outdoor world by alleged stranger-danger so the toy and entertainment industries benefit from that enclosure, while even the streets – the commons of the urban child – have been closed off to them. Society owes it to children to repeal all acts of enclosure, literal and metaphoric, which have fenced in childhood with barbed wire.

Children are victims of a contemporary work 'ethic' which puts the needs of consumerism ahead of the needs of a crying child, an ideology which drives Ferberization and Controlled Crying; and today's children need the Romantic ethic of a kinder political vision.

Relationships with animals make children happy, they say, simply and repeatedly, and they mean it; children need to be able to play with, and to play *like*, the animals they so adore. They also deserve access to public play in carnival and, like kittens with their whiskers twitching, may they be given back their rightful positions as chiefs of mischief nights and lords of misrule. Play is at the core of human nature, the play of the mind is the beginning of art, as the historical Romantics so explicitly maintained, yet the suffocating playless spirit of the gamekeeper stalks childhood, docking children at a desk, clock-worked, workbound and un-enreveried.

Liberty and freedom are the demands of childhood as of Romanticism, and children instinctively seek their fortune, taking the risks which are theirs to take, learning autonomy, self-rule and independence, those characteristics so much more vital and important than the subliminal political messages of control and command which a risk-averse society teaches its children.

The shocking laws imposed on children and the dishonest public portrayals of them present a terrible contrast to the way in which almost all societies throughout history have regarded their young. The historical Romantics paid attention to the thoughtways of indigenous cultures: today, if there is one pool of wisdom as deep as it is neglected, it is the collective philosophies of childhood of those indigenous cultures which, while never identical, have striking commonalities: the closeness of infants; the freedom of older children; the widespread condemnation of physical punishment; a willingness to allow children to own their own time and to be captains of their own souls, following their own will, knowing that such a child will better be able to respect the will of others.

Children like thinking and want to learn, but not to be taught a hidden curriculum of hierarchy and obedience in schooling which damages their psyche with stress and overwork. In Euro-American societies, children's minds are in pain – they tell us this over and over again in all the languages they know, including the language of silence, spoken so eloquently by the deeply depressed – yet they are denied many of the psyche's helpers: animal companions; rites of passage in the wild world for their mysterious transitions into adulthood; and the secret places of soul privacy to cocoon themselves, to nurture their butterfly psyche. They are instead given the opposite, the brutal inquisition of surveillance. Each child needs to be able to hear the voice of their inner daemon, so that they can find their happiness, their *eudaimonia*: but that exquisitely specific voice is dinned out by the cacophony of identikit consumer identities and mass-produced celebrity role-models. Instead of the unmediated fairy tales that demonstrate to the child's mind the magic of their own metaphor-making ability, they are sold pre-packaged, literal fairies and stories which have been actualized for them on-screen.

Children suffer from the utilitarianism of today; they are impoverished by modernity's literalism. For children dwell not in the concrete world of utilitarianism but with the Romantics in metaphor's green meanings, and the rest of this chapter will suggest how answers to the riddle of childhood unhappiness can be found in that evergreen Romantic childscape: the mind.

~

Written in bone, sung in fire and painted in electric feeling, historical Romanticism was forced, by the uglinesses of its time, to furious beauty. It had to articulate its truths precisely because those truths were subject to such attack. The force of that Romantic insight is needed again today. Romanticism was not merely a style of art, a passing philosophy or a historically specific sensibility, but rather a perennial truth about the human mind – and never more so than in its portrayal and championing of childhood. Romanticism expressed its orientation towards childhood and nature because it comprehended authentic human nature and saw how that spirit was being brutalized in childhood.

Utilitarianism and the Industrial Revolution militated against the mind at play; the Romantics revered reverie. (Thomas Chatterton, for one, was a spectacular daydreamer as a child.) 'The dreaming child knows the cosmic reverie which unites us to the world,' writes Gaston Bachelard, defender of childhood's Romanticism, and he describes 'the continuity of the great childhood reveries with the reveries of the poet'. But forbidden their time of reverie, children are told this inner wandering out to the stars is a sin against the Useful Use of time by the utilitarians of today, who set themselves against the play of thought – and the ludic in general. Childhood and Romanticism link arms in play, in Blake's 'eternal delight', Wordsworth's 'joy' or Tagore's '*ananda*' (bliss), all of which acknowledged the vital play of creation. Setting Schiller's 'Ode to Joy' to music, Beethoven's Ninth Symphony represented joy's unifying force, the political generosity of rapture. Schiller thought that re-visioning the political landscape (another world is possible) was like the play of children and that joy could overthrow the given reality.

Play is crescive, burgeoning from the earth, self-augmenting, opening skyward to the unrivalled simplicity of sunlight. Happiness, as if by sympathetic magic, tunes the world-spiral up, up and away and the human spirit runs reckless torrents in reverse, cascading upwards, gravity-defying in an irresistible force of irrepressible energy, as laughter defies gravity and denies solemnity in the send-up of comedy.

Play is a form of freedom, understood by Romantics and children who, freedom fighters all, are in-arms for a principle of freedom, a politics of freedom and a poetics of freedom. Children assume their freedom as their right to breathe, 'born free' in Rousseau's declaration of independence, free as a nation declaring self-sovereignty, free as Huckleberry Finn, envied by all the other children because 'he was idle, and lawless, and vulgar, and bad', but most of all because he was free: 'Huckleberry came and went at his own free will . . . he did not have to go to school or to church, or call any being master, or obey anybody . . . Tom hailed the romantic outcast.' Twain, incidentally, uses the word 'romantic' at least six times to describe Tom and Huck's world-view, while A. N. Whitehead refers to the wonder-lit ages of eightish to thirteenish as 'by far the greatest stage of romance which we ever experience'.

Both Romantics and children find the ordinary mysterious and have a sense of infinity. Children may be enraptured by enormity – a million, trillion, billion, and, as my godson is delighted to know, a nonillion. Children may be on good terms, as Coleridge was, with the Vast, or they may be troubled by it, the extent of the universe a devastation of stars which frightens my god-daughter with the insignificance of her world. Either way, vastness touches them.

For those habituated to the Vast, enclosure is deadly. The historical Romantics detested the factory-prisons, and the Acts and spirit of enclosures which limited childhood's freedom. It was as if adults, caged and suffocating, could still just about make out the freedom which childhood was born for and, peering over the fences not of biological age but of social construction, they could see the human spirit most lively, green and vigorous in the child. On the cusp between childhood and adulthood, D. H. Lawrence's character Paul in *Sons and Lovers* 'looked wistfully out of the window. Already he was a prisoner of industrialism. Far off on the hills were the woods of Annesley, dark and fascinating. Already his heart went down. He was being taken into bondage. His freedom in the beloved home valley was going now.'

At least he knew. Many of today's children may not even know how gravely they are interred indoors and may never fully understand their insidious enclosure. They may never experience the wild divinity of nature – its cliffs and forests and storms – which the Romantics so passionately honoured. The 'essential love of *Nature*,' wrote Ruskin of his childhood, was 'the root of all that I have usefully become, and the light of all that I have rightly learned.'

The wild child of Aveyron deeply affected Coleridge in his uninhibited empathy and communication with nature, the sort of instinctive trespass of sympathy by which the Romantic mind, in poet or child, does not acknowledge the mind-fences. Similarly, Blake pictures a child watching an ant, in oneness with it, and Shelley implores the West Wind to *become* him. This insight is shared by Wordsworth and Whitman: children are part-created by the nature that surrounds them and they become what they see. Like bower-birds of the forget-me-not variety, children create the nest of their own selves, building it with whatever they can find, intimate twigs, leaves, fur and objects of blue, the unforgotten flowers of waysides.

Children want what is authentic. (They loathe fake characters, forced laughs, false smiles and forged emotions.) For the historical Romantics, the authentically natural world was being lost in increasing artifice, and for many children today, the authentic is almost out of reach: they are given a tinny plastic keyboard with pre-recorded sound when they deserve to hear the dog-otter bark or the knock-on-wood drilling of a woodpecker. They demand the heartwood truth of trees but are instead given plastic trees, mechanical flowers and photographs of rivers, waterless and unspeaking.

Empiricism is the mental equivalent of the Enclosures, and Wordsworth loathed it for its conceptual hostility to childhood, freedom, poetry and imagination all at once. The empiricist philosopher John Locke advised that if a child should have a feeling for poetry, 'the parents should labour to have it stifled and suppressed as much as may be.' Instead, children and Romantics alike hold a candle for the intuitive fire. Blake writes that 'Innate Ideas are in Every Man Born with him.' Against excessive rationalism and mechanistic philosophy, the Romantics believe in the inner light of the mind. The 'tygers' of intuitive wrath growl in the hedge margins as the horses of instruction (*Locked* into harness) plough the fields in strict furrows traced for them by someone else. I see it as a page in a school exercise book. The narrow margin. The ruled page. In the straight lines, the horses of instruction are the words dictated by another, while in the margins the doodles spring to life: curly, starry, full of faces, flowers, rabbits *and tygers*. Nature, in the history of European schooling, is relegated to the margins, but children instinctively perceive, and Romanticism declares, that all life is in that margin, so they redraw it until the margin takes over the whole page, overgrown with ivy and wet as a riverbank.

'Let nature be your teacher,' wrote Wordsworth, and this was also a school principle for Tagore. Rousseau likewise considered the sources of educational authority to be in nature and in the child. Romanticism is concerned with how we learn and how we perceive, the human mind reflecting on itself, but it refuses to disembody the mind, for the Compleat Human includes not only nature but the senses and the importance of feeling. 'I feel therefore I am' was the nineteenth-century Romantic revolt against the strictures of eighteenth-century Reason. We know that we know because we feel, but hyper-rationalists don't want to admit it. The terms themselves suggest that feelings are connected to knowings, so we 'have a feeling' something is true, we 'feel it in our bones', we have 'gut feelings' or 'a feeling for' a subject. Language, here, a beautiful partisan, waits with rifle and song to ambush us into remembering what we used to know as children.

The ethos of the Industrial Revolution and factory schooling intended to make a machine of even moonlight, to drill a nightingale in scales and arpeggios, to line up imaginations in rows and to require a butterfly to fit the grid. The historical Romantics saw with horror the conceptual threat to Imagination when the mind goes where it lists of its own free – wild – will, the psyche's right to roam, where wondering rhymes with wandering, twin rights of the mind and body to think and to walk unenclosed. They understood – as contemporary Romantics also do – that children were imaginatively vulnerable to machine-mindedness and that what was being enclosed was the free play of thought. Romanticism, then and now, is on a serious mission, attempting to tear down the fences of enclosure established not only on the common land but in that most enigmatic and vibrant landscape, the commons of the human mind.

The 'vast majority' of children, according to Blake, are on the 'side of Imagination or Spiritual Sensation'. In D. H. Lawrence's *The Rainbow*, the child Ursula has waking dreams where she is on a quest, 'gifted with magic' – that word connected to imagination – in an animated world where a doe speaks to her 'as if the sunshine spoke'. The twentieth-century Romantic Dylan Thomas conjures the imagination of children watching 'the ships steaming away into wonder and India, magic and China, countries bright with oranges and loud with lions'. Vertigo sheers into ecstasy. Romanticism has never ended, any more than childhood, and it draws on the features of childhood fascination with the sublime, the beyond, endowing nature with *anima*, seeing the universe animated, messageful and alive – that vision so maligned by the objective, mechanical and utilitarian view.

Childhood and Romanticism alike put the mind's own life at the heart of experience. Wordsworth writes of his childhood ways of thinking as 'the hiding-places of my power' and says that the paths to them seem 'open' until he approaches, at which point they close, tantalizingly, so 'I see by glimpses now.' As if only in those brief moments when the guards are off duty can he nip back to the light. But Romanticism finds too often that this way (of thinking) has been barred and padlocked, no way through, and those who try to cross over are mocked and attacked like Wordsworth and Coleridge, despised and ignored like Blake or Keats or Ibsen. John Clare found the TRESPASSERS WILL sign nailed up in his own mind, as so completely does he identify with his land that the paths on the ground are fused with the pathways of his mind, the tracks of his memory.

On paths to freedom and to childhood dear
A board sticks up to notice 'no road here'.

Novalis thought of fairy tales as 'that homeland which is everywhere and nowhere'. Where is that? Right inside the mind, in the cosmic trespass of imagination. This is the heart of it: this is why Romanticism, now, here, is necessary as a way of understanding childhood, not as a passing interest in the past but because Romanticism comprehends what is perennially important, beautiful, valuable and good in the human condition, and finds those treasures within us all.

Romanticism intuits the perennial truths of childhood because it is attuned to the workings of *mind itself*. Nothing less. As psychiatrist Iain McGilchrist, in his extraordinary book on the brain, *The Master and His Emissary*, writes: 'many of the features of Romanticism are in fact potentially universals, part of the structure of the human mind and brain, not just aspects of a culture-bound syndrome'.

Until the age of about four, children dwell very much in the instinctive and empathic realm of the brain, its right hemisphere. They gradually develop the skills of reason and logic more associated with the left hemisphere and then they will be able to flow between the two, as the corpus callosum – the gate at the back of the head – is open to both hemispheres. In *The Lion, the Witch and the Wardrobe*, the Professor warns the children at the end: 'I don't think it will be any good trying to go back through the wardrobe . . . You won't get into Narnia again by *that* route.'

Philip Pullman's character Lyra traces a journey of the mind. At first, her wisdom is intuitive. She possesses an instinctive ability to read the truth-meter, the alethiometer. At the start, she thinks with unteachable grace but this intuitive ability abandons her as she grows up: later she must study consciously, with difficulty and hard work. For, as an angel-messenger tells her, she can learn to read it, and learning with conscious effort is grace of another and deeper order. 'Grace attained like that is deeper and fuller than grace that comes freely, and furthermore, once you've gained it, it will never leave you.' This, Pullman's writing argues, is what growing up is about, and children *want* to grow up, he knows, moving from innocence to experience. It is a portrait of the mind's development.

One cannot either retain or regain that innocence, argues Pullman, but must work at finding, questioning, questing for *tuited* grace. Pullman says he was influenced by Heinrich von Kleist's 'Essay on the Puppet Theatre' of 1811, which also hints at the importance of the search when Eden is no longer within reach. 'Paradise is bolted, and the cherub is behind us; we must make a voyage around the earth and see if, perhaps, it is open again at the back.' In terms of the mind-world, there *is* a gate at the back: the corpus callosum, which admits both instinct and reason, both the right hemisphere and the left.

The machine-making, utilitarian, pragmatic way of thinking is founded in the left hemisphere. It has a narrow, focused attention, impersonal and abstract. It deals in The Useful, tools, and the mechanical; measurement and artifice, the logic of language, what is routine and familiar. It is the right hemisphere which comprehends the world of imagination, divinity, metaphor, music and enchantment, which responds to the vitality of things, which considers nature and animals important in their own right – much as the fairy-tale mind does. It deals in connotation, puns and uncertainty. It has a feeling for the foreign and the beyond. Here is where the psyche prefers its modal verbs, its moods: 'could', 'should', 'might' or 'may'; the endless grace of perhaps. Here is where the enfolded truths offer layers of meaning. Here, right in the heart of the mind, we can see things Otherwise, as the fairy tales suggest, in moments of open-hearted epiphany, brave to the world, suddenly knowing there is a different way, other than the enclosure of habitual responses and ritual behaviours. Here is transformation and possibility: life not subject to immutable destiny but alive to wild grace.

Children are Romantics before they are Utilitarians; visionaries before they are Gradgrinds. They think in the right hemisphere before the left. We humans sang before we spoke. Poetry came before prose. The depth was there before the shallowness, the extraordinary before the ordinary, metaphysics before physics. Metaphor before all.

~

As children, my brothers and I were buccaneers, digging up much of the garden for buried treasure and it seems to me now that this common activity represents how children delve into earth and mind at the same time. With an instinct for rich and secret wealth from the past, they are perhaps seeking the treasure of their own history, the florins, ducats and gems which glint, ambiguous and precious, in their own first wisdom. The invisible, inaudible, unliteral gems are uncovered only in metaphor. Seeking in darkness, in a night vouchsafed with vows, looking for gold and maps and rings, treasure forgotten by adults and found by children: this is an uncannily apt metaphor for the treasures of the mind, perhaps for the primacy of the right hemisphere's wisdom, which adults (it seems to children) often bury and lose. Did we ever find any treasure? We did. All children do. And I think we have those gems still, self-safed, somewhere in mind.

'In Bimini, on the old Spanish Main,' writes Loren Eiseley, 'a black girl once said to me: "Those as hunts treasure must go alone, at night, and when they find it they have to leave a little of their blood behind them." I have never heard a finer, cleaner estimate of the price of wisdom. I wrote it down at once under a sea lamp, like the belated pirate I was, for the girl had given me unknowingly the latitude and longitude of a treasure.'

Both children and Romantics are fascinated by ruins because something is left to the imagination. 'The olden days' is a phrase that spellbinds children. Children read runes and invent history until their myths prickle into life. Our local streets were stuffed full of stabbings and explosions and sightings of ghosts, places where people had died gory deaths and seen flying saucers, all of which happened some vague time ago, as we honoured an imaginary past. Unlike the spirit of the eighteenth century, which was contemptuous towards the past, both Romanticism and childhood cherish it. The medieval period which so appeals to children was a Golden Age for the Romantics too: Novalis's hero was a medieval poet; Thomas Chatterton as a teenager adopted the persona of an imaginary medieval monk; William Blake, only ten, was deeply impressed by Chatterton's medievalism.

When an earlier age had so detested the past that it invoked original sin to punish children with the idea that their souls were rat-gnawed even before they drew breath, the Romantics perceived a child's original innocence, treasuring the personal past. Not only is the recollection of childhood and the memory of its illuminated moments precious to the Romantics, but a very particular grief for the past yearns through their work in a torque of loss and a gyre of longing.

Its colour is blue. A. E. Housman wrote of the 'blue remembered hills'; Hazlitt's sense of longing was provoked by blue hills, and Dylan Thomas wrote of the 'radiant, rainless, lazily rowdy and skyblue summers departed', while the enigmatic blue flower at the heart of Romanticism is (for me) the blue and unforgotten forget-me-not of my childhood. Novalis's hero, the medieval poet, seeks the mysterious Blue Flower which awakes 'an inexpressible longing', and the blue flower became a Romantic symbol of longing for what is ever unattainable. C. S. Lewis refers to the Blue Flower when he expresses the yearning which beauty evoked in him when he was six.

Nostalgia floods *Peter Pan* (1904), while *The Wind in the Willows*, published in 1908, opens with a description of spring's 'spirit of divine discontent and longing'. C. S. Lewis, whose childhood coincided with these milestones in children's literature, would write of the ever-unsatisfiable desire as 'a longing for the longing'. When Schiller called the Romantics 'exiles pining for a homeland', he expressed their longing for *be*longing, homesick for the childhood home, the kith as well as the kin. But more, the kindred spirits of the Romantics and children are exiles pining for a homeland *in the mind*, where dwelling means both thinking and inhabiting, in ways which the very young child, the poet, the artist, the dreamer and the seer all understand. It is a habit of thinking which can really be registered only when it ceases to be the mind's sole habitation. It is a way of thinking which is both known and unknowable, impossible to find, impossible to ignore. Both inwritten and indescribable, its canticles are inaudible in the mind by twilight, the truant twilight playing double meanings of paradox, longing to unite sight with insight.

Childhood itself is the quintessential Romanticism, and every child needs to be allowed to live in that state of grace, but wider society also needs the romance of childhood for its very creativity, requiring the reckless rapture of the *puer* figure, the eternal child within culture, whose incandescence must be tended and attended to, so that its light can flare in the storyteller or dancer, so that the risk-taking, anarchic and flame-like quality, the eternal return of the great romance of childhood which exists within us all, can flame in a resurgent romantic revolution. The chill of our utilitarian age needs that fire.

Though all adults need this, it is perhaps artists who most clearly express its presence. John Ruskin said of Kate Greenaway that she 'lives with her girlhood as with a little sister'. Writing of Wordsworth, Coleridge saluted the capacity of the poet 'To carry on the feelings of childhood into the powers of manhood; to combine the child's sense of wonder and novelty with the appearances which every day for perhaps forty years had rendered familiar . . . this is the character and privilege of genius.' The Romantics, said critic William Empson, 'kept a sort of tap-root going down to their experience as children', believing that childhood's intuition 'contains what poetry and philosophy must spend their time labouring to recover'. Von Kleist and Pullman and every other self-respecting Romantic would understand this, knowing that the past is not behind us but within us. We do not go back to childhood but spiral in towards it. And must. Because the Romantic protest, then as now, is on the side of life: brilliant, impassioned, quickening *life*. From the exuberance of Mark Twain to the vision of Blake, from the profundity of Wordsworth to the scorching satire of Dickens, the Romantic fight for the human spirit burns in defence of vitality. Coleridge furiously called the eighteenth century's deanimating of nature as 'the philosophy of mechanism, which strikes DEATH'.

Reckless with divinity, childhood knows itself to share the resonant frequency of life in a riff, a rhythm and a rhyme of the mind, and it holds to that truth, kin to the wind or the life of water. Life is sheer, sudden presence, to a child. A transcendence into a feeling of oneness so powerful that the senses themselves become one. Synaesthesia.

A cat's paw blooms into blue flowers which burn the innermost blue of a candle flame while the wind is staves of music with birdsong written on it. The inseeing song.

A child's hearing is better than ours, in two senses. A child can hear at a pitch far higher into the sheer beyond and can also hear the earth singing to herself when life resolves into music. Pitched above pitch of intensity into translucency as light comes through them like bluebells at twilight, each bluebell's bell ringing itself, without end or beginning, children hear a rhapsody in green, for they can hear so well that they can hear what they see, in sea-green and ivy, hearing star chimes or the cascade of bells in one lily of the valley.

Songstruck by the wood canticles of a thrush or wren, children first hear the music in duet when it sings outside them and inside them, in the unceasing song willow-voiced and grass-strung, when they hear the bells ring like a stone thrown into water ringing out in ring-cycles its circles to eternity, and when those bells, which should be pealing now and always inside a child's mind, are jarred and cracked into hollow broken barrels, then children will be wordlessly, riddlingly, grief-struck as they try to remember the meaning of the blue flower, spoken in so many languages to name it the same, that speaking blue flower of childhood by which children are charged with a lifelong loyalty, never to forget this insight that life itself whispers to every listening child: *forget-me-not*.

NOTES

Chapter One: Kith

The Maori word for placenta ... back in the mothering earth: Kiwi Tamasese, Flora Tuhaka, Charles Waldegrave, the Just Therapy Team, 'Culture, Attachment and Belonging', interview for *Context* by Jan Parker, 2005.

India, the qualities of different aspects of nature ... right down to the earthworm: Chuden Tshering-Misra, 'India: Development Process and Indigenous Children', *Cultural Survival Quarterly*, 1986 (10).

Story and song weave the child into the subtle world of the Dreaming: Hannah Rachel Bell, *Men's Business, Women's Business: The Spiritual Role of Gender in the World's Oldest Culture*, Inner Traditions International, 1998.

some Indigenous Australians were forced to give birth in morgues: Allan Collins (dir.), *Spirit Stones*, 2008.

a child's conception site as the origin of their selfhood: A vexing issue of pronouns. The insistent use of 'he or she, himself or herself' is laborious. Using 'he' as default is unjust. The random use of 'he' or 'she' can be distracting. While a baby can be an 'it', calling a child 'it' seems dehumanizing. 'A child ... they' may be grammatically incorrect (singular followed by plural) but seems better than the alternatives. I have generally used this.

Kunjen elder describes the conception site as 'the home place for your image': Veronica Strang, *Uncommon Ground: Cultural Landscapes and Environmental Values*, Berg, 1997.

'... the Moon bird, the fish or any other thing that makes me what I am': Kevin Gilbert (ed.), *Inside Black Australia: An Anthology of Aboriginal Poetry*, Penguin, 1988.

childbirth should always take place in the forest-gardens: Gerardo Reichel-Dolmatoff, *The Forest Within: The World-View of the Tukano Amazonian Indians*, Themis Books, 1996.

Nature near the home . . . promoting the psychological well-being of children: Nancy Wells and Gary Evans, 'Nearby Nature: A Buffer of Life Stress among Rural Children', *Environment and Behavior*, May 2003 (35).

asphalt seems to generate more conflict . . . greenery promotes more harmony: Gary Paul Nabhan and Stephen Trimble, *The Geography of Childhood: Why Children Need Wild Places*, Beacon Press, 1994.

the Emu waterhole . . . went dry with grief: Veronica Strang, *Uncommon Ground: Cultural Landscapes and Environmental Values*, Berg, 1997.

susto as a sickness of soul . . . cured by 'the great without': Linda Hogan, 'The Great Without', *Parabola* 24, 1999.

Chapter Two: The Patron Saint of Childhood

Enclosures have brought a bleak, cold, unseasonable season, 'strange and chill': John Clare, 'Remembrances', *Major Works*, Oxford University Press, 1984.

'maintain themselves and their Families in the Depth of Winter': Northamptonshire petition against the Enclosure Act of 1797, in J. L. and Barbara Hammond, *The Village Labourer*, Nonsuch Publishing, 2005, first published 1911.

both the sites of carnival and the customs themselves disappeared: Bob Bushaway, *By Rite: Custom, Ceremony and Community in England 1700–1880*, Junction Books, 1982.

boys were made to stand on their heads in holes . . . the extent of their land: *Gentleman's Magazine*, 1833.

Scottish artist Matthew Dalziel: personal communication with the author.

'Giant Grum': 'B. B.' (D. J. Watkins-Pitchford), *The Little Grey Men*, Eyre and Spottiswoode, 1942.

ideology of the Enclosures . . . less likeable attitudes of the Enlightenment: J. L. and Barbara Hammond, *The Village Labourer*, Nonsuch Publishing, 2005, first published 1911.

Chapter Three: Textures of Tenderness

'They teach their children to cry!': H. Scudder Mekeel, in Erik Erikson, *Childhood and Society*, Paladin, 1977, first published 1951.

Ache people . . . never set down on the ground or left alone: Kim Hill and A. Magdalena Hurtado, *Ache Life History: The Ecology and Demography of a Foraging People*, Aldine de Gruyter, 1996.

caressing, stroking and sensual pleasure . . . infancy among the Huaorani: Laura Rival, 'What Kind of Sex Makes People Happy?', in R. Astuti, J. Parry and C. Stafford (eds.), *Questions of Anthropology*, Berg, 2007.

!Kung people say that the closeness . . . strength and emotional security: Marjorie Shostak, *Nisa: The Life and Words of a !Kung Woman*, Harvard University Press, 1981.

Richard B. Lee and Irven DeVore (eds.), *Kalahari Hunter-Gatherers: Studies of the !Kung San and Their Neighbors*, Harvard University Press, 1976.

Leaving a baby to cry will damage . . . argues the psychotherapist Sue Gerhardt: Sue Gerhardt, *Why Love Matters: How Affection Shapes a Baby's Brain*, Routledge, 2004.

sling-carried babies . . . secure in their attachment: Oliver James, *They F*** You Up: How to Survive Family Life*, Bloomsbury, 2002.

High levels of maternal affection . . . lower levels of distress: J. Maselko, L. Kubzansky, L. Lipsitt, S. L. Buka, *Journal of Epidemiology and Community Health, BMJ*, 2010.

studies of Romanian orphans: Chugani et al, in Sue Gerhardt, *Why Love Matters: How Affection Shapes a Baby's Brain*, Routledge, 2004.

'a virtual black hole where their orbitofrontal cortex should be': Sue Gerhardt, *Why Love Matters: How Affection Shapes a Baby's Brain*, Routledge, 2004.

boarding schools, with terrible emotional consequences: Joy Schaverien, 'Boarding School Syndrome', *British Journal of Psychotherapy*, May 2011 (27).

Short working hours . . . a feature of many indigenous societies: see the work of Professor Richard Lee and others.

a 'private' individual as one *deprived* of public life: Hannah Arendt, *The Human Condition*, University of Chicago Press, 1958.

Chapter Four: By the Mark, Twain!

Paris, 1840 . . . Béasse is having a run-in with the courts: first reported in *La Phalange*, then in Michel Foucault, *Discipline and Punish: the Birth of the Prison*, Gallimard, 1975.

supposedly from the speech of Patrick Henry . . . in the American Revolution: Bill Bryson in *Made in America*, Black Swan, 1998, says there is no evidence Patrick Henry ever said this.

'games that the night demanded': Laurie Lee, *Cider with Rosie*, Hogarth Press, 1959.

Native American children were traditionally free to wander: see reports of Pierre de Charlevoix, Jesuit missionary in Canada, 1761.

'spadgering', casting a net over a whole hedge to catch sparrows: Flora Thompson, *Lark Rise to Candleford*, Oxford University Press, 1939–43.

Alacaluf children of Patagonia fend for themselves early: Eric Shipton, *Land of Tempest: Travels in Patagonia 1958–62*, Hodder and Stoughton, 1963.

Inuit children may use a whip to hunt ptarmigans: Simon Tookoome with Sheldon Oberman, *The Shaman's Nephew: A Life in the Far North*, Stoddart, 1999.

Ache children of Paraguay learn early . . . very independent of their parents: Kim Hill and A. Magdalena Hurtado, *Ache Life History: The Ecology and Demography of a Foraging People*, Aldine de Gruyter, 1996.

'Wild About Play' . . . to collect and eat wild foods: Tim Gill, 'Let Our Children Roam Free', *The Ecologist*, October 2005.

artists . . . an ecstatic knowledge of nature: Louise Chawla, *In the First Country of Places: Nature, Poetry, and Childhood Memory*, State University of New York Press, 1994.

American psychiatrist, Herbert Hendin . . . suicide statistics in Scandinavia: Herbert Hendin, *Suicide and Scandinavia*, Anchor Books, 1965.

Norwegian children now spend more time indoors: Astrid N. Sjolie and Frode Thuen, *Health Promotion International*, Oxford University Press, 2002.

under house arrest . . . complaining that they have 'nowhere to go': Richard Layard and Judy Dunn, *A Good Childhood: Searching for Values in a Competitive Age*, Report for the Children's Society, Penguin, 2009.

netball hoop . . . 'because residents didn't want to attract children': *ECOS* 24, Journal of the British Association of Nature Conservationists, 2003.

children . . . told off for playing outdoors: Survey for The Children's Society, 2003.

time (particularly with families), friendships and, yearningly, 'outdoors': UNICEF-commissioned report from IPSOS/MORI and Dr Agnes Nairn, 2011.

unstructured play in nature . . . freedom, independence and inner strength: N. Wells and K. S. Lekies, 'Nature and the Life Course: Pathways from

Childhood Nature Experiences to Adult Environmentalism', *Children, Youth and Environments*, 2006 (16).

less stressed but also bounce back from stressful events more readily: Nancy Wells and Gary Evans, 'Nearby Nature: A Buffer of Life Stress among Rural Children', *Environment and Behavior*, May 2003 (35).

reduction in available open spaces for children to play: UK Children's Commissioners' Report to the UN Committee on the Rights of the Child, 2008.

USA, the home turf of children shrank … between 1970 and 1990: S. Gaster, 1991, quoted by Stephen Moss, *Naturalworld*, 2009.

in Britain, children have one-ninth of the roaming room: UK Children's Commissioners' Report to the UN Committee on the Rights of the Child, 2008.

less than ten per cent of children now spending time playing in woodlands: Natural England, 'Our Natural Health Service', 2009.

'The countryside – I've been there, maybe about once': Guy Thompson, *ECOS* 26, Journal of the British Association of Nature Conservationists, 2005.

cycled to school alone … social services: BBC News, 5 July 2010.

Mary Bousted … 'not allowed the freedom to play and learn unwatched': *Independent*, 11 March 2008.

GPS devices … British parents are in favour of their children using: Information from The Future Foundation.

media stories about young people are negative … about crime: UK Children's Commissioners' Report to the United Nations Committee on the Rights of the Child, 2008.

'stop and search' power … disproportionately used against children: Under-eighteens comprise 18–20 per cent of London's population but 40 per cent of stops and 30 per cent of searches were made on children, in figures from 2007.

Children are discriminated against on public transport and by public services: According to Young Equals, a coalition of leading children's charities.

curfew powers … kids who have committed no crime whatsoever: The Crime and Disorder Act, 1998, Section 14, and the Anti-social Behaviour Act, 2003, Section 30.

power may be disproportionately used … 'may penalize law-abiding children': UK Children's Commissioners' Report to the United Nations Committee on the Rights of the Child, 2008.

emigrating 'mainly because of young people hanging around': British Crime Survey, 2004–5.

children excluded from school can be effectively subject to house arrest: Education and Inspections Act, 2006.

Johan Huizinga ... 'close to the realm of the sacred': Johan Huizinga, *Homo Ludens: A Study of the Play Element in Culture*, Roy Publishers, 1950.

teenagers now don't even know how to find water: Melanie Challenger, *On Extinction: How We Became Estranged from Nature*, Granta, 2011.

Many Inuit children who have attempted suicide ... they were bored: Melanie Challenger, *On Extinction: How We Became Estranged from Nature*, Granta, 2011.

The rate of suicide among Inuit youth ... eleven times the national average: 2012 data from Health Canada, public health department of the government of Canada.

In Sámi tradition, trial and error ... often quite dangerous situations: Asta Balto, *Traditional Sámi Child Rearing in Transition: Shaping a New Pedagogical Platform*, Sámi University College, 2005.

Indigenous Australian Bob Randall: see Melanie Hogan (dir.), *Kanyini*, 2006.

Chapter Five: Wolf Milk in the Ink

pets were one of the top four most important things for their happiness: UNICEF, 'Child Poverty in Perspective: An Overview of Child Well-being in Rich Countries', UNICEF Innocenti Research Centre, 2007.

Stealthily, heartfeltedly, he kissed the lion's nose: Francis Spufford, *The Child that Books Built*, Faber, 2002.

Birds and animals come into our lives as 'guests', say Mohawk tales: Ernest Benedict (Mohawk) in Sylvester M. Morey and Olivia L. Gilliam (eds.), *Respect for Life: The Traditional Upbringing of American Indian Children*, Report of a Conference at Harper's Ferry, West Virginia, Waldorf Press, 1972.

'beevis have pouchis at the baof side ... the bughunt was amingszing': I freely admit that the sole reason for this sentence is to include this amingszing spelling.

Eighty per cent of the dreams of children under six are about animals: Bill Plotkin, *Nature and the Human Soul: Cultivating Wholeness and Community in a Fragmented World*, New World Library, 2008.

Koyukon world-view, children have an especial sensitivity towards nature: Richard K. Nelson, *Make Prayers to the Raven: A Koyukon View of the Northern Forest*, University of Chicago Press, 1983.

wise to raise a hawk owl around them: I bid.

Henry Old Coyote: Sylvester M. Morey and Olivia L. Gilliam (eds.), *Respect for Life: The Traditional Upbringing of American Indian Children*, Report of a Conference at Harper's Ferry, West Virginia, Waldorf Press, 1972.

animal companionship . . . self-esteem, self-control and autonomy: B. M. Levinson, 'Pets and Personality Development', *Journal for the Study of Animal Problems*, 1978 (3).

children treat their pets as they themselves would like to be treated: V. Morrow, 'My Animals and Other Family: Children's Perspectives on Their Relationships with Companion Animals', *Anthrozoos* 17, 1998 (4).

children who have pets feel more empathy towards other people: V. Vidovic, V. Stetic and D. Brathko, 'Pet Ownership, Type of Pet, and Socio-Emotional Development of School Children', *Anthrozoos* 12, 1999 (4).

'enjoyed killing the unwanted newborn puppies': Jean L. Briggs, *Never in Anger: Portrait of an Eskimo Family*, Harvard University Press, 1970.

'will gauge our intentions . . . from the way we spontaneously treat his teddy bear': Bruno Bettelheim, *A Home for the Heart*, Knopf, 1974.

'Sometimes he was a panther' . . . John Joseph Mathews: quoted in Patricia Riley (ed.), *Growing Up Native American: An Anthology*, William Morrow, 1993.

Pueblo Indian children . . . lyrics, choreography and costume: Gary Paul Nabhan and Stephen Trimble, *The Geography of Childhood: Why Children Need Wild Places*, Beacon Press, 1994.

Chapter Six: A Ludic Revolution (and a doodle)

Play on the urban commons, the street, has today 'mostly disappeared': Andrew Burn, 'Children's Playground Games and Songs in the New Media Age,' Institute of Education, University of London, 2009–11.

school playground is crucial to the continuance of aspects of children's culture: Andrew Burn, 'Children's Playground Games and Songs in the New Media Age', Institute of Education, University of London, 2009–11.

schools are now being built without playgrounds: UK Children's Commissioners' Report to the UN Committee on the Rights of the Child, 2008.

'I never thought I'd see them laugh again': Jo Wilding, *Taking a Circus to the Children of Iraq*, New Internationalist Publications, 2006.

children play imaginatively . . . the ability to self-regulate: Howard Chudacoff, cultural historian, with Alix Spiegel on *NPR*, 21 February 2008.

In structured play, this private speech declines: Alix Spiegel on *NPR*, 21 February 2008.

Playfully taking a line for a walk: Paul Klee defined drawing as taking a line for a walk, Paul Klee, *Pedagogical Sketchbook*, 1925.

Johan Huizinga . . . *lila* is used in the sense of 'as if', to denote 'seeming': Johan Huizinga, *Homo Ludens: A Study of the Play Element in Culture*, Roy Publishers, 1950.

Internet site on doodling comes complete with a 'Disclaimer': Oh dearie me.

Gaston Bachelard . . . 'for a reverie which knows the price of solitude': Gaston Bachelard, *The Poetics of Reverie*, Viking, 1969, first published 1960.

educational psychologists . . . daydreaming could cause neurosis and psychosis: Eric Klinger, *Psychology Today*, October 1987.

Daydreams . . . complex problem-solving: K. Christoff, A. M. Gordon, J. Smallwood, R. Smith and J. W. Schooler, in *Proceedings of the National Academy of Sciences*, 2009.

Chapter Seven: A Clockwork Child

ideal school . . . hatred of timetables: Edward Blishen (ed.), *The School That I'd Like*, Penguin, 1969.

UNICEF . . . one of their top three needs, they said, was *time*: UNICEF-commissioned report from IPSOS/MORI and Dr Agnes Nairn, 2011.

because, Sámi people say, children would grow up more self-reliant: Asta Balto, *Traditional Sámi Child Rearing in Transition: Shaping a New Pedagogical Platform*, Sámi University College, 2005.

Bells, whistles, gongs and clappers: Basil Johnston (Ojibwa) in Patricia Riley (ed.), *Growing Up Native American: An Anthology*, William Morrow, 1993.

Chapter Eight: The Will of the Wild

the root of 'wild' is in 'will': what is self-willed: Roderick Frazier Nash, *Wilderness and the American Mind*, Yale University Press, 1967.

The stem of 'well' is identical to that of the verb 'will': *The Oxford English Dictionary*.

wilderness therapy produces positive outcomes for teenagers: J. Hattie, H. W. Marsh, J. T. Neill, and G. E. Richards, 'Adventure Education and Outward Bound: Out-of-Class Experiences that Make a Lasting Difference', *Review of Educational Research*, 67(1), 1997.

lessen distress both within themselves and in their relationships with others: K. C. Russell, 'An Assessment of Outcomes in Outdoor Behavioral Healthcare Treatment', *Child and Youth Care Forum*, 32(6), 2003.

K. C. Russell, 'Two Years Later: A Qualitative Assessment of Youth Well-being and the Role of Aftercare in Outdoor Behavioral Healthcare Treatment', *Child and Youth Care Forum*, 34(3), 2005.

helpful, effective treatment for problematic – difficult – adolescents: S. Crisp and C. Hinch, 'Treatment Effectiveness of Wilderness Adventure Therapy: Summary Findings', *Neo Psychology*, 2004.

In the wilds, self-awareness and communication . . . enhanced: M. Conner, 'What is Wilderness Therapy and a Wilderness Program?', 2007, see <wildernesstherapy-org.>

adventure therapy improves . . . self-conception and sense of self-control: D. Cason and H. L. Gillis, 'A Meta-analysis of Outdoor Adventure Programming with Adolescents', *Journal of Experiential Education*, 17, 1994.

adventure therapy . . . guiding them towards better social skills: J. Hattie, H. W. Marsh, J. T. Neill, and G. E. Richards, 'Adventure Education and Outward Bound: Out-of-Class Experiences that Make a Lasting Difference', *Review of Educational Research*, 67(1),1997.

!Kung children of the Kalahari were customarily not forced into obedience: Marjorie Shostak, *Nisa: The Life and Words of a !Kung Woman*, Harvard University Press, 1981.

Richard B. Lee and Irven DeVore (eds.), *Kalahari Hunter-Gatherers: Studies of the !Kung San and Their Neighbors*, Harvard University Press, 1976.

Among the Yequana people of Venezuela, coercion was traditionally absent: Jean Liedloff, *The Continuum Concept*, Duckworth, 1975.

Huaorani childhood in Ecuador . . . no stain of authoritarianism: Laura Rival, 'What Kind of Sex Makes People Happy?', in R. Astuti, J. Parry and C. Stafford (eds.), *Questions of Anthropology*, Berg, 2007.

'I'm boss for meself': Diane Bell, *Daughters of the Dreaming*, George Allen and Unwin, 1983.

self-directed, acting by their 'own idea', according to Pintupi people: Fred R. Myers, *Pintupi Country, Pintupi Self: Sentiment, Place, and Politics among Western Desert Aborigines*, Smithsonian Institution Press, 1986.

domination of any sort ... regarded as being against the law of nature: Hannah Rachel Bell, *Men's Business, Women's Business: The Spiritual Role of Gender in the World's Oldest Culture*, Inner Traditions International, 1998.

autonomy and self-expression were important ... coercion was a last resort: J. R. Miller, *Shingwauk's Vision: A History of Native Residential Schools*, University of Toronto Press, 1996.

strength of mind, independence and potency: see Howard Zinn, *A People's History of the United States, 1492–Present*, Harper and Row, 1980.

Iroquois children were encouraged ... not to submit to authoritarian behaviour: Ibid.

Laguna Pueblo of New Mexico forbids forcing children ... against their will: Victor Sarracino (Laguna Pueblo) in Sylvester M. Morey and Olivia L. Gilliam (eds.), *Respect for Life: The Traditional Upbringing of American Indian Children*, Report of a Conference at Harper's Ferry, West Virginia, Waldorf Press, 1972.

Among the Navajo ... which they adamantly refused to do: Dorothy Lee, *Freedom and Culture*, Prentice-Hall, 1959.

Wintu language ... 'I participated in my child's eating': Ibid.

Ngarinyin children ... from a young age they learned socialization: Hannah Rachel Bell, *Men's Business, Women's Business: The Spiritual Role of Gender in the World's Oldest Culture*, Inner Traditions International, 1998.

Huaorani ... appreciate the unique and idiosyncratic characteristics: Laura Rival, 'What Kind of Sex Makes People Happy?', in R. Astuti, J. Parry and C. Stafford (eds.), *Questions of Anthropology*, Berg, 2007.

reason, mind or thought which the Utkuhikhalingmiut people ... call *ihuma*: Jean L. Briggs, *Never in Anger: Portrait of an Eskimo Family*, Harvard University Press, 1970.

Sámi children are trained to control anger, sensitivity, aggression and shame: Asta Balto, *Traditional Sámi Child Rearing in Transition: Shaping a New Pedagogical Platform*, Sámi University College, 2005.

Amazonian myths place huge importance on self-restraint and self-discipline: Laura Rival, 'What Kind of Sex Makes People Happy?', in R. Astuti, J. Parry and C. Stafford (eds.), *Questions of Anthropology*, Berg, 2007.

Proceedings of the National Academy of Sciences of the United States of America: Terrie E. Moffitt, Louise Arseneault, Daniel Belsky, Nigel Dickson, Robert J. Hancox, HonaLee Harrington, Renate Houts, Richie Poulton, Brent W. Roberts, Stephen Ross, Malcolm R. Sears, W. Murray Thomson and Avshalom Caspi, 'A gradient of childhood self-control predicts health, wealth, and public safety', *Proceedings of the National Academy of Sciences of the United States of America*, 108(7), 2011.

San Bushmen would kill a baby if it was born deformed . . . unable to support it: Elizabeth Marshall Thomas, *The Harmless People*, Secker and Warburg, 1959.

nineteenth-century European cities, a third or even half . . . abandoned: Colin Heywood, *A History of Childhood*, Polity, 2001.

the training of young Samurai . . . the decapitated head: Inazō Nitobe, *Bushidō: The Soul of Japan*, Oxford University Press, 2002, first published 1905.

'the man I didn't want was my first experience': Rosie Iqalliyuq, *Interview for the Igloolik Oral History Project*, Igloolik Research Centre, 1987.

'once they did that the tribe had no more use for them': Dorothy Haegert, *Children of the First People*, Tillacum Library, 1983.

the Stubborn Child Act, by which parents were allowed to kill a child: cited in C. E. Walker, B. L. Bonner and K. L. Kaufman, *The Physically and Sexually Abused Child: Evaluation and Treatment*, Pergamon Press, 1988.

As a mother is to a child, so is the poet to (a radiant) god: Sudhir Kakar, *The Inner World: A Psycho-analytic Study of Childhood and Society in India*, Oxford University Press, 1981.

'And the brilliance of millions of bits of the universe': Sūrdās, *The Memory of Love: Sūrdās Sings to Krishna*, trans. John Stratton Hawley, Oxford University Press, 2009.

In the Bhakti tradition, creativity is centred around childhood: Sudhir Kakar, *The Inner World: A Psycho-analytic Study of Childhood and Society in India*, Oxford University Press, 1981.

Shamanic creatures are overwhelmingly the wildest within any region: Åke Hultkrantz, *Native Religions of North America*, Waveland Press, 1987.

Chapter Nine: The Fractal Politics of Childhood

the two great sins are picking wild flowers and threatening children: Peter Matthiesen, *The Snow Leopard*, Viking, 1978.

Gypsy children ... treated with notable indulgence and freedom: Denis Harvey, *The Gypsies: Waggon-time and After*, Batsford, 1979.

!Kung children almost never received physical punishment: Marjorie Shostak, *Nisa: The Life and Words of a !Kung Woman*, Harvard University Press, 1981. Richard B. Lee and Irven DeVore (eds.), *Kalahari Hunter-Gatherers: Studies of the !Kung San and Their Neighbors*, Harvard University Press, 1976.

Tylwyth Teg, the fair folk, in Wales, or the piskies in Cornwall would steal them: W. Y. Evans-Wentz, *The Fairy-faith in Celtic Countries*, Oxford University Press, 1911.

In traditional Maori culture children were almost never beaten ... tyrannical: Linda Tuhiwai Smith, 'Nga Aho o te Kakahu Matauranga: The Multiple Layers of Struggle by Maori in Education', PhD thesis, University of Auckland, 1996.

Laguna Pueblo ... reprimanded by a family member but not the parents: Sylvester M. Morey and Olivia L. Gilliam (eds.), *Respect for Life: The Traditional Upbringing of American Indian Children*, Report of a Conference at Harper's Ferry, West Virginia, Waldorf Press, 1972.

the dreamcatcher ... sacred to that parent–child relationship: Guy W. Jones and Sally Moomaw, *Lessons from Turtle Island: Native Curriculum in Early Childhood Classrooms*, Redleaf Press, 2002.

'For an elder person in the Lakota tribe' ... Luther Standing Bear: Luther Standing Bear, *Land of the Spotted Eagle*, University of Nebraska Press, 1978, first published 1933.

no word for punishment ... they would be tolerated: Theodore Zeldin, *An Intimate History of Humanity*, Sinclair-Stevenson, 1994.

seek to earn a child's respect ... never need to use coercion, let alone violence: Allen Quetone (Kiowa) in Sylvester M. Morey and Olivia L. Gilliam (eds.), *Respect for Life: The Traditional Upbringing of American Indian Children*, Report of a Conference at Harper's Ferry, West Virginia, Waldorf Press, 1972.

missionary ... preparing to thrash an Ayoreo child: Norman Lewis, *The Missionaries*, Arena, 1989.

timid and submissive, in contrast to ... pride, independence and bravery: Steven Mintz, *Huck's Raft: A History of American Childhood*, The Belknap Press, 2004.

A child granted respect will accord it to others: Simon Tookoome with Sheldon Oberman, *The Shaman's Nephew: A Life in the Far North*, Stoddart, 1999.

loving-songs, *aqausiit* ... their own songs which people sing to them: Naqi Ekho and Uqsuralik Ottokie in Jean Briggs (ed.), *Interviewing Inuit Elders: Childrearing Practices*, Nunavut Arctic College, 2000.

'snuffed, cuddled, cooed at . . . a passing titter or a moo of disapproval': Jean L. Briggs, *Never in Anger: Portrait of an Eskimo Family*, Harvard University Press, 1970.

Fridtjof Nansen . . . 'more European than Eskimo': Fridtjof Nansen, *The First Crossing of Greenland*, Longmans, 1890.

G. F. Lyon . . . a childhood of devoted fondness: Captain G. F. Lyon, *The Private Journal of Captain G. F. Lyon of HMS* Hecla *during the Recent Voyage of Discovery under Captain Parry 1821–1823*, Imprint Society Barre-Massachusetts, 1970.

natural both to take care of others . . . and to expect to be cared for: Sudhir Kakar, *The Inner World: A Psycho-analytic Study of Childhood and Society in India*, Oxford University Press, 1981.

'These Barbarians cannot bear to have their children punished': Martin Daunton and Rick Halpern (eds.), *Empire and Others: British Encounters with Indigenous Peoples, 1600–1850*, University College London Press, 1999.

Lewis Hennepin, in 1699 . . . 'They are perpetually belching': Ibid.

Colonist children who were captured by Native Americans . . .: 'Holley Swallowed up with the Indians': Steven Mintz, *Huck's Raft: A History of American Childhood*, The Belknap Press, 2004.

Time after time the settler children refused to return: Natty Bumppo, the white man raised by Mohicans, is the most famous fictional representation of this phenomenon, in James Fenimore Cooper's *The Last of the Mohicans: A Narrative of 1757*, first published 1826.

James McCullough . . . So ferocious was his desire to escape: Steven Mintz, *Huck's Raft: A History of American Childhood*, The Belknap Press, 2004.

Colonel Henry Bouquet . . . the children, had to be bound hand and foot: James W. Loewen, *Lies My Teacher Told Me: Everything Your American History Textbook Got Wrong*, The New Press, 1995.

returning to their own people 'with great signs of joy': Frederick Turner, *Beyond Geography: The Western Spirit against the Wilderness*, Rutgers University Press, 1983.

Benjamin Franklin . . . 'one Indian Ramble': Steven Mintz, *Huck's Raft: A History of American Childhood*, The Belknap Press, 2004.

Comanche raids, for example, men were killed . . . children were frequently adopted: S. C. Gwynne, *Empire of the Summer Moon: Quanah Parker and the Rise and Fall of the Comanches, the Most Powerful Indian Tribe in American History*, Scribner, 2010.

in Norwich, a seven-year-old girl stole a petticoat and was hanged: Neil Postman, *The Disappearance of Childhood*, Delacorte Press, 1982.

After the Gordon Riots of 1780 . . . contemporary observer George Selwyn:
quoted in Neil Postman, *The Disappearance of Childhood*, Delacorte Press, 1982.

education became increasingly hierarchical . . . monarchical absolutism:
Philippe Ariès, *Centuries of Childhood: A Social History of Family Life*,
Jonathan Cape, 1962, first published 1960.

In Han China, the word for slave was derived from the word for child: Theodore
Zeldin, *An Intimate History of Humanity*, Sinclair-Stevenson, 1994.

'Its spirit carried out in society would . . . inaugurate universal lawlessness':
The school committee of Beverly, Report for 1867–8.

director of the Union Banking Corporation, a firm involved with the financial
architects of Nazism: *Guardian*, 25 September 2004.

you cannot 'discipline' a baby: Sue Gerhardt, *Why Love Matters: How Affection
Shapes a Baby's Brain*, Routledge, 2004.

'a true, wounded, submissive whimper': Michael and Debi Pearl, *To Train Up a
Child*, No Greater Joy Ministries, 1994.

'Hold the resisting child . . . rule over him as a benevolent sovereign': Ibid.

Alice Miller . . . 'poisonous pedagogy': Alice Miller, *For Your Own Good: The
Roots of Violence in Child-rearing*, Faber, 1983, first published 1980.

Even low rates of physical punishment predict psychological distress . . . a
worsening of the parent–child relationship: Elizabeth Gershoff, 'Report
on Physical Punishment in the United States: What Research Tells Us about
Its Effects on Children', *Columbus Center for Effective Discipline*, 2008.
For an excellent exploration of the ill effects of physical punishment, see Jan
Parker and Jan Stimpson, *Raising Happy Children: What Every Child Needs
Their Parents to Know*, Hodder, 1999.

Fear, anger, hate . . . paranoia and extreme dissociation: Philip Greven, *Spare
the Child: The Religious Roots of Punishment and the Psychological Impact of
Physical Abuse*, Knopf, 1991.

'A child can be turned back from the road to hell through proper spankings':
Michael and Debi Pearl, *To Train Up a Child*, No Greater Joy Ministries, 1994.

beating babies with a branch . . . flogged with a cutting from a shrub: Ibid.

'as easy as putting a rag doll to bed': Ibid.

'Very few ever became more than very confused, ambivalent, and immobilized
individuals': Clyde Warrior (Ponca) in Wayne Moquin and Charles Van
Doren, *Great Documents in American Indian History*, Da Capo Press, 1995.

called genocidal by the Human Rights Commission Inquiry: Human Rights and Equal Opportunity Commission Report, *Bringing Them Home*, Report of the National Inquiry into the Separation of Aboriginal and Torres Strait Islander Children from Their Families, 1997.

life stories from the Stolen Generations: Carmel Bird (ed.), *The Stolen Children: Their Stories*, Random House, 1998.

One in five stolen children was sexually abused in care: Human Rights and Equal Opportunity Commission Report, *Bringing Them Home*, Report of the National Inquiry into the Separation of Aboriginal and Torres Strait Islander Children from Their Families, 1997.

'We are civilized today and they are not': Russell Ward, *Man Makes History*, Shakespeare Head Press, 1952.

Nils-Aslak Valkeapää ... '... machine guns and Hunter jets. That's education, that is': Nils-Aslak Valkeapää, *Greetings from Lappland: The Sámi, Europe's Forgotten People*, Zed Press, 1983.

Native American Assiniboine chief: Dan Kennedy (Ochankugahe), *Recollections of an Assiniboine Chief*, James R. Stevens (ed.), McClelland and Stewart, 1972.

Douglas George-Kanentiio (Mohawk-Iroquois): Huston Smith, *A Seat at the Table: Huston Smith in Conversation with Native Americans on Religious Freedom*, Phil Cousineau (ed.), University of California Press, 2006.

'They might be encouraged to have little gardens, and be gradually brought into habits of civilization': Little gardens. So that's okay then. As long as there are a couple of gnomes, who can complain?

'It is impossible to persuade the men to give up their wandering life': W. N. Gray, JP of Port Macquarie, to the Select Committee on the Condition of Aborigines, 1845.

'at liberty to roam about ... useless afterwards': Select Committee of the Western Australia Legislative Council, 1886.

traditional connections to the land can have preventative effects on suicidality: see the work of Suicide Prevention, Australia.

Chapter Ten: Who Owns a Child?

'little grammas and little grampas': Inés Hernandez in Patricia Riley (ed.), *Growing Up Native American: An Anthology*, William Morrow, 1993.

damaging the ancestor's *mana*, their spiritual power: Linda Tuhiwai Smith, 'Nga Aho o te Kakahu Matauranga: The Multiple Layers of Struggle by Maori in Education', PhD thesis, University of Auckland, 1996.

belief that the soul of an elder resides within the child: Kaj Birket-Smith, *The Eskimos*, Methuen, 1936, first published 1927.

namesake links the present and the past: Naqi Ekho and Uqsuralik Ottokie in Jean Briggs (ed.), *Interviewing Inuit Elders: Childrearing Practices*, Nunavut Arctic College, 2000.

their relationship with their ancestors: Linda Richter and Robert Morrell (eds.), *Baba: Men and Fatherhood in South Africa*, Human Sciences Research Council Press, 2006.

kin terms of the Kunjen people . . . a grandmother might call her great grand-daughter 'Little Auntie': Alma Wason in Veronica Strang, *Uncommon Ground: Cultural Landscapes and Environmental Values*, Berg, 1997.

Simon Tookoome's granddaughter . . . 'I do things for her as if my sister was asking': Simon Tookoome with Sheldon Oberman, *The Shaman's Nephew: A Life in the Far North*, Stoddart, 1999.

If a child's *atiq* drowned . . . this cautioning fear is passed on: Naqi Ekho and Uqsuralik Ottokie in Jean Briggs (ed.), *Interviewing Inuit Elders: Childrearing Practices*, Nunavut Arctic College, 2000.

they may notice that a particular child needs some of their own qualities: Ruthie Piungittuq, *Interview for the Igloolik Oral History Project*, Igloolik Research Centre, 1991.

Among the Yequana . . . the concept of 'my child' is non-existent: Jean Liedloff, *The Continuum Concept*, Duckworth, 1975.

the idea of ownership does not exist in Ngarinyin life: Hannah Rachel Bell, *Men's Business, Women's Business: The Spiritual Role of Gender in the World's Oldest Culture*, Inner Traditions International, 1998.

Many teenagers . . . moved to other households as apprentices or servants: John Gillis, *A World of Their Own Making: Myth, Ritual and the Quest for Family Values*, Basic Books, 1996.

among the !Kung . . . Children would readily and happily move to live with grandparents, aunts or other close relatives: Marjorie Shostak, *Nisa: The Life and Words of a !Kung Woman*, Harvard University Press, 1981.
Richard B. Lee and Irven DeVore (eds.), *Kalahari Hunter-Gatherers: Studies of the !Kung San and Their Neighbors*, Harvard University Press, 1976.

In Indigenous Australia ... no single adult had the full-time care of any child: Jan Kociumbas, *Australian Childhood: A History*, Allen and Unwin, 1997.

Pintupi ... adulthood itself is defined by the ability to take care of others: Fred R. Myers, *Pintupi Country, Pintupi Self: Sentiment, Place and Politics among Western Desert Aborigines*, Smithsonian Institution Press, 1986.

For the Ngarinyin people, everyone is responsible for a baby: Hannah Rachel Bell, *Men's Business, Women's Business: The Spiritual Role of Gender in the World's Oldest Culture*, Inner Traditions International, 1998.

Children in traditional Welsh villages ... considered 'village property': Sylvia Prys Jones in F. Bowie and O. Davies, (eds.), *Discovering Welshness*, Gomer, 1992.

African societies ... these terms pledge people to take responsibility for each other: Nhlanhla Mkhize, 'African Traditions and the Social, Economic and Moral Dimensions of Fatherhood', in Linda Richter and Robert Morrell (eds.), *Baba: Men and Fatherhood in South Africa*, Human Sciences Research Council Press, 2006.

'Thou hast no sense. You French people love only your own children': Theodore Zeldin, *An Intimate History of Humanity*, Sinclair-Stevenson, 1994.

In traditional Dakota life ... great security and self-assurance: Ella Cara Deloria, *Waterlily*, University of Nebraska Press, 1988, written in 1940s.

When such a connection is broken, people experience internal trauma: Douglas George-Kanentiio (Mohawk-Iroquois) in Huston Smith, *A Seat at the Table: Huston Smith in Conversation with Native Americans on Religious Freedom*, Phil Cousineau (ed.), University of California Press, 2006.

a breastfeeding infant would reach into the blouse of any nursing mother: Erik Erikson, *Childhood and Society*, Paladin, 1977, first published 1951.

Huaorani ... may breastfeed her child, a sister's child and a grandchild: Laura Rival, 'What Kind of Sex Makes People Happy?', in R. Astuti, J. Parry and C. Stafford (eds.), *Questions of Anthropology*, Berg, 2007.

segregated out of public life ... as a result becoming less capable: see Philippe Ariès, Shulamith Firestone and others.

D. J. Williams ... the merry-young-uncle-in-search-of-a-wife: D. J. Williams, *The Old Farmhouse/Hen Dŷ Ffarm*, translated by Waldo Williams, Harrap and Co., 1961.

in the UK ... one in ten children aged five to sixteen has clinically significant mental health difficulties: H. Green et al, 2005, quoted in Richard Layard and Judy Dunn, *A Good Childhood: Searching for Values in a Competitive Age*, Report for the Children's Society, Penguin, 2009.

Britain ranks lowest of twenty-one industrialized nations for childhood well-being: UNICEF, *Child Poverty in Perspective: An Overview of Child Well-being in Rich Countries*, UNICEF Innocenti Research Centre, 2007.

A 2007 Cambridge University study ... a 'loss of childhood': see the work of Professor Robin Alexander, the Cambridge Primary Review, Cambridge University Faculty of Education.

the amount of television which children watch correlates with measures of body fat: Richard Louv, *Last Child in the Woods: Saving Our Children from Nature-Deficit Disorder*, Algonquin Books of Chapel Hill, 2005.

seeing violence on television increases children's aggression: Philip Greven, *Spare the Child: The Religious Roots of Punishment and the Psychological Impact of Physical Abuse*, Knopf, 1991.

more television when they are four are more likely to tease and bully: Juliet B. Schor, *Born to Buy*, Scribner, 2004.

fifty-two per cent of American children go shopping each week, while only seventeen per cent play outdoors: Ibid.

In Britain, the pressure to buy 'stuff' is more acutely felt in poorer households: UNICEF-commissioned report from IPSOS/MORI and Dr Agnes Nairn, 2011.

Argentina ... the civil registry removed people's indigenous names: Eduardo Galeano, *Upside Down: A Primer for the Looking-Glass World*, Picador, 1998.

three-year-olds can recognize an average of one hundred logos: *New Internationalist*, September 2006.

Only half of British children can identify an oak leaf ... cannot identify a frog: Stephen Moss, quoting a National Trust study, in *Naturalworld*, spring 2009.

Chapter Eleven: The Tribe of Children

for most of human history, children have roamed in packs, playing together: Howard Chudacoff, *Children at Play: An American History*, NYU Press, 2007.

Iona and Peter Opie: Iona and Peter Opie, *The Lore and Language of Schoolchildren*, Oxford University Press, 1959.

Iona Opie, *The People in the Playground*, Oxford University Press, 1993.

A recent study into childhood lore and play: Andrew Burn, 'Children's Playground Games and Songs in the New Media Age,' Institute of Education, University of London, 2009–11.

Chapter Twelve: On the Character Fault of Exuberance

Plato's *Republic* **... a founding text on the education of boys**: What use, by the way, are women? Their greatness lies in the making of pancakes and preserves, says Plato. How shockingly unfair. I can't make marmalade to save my life.

has the temerity to censor Homer: Homer the Greek, not Homer the Simpson, ye gods, Plato would shiver in his chilly tomb.

'the child must be beaten harder if he screams': Philippe Ariès, *Centuries of Childhood: A Social History of Family Life*, Jonathan Cape, 1962, first published 1960.

The Jesuit Fathers armed their servants ... hit by a bullet in the thigh: Ibid.

School mutinies in England ... Marlborough in 1851: Ibid.

student loans ... disproportionately deter people from poorer backgrounds: Leicester University study quoted by Sean Coughlan, *BBC News*, 21 September 2010.

explicitly yearning for classrooms in the form of domes: Edward Blishen (ed.), *The School That I'd Like*, Penguin, 1969.

'... constant supervision ... calculated to make them think one loves them': Philippe Ariès, *Centuries of Childhood: A Social History of Family Life*, Jonathan Cape, 1962, first published 1960.

'The hamlet children hated school. It was prison to them ...': Flora Thompson, *Lark Rise to Candleford*, Oxford University Press, 1939–43.

on reaching age seventeen, children are sent to jail for non-payment: Chris McGreal, 'The US Schools with Their Own Police', *Guardian*, 9 January 2012.

A child may be seen as having eight intelligences: see the work of the educator Kurt Hahn and the Harvard psychologist Howard Gardner, the idea popularized by Anthony Seldon, headteacher at Wellington College, in, e.g., speech to the College of Teachers, March 2009.

review of research on teenagers ... very little sign of disturbance and anti-social behaviour: A. Schlegel and H. Barry, 'A Cross-cultural Approach to Adolescence' *Ethos*, 23 (1), 1995.

historians have remarked on this generally peaceful transition to adulthood: Robert Epstein, 'The Myth of the Teen Brain', *Scientific American Mind*, April/May 2007.

teenage trouble appears soon after ... influences, particularly television and schooling: Ibid.

'There is not one Indian child who has not come home in shame and tears': Rupert Costo in Miriam Wasserman, *Demystifying School: Writings and Experiences*, Praeger, 1974.

Children's Hospital and Regional Medical Center in Seattle . . . increases the likelihood of developing ADHD: Richard Louv, *Last Child in the Woods: Saving Our Children from Nature-Deficit Disorder*, Algonquin Books of Chapel Hill, 2005.

Juliet B. Schor, *Born to Buy*, Scribner, 2004.

Inuit elders say that hyperactivity is a result of being physically separated from mothers in infancy: Uqsuralik Ottokie in Jean Briggs (ed.), *Interviewing Inuit Elders: Childrearing Practices*, Nunavut Arctic College, 2000.

Black children, boys, and working-class children are disproportionately diagnosed: On disproportionate diagnosis of ADHD see David Pilgrim, *Psychotherapy and Society*, Sage Publications, 1997.

Family psychotherapist and author Jan Parker: personal communication with author.

'a medical treatment that . . . drugs their specialness into submission': J. Wilson, 'Attention Deficit Hyperactivity Disorder: Ethical, Political and Practical Considerations of a Sceptic', *Journal of Family Therapy*, 2012.

hand movements are related to thinking and talking; gestures help constitute thought: Iain McGilchrist, *The Master and His Emissary: The Divided Brain and the Making of the Western World*, Yale University Press, 2009.

restricting hand gestures impacts negatively on speech: Ibid.

Babies and young children point while they babble and . . . to name things: M. Kinsbourne, (ed.), *Asymmetrical Function of the Brain*, Cambridge University Press, 1978.

'strong psychotropic drugs' were being handed out to children 'like sweets': see *Guardian*, 11 May 2010 and 18 March 2011.

the 'real me' is the 'me' not taking drugs: G. Brady in Craig Newnes and Nick Radcliffe (eds.), *Making and Breaking Children's Lives*, PCCS Books, 2005.

Chapter Thirteen: Mirrors of the Mind

a student could encounter . . . couldn't move for meeting someone: Pulak Dutta, 'Public Nature of Art Practices: Can Art Have a Public Life?', *International Yearbook of Aesthetics*, 2008 (12).

A. N. Whitehead . . . 'that is Life in all its manifestations': Alfred North Whitehead, *The Aims of Education and Other Essays*, Macmillan, 1929.

'We may become powerful by knowledge, but we attain fullness by sympathy':
Rabindranath Tagore, 'A Poet's School' from 'Thoughts on Education', *The
Visva-Bharati Quarterly*, May–October 1947.

'learned that a person thinks with his head instead of his heart': Don C.
Talayesva (Hopi) in Wayne Moquin and Charles Van Doren, *Great Documents in American Indian History*, Da Capo Press, 1995.

A Kiowa child's learning . . . 'strictly from a feeling point of view': Allen
Quetone (Kiowa) in Sylvester M. Morey and Olivia L. Gilliam (eds.), *Respect
for Life: The Traditional Upbringing of American Indian Children*, Report of a
Conference at Harper's Ferry, West Virginia, Waldorf Press, 1972.

'the conviviality between the child and the animate earth': David Abram,
Becoming Animal, Pantheon, 2010.

physical stamina . . . observance and insight into nature: Liz O'Brien and Richard Murray, 'Forest School and Its Impacts on Young Children: Case Studies
in Britain', *Urban Forestry and Urban Greening*, 2007 (6).

Outdoor education leads to improved cognitive outcomes: B. A. Sibley and
J. L. Etinier, 'The Relationship between Physical Activity and Cognition in
Children: A Meta-analysis', *Pediatric Exercise Science*, 2003 (15).

attitudes, self-perceptions, interpersonal skills and memory: M. Rickinson,
J. Dillon, K. Teamey, M. Morris, M. Choi, D. Sanders and P. Benefield,
A Review of Research on Outdoor Learning, Field Studies Council, 2004.
M. C. Berman, J. Jonides and S. Kaplan, 'The Cognitive Benefits of Interact-
ing with Nature', *Psychological Science*, 2008 (19).

no legal obligation for nurseries to have any outdoor play area: Statutory
Framework for the Early Years Foundation Stage, May 2008.

'But you, who are wise, must know . . . make Men of them': T. C. McLuhan
(compiler), *Touch the Earth: A Self-portrait of Indian Existence*, Abacus, 1973,
recorded in Benjamin Franklin, *Remarks Concerning the Savages of North
America*, pamphlet of 1784.

the role of older Ngarinyin men in Australia to educate through stories: Hannah Rachel Bell, *Men's Business, Women's Business: The Spiritual Role of
Gender in the World's Oldest Culture*, Inner Traditions International, 1998.

Salish educator Julie Cajune spoke of stories as teaching survival skills: personal communication with the author.

Inuit people were happier with children who took their time learning to talk: Uqsuralik Ottokie in Jean Briggs (ed.), *Interviewing Inuit Elders: Childrearing Practices*, Nunavut Arctic College, 2000.

'Silence, love, reverence – this is the trinity of first lessons': Charles Alexander Eastman (Ohiyesa), *The Soul of the Indian: An Interpretation*, University of Nebraska Press, 1911.

'The word is all-powerful ... taught to use words tenderly and never against anyone': Henry Old Coyote (Crow) in Sylvester M. Morey and Olivia L. Gilliam (eds.), *Respect for Life: The Traditional Upbringing of American Indian Children*, Report of a Conference at Harper's Ferry, West Virginia, Waldorf Press, 1972.

Inuit children were taught not to be stingy about anything, especially food: Uqsuralik Ottokie in Jean Briggs (ed.), *Interviewing Inuit Elders: Childrearing Practices*, Nunavut Arctic College, 2000.

'the contempt and disgrace falling upon the ungenerous and mean man': Charles Alexander Eastman (Ohiyesa), *The Soul of the Indian: An Interpretation*, University of Nebraska Press, 1911.

a sense of their ideal selves, their truest identity, practising honour: Erik Erikson, *Childhood and Society*, Paladin, 1977, first published 1951.

speak to a tree before cutting it down, treating it 'like a person coming home': John Thomas (Nitinaht) in Dorothy Haegert, *Children of the First People*, Tillacum Library, 1983.

never to abuse or mistreat an animal ... lose their ability to hear birds: Uqsuralik Ottokie in Jean Briggs (ed.), *Interviewing Inuit Elders: Childrearing Practices*, Nunavut Arctic College, 2000.

Pray while walking, George Louis ... was told by his grandmother: George Louis (Ahousaht) in Dorothy Haegert, *Children of the First People*, Tillacum Library, 1983.

literalist Christian teachers mock the traditional religion ... rituals undermined: anthropologist Dilwyn Jenkins, personal communication with author.

Theodore Zeldin notes how missionaries use children ... humiliating the fathers: Theodore Zeldin, *An Intimate History of Humanity*, Sinclair-Stevenson, 1994.

'the magic art of writing ... Why even the medicine men of our tribe cannot perform such miracles!': Dan Kennedy (Ochankugahe), *Recollections of an Assiniboine Chief*, James R. Stevens (ed.), McClelland and Stewart, 1972.

the training of the *Mamas*, the spiritual leaders of the Kogi people in Colombia: Alan Ereira, *The Heart of the World*, Cape, 1990.

Chapter Fourteen: The Woods and the Quest

Only two out of the forty had ever been to a woodland before: *ECOS* 26, Journal of the British Association of Nature Conservationists, 2005.

Karen . . . 'life tree' to teach the child to care for it: Seri Thongmak and David L. Hulse, 'The Winds of Change: Karen People in Harmony with World Heritage', in Elizabeth Kemf (ed.), *Indigenous Peoples and Protected Areas: The Law of Mother Earth*, Earthscan, 1993.

anti-road protesters: for a good account of these protests see Jim Hindle, *Nine Miles: Two Winters of Anti-Road Protest*, Underhill Books, 2006.

Charter of the Forests . . . commoning, including grazing and gleaning: Peter Linebaugh, *The Magna Carta Manifesto: Liberties and Commons for All*, University of California Press, 2008.

Dang people felt that time itself had been split apart . . . This time was called *moglai*: Ibid.

Hopi . . . still tell stories of orphans abandoned in the wilderness: Francis Spufford, *The Child That Books Built*, Faber, 2002.

'the Great Spirit' sometimes 'spoke to us through . . . thunder, or the changing seasons': Chief John Snow in J. R. Miller, *Shingwauk's Vision: A History of Native Residential Schools*, University of Toronto Press, 1996.

John Fire Lame Deer . . . 'I felt the power surge through me like a flood': John Fire Lame Deer and Richard Erdoes, *Lame Deer: Sioux Medicine Man*, Davis-Poynter, 1973.

attention to that threshold . . . to help young people to make meaning of their lives: see, for example, the work of Robert Bly, Joseph Campbell, Bill Plotkin, Eric Maddern, and many others.

Chapter Fifteen: The Ship That Goes as Well on Land as on Water

'I love this Earth. It's the only one with magic': Kim Stafford 'Wild Child Words', in Christian McEwen and Mark Statman (eds.), *The Alphabet of the Trees: A Guide to Nature Writing*, Teachers and Writers Collaborative, 2000.

In traditional Hindu medicine, someone who was psychically disoriented would be given a fairy tale: Bruno Bettelheim, *The Uses of Enchantment: The Meaning and Importance of Fairy Tales*, Thames and Hudson, 1976.

Goethe's mother was a renowned storyteller . . . 'so my imagination often was replaced by his': Ibid.

Subcomandante Marcos . . . 'The greatest knight-errant the world has ever seen': Subcomandante Insurgente Marcos, *Our Word is Our Weapon*, Serpent's Tail, 2001.

Rima Staines . . . 'has always had one foot in Early Medieval Europe': see <intothehermitage.blogspot.com>

good actions resonate with – and sustain – the impetus of life: Hannah Rachel Bell, *Men's Business, Women's Business: The Spiritual Role of Gender in the World's Oldest Culture*, Inner Traditions International, 1998.

Little Red Riding Hood . . . something horrible happened to her story along its path: see the work of Heide Göttner-Abendroth in Jack Zipes, *Fairy Tales and the Art of Subversion*, Heinemann, 1983.

oral folk tales had their goddesses . . . The child-hero became, most often, male: Ibid.

Spell, commented J. R. R. Tolkien: J. R. R. Tolkien who sadly did not have a grandson called Tolkien JR Jr Jr.

'Of this world-wide animism the fairy-faith is an expression': Kathleen Raine in an introduction to W. Y. Evans-Wentz, *The Fairy-faith in Celtic Countries*, Oxford University Press, 1911.

Chapter Sixteen: The Secret World of a Child's Soul

children make dens from the age of about six . . . in a worldwide habit of childhood: David Sobel, *Children's Special Places: Exploring the Role of Forts, Dens and Bush Houses in Middle Childhood*, Zephyr Press, 1993.

children make nests with lookouts because they are genetically programmed to do so: Gary Paul Nabhan and Stephen Trimble, *The Geography of Childhood: Why Children Need Wild Places*, Beacon Press, 1994.

Kim Stafford . . . 'held secret by my own soul as a rehearsal for departure': Kim Stafford, *Having Everything Right: Essays on Place*, Confluence, 1986.

study of how creative thinkers recall childhood . . . profound immersion in the world: Edith Cobb, *The Ecology of Imagination in Childhood*, Columbia University Press, 1977.

'I looked right at her face, and I said, "At God." Then she looked up at the sky, and then she looked at me, and she didn't call me any more names': Robert Coles, *The Spiritual Life of Children*, Houghton Mifflin, 1990.

an ash wand . . . and crow feathers to represent unerring flight: Ella Cara
Deloria, *Waterlily*, University of Nebraska Press, 1988, written in 1940s.

Alice Walker's earliest memory: Interview in *New Internationalist*, September
2012.

An eight-year-old Hopi girl . . . waving to the sun and stars: Robert Coles, *The
Spiritual Life of Children*, Houghton Mifflin, 1990.

stories . . . 'shone with a kind of moonlight radiance': Flora Thompson, *Lark
Rise to Candleford*, Oxford University Press, 1939–43.

Chapter Seventeen: Eureka!

Wordsworth . . . 'Hence my obeisance, my devotion hence': William Wordsworth, *The Prelude*, Part Two, 1799.

James Hillman in his beautiful book *The Soul's Code*: James Hillman, *The Soul's
Code: In Search of Character and Calling*, Bantam, 1996.

Pablo Neruda . . . 'fever or forgotten wings': Pablo Neruda, *Poems*, trans.
Stephen Tapscott, W. S. Merwin, Alastair Reid, Nathaniel Tarn, Ken Krab-
benhoft and Donald D. Walsh, The Harvill Press, 1995.

Jonathan Bate's beautiful biography: Jonathan Bate, *John Clare: A Biography*,
Picador, 2003.

Ed O'Brien: personal communication with the author.

'My Muse willed it – so I obeyed, and wrote': Beethoven letter to the Elector of
Cologne, Frederick Maximilian.

Philip Pullman: personal communication with the author.

Coleridge . . . 'by a sort of transference and transmission of my consciousness
to identify myself with the Object': Coleridge in a letter of 1820.

Nikolai Fraiture: personal communication with the author.

Nils-Aslak Valkeapää . . . an elusive, bookish, dreamy child who played with
animals and spoke with birds: Nils-Aslak Valkeapää, *The Sun, My Father
(Beaivi, Áhčážan)*, trans. Harald Gaski, University of Washington, 1997, first
published 1988.

Dedication

The faerie beam upon you . . . And the luckier lot betide you: Ben Jonson, 'The
Gypsies Metamorphosed'.

BIBLIOGRAPHY

Abram, David, *The Spell of the Sensuous: Perception and Language in a More-than-Human World*, Vintage Books, 1997.
—, *Becoming Animal*, Pantheon, 2010.
Ackroyd, Peter, *Blake*, Sinclair-Stevenson, 1995.
Agnelli, Susanna, *Street Children: A Growing Urban Tragedy*, Report for the Independent Commission on International Humanitarian Issues, Weidenfeld and Nicolson, 1986.
Alain-Fournier, *Le Grand Meaulnes*, 1912.
Anderson, Lindsay (dir.), *If*, 1968.
Arendt, Hannah, *The Human Condition*, Chicago Press, 1958.
Ariès, Philippe, *Centuries of Childhood: A Social History of Family Life*, Jonathan Cape, 1962, first published 1960.
Asbjørnsen, Peter Christen and Moe, Jørgen, *Norwegian Folktales*, Pantheon, 1960, first published 1888.
Auden, W. H., 'Amor Loci' in *Collected Poems*, Faber, 1976.

Bachelard, Gaston, *The Poetics of Space*, Beacon Press, 1969, first published 1958.
—, *The Poetics of Reverie*, Viking, 1969, first published 1960.
Balto, Asta, *Traditional Sámi Child Rearing in Transition: Shaping a New Pedagogical Platform*, Sámi University College, 2005.
Bashir, Halima and Lewis, Damien, *Tears of the Desert*, Hodder and Stoughton, 2008.
Bate, Jonathan, *John Clare: A Biography*, Picador, 2003.
'B.B.' (D. J. Watkins-Pitchford), *The Little Grey Men*, Eyre and Spottiswoode, 1942.
Bell, Diane, *Daughters of the Dreaming*, George Allen and Unwin, 1983.

Bell, Hannah Rachel, *Men's Business, Women's Business: The Spiritual Role of Gender in the World's Oldest Culture*, Inner Traditions International, 1998.

Berger, John, *Here is Where We Meet*, Bloomsbury, 2005.

Bergman, Ingmar (dir.), *Fanny and Alexander*, 1982.

Berman, M. C., Jonides, J. and Kaplan, S., 'The Cognitive Benefits of Interacting with Nature', *Psychological Science*, 2008 (19).

Bettelheim, Bruno, *A Home for the Heart*, Knopf, 1974.

—, *The Uses of Enchantment: The Meaning and Importance of Fairy Tales*, Thames and Hudson, 1976.

Bird, Carmel (ed.), *The Stolen Children: Their Stories*, Random House, 1998.

Birket-Smith, Kaj, *The Eskimos*, Methuen, 1936, first published 1927.

Blake, William, *Complete Poems*, Penguin 1977.

Blishen, Edward (ed.), *The School That I'd Like*, Penguin, 1969.

Bookchin, Murray, *The Ecology of Freedom*, AK Press, 2005.

Bowie, F. and Davies, O. (eds.), *Discovering Welshness*, Gomer, 1992.

Brave Heart, Maria Yellow Horse, *Wakiksuyapi: Carrying the Historical Trauma of the Lakota*, Tulane University School of Social Work, 2000.

Briggs, Jean L., *Never in Anger: Portrait of an Eskimo Family*, Harvard University Press, 1970.

Brody, Hugh, *The Other Side of Eden: Hunter-gatherers, Farmers and the Shaping of the World*, Douglas and McIntyre, 2000.

—(dir.), *The Meaning of Life*, 2008.

Buliard, Roger P., *Inuk*, Macmillan, 1956.

Burn, Andrew, 'Children's Playground Games and Songs in the New Media Age', Institute of Education, University of London, 2009–11.

Burnett, Frances Hodgson, *The Secret Garden*, first published 1911.

Burningham, John, *When We were Young: A Compendium of Childhood*, Bloomsbury, 2004.

Burnside, John, *A Lie about My Father*, Random House, 2007.

Bushaway, Bob, *By Rite: Custom, Ceremony and Community in England 1700–1880*, Junction Books, 1982.

Calvino, Italo, *Italian Folktales*, Harcourt, 1980.

Campbell, Joseph, *The Hero with a Thousand Faces*, Bollingen Foundation, 1949.

Carroll, Lewis, *Complete Illustrated Works*, Chancellor Press, 1982.

Carson, Rachel, *The Sense of Wonder*, HarperCollins, 1998.

Carter, Angela, *The Bloody Chamber*, Gollancz, 1979.

Cary, Joyce, *A House of Children*, Everyman, 1995, first published 1941.

Cason, D. and Gillis, H. L., 'A Meta-analysis of Outdoor Adventure Programming with Adolescents', *Journal of Experiential Education*, 1994 (17).

Challenger, Melanie, *On Extinction: How We Became Estranged from Nature*, Granta, 2011.

Chawla, Louise, *In the First Country of Places: Nature, Poetry and Childhood Memory*, State University of New York Press, 1994.

Chomsky, Noam, *Failed States*, Metropolitan Books, Henry Holt, 2006.

Christoff, K., Gordon, A. M., Smallwood, J., Smith, R. and Schooler, J. W., 'Experience Sampling during fMRI Reveals Default Network and Executive System Contributions to Mind Wandering', *Proceedings of the National Academy of Sciences*, 2009.

Chudacoff, Howard, *Children at Play: An American History*, NYU Press, 2007.

Clare, John, *Major Works*, Oxford University Press, 1984.

Cobb, Edith, *The Ecology of Imagination in Childhood*, Columbia University Press, 1977.

Cocteau, Jean, *Les Enfants Terribles*, Harvill, 1955, translated by Rosamond Lehmann, first published 1929.

Coles, Robert, *The Spiritual Life of Children*, Houghton Mifflin, 1990.

Collins, Allan (dir.), *Spirit Stones*, 2008.

Cooper, James Fenimore, *The Last of the Mohicans: A Narrative of 1757*, first published 1826.

Coveney, Peter, *Poor Monkey: The Child in Literature*, Rockliff, 1957.

Crompton, Richmal, *Just William*, first published 1922.

Crossley-Holland, Kevin, *The Seeing Stone*, Orion Children's Books, 2000.

Crisp, S. and Hinch, C., 'Treatment Effectiveness of Wilderness Adventure Therapy: Summary Findings', *Neo Psychology*, 2004.

Daunton, Martin and Halpern, Rick (eds.), *Empire and Others: British Encounters with Indigenous Peoples, 1600–1850*, University College London Press, 1999.

Davis, Wade, *The Wayfinders: Why Ancient Wisdom Matters in the Modern World*, House of Anansi Press, 2009.

Deakin, Roger, *Wildwood: A Journey through Trees*, Hamish Hamilton, 2007.

de Graaf, John (ed.) *Take Back Your Time: Fighting Overwork and Time Poverty in America*, Berrett-Koehler Publishers, 2003.

Deloria, Ella Cara, *Waterlily*, University of Nebraska Press, 1988, written in 1940s.

Dibb, Mike (dir.), *Fields of Play*, BBC Television, 1982–3.

Dickens, Charles, *Hard Times*, first published 1854.

Dobson, James, *The New Strong-willed Child*, Tyndale House Publishers, 2004, first published 1978.

Dutta, Pulak, 'Santiniketan: Birth of an Alternative Cultural Space', *Folklore, Public Sphere and Civil Society*, 2004.

—, 'Public Nature of Art Practices: Can Art Have a Public Life?', *International Yearbook of Aesthetics*, 2008 (12).

Eastman, Charles Alexander, *The Soul of the Indian: An Interpretation*, University of Nebraska Press, 1911.

ECOS 24, Journal of the British Association of Nature Conservationists, 2003.

ECOS 26, Journal of the British Association of Nature Conservationists, 2005.

Edwards, C., Gandini, L. and Forman, G. (eds.), *The Hundred Languages of Children: The Reggio Emilia Approach*, Ablex Publishing, 1998.

Eiseley, Loren, *The Mind as Nature*, Harper and Row, 1962.

Ekho, Naqi and Ottokie, Uqsuralik, *Interviewing Inuit Elders: Childrearing Practices*, Nunavut Arctic College, 2000.

Empson, William, *Some Versions of Pastoral*, Chatto and Windus, 1935.

Epstein, Robert, 'The Myth of the Teen Brain', *Scientific American Mind*, April–May 2007.

Ereira, Alan, *The Heart of the World*, Cape, 1990.

Erikson, Erik, *Childhood and Society*, Paladin, 1977, first published 1951.

Etchells, Tim, *That Night Follows Day*, Carl Gydé, 2007.

Evans-Wentz, W. Y., *The Fairy-faith in Celtic Countries*, Oxford University Press, 1911.

Evens, G. Bramwell, *A Romany and Raq, A Romany in the Fields*, The Epworth Press, 1929.

Fan, Lixin (dir.), *Last Train Home*, 2009.

Feinstein, Adam, *Pablo Neruda: A Passion for Life*, Bloomsbury, 2004.

Firestone, Shulamith, *The Dialectic of Sex: The Case for Feminist Revolution*, Jonathan Cape, 1971.

Foucault, Michel, *Discipline and Punish: The Birth of the Prison*, Gallimard, 1975.

Franklin, Benjamin, *Remarks Concerning the Savages of North America*, pamphlet of 1784.

Freeman, Minnie Aodla, *Life among the Qallunaat*, Hurtig, 1978.

Galeano, Eduardo, *Upside Down: A Primer for the Looking-glass World*, Picador, 1998.

Garner, Alan, *The Owl Service*, Collins, 1967.

Gerhardt, Sue, *Why Love Matters: How Affection Shapes a Baby's Brain*, Routledge, 2004.

Gershoff, Elizabeth, 'Report on Physical Punishment in the United States: What Research Tells Us about Its Effects on Children', Columbus Center for Effective Discipline, 2008.

Gibson, Ian, *Federico García Lorca: A Life*, Faber, 1989.

Gilbert, Kevin (ed.), *Inside Black Australia: An Anthology of Aboriginal Poetry*, Penguin, 1988.

Gill, Tim, *The Ecologist*, October 2005.

Gillis, John, *A World of Their Own Making: Myth, Ritual and the Quest for Family Values*, Basic Books, 1996.

Golding, William, *Lord of the Flies*, Faber, 1954.

Grahame, Kenneth, *Dream Days*, John Lane, 1898.

—, *The Wind in the Willows*, Methuen, 1908.

Greene, Graham, *Lost Childhood*, Eyre and Spottiswoode, 1951.

Greven, Philip, *Spare the Child: The Religious Roots of Punishment and the Psychological Impact of Physical Abuse*, Knopf, 1991.

Griffiths, Niall, *Runt*, Jonathan Cape, 2007.

Gwynne, S. C., *Empire of the Summer Moon: Quanah Parker and the Rise and Fall of the Comanches, the Most Powerful Indian Tribe in American History*, Scribner, 2010.

Haegert, Dorothy, *Children of the First People*, Tillacum Library, 1983.

Hætta, Odd Mathis, *The Ancient Religion and Folk-beliefs of the Sámi*, Alta Museum Pamphlets, 1994.

Hammond, J. L. and Hammond, Barbara, *The Village Labourer*, Nonsuch Publishing, 2005, first published 1911.

Harrison, Robert Pogue, *Forests: The Shadow of Civilization*, University of Chicago Press, 1992.

Hart, Roger, *Children's Experience of Place*, Irvington Publishers, 1979.

Harvey, Denis, *The Gypsies: Waggon-time and After*, Batsford, 1979.

Hattie, J., Marsh, H. W., Neill, J.T. and Richards, G. E., 'Adventure Education and Outward Bound: Out-of-Class Experiences That Make a Lasting Difference', *Review of Educational Research*, 67 (1), 1997.

Heelas, Paul and Lock, Andrew (eds.), *Indigenous Psychologies: The Anthropology of the Self*, Academic Press, 1981.

Hendin, Herbert, *Suicide and Scandinavia*, Anchor Books, 1965.

Herrera, Hayden, *Frida: A Biography of Frida Kahlo*, Harper and Row, 1983.

Heywood, Colin, *A History of Childhood*, Polity, 2001.

Hightower, James, *Happy Hunting Grounds*, Colorado Springs, 1910, published by the author.

Higonnet, Anne, *Pictures of Innocence: The History and Crisis of Ideal Childhood*, Thames and Hudson, 1998.

Hill, Kim and Hurtado, A. Magdalena, *Ache Life History: The Ecology and Demography of a Foraging People*, Aldine de Gruyter, 1996.

Hillman, James, *The Soul's Code: In Search of Character and Calling*, Bantam, 1996.

Hindle, Jim, *Nine Miles: Two Winters of Anti-Road Protest*, Underhill Books, 2006.

Hobbes, Thomas, *The Elements of Law*, first published 1650.

Hodgkinson, Tom, *The Idle Parent*, Hamish Hamilton, 2009.

Hogan, Linda, 'The Great Without', *Parabola* 24, 1999.

Hogan, Melanie (dir.), *Kanyini*, 2006.

Holmes, Richard, *The Age of Wonder: How the Romantic Generation Discovered the Beauty and Terror of Science*, HarperPress, 2008.

Home, Henry (Lord Kames), *Loose Hints upon Education, Chiefly Concerning the Culture of the Heart*, Edinburgh, 1781.

Hornung, Eva, *Dogboy*, Text Publishing, 2009.

Huda, Menhaj (dir.), *Kidulthood*, 2006.

Hughes-Hallett, Penelope (ed.), *Childhood: A Collins Anthology*, Collins, 1988.

Huizinga, Johan, *Homo Ludens: A Study of the Play Element in Culture*, Roy Publishers, 1950.

Hultkrantz, Åke, *Native Religions of North America*, Waveland Press, 1987.

Human Rights and Equal Opportunity Commission Report, *Bringing Them Home*, Report of the National Inquiry into the Separation of Aboriginal and Torres Strait Islander Children from Their Families, 1997.

Illich, Ivan, *Deschooling Society*, Calder and Boyars, 1971.

Iqalliyuq, Rosie, *Interview for the Igloolik Oral History Project*, Igloolik Research Centre, 1987.

Itard, Jean, *Of the First Developments of the Young Savage of Aveyron*, 1799, translated 1802.

James, Oliver, *They F*** You Up: How to Survive Family Life*, Bloomsbury, 2002.

Jenks, Chris (ed.), *Childhood: Critical Concepts in Sociology*, Routledge, 2005.

Jones, Guy W. and Moomaw, Sally, *Lessons from Turtle Island: Native Curriculum in Early Childhood Classrooms*, Redleaf Press, 2002.

Jones, Noragh, *Living in Rural Wales*, Gomer Press, 1993.

Jordan, Neil (dir.), *The Company of Wolves*, 1984.

Kahn, Peter H. and Kellert, Stephen R. (eds.), *Children and Nature: Psychological, Sociocultural and Evolutionary Investigations*, MIT Press, 2002.

Kakar, Sudhir, *The Inner World: A Psycho-analytic Study of Childhood and Society in India*, Oxford University Press, 1981.

Kartinyeri, Doris, *Kick the Tin*, Spinifex, 2000.

Kast, Verena, *Through Emotions to Maturity: Psychological Readings of Fairy Tales*, Walter-Verlag, 1982.

Kemf, Elizabeth (ed.), *Indigenous Peoples and Protected Areas: The Law of Mother Earth*, Earthscan, 1993.

Kennedy, Dan (Ochankugahe), *Recollections of an Assiniboine Chief*, James R. Stevens (ed.), McClelland and Stewart, 1972.

Kieran, Dan, *I Fought the Law: A Riotous Romp in Search of British Democracy*, Bantam, 2007.

Kinsbourne, M. (ed.), *Asymmetrical Function of the Brain*, Cambridge University Press, 1978.

Kipling, Rudyard, *The Jungle Book*, first published 1894.

—, *The Second Jungle Book*, first published 1895.

—, *Puck of Pook's Hill*, first published 1906.

Klee, Paul, *Pedagogical Sketchbook*, 1925.

Kociumbas, Jan, *Australian Childhood: A History*, Allen and Unwin, 1997.

Krüger, J. G., *Some Thoughts on the Education of Children*, 1752.

Lame Deer, John Fire and Erdoes, Richard, *Lame Deer: Sioux Medicine Man*, Davis-Poynter, 1973.

Lane, Margaret, *The Tale of Beatrix Potter*, Penguin, 1946.

Lawrence, D. H., *The Rainbow*, Methuen, 1915.

—, 'Education of the People', in *Phoenix: The Posthumous Papers of D. H. Lawrence*, Heinemann, 1936.

—, 'Pan in America', in *Phoenix: The Posthumous Papers of D. H. Lawrence*, Heinemann, 1936.

Layard, Richard and Dunn, Judy, *A Good Childhood: Searching for Values in a Competitive Age*, Report for the Children's Society, Penguin, 2009.

Ledda, Gavino, *Padre Padrone: The Education of a Shepherd*, translated by George Salmanazar, Allen Lane, 1978, first published 1975.

Lee, Dorothy, *Freedom and Culture*, Prentice-Hall, 1959.

Lee, Laurie, *Cider with Rosie*, Hogarth Press, 1959.

—, *As I Walked Out One Midsummer Morning*, André Deutsch, 1969.

Lee, Richard B. and DeVore, Irven (eds.), *Kalahari Hunter-gatherers: Studies of the !Kung San and Their Neighbors*, Harvard University Press, 1976.

Le Guin, Ursula, Earthsea novels, published by Parnassus from 1968.

Lehtola, Veli-Pekka, *The Sámi People: Traditions in Transition*, University of Alaska Press, 2004.

Levi, Primo, *The Truce*, Penguin, 1979, first published Italy, 1963.

Levinson, B. M., 'Pets and Personality Development', *Journal for the Study of Animal Problems*, 1978 (3).

Lewis, C. S., *The Lion, the Witch and the Wardrobe*, Geoffrey Bles, 1950.

—, *The Magician's Nephew*, Bodley Head, 1955.

—, *Surprised by Joy: The Shape of My Early Life*, Harcourt, 1955.

Lewis, Norman, *The Missionaries*, Arena, 1989.

Lewis, Richard, *Living by Wonder: Writings on the Imaginative Life of Childhood*, Parabola, 1998.

Liedloff, Jean, *The Continuum Concept*, Duckworth, 1975.

Linebaugh, Peter, *The Magna Carta Manifesto: Liberties and Commons for All*, University of California Press, 2008.

Locke, John, *Some Thoughts Concerning Education*, Yolton and Yolton (eds.), Clarendon Press, 1989.

Loewen, James W., *Lies My Teacher Told Me: Everything Your American History Textbook Got Wrong*, The New Press, 1995.

Lopez, Barry, *Crossing Open Ground*, Random House, 1988.

Lorde, Audre, *Zami: A New Spelling of My Name*, Persephone Press, 1982.

Louv, Richard, *Last Child in the Woods: Saving Our Children from Nature-Deficit Disorder*, Algonquin Books of Chapel Hill, 2005.

—, 'A Walk in the Woods', in *Orion* magazine, March–April 2009.

Lyon, Captain G. F., *The Private Journal of Captain G. F. Lyon of HMS* Hecla *during the Recent Voyage of Discovery under Captain Parry 1821–1823*, Imprint Society Barre-Massachusetts, 1970.

Marcos, Subcomandante Insurgente, *Our Word is Our Weapon*, Serpent's Tail, 2001.

Marshall Thomas, Elizabeth, *The Harmless People*, Secker and Warburg, 1959.

Maselko, J., Kubzansky, L., Lipsitt, L. and Buka, S. L., *Journal of Epidemiology and Community Health*, BMJ, 2010.

Matthiesen, Peter, *The Snow Leopard*, Viking, 1978.

McEwen, Christian and Statman, Mark (eds.), *The Alphabet of the Trees: A Guide to Nature Writing*, Teachers and Writers Collaborative, 2000.

McGilchrist, Iain, *The Master and His Emissary: The Divided Brain and the Making of the Western World*, Yale University Press, 2009.

McIntosh, Alastair, *Hell and High Water: Climate Change, Hope and the Human Condition*, Birlinn, 2008.

McLuhan, T. C. (compiler), *Touch the Earth: A Self-portrait of Indian Existence*, Abacus, 1973.

Miller, Alice, *The Drama of being a Child*, Faber, 1983.

—, *For Your Own Good: The Roots of Violence in Child-rearing*, Faber, 1983.

Miller, J. R., *Shingwauk's Vision: A History of Native Residential Schools*, University of Toronto Press, 1996.

Miller, Laura, *The Magician's Book: A Skeptic's Adventures in Narnia*, Little, Brown, 2008.

Mintz, Steven, *Huck's Raft: A History of American Childhood*, The Belknap Press, 2004.

Momaday, N. Scott, *The Way to Rainy Mountain*, University of New Mexico Press, 1969.

Monbiot, George, *No Man's Land: An Investigative Journey through Kenya and Tanzania*, Macmillan, 1994.

Montaigne, Michel de, *Essays*, 1580.

—, *Autobiography*, Marvin Lowenthal (ed.), Nonpareil Books, 1999.

Moore, Robin C., *Childhood's Domain: Play and Place in Child Development*, Croom Helm, 1986.

Morden, Daniel, *Dark Tales from the Woods*, Gomer Press, 2006.

Morey, Sylvester M. and Gilliam, Olivia L. (eds.), *Respect for Life: The Traditional Upbringing of American Indian Children*, Report of a Conference at Harper's Ferry, West Virginia, Waldorf Press, 1972.

Moquin, Wayne and Van Doren, Charles, *Great Documents in American Indian History*, Da Capo Press, 1995.

Morpurgo, Michael, *War Horse*, Kaye and Ward, 1982.

Morrow, V., 'My Animals and Other Family: Children's Perspectives on Their Relationships with Companion Animals', *Anthrozoos* 17, 1998 (4).

Moss, Rod, *The Hard Light of Day: An Artist's Story of Friendships in Arrernte Country*, University of Queensland Press, 2010.

Mowat, Farley, *People of the Deer*, Little, Brown, 1952.

Muir, John, *Travels in Alaska*, Houghton Mifflin, 1915.

Myers, Fred R., *Pintupi Country, Pintupi Self: Sentiment, Place and Politics among Western Desert Aborigines*, Smithsonian Institution Press, 1986.

Nabhan, Gary Paul and Trimble, Stephen, *The Geography of Childhood: Why Children Need Wild Places*, Beacon Press, 1994.

Nansen, Fridtjof, *The First Crossing of Greenland*, Longmans, 1890.

Nash, Roderick Frazier, *Wilderness and the American Mind*, Yale University Press, 1967.

Nasook, Martha, *Interview for the Igloolik Oral History Project*, Igloolik Research Centre, 1990.

Neihardt, John G., *Black Elk Speaks: Being the Life Story of a Holy Man of the Oglala Sioux*, William Morrow, 1932.

Nelson, Richard K., *Make Prayers to the Raven: A Koyukon View of the Northern Forest*, University of Chicago Press, 1983.

Neruda, Pablo, *Poems*, The Harvill Press, 1995.

Newnes, Craig and Radcliffe, Nick (eds.), *Making and Breaking Children's Lives*, PCCS Books, 2005.

Newton, Michael, *Savage Girls and Wild Boys: A History of Feral Children*, Faber, 2002.

Niall, Ian, *A Galloway Childhood*, Heinemann, 1967.

Nitobe, Inazō, *Bushidō: The Soul of Japan*, Oxford University Press, 2002, first published 1905.

Obama, Barack, *Dreams from My Father*, Times Books, 1995.

O'Brien, Liz and Murray, Richard, 'Forest School and Its Impacts on Young Children: Case Studies in Britain', *Urban Forestry and Urban Greening*, 2007 (6).

O'Driscoll, Dennis, *Stepping Stones: Interviews with Seamus Heaney*, Faber, 2008.

Opie, Iona, *The People in the Playground*, Oxford University Press, 1993.

Opie, Iona and Peter, *The Lore and Language of Schoolchildren*, Oxford University Press, 1959.

Paffard, Michael, *Inglorious Wordsworths: A Study of Some Transcendental Experiences in Childhood and Adolescence*, Hodder and Stoughton, 1973.

Parker, Jan and Stimpson, Jan, *Raising Happy Children: What Every Child Needs Their Parents to Know*, Hodder, 1999.

Parker, Jan, 'Culture, Attachment and Belonging', Interview of the Just Therapy Team, (Kiwi Tamasese, Flora Tuhaka, Charles Waldegrave) for *Context*, 2005.

Paterson, Fiona M. S., *Out of Place: Public Policy and the Emergence of Truancy*, The Falmer Press, 1989.

Pearl, Michael and Debi, *To Train Up a Child*, No Greater Joy Ministries, 1994.

—, <http://www.nogreaterjoy.org/articles/general-view/archive/2001/october/01/in-defense-of-biblical-chastisement-part-2/>

Philibert, Nicolas (dir.), *Être et Avoir*, 2002.

Pilgrim, David, *Psychotherapy and Society*, Sage Publications, 1997.

Piungittuq, Ruthie, *Interview for the Igloolik Oral History Project*, Igloolik Research Centre, 1991.

Plotkin, Bill, *Nature and the Human Soul: Cultivating Wholeness and Community in a Fragmented World*, New World Library, 2008.

Porteous, Alexander, *The Lore of the Forest: Myths and Legends*, George Allen and Unwin, 1928.

Pospisil, Leopold, *The Kapauku Papuans of West New Guinea*, Holt, Rinehart and Winston, 1963.

Postman, Neil, *The Disappearance of Childhood*, Delacorte Press, 1982.

Prescott, James W. (scientific director), *Rock A Bye Baby*, 1970.

Pretty, J., Angus, C., Bain, M., Barton, J., Gladwell, V., Hine, R., Pilgrim, S., Sandercock, S. and Sellens, M., 'Nature, Childhood, Health and Life Pathways', Interdisciplinary Centre for Environment and Society Occasional Paper, University of Essex, 2009.

Prichard, Caradog, *One Moonlit Night*, Canongate, 2009, first published 1961.

Pullman, Philip, *Northern Lights*, Scholastic, 1995.

—, *The Subtle Knife*, Scholastic, 1997.

—, *The Amber Spyglass*, Scholastic, 2000.

Ramsay, Lynne (dir.) *Ratcatcher*, 1999.

Rasmussen, Knud, *Report of the Fifth Thule Expedition, 1921–24*, Gyldendal, published from 1929.

Ray, Satyajit (dir.), *Pather Panchali (Song of the Little Road)*, 1955.

Reichel-Dolmatoff, Gerardo, *The Forest Within: The World-View of the Tukano Amazonian Indians*, Themis Books, 1996.

Rhys, Ernest, *Rabindranath Tagore: A Biographical Study*, Macmillan, 1915.

Richter, Linda and Morrell, Robert (eds.), *Baba: Men and Fatherhood in South Africa*, Human Sciences Research Council Press, 2006.

Rickinson, M., Dillon, J., Teamey, K., Morris, M., Choi, M., Sanders, D. and Benefield, P., *A Review of Research on Outdoor Learning*, Field Studies Council, 2004.

Riley, Patricia (ed.), *Growing Up Native American: An Anthology*, William Morrow, 1993.

Rival, Laura, 'What Kind of Sex Makes People Happy?', in R. Astuti, J. Parry and C. Stafford (eds.), *Questions of Anthropology*, Berg, 2007.

Roeg, Nicolas (dir.), *Walkabout*, 1971.

Rosenthal, T. G., *Paula Rego: The Complete Graphic Work*, Thames and Hudson, 2003.

Roszak, Theodore, *The Voice of the Earth: An Exploration of Ecopsychology*, Simon and Schuster, 1992.

Rousseau, Jean-Jacques, *Émile: or On Education*, Basic Books, 1979, first published 1762.

Russell, Bertrand, 'Freedom versus Authority in Education', in *Sceptical Essays*, George Allen and Unwin, 1928.

Russell, K. C., 'An Assessment of Outcomes in Outdoor Behavioral Healthcare Treatment', *Child and Youth Care Forum*, 32(6), 2003.

—, 'Two Years Later: A Qualitative Assessment of Youth Well-being and the Role of Aftercare in Outdoor Behavioral Healthcare Treatment', *Child and Youth Care Forum*, 34 (3), 2005.

Saban, Sinem (dir.), *Our Generation*, 2011.

Sakolsky, Ron and Koehnline, James (eds.), *Gone to Croatan: Origins of North American Dropout Culture*, Autonomedia/AK Press, 1993.

Salon.com on the death of Lydia Schatz, <http://www.salon.com/life/feature/2010/02/22/no_greater_joy>

Sarkar, Sunil Chandra, *Tagore's Educational Philosophy and Experiment*, Visva-Bharati, 1961.

Schaverien, Joy, 'Boarding School Syndrome', *British Journal of Psychotherapy*, May 2011 (27).

Schlegel, A. and Barry, H., 'A Cross-cultural Approach to Adolescence', *Ethos*, 23 (1), 1995.

Schor, Juliet B., *Born to Buy*, Scribner, 2004.

Seierstad, Åsne, *The Bookseller of Kabul*, Back Bay Books, 2002.

Seldon, Anthony, Address to the College of Teachers, March 2009.

Sewell, Anna, *Black Beauty*, Jarrold and Sons, 1877.

Sewell, Elizabeth, *The Human Metaphor*, University of Notre Dame Press, 1964.

Shakespeare, William, *A Midsummer Night's Dream*.

Shelley, Mary, *Frankenstein*, first published 1831.

Shelley, P. B., 'Ode to the West Wind', 1819.

Shepard, Paul, *The Only World We've Got: A Paul Shepard Reader*, Sierra Club Books, 1996.

—, *The Others: How Animals Made Us Human*, Island Press, 1996.

—, *Coming Home to the Pleistocene*, Island Press, 1998.

Shipton, Eric, *Land of Tempest: Travels in Patagonia 1958–62*, Hodder and Stoughton, 1963.

Shiva, Vandana, *Staying Alive: Women, Ecology and Survival in India*, Zed Books, 1988.

Shostak, Marjorie, *Nisa: The Life and Words of a !Kung Woman*, Harvard University Press, 1981.

Sibley, B. A. and Etinier, J. L., 'The Relationship between Physical Activity and Cognition in Children: A Meta-analysis', *Pediatric Exercise Science*, 2003 (15).

Sissay, Lemn, *Rebel Without Applause*, Bloodaxe, 1992.

—, *Morning Breaks in the Elevator*, Canongate, 1999.

Sjolie, Astrid N. and Thuen, Frode, *Health Promotion International*, Oxford University Press, 2002.

Smith, Huston, *A Seat at the Table: Huston Smith in Conversation with Native Americans on Religious Freedom*, Phil Cousineau (ed.), University of California Press, 2006.

Smith, Linda Tuhiwai, 'Nga Aho o te Kakahu Matauranga: The Multiple Layers of Struggle by Maori in Education', PhD thesis, University of Auckland, 1996.

Smith, Robert Paul, *Where Did You Go? Out. What Did You Do? Nothing*, The World's Work, 1957.

Snow, Chief John, *These Mountains are Our Sacred Places: The Story of the Stoney Indians*, Samuel Stevens, 1977.

Snyder, Gary, *A Place in Space: Ethics, Aesthetics and Watersheds*, Counterpoint, 1995.

Sobel, David, *Children's Special Places: Exploring the Role of Forts, Dens and Bush Houses in Middle Childhood*, Zephyr Press, 1993.

Soyinka, Wole, *Aké: The Years of Childhood*, Rex Collings, 1981.

Sparkes, Russell (ed.), *Prophet of Orthodoxy: The Wisdom of G. K. Chesterton*, HarperCollins, 1997.

Spufford, Francis, *The Child That Books Built*, Faber, 2002.

Stafford, Kim, *Having Everything Right: Essays on Place*, Confluence, 1986.

Staines, Rima, <intothehermitage.blogspot.com>

Standing Bear, Luther, *Land of the Spotted Eagle*, University of Nebraska Press, 1978, first published 1933.

Stefansson, Vilhjalmur, *My Life with the Eskimos*, Harrap, 1924.

Stone, Lawrence, *The Family, Sex and Marriage in England 1500–1800*, Weidenfeld and Nicolson, 1977.

Strang, Veronica, *Uncommon Ground: Cultural Landscapes and Environmental Values*, Berg, 1997.

Sūrdās, *The Memory of Love: Sūrdās Sings to Krishna*, translated by John Stratton Hawley, Oxford University Press, 2009.

Szirtes, George, 'Thin Ice and the Midnight Skaters', the T. S. Eliot Lecture, 2005.

Tagore, Rabindranath, 'A Poet's School' from 'Thoughts on Education', *The Visva-Bharati Quarterly*, May–October 1947.

—, *On Art and Aesthetics*, Longman, 1961.

Taviani, Paolo and Vittorio (dirs.), *Padre Padrone* (*My Father, My Master*), 1977.

Tench, Watkin, *1788*, Tim Flannery (ed.), Text Publishing, 2009, first published 1789.

Thomas, Dylan, *Quite Early One Morning*, New Directions, 1954.

Thompson, Flora, *Lark Rise to Candleford*, Oxford University Press, 1939–43.

Thompson, Guy, *ECOS* 26, Journal of the British Association of Nature Conservationists, 2005.

Tolkien, J. R. R., *Tree and Leaf*, George Allen and Unwin, 1964.

Tookoome, Simon with Oberman, Sheldon, *The Shaman's Nephew: A Life in the Far North*, Stoddart, 1999.

Trench, Archbishop Richard, *On the Study of Words*, Macmillan, 1864.

Truffaut, François (dir.), *Les Quatre Cents Coups* (*The Four Hundred Blows*), 1959.

—(dir.), *L'Enfant Sauvage* (*The Wild Child*), 1970.

—(dir.), *L'Argent de Poche* (*Small Change*), 1976.

Tshering-Misra, Chuden, 'India: Development Process and Indigenous Children', *Cultural Survival Quarterly*, 1986 (10).

Turner, Frederick, *Beyond Geography: The Western Spirit against the Wilderness*, Rutgers University Press, 1983.

Twain, Mark, *The Adventures of Tom Sawyer*, first published 1876.

—, *The Adventures of Huckleberry Finn*, first published 1884.

UK Children's Commissioners' Report to the UN Committee on the Rights of the Child, 2008.

UNICEF, 'Child Poverty in Perspective: An Overview of Child Well-being in Rich Countries', UNICEF Innocenti Research Centre, 2007.

UNICEF-commissioned report from IPSOS/MORI and Dr Agnes Nairn, 2011.

Valkeapää, Nils-Aslak, *Greetings from Lappland: The Sámi, Europe's Forgotten People*, Zed Press, 1983, first published 1971.

—, *The Sun, My Father (Beaivi, Áhčážan)*, translated by Harald Gaski, University of Washington, 1997, first published 1988.

Vidovic, V., Stetic, V. and Brathko, D., 'Pet Ownership, Type of Pet, and Socio-Emotional Development of School Children', *Anthrozoos* 12, 1999 (4).

Vigo, Jean (dir.), *Zéro de Conduite (Zero for Conduct)*, 1933.

Walker, C. E., Bonner, B. L. and Kaufman, K. L., *The Physically and Sexually Abused Child: Evaluation and Treatment*, Pergamon Press, 1988.

Wasserman, Miriam, *Demystifying School: Writings and Experiences*, Praeger, 1974.

Watson, John B., *Psychological Care of Infant and Child*, W. W. Norton, 1928.

Wells, N. and Evans, G., 'Nearby Nature: A Buffer of Life Stress among Rural Children', *Environment and Behavior*, May 2003 (35).

Wells, N. and Lekies, K. S., 'Nature and the Life Course: Pathways from Childhood Nature Experiences to Adult Environmentalism', *Children, Youth and Environments*, 2006 (16).

White, T. H., *The Sword in the Stone*, Collins, 1938.

Whitehead, Alfred North, *The Aims of Education and Other Essays*, Macmillan, 1929.

Whitman, Walt, *Leaves of Grass*, 1892.

wildernesstherapy.org

Wilding, Jo, *Taking a Circus to the Children of Iraq*, New Internationalist Publications, 2006.

Williams, D. J., *The Old Farmhouse/Hen Dŷ Ffarm*, translated by Waldo Williams, Harrap and Co., 1961.

Wilson, J., 'A Social Relational Critique of the Biomedical Definition and Treatment of ADHD: Ethical, Practical and Political Implications' published online, *Journal of Family Therapy*, 2012.

Woodroffe, John, *Shakti and Shakta*, Luzaz and Co., 1929.

—, *The Serpent Power*, Ganesh and Co., 1931.

Wordsworth, William, *The Prelude*, 1799.

Wordsworth, William and Coleridge, Samuel Taylor, *Lyrical Ballads*, 1798.

Zeldin, Theodore, *An Intimate History of Humanity*, Sinclair-Stevenson, 1994.

Zinn, Howard, *A People's History of the United States, 1492–Present*, Harper and Row, 1980.

Zipes, Jack, *Fairy Tales and the Art of Subversion*, Heinemann, 1983.

INDEX

IN THANKS

Thank you to the following for friendship in so many forms while I was writing this book: Adrian, Andy S. and Tuppin, Andy W., Ann, Annie and George, Boff and Casey, Buz and Thoby, Clare, Ed and Susan, Eddie, George M., Gideon, Giuliana, Hannah and Ralph, Jan, Lemn, Marg, Mike and Nisha, Naomi and Narayan, Niall and Deborah, Nicoletta, Nikolai, Rima and Tom, Shane, Thea and Vic. In the elected solitude of the writer's psyche, I am profoundly grateful for your enthusiasm for this book.

My thanks are due to the ever-helpful Authors' Foundation of the Society of Authors, which provided financial assistance. With quite astonished gratitude for its munificence, my thanks go to the Royal Literary Fund.

My particular thanks are due to George Monbiot and Jan Parker for second-guessing my interests and suggesting books and articles; and to Mel McCree and Jules Pretty for providing pointers to academic papers. My delighted gratitude goes to Jessica Woollard at the Marsh Agency and to Simon Prosser at Hamish Hamilton, for your unstinting belief, as keen as it was patient, in this book.

I will always hold a candle to the memory of my grandmothers, Pankhurst and Day, who gave me so much. To Philip Pullman, I offer my deep and happy respect for your transformative writing on childhood, which means the world to me. And to Gareth Evans, a literary guardian angel, thank you with all my heart.

DEDICATION

In glad gratitude for sharing your childhoods with me and giving me the cherished roles of aunt and godmother, this book is dedicated with love to David, Timothy, Euan, Laurel, Elsa, Ned, Erica, Emily and Tanushka.

The faerie beam upon you,
The stars to glister on you;
A moon of light
In the noon of night . . .
And the luckier lot betide you

He just wanted a decent book to read ...

Not too much to ask, is it? It was in 1935 when Allen Lane, Managing Director of Bodley Head Publishers, stood on a platform at Exeter railway station looking for something good to read on his journey back to London. His choice was limited to popular magazines and poor-quality paperbacks – the same choice faced every day by the vast majority of readers, few of whom could afford hardbacks. Lane's disappointment and subsequent anger at the range of books generally available led him to found a company – and change the world.

'We believed in the existence in this country of a vast reading public for intelligent books at a low price, and staked everything on it'
Sir Allen Lane, 1902–1970, founder of Penguin Books

The quality paperback had arrived – and not just in bookshops. Lane was adamant that his Penguins should appear in chain stores and tobacconists, and should cost no more than a packet of cigarettes.

Reading habits (and cigarette prices) have changed since 1935, but Penguin still believes in publishing the best books for everybody to enjoy. We still believe that good design costs no more than bad design, and we still believe that quality books published passionately and responsibly make the world a better place.

So wherever you see the little bird – whether it's on a piece of prize-winning literary fiction or a celebrity autobiography, political tour de force or historical masterpiece, a serial-killer thriller, reference book, world classic or a piece of pure escapism – you can bet that it represents the very best that the genre has to offer.

Whatever you like to read – trust Penguin.

JAY GRIFFITHS

WILD: AN ELEMENTAL JOURNEY

'I took seven years over this work, spent all I had, my time, money and energy. Part of the journey was a green riot and part a deathly bleakness. I got ill, I got well. I went to the shamans in the Amazon for their hallucinogenic medicine and went to the freedom fighters of West Papua to sing my head off in their highlands. I met cannibals infinitely kinder than the murderous missionaries who evangelize them. I anchored a boat to an iceberg where polar bears slept; ate witchetty grubs and visited sea gypsies. I found a paradox of wildness in the glinting softness of its charisma, for what is savage is in the deepest sense gentle and what is wild is kind. In the end – a strangely sweet result – I came to a wild home...'

'Wholly original, undefinable, untameable, profound and extraordinary' *Observer*

'Utterly compelling, easily the best travel book that I have read in the last ten years' *Guardian*

'Incandescent, exhilarating, sensuous, cocky, magnificent, explosive. A raging oratorio' **Richard Mabey**, *The Times*